PAPERDOLLS
&
COWBOY BOOTS

The Original
**Paperdolls: Healing From Sexual
Abuse in Mormon Neighborhoods**
&
**The True Events of the
Subsequent Decades**

April Daniels & Carol Scott

**The Paperdolls Foundation
2024**

Palingenesia Press, Printed 1992 | Recovery Publications, Inc., Printed 1993 |
The Paperdolls Foundation, Revised and Reprinted 2024

Cover Design: April Daniels and Debbie O'Byrne
Cover Photo by Jason Shepherd
Interior Design: Jetlaunch Publishing

Paperdolls Foundation
P.O. Box 58812
Salt Lake City, Utah 84158

Quantity discounts available for therapeutic agencies.
Copyright 1992, 1993, 2024 by April Daniels and Carol Scott.
Published by: The Paperdolls Foundation

Websites: www.paperdollsbook.org | www.paperdolls.today

Acknowledgments

For their help in a variety of ways, we would like to express our gratitude to the therapists who helped in the healing processes here described: the late Karen Fisher, LCSW; Dr. Paul Whitehead, Sr; Dr. Johanna McManemin; Dr. Katy O'Bannion; the late Dr. Jan Stout; Dr. Janine Wanlass; Dr. Lorna Smith-Benjamin; and Merritt Stites.

Thank you to Lisa Bednarz for her diligence in proof reading and initial editing. Thank you to Jason Shepherd for granting us permission to use his gorgeous photo of the Salt Lake Valley on the cover.

We also wish to thank most deeply those irreplaceable loved ones whose enduring support give our lives and this book significance and hope.

To Elizabeth Smart
for requesting her perpetrator be gagged
and remain in the courtroom
to hear her testimony

and

To Kacie Woody
honoring her sacred memory
and the vibrancy of her life
We will never forget her tragic end.

"Crimes That Never Should Have Happened"

Contents

Authors' Prologues

LIKE THE SINGLE WORD *Paperdolls*, we are all connected. I believe that this book can be beneficial to anyone who has experienced pain. Healing and growth happen when we have the courage to experience what Scott Peck defines as "legitimate suffering." The healing process is the same for all of us, even if the degree and the specifics of the pain are different.

The main person in this book who has retained her real name is Karen Fisher. She was my therapist for three years before I even remembered. Then with infinite patience, she skillfully supported me through the events described in this book. She had the courage to be authentic, which has been a significant contribution to my road to freedom.

Most of the names of other people, places and identifying details have been changed or redacted. A few valiant souls dedicated to combating sexual assault have given approval to use their real names. Perpetrators who chose to continue into adulthood victimizing children and who have become monsters in the public domain are identified. I know that the abuse in my childhood will always be with me, but I do not wish to be known as merely a sexual abuse survivor—I am so much more than that. I also want to protect a handful of wounded adults walking around who have or have not dealt with the abuse of our childhood neighborhood. Possibly some have repressed these memories. I believe that revealing these facts about individuals before they are ready to remember is a violation. I do not want to be part of any more violations or victimization of others.

This is not fiction. I am not an author. If this reads emotionally and illogically, it is because this was how my mind was working. Sexual abuse and the healing process are not neat and tidy. Confusing—out of sync—that is how thoughts occur. Healing does not occur in logical sequence.

The initial publication of *Paperdolls: Healing from Sexual Abuse in Mormon Neighborhoods* in 1992, highlights the stages of grief. The stages—denial, despair, rage, confrontation and acceptance—weave incoherently back and forth like my mind. Healing does not follow a clean plan with a smooth inclined plane. It is a jagged, up and down ascent. Only over time can survivors see patterns and progression. Over time, slowly, back and forth, healing finally occurs—and growth can begin.

When contemplating this next ideation of *Paperdolls*, Carol and I joked that it would be like the Old and New Testament. Both of us had to evolve and make changes in order to grow, experience joy, and gain wisdom.

—April Daniels

WHEN THE EVENTS CHRONICLED in this book occurred, I was a 55-year-old psychology professor with four grown children and several grandchildren. My husband and I had challenging jobs and many interests. Our lives seemed secure and good. I'm sure that to many people we looked like the storybook family.

I had known April Daniels as a friend of my daughter, Susy. Like many of our children's friends, April spent a considerable amount of time in our home during her growing up years. But nothing I saw in her behavior as an adolescent prepared me for the personal narrative she finally revealed to me.

April's brother, Tom, and Hank, who married and then was divorced from my daughter Lorraine, were best friends. Tom and Hank are central characters in *Paperdolls*. April's life collided and meshed with mine because of the actions of Tom and Hank.

Child sexual abusers adapt to any culture like chameleons; they use protective coloring. Close-knit Mormon neighborhoods provide a lot of access to children due to the trusting and communal nature of ward structure. Perhaps because of that, they are good environments for child abusers to thrive in. In addition to the close nature of the neighborhoods, denial can thrive within the wards. No one wants to believe their fellow "saints" could be involved in such behavior. All of us find it difficult to believe, but facing the truth can lead to healing.

As in April's account, I have changed the names, locations and other identifying details in my story. I am particularly concerned to protect the anonymity of children.

I have a friend who was molested as a child. She read this manuscript and said, "Tell the perpetrators our greatest weapon against them is our voices. When we were little, we had only silence. We have to find our voices." It is with their voices that April and I have tried to speak.

—Carol Scott

Therapeutic Commentary

THE EVENTS CHRONICLED by these two authors are straightforward accounts of one of society's most pervasive and disturbing problems: the sexual abuse of children. Shattered lives, fragmented families and dysfunctional adults are the all-too-often consequences. Abuse of children by a parent, with its blatant betrayal of trust, is even more traumatizing than rape of a child by a stranger. Because we tend to avoid and deny those things that are distressing to us, sexual abuse of children has been recognized only in recent years as a fact of life. Even today, many people are still unable to accept the reality of its existence. As a therapist for three of the children described in this book, I can verify the accuracy of their horrific experiences.

—Paul L. Whitehead, M.D. *January 1992*
Child, Adolescent, and Adult Psychiatrist

THIS BOOK WILL BE HARD to read. It is the heart wrenching story of incest and child sexual abuse. All of us involved in its publication, authors, editors, and therapists, have struggled with finding that place where the overwhelming devastation of the child's experience can be accurately portrayed without assaulting the reader.

I can promise this: you will come to understand that underneath the painful, tormenting theme of abuse and betrayal, there is love and courage.

Incest and child abuse is a soul-ripping reality endured by thousands of our children on a daily basis. We are, even now, unprepared to recognize it, name it, and rid ourselves of its brutal agony.

As her therapist, I was fortunate to be a part of the healing of one of these women, but I marvel still at the resilience of the human soul, of April Daniel's soul. She and the other children in this book suffered the ultimate betrayal of trust and innocence that was their birthright.

Their child's bodies, minds, and spirits were violated, and they will forever carry the inner scar. Fortunately, they are recovering from their traumas and will one day be capable of sharing in loving, committed relationships.

We must all bear the burden of helping to heal and, better yet, prevent the cataclysmic wound of child sexual abuse.

It is my sincere belief that by sharing their stories with you, April Daniels and Carol Scott will have helped remove one more critical layer of the denial system that keeps our children in peril.

—Karen Fisher, L.C.S.W.
January 1992

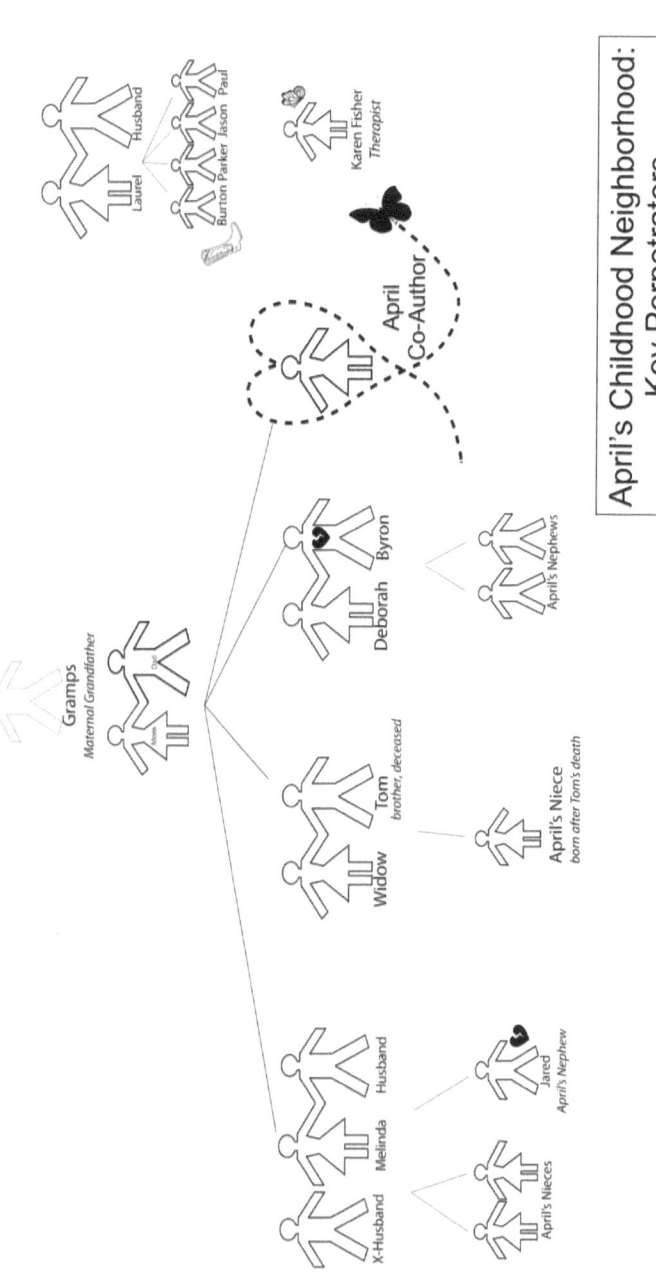

Gramps
Maternal Grandfather

Laurel
Husband
Burton Parker Jason Paul

Karen Fisher
Therapist

April
Co-Author

Deborah Byron
April's Nephews

Widow
Tom
brother, deceased

April's Niece
born after Tom's death

Melinda
X-Husband Husband
April's Nieces

Jared
April's Nephew

April's Childhood Neighborhood:
Key Perpetrators

- **Hank** *(Tom's Friend who married Lorraine Scott)*
- **David Fuller** *(real name - murdered Kacie Woody)*
- **Brian David Mitchell** *(real name - abducted Elizabeth Smart)*
- **Charles** *(April's cousin)*
- **Toy Box Man**
- **Architect**

For more information visit:
❤ https://www.paperdolls.today/p/butterflies-not-blood 🦋

Relationship Charts
of Key Individuals

❤ = perpetrators

🦋 = victims/survivors/healing

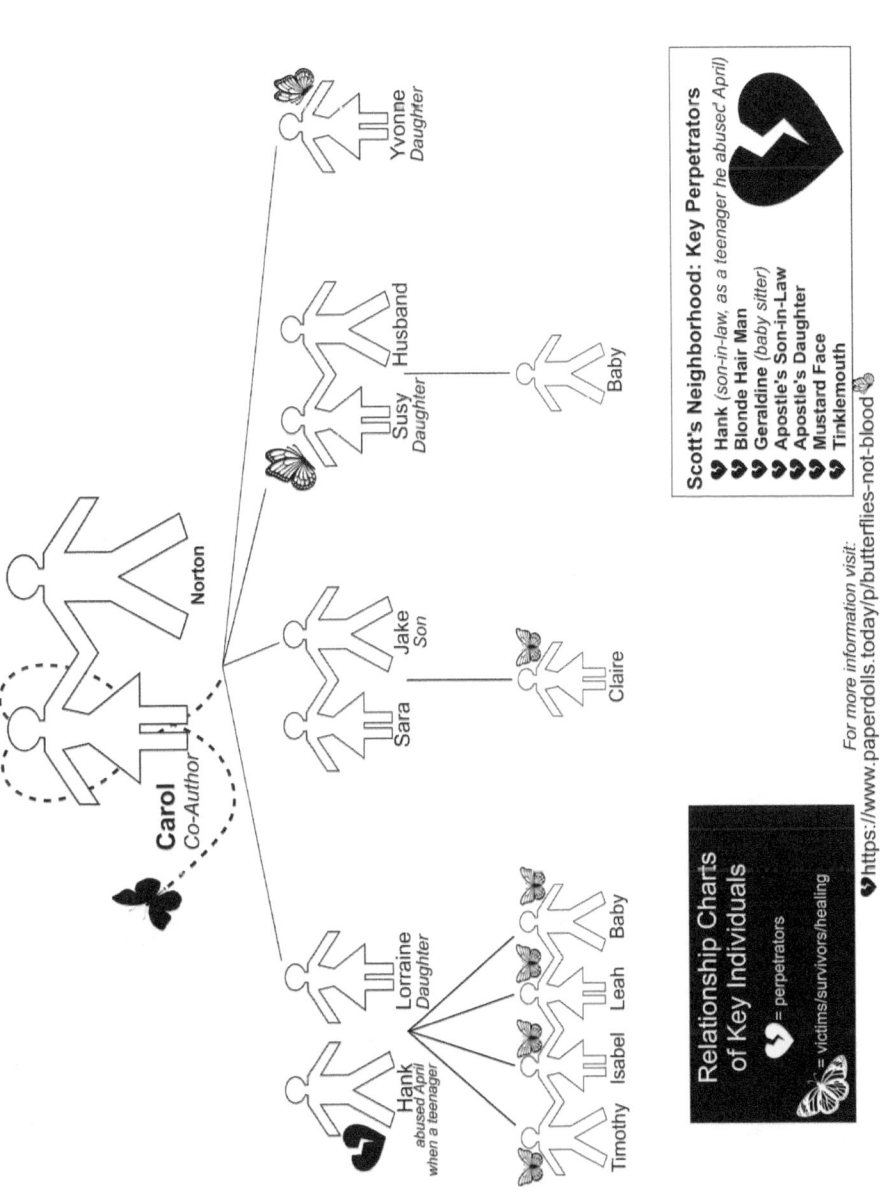

Carol
Co-Author

Norton

Lorraine
Daughter

Hank
*abused April
when a teenager*

Timothy Isabel Leah Baby

Jake
Son

Sara

Claire

Susy
Daughter

Husband

Baby

Yvonne
Daughter

**Relationship Charts
of Key Individuals**

= perpetrators

= victims/survivors/healing

Scott's Neighborhood: Key Perpetrators

❯ **Hank** *(son-in-law, as a teenager he abused April)*
❯ **Blonde Hair Man**
❯ **Geraldine** *(baby sitter)*
❯ **Apostle's Son-in-Law**
❯ **Apostle's Daughter**
❯ **Mustard Face**
❯ **Tinklemouth**

For more information visit:
❤https://www.paperdolls.today/p/butterflies-not-blood 🦋

April

A TEAR COULD HAVE WASHED her away. In the attic, underneath layers of dust, I found her. I carefully brushed the dirt from her face. She was water-colored by my grandmother's hand, evidently for my mother when she was a little girl. The floor creaked as I walked past some tarnished brass. I took her away from the dark attic. Only then could I see her beauty.

An antique paper doll, salvaged from a hundred-year-old home. Her hair is blond and her eyes hazel—like my mother's. Like mine. I am a 32-year-old woman now living in the home where my mother was raised. I am as old as my mother was when she bore me. I wonder, if my mother had kept this doll, would things have been different for her?

I'll keep her. My life is different. She's fragile, mere paper and watercolors. Forgotten in a dusty attic for decades. I am going to display her, protected, under glass. I want to display her resilience. Somewhere where I can always see her. To remind me to never forget.

DENIAL

"What awful lives children live!"
"Yes … And they can't tell anybody."

—Virginia Woolf from *The Years*

Carol

WHEN YOU'RE TELLING A STORY, anywhere can be the beginning. Like the blankets in the recovery room. They warm them so they're wonderfully comforting. The blankets hold you and caress your body. Nurses come in to check your packing and take your blood pressure. They push on your stomach and the after-birth contractions won't leave you alone, but mostly you doze in a half-world of druggedness feeling utter irresponsibility. For a few hours there is no one in the world who can ask you for anything. There is no calendar, no list to check off. Basking in the good fatigue of a job well done, you don't care about the baby or any of the others at home, only the heat of the cotton blankets. As soon as they wheel you to your room, the baby will be there forever and ever on until you're 80. But now there can be only warmth and soft light and someone taking care of you. It's worth having a birth to earn this blanket. I want to be in the recovery room again, but instead I am here, now, telling my story.

It took me some time to tell April, years in fact. I remember when we began to keep in touch. I wondered, of course, why she had made the appointment. I was a professor in the psychology department at the university. She was my daughter Susy's friend. She was Susy's age, 25, but not someone I knew well. She was attractive, intelligent and competent. She had a good job in her family's bank. She exuded health and always had. The Scandinavian, scrubbed-clean look. Her looks fit with her being a champion runner with all kinds of school and state trophies - even training for the Olympics - and a swimmer and biker too.

Besides knowing Susy well, April had a connection with Lorraine, our oldest daughter. April's brother, who had passed away at a young age, had been Lorraine's husband's best friend. Hank was still always talking about April's brother Tom, almost worshipped him it seemed to us. Hank cared about April too. And April and Lorraine seemed to have some kind of attraction despite their age difference.

I remembered that April had come to Lorraine's and Hank's wedding breakfast almost ten years ago, one of the few guests who wasn't family. I remembered because at the Lion House Restaurant we went around the room, and everyone told how they were connected to Hank and Lorraine and something funny or tender about them. April said a strange thing that morning. "I'm here"—she laughed—"because I don't like the groom, but I really like Lorraine." We all tried to laugh, but the joke didn't quite fly and April looked embarrassed.

A few months before Lorraine's wedding, April's brother Tom was diagnosed with cancer. Hank and Lorraine were devastated. Tom had a new wife, and she was pregnant. He was so young, and everyone seemed to adore him. His death was extremely hard on April.

Now here she was sitting in my office on the tan corduroy sofa where students always sat, facing me. Why is she really here, I kept wondering. She claimed she had come for business advice, but she had a hundred people who could give her better advice than I. And why make a formal appointment instead of dropping in at home as she surely knew she could have done?

The setting and the formality of her scheduling an appointment made me inclined to prod a little. "Tell me how you are, April."

It seemed only seconds before April's happy, contagious smile (nice teeth, I noted in passing) had vanished, and she was sobbing and clutching for my ever-present Kleenex box.

"It's my parents," she moaned.

Of course. Whatever else, old Sigmund sure got that one right. Always the parents. I knew her parents a little. They were known to be religious, "temple-going" as the phrase went. So, when the story of them staying soused in their room for days at a time came tumbling out, I was astonished. You think you've heard it all in my job and still you never cease to be amazed. I remembered that Susy would giggle about April's parents "always locked in their bedroom, even in the daytime!"

"Call me whenever you want," I assured her as I hugged her when she left my office. I wondered if my girls had any idea. I wondered when I'd see her again.

April

MY BROTHER'S FACE BEFORE THEY closed his casket. I didn't realize I had retained that memory until today. I went to lunch today with Carol Scott and we talked about my brother Tom's funeral. We talked about Hank.

It's really late at night. I can't sleep. I am so rattled. I'll write it down and figure it out later. What happened today at lunch? And why can't I get the image of Tom in the casket out of my mind? I keep seeing it. My head is spinning with images of Tom, Hank, the funeral, the casket. I haven't thought about this stuff in such a long time. I'm over it. What did Carol say that brought all this zooming up again?

Carol Scott is someone I really trust. I tell her things. Real personal things. She was the first person I told about my parents' alcoholism. I still remember the day; it was sometime in August 1985.

I made a formal appointment to talk with her. I can hardly remember any preliminary conversation. I blurted out the words "My parents are alcoholics," and then just cried. Carol was the only one I knew who might understand. She knew about psychological things. When people had problems, they'd talk to Carol.

I didn't know where else to go. I had only figured it out the previous year. I was student teaching in my last year of college, when I realized that my parents were drinking. My parents were dogmatic Mormons, a religion that forbids alcohol. I was living with them while I was student teaching, and although I was busy their drinking had escalated to a point where I had to notice. One day I finished up at the high school early and went to my sister's office. I sat across from her and skeptically stated, "I think Mom and Dad are drinking." Melinda looked at me evenly in the eyes and calmly said, "Close the door."

I was afraid. I was so scared I felt like running out. But I wanted to know more than I wanted to run. Melinda stayed behind her big oak desk as she waited for me to sit down. "Dad and Mom have been drinking all of your life."

Melinda is twelve years older than I. She said that she used to steal liquor from our parents' bedroom. I was stunned. I was relieved. I was terrified. It was my fault. My parents had ingrained into the very fiber of my thought patterns that alcohol was bad, anyone who drank was immoral, and that they had never touched the stuff.

My dad was a temple worker! Every Friday morning for as long as I could remember my father got up before dawn and went down to the Salt Lake Temple and did work for the dead. It is a very sacred place, and only the most righteous saints are allowed through those hallowed doors. It was a tremendous honor to be asked to work in the temple.

However, my dad and I never got along. I thought maybe I was a bad kid, but even when I tried to be good, we didn't get along. I decided our personalities clashed. Sometimes I'd think the problem was my dad and I were so much alike. This always made me sick because my dad is a real ornery man, and I always tried to please people, to be nice. Still, saying we were alike was an easy explanation and the only reason for the tension between us. My dad was cranky and controlling; he always ordered people around, but he was a righteous man. He worked in the temple, and that meant this was my problem, not his.

Melinda, my only sister, told me this was all a lie. My dad and my mom were alcoholics and had been drinking all my life. My dad lied to get into the temple. They have interviews to determine worthiness, and my dad just lied his way through it. The reason my dad and I didn't get along was because he was usually drunk or hung over.

My sister's words sunk in like lead. I sat heavy and bewildered. I didn't know what to say; the truth anchored me to the chair.

I don't know how or when I left Melinda's office. Reality dawned on me. We had to make them stop. Or do something. Maybe that is why I made the appointment with Carol. She was the only one I could possibly tell. Maybe she'd know what to do.

She understood. She told me to read *Adult Children of Alcoholics.* For some reason, I felt better. Just telling and having the name of a book helped. I planned to read up on the subject. I knew I could get my parents to stop drinking.

When Carol walked me to the door, I noticed crayons and paper. I asked Carol about them. She said she saw a couple of students privately in her office, and it sometimes helped them to draw. I dropped the subject. I couldn't imagine drawing to help with problems.

Then I remembered a time in kindergarten when my teachers made me color over the big penis I had drawn. I sometimes drew Daddy with a big, red penis. Sometimes it spit up. I flinched at the memory of my nastiness in kindergarten. I decided not to mention to Carol that I had drawn big red penises when I was little or that sometimes they spit up. I knew Carol would think I was crazy or just a nasty girl. I thanked her for listening to me ramble on about my parents and their alcoholism, and I left. But I remembered. And I remembered never to lose contact with Carol Scott.

And I haven't lost contact with Carol. I trust her. Why am I so upset tonight? What happened at lunch? Did she know how upset I was? Why do I keep seeing Tom's face in the coffin? What about Hank? Carol asked me what I know about Hank. Hank, the groom at whose wedding breakfast I stood up and said, "I hate the groom." I didn't remind Carol about the wedding breakfast. No need bringing up events which strangely still shame me. Maybe that's why I'm upset; something reminded me of what a flippant teenager I had been. No, that's not it.

What did Carol say at lunch today about Hank? Calm down April—retrace your steps—figure this out—get it all on paper, and then you can make sense of it all. You'll be able to sleep tonight. Start with lunch.

Carol and I went to one of the nicest restaurants in the city. Carol likes to talk about ideas and feelings—she is a deep person. I think she asked me something too deep today. That's why I am so rattled. What did she ask me? She asked me if I knew anything about Hank. Automatically I replied, "No, he never touched me."

My mind flashed to my brother and the casket. Hank was one of my brother's closest friends. Hank was a pall bearer at Tom's funeral. Hank helped carry Tom's body to his grave. For me the fourteen years dissolved instantly. I felt like a teenager standing in the shadows of the hospital corridor watching Hank cry. He was clutching a plastic bag filled with Fernwood's starlight mint ice cream. He brought it to the hospital because it was Tom's favorite. Tom died before Hank could give it to him. Hank stood outside the intensive care unit and cried. I noticed a small drop of water fall from the plastic to the floor.

Then my mother collapsed in the waiting room. Silently I walked into the intensive care unit. The doctors were "cleaning up" my brother. Dazed, I waited for the tubes to be pulled from his lungs and the equipment to be unplugged. One doctor was crying as he pulled the plastic from Tom's skin. I went to my brother and gently touched his face. He was still hot. His mouth was not completely closed, and I could see the white of his teeth. I felt the moisture of his perspiration on my fingertips, and I knew I would never feel any moisture from his body again.

I said all of this to Carol at lunch today. My memory of the day Tom died was crystal clear when I told her. I forgot momentarily where I was—at the restaurant. Carol's eyes teared as she listened. I told her about Tom's face before they closed his casket. He looked plastic and he was very, very cold. They put make-up on him, and his body creaked when they put a white hat on his head. I was cold and creaky also. The coffin closed, and I was jealous it wasn't me inside. Carol's daughter, Lorraine, was there. She was the only one who noticed me. She took my cold hands and tried to warm them. A few months later Lorraine married Hank. I never forgot her quiet kindness the day of Tom's funeral.

I stood tall, blond, and beautiful at my brother's viewing. It's important to look good at a viewing, so I did my hair, decorated my body with a new dress, and put on make-up (for the first time). I did look good. I kept the mask intact as I watched my father pop Valium, my mother collapse and my pregnant sister-in-law hold my brother's cold, lifeless hand. Only Lorraine noticed me, posed perfectly masking the pain. She took my cold hands into her own and began to warm them. A moment of shared grief. As she gently held my hands, I let myself crumble.

Lorraine Scott, I feel so bad for her. Carol asked me if I ever knew anything about Hank. I wish I could have warned her about Hank. I think that is why I am so upset tonight. I wish I could have warned Lorraine about Hank.

March 12, 1989

Today is my thirtieth birthday. I am in Kauai with Jennifer and Lilly. I chuckle whenever I think of Jennifer in our seventh-grade math class. She was a performer back then, and now she's living in New York and acting. She is inspiring. It is a tough profession, and she is making it. She is talented. I love Jennifer, but it's her daughter Lilly who captivates me. Lilly is three years old, and I am having a blast with her. I've been teaching her how to swim, and she's like a little fish. We have so much fun. I can't think of a better birthday.

This morning Lilly and I warmed up—a little stretching. Then we jogged down the sidewalk together and back to our hotel room. She is so darling! Yesterday I bought her a little Lycra jogging suit. We were quite a pair, jogging along the sidewalk on the beach. I don't know who was smiling more, Lilly or me. Then I went for a long run by myself. Lilly put on some headphones, stood at the window and waited for me to come back. Jennifer said that she stood there and danced to the music while she waited. So cute!

I ran for about 10 miles. It was beautiful. I wrote a poem in my head. I'll write it down when it comes together more; one of the lines has to do with "wind upon my hair."

When I got back to the hotel, Lilly wanted to shower with me. Why was I uncomfortable with that? She is just a little girl, but it made me nervous. Jennifer seemed just fine with it, so I took Lilly in the shower with me. Lilly exclaimed, "You got really big boobs." It was cute and funny, but I was embarrassed. I washed her hair while she sang. I didn't really feel like singing with her. I don't know, I must be extra modest or something, but I was still uncomfortable with the whole thing. I know it's stupid. After all I am 10 times older than Lilly. I am thirty, and she is three. I guess old habits die hard.

After we got dressed, we were going to do a little shopping. There is a large field right by our hotel. We were walking to the car, and Lilly ran through this green field of flowers chasing after some birds. She didn't catch any, but it was a beautiful sight to watch her running through the field as the birds took flight.

Lilly is so outgoing and free. She is such a happy, trusting little girl. She has long hair and she sucks her thumb. She reminds me of me when I was a little girl. I sucked my thumb until I was eight. I feel a bond with her.

April 15, 1989

I am totally redecorating my apartment. It's something I wanted to do for years, and now I'm doing it. I feel like I've overcome a "rhetoric block" that I inherited from my mother. I've watched her talk and talk and talk about things and then never take action. I have talked about redoing my apartment for years but haven't done anything. It was not feminine enough for me, and I made plans and talked about it a lot. But I never really did anything. For some reason, my old "hand-me-down" apartment was okay. After all Gramps did take pride in it, and he has such a hard time with change. Why rock the boat?

I live in the top floor of this fascinating old house. Gramps lives on the bottom. He is my mom's father. All my friends and everyone at the bank call him Gramps. He is the only male authority figure in my life who exudes any real emotion. Gramps is 88 years old, and I can talk with him more easily than I can talk to my brother Byron. We talk about religion, money and the meaning of life. We talk about my parents. We both have a great deal of remorse and sadness about my parents. Gramps can't understand why they can't stop drinking. He doesn't understand the concept of addiction. Sometimes I try to explain it to him. Other times I just let it go. And I listen to him express his feelings of sadness and loneliness.

It's been seven years since Grandmother's funeral, and Gramps occasionally talks about how much he loved her. I am touched when he talks about my grandmother. Gramps is the only man I know who talks about love.

I don't want to hurt Gramps's feelings. He did this place all by himself, long before I moved in. But I live here, and I want it to be nice enough for me. I don't need the old, tattered couches. I don't need the orange drapes that are falling from the curtain rods. I don't need the red and green squares nailed to the ceiling. And above all, I don't need the dark brown paneling. It is so dark in here. I am getting rid of the darkness.

I've picked out my wallpaper. It is light crème with tiny pink and green flowers. I am going to have a theme of flowers. I am going to re-carpet, buy all new furniture, paint (pearl tint is the color), and redo this entire place. For some reason, this has been very therapeutic for me. I don't know, something about this being the house where my mother grew up, where my mom and dad lived when they first got married, even where Melinda was born. Melinda and her husband lived here when they first got married. I'm totally changing it, making it a reflection of me.

The only rule I have is "Do I like it?" I know it will be beautiful. I've made a deal with Gramps—he has promised not to come up until it is all done. I think that if he misses out on the ripped-up look and only sees the end result he'll be okay. The place is gutted, and it would be hard for him to imagine what it will look like at the end. In my exhausted moments even, I have a hard time visualizing the end result. Sometimes I wonder why I started this enormous project. But I know it will be beautiful.

May 21, 1989

I'm back in Maui right now with Jennifer. I came for a fiscal investment convention, and Jennifer left Lilly and met me for a getaway. I have a great time with Jennifer. But it's not the same without her darling little girl. I love Lilly so much.

I'm sitting out here on the beach tonight—just writing. I am peaceful and content, yet I have a longing. A longing for something, but I don't know what.

I remember sitting on the shores of the Sea of Galilee with the same feeling. I guess I will always have this feeling until I meet my Heavenly Father again. Abraham felt this way when he asked the Lord for more—more understanding, more knowledge and more inspiration. And the Lord replied that our minds are too finite, and until we leave this state, we cannot understand any more.

There is always more. One of my greatest weaknesses is my impatience. I need to turn that into a strength. Instead of hungering for more, I need to fill my soul with the beauty and goodness surrounding me. I need to embrace the love continually encircling my heart.

Life is like sand. The more tightly you grip on to it, the quicker it slips through your hands. But if you open your palms, the sand will leave only a little at a time. It will still diminish, but gradually, and finally you will be left with an open palm. Not a closed, clenched fist—which will never hold anything again.

The sand, oh how I love to feel the sand sift through my fingers.

May 29, 1989

I got back from Hawaii on Sunday; I am over the jet lag.

I have a strange feeling of contentment now. Maybe I have developed the maturity to distinguish the important from the unimportant and to let the unimportant go. I also feel the soothing power of forgiveness. Forgiving others comforts me.

Monday night I was so tired, but I felt an urge to go and visit my dad. So I drove up there. My mom and Gramps are up at East Canyon Reservoir. My dad was the only one home. He was a little fidgety, but then we sat down, had some strawberry shortcake and a chat. It's the first time in my life I remember my dad and myself sitting down and having a talk. It wasn't major; it was just nice.

I believe in forgiveness and love and letting go of negativity. I believe in me.

June 17, 1989

My little apartment is almost done. I've been redecorating for two months. It is beautiful. And I have done everything myself!

A guy I've been dating, Brent, walked in, and he said it was so elegant it looked like a museum. This place has so much of me written all over that I am only letting special people in to see it. Brent is, Brent is—well, not counting my brothers, the only male I have ever sustained a relationship with. This relationship entails several gaps of several months, primarily because of my "push-pull" syndrome. This adult child of alcoholics' lingo describes my problems with intimacy so well.

I don't plan on letting just anyone into my space. I must have a certain level of trust. I had a beautiful wall of glass etched between my bedroom and living room. The etching on the glass is from 1050 A.D., and it is called "Invocation."

God within me God without
How shall I ever be in doubt?
There is no place where I may go
And not there see God's face, not know

I am God's vision and God's ears
So through the harvest of my years
I am the sower and the sown
God's self unfolding and God's own.

I have flowers all over and statues, figurines and brass. I love it. My mom said it was darling and light and cozy. It is. It is a reflection of me. I am beautiful and light and open and comfortable and elegant and feminine and me!

July 5, 1989

I'm a little down today—maybe I'm tired. Or maybe I'm sad to see my project completed. I don't know; maybe I'm lonely.

I feel like I've gained weight, and that always bugs me. I'm far too old to be bulimic. After all of my understanding and therapy, what am I doing? This doesn't make sense. I'm humiliated to admit it.

July 6, 1989

I'm still trying to shrug this mood. I think it has a lot to do with Lilly. I miss her. I feel really bad about it. So maybe I need to just cry for a while.

Always in the past, whenever I felt hurt or sad or lonely, I would panic and rush into something—buy things, eat and purge, and talk to everyone around me. Now I've learned to simply let myself feel the hurt. I feel abandoned by Lilly. I know this is irrational. I am the adult, and Lilly is the child; but it's how I feel. By allowing myself to feel the hurt, I find strength in me. It is still morning, and I am twirling a pen around and just looking at it, not feeling.

July 7, 1989

I miss Lilly. I feel such a bond with her. When we were in Hawaii, Jennifer told me about Lilly's father showering with Lilly. Jennifer encourages them to be "natural" in the shower. Jennifer said, "It is better to be natural so that Lilly doesn't feel ashamed of the differences between boys and girls." When I heard about Lilly showering with her father, I literally got sick inside. I don't know why, but I think the father might be sexually abusing Lilly. He is so demanding and controlling of her. He is jealous of her. I've seen the father pout and pinch Lilly until she cries. Lilly always clings to me or her mother when her dad is around. I think the whole thing is weird. I don't know why I have such a strong feeling about this. I want to take Lilly away and protect her. It makes me sick to think of beautiful, beautiful Lilly in the shower with him and his big thing hanging down in her face.

July 13, 1989

I woke up a little depressed today—and I'm not sure why. I've been dreaming about Lilly. I am worried about her.

July 14, 1989

I am still very shame based. I try to be perfect—I have a lot of grandiose thinking—I worry too much about what other people think.

My brain is a little scrambled right now. I think I've been trying to people-please too much lately. I just want a simple, beautiful weekend. I am tired of confusion, anger and crisis. I am tired of all the emotional turmoil and blackmail I experience when dealing with my father. He has a beautiful home up in East Canyon Reservoir. He has left an open door for anyone in the family to use it, but every summer I am the only one who goes. I love to water ski, but I'm starting to wonder if it's worth it.

My parents proclaim, "Feel free to use the cabin anytime. You have a great time!" But my father wants to control every detail of the happenings in that cabin. He even wants to know what soda pop we'll be drinking. After (and only after) I make plans to go up to East Canyon does he start to intervene. Now he's on a rampage about not launching the boat until it's in "perfect" condition. Well, I'm sorry, but a seven-year-old boat is not going to be in perfect condition. I approached my mother about buying the boat from my dad, but I don't know how that will go. I don't think my dad can release control over the boat. He never drives it, but he knows that I love it. If he keeps it, he can have some pull on my life. Maybe I should just buy my own boat. Anyway, I'm tired of dealing with my father in any fashion.

July 15, 1989

I am so sad. I went to therapy with Karen Fisher yesterday, and she said I need to have a heart-to-heart with Jennifer. There is a wedge between us, and the wedge is my fear. My fear of intimacy, my fear that I will lose myself, my fear that I will be judged, my fear that I will lose our friendship, my fear that I will lose Lilly. My fear that Lilly will be hurt. I miss her.

Denial

I woke up late today. I have had some fairly rough nights lately. Whenever I am upset, I have trouble sleeping. I wish I could figure out what is bothering me.

I am watching Gramps saw up the yard right now. Really, he has his saw out—not hedgers. I guess you use whatever works. The dog is watching too. I love my apartment. I am happy to be here. This is my home. I enjoy sitting here and just being. Watching Gramps has raised my spirits.

Carol

I HAD A BABY SHOWER for my daughter Susy tonight. I look at her rounded stomach, and I can almost feel the kicking, the new life. New life. Hope.

I cannot remember a time when I didn't want babies more than anything. I think I was in kindergarten, and it was Christmastime, and we were doing a Sub-for-Santa. In an effort to teach us altruism, Mother had asked each of us to give a favorite toy. I don't know what my sister chose; but it was impossible for me to believe she loved anything the way I loved my dolls, except possibly her bike, which Mother would have refused as too expensive. I looked at each doll and tried to make a choice, but I couldn't give away one of my own babies. Every night I slept with them all so none would feel left out. With their heads peeking up above the covers so they wouldn't smother, I couldn't turn over the whole night. The most beautiful ones, like Frenchie, I scarcely touched because I was saving them for my own little girls. But I loved them all with a passion bestowed on nothing else. Each Christmas I washed and ironed all their clothes and dressed them in their best and put them out for Santa Claus to see what good care I had taken of them so that he would leave me yet another.

Mother said, "Your sister knows how happy some little child would be, and that means more to her than the toy. Can't you do that too?" I could not. Manipulate me as she might, I was not going to sacrifice a doll to my mother's sense of being a good mother. Instead, I would give doll dishes, a book, a game—anything but a doll. Even then I knew you don't give away your children.

As I watched Susy opening her presents at the shower, I thought of the call a few years ago from Sara, my son Jake's wife. She called from a hospital in Mexico City, where she and Jake were traveling. She had a miscarriage there. All the memories I felt when Sara called came back to me now looking at Susy. How much I needed to hold Sara. Memories of when I was little.

I must have been seven because I wasn't baptized yet. Mother had been in her bedroom for a very long time it seemed, and I was told all day long to be quiet so she could sleep. I worried she might die, but no one I knew had died. What was awful was not being allowed to ask what was the matter. All the quiet, a bad quiet. Finally, my sister told me.

"You have to be really good now because Mother feels so bad. She had a little baby inside her and it died and now she's very sick."

"But she wasn't fat like Aunt Emily!"

"The baby starts out little and then when it gets so big you might pop, they take it out of you."

"But where is it if it's dead? What happened to it? What made it die?"

My sister referred me to Daddy. I never asked him, so I am left still with my questions. All I could think was how bad my mother must feel, worse than when I left my doll outside, and a dog chewed her up. It was quiet, and nobody cared if I knew or not. It seemed the saddest thing that could happen.

Then the memory of being 21 and married six months. I was in our small white house cleaning our kitchen with the red daisy fabric on the ceiling matching the ruffled curtains. Not a crumb or smudge anywhere, but I was scrubbing anyway before we left it to the renters. We were leaving Salt Lake. Norton was going to graduate school in New York.

I had skipped lunch, and in the logic of the guilty that has always seemed a relevant fact to me. Norton was eating a sandwich at our gray Formica table when I went into the bathroom. I came back and sat by him and watched him eat. It wasn't until he got to dessert that I could say, "There's some blood. I don't know what it means. Do you think I should call the doctor?"

The cramps and the blood started hard, and the doctor sent an ambulance. Norton sat in back by me and held my hand, and I felt sort of foolish, almost amused, but mostly empty and scared. They put me in the maternity ward where I could hear the insistent wail of the newborn at feeding times. Even now my uterus, removed since by a hysterectomy, contracts and my milk almost rushes to my breasts when I hear that sound. A day or so later the doctor decided I had lost the baby.

We walked across South Temple to First Avenue where Norton's mother lived to tell her; and like the blood, the tears and pain poured out of me. She had three miscarriages before Norton. Norton grieved for me, but together she and I mourned the baby.

The miscarriage left me with an all-consuming passion to have a baby. I had wanted one since I tucked all the dolls under their covers, but now it became an obsession.

Lorraine was conceived. The first three months went well enough, aside from the fish factory down the block which burned down when I was most nauseated. But then again came the pale pink spotting, the prayers and fasting, the hours flat in bed, the embarrassed telephone explanation to my boss, and the long subway ride to 108th Street, where the medical center was. As I walked slowly to the subway, I worried if I had to stand mashed among all those impersonal sweating bodies, each trying to squeeze into its own protected space, I would lose the baby. But it was mid-morning, and I found a seat. Then there was only a transfer at 42nd Street and climbing the subway steps at 108th, carefully resting in between, calculating every step. Please God, let me get to the doctor. Just let him give me the shots before anything happens. Pretending to look at the *New Yorker* in his crowded waiting room, I tried to take deep relaxing breaths. At last, his patient, tired eyes saying he thought we'd make it.

The first three months were the same for me with Susy. Even after I was halfway convinced by the best medical opinion that nothing I could do would make any difference, whenever I lifted a heavy child or was too tired or felt sharp cramps, there was the lonely gnawing panic and the quick guilt. Each bathroom visit for the first three months was a hasty search for red and a thanksgiving prayer. Nausea, exhaustion, backache, pain—they counted nothing against the toilet tissue's whiteness.

I know the value of your baby, Susy. In the pressure and waste of getting and spending, the headlines blazing politics and crime, the clatter of dirty dishes and small useless words, some things are sure: a husband's touch or glance across a room, the sun dipping into the Great Salt Lake, Susy at 10 grabbing her black puppy to her throat, and, almost more than all, that growing, pulsating, living being, deep beyond all deepness within you. Mother, Norton's mother, Lorraine, Sara, Susy and I—bound tight in this sure knowledge. I have always secretly believed I share more with a Guatemalan peasant in labor in a ditch behind her hut than with the childless, cultured, interesting neighbor down the street. Even now, after everything.

All this passed through me as I watched Susy and her friends. Some of them I'd known before they were in high school. April was there. She seemed happy to see everyone. She knew most of those old friends, but she seemed tense. Maybe it was seeing Lorraine. Lorraine must always remind her of her brother Tom, of his death, because Hank and Tom were so close.

Lorraine looked lovely in a new lavender silk dress. Only I knew how hard it was for her to be around people, to make small talk, to seem normal. I remembered the baby shower I had for Lorraine before Timothy was born. Hank had just passed his CPA exam. Everything seemed so promising. I thought of them in white kneeling at the temple altar, promising to be together for ever and ever.

Something's going on with April. I know it. I wish she'd talk to me. She gave Susy a ton of practical stuff like baby wipes and diapers. I hope people had fun. It was fun for me. I care about my kids' old friends, at least some of them.

April

I JUST GOT BACK FROM a baby shower for Susy Scott. The shower was up at Carol's new home in Deer Valley. It's the first time I've seen this house, and typical for Carol, it is beautiful.

Deer Valley is so secluded. It would be great to jog there.

The first person I saw at the shower was Jennifer. I wasn't sure if she'd make it from New York. I think I was nervous because I wanted to talk to her about Lilly.

I had to tell her I think Lilly is being sexually abused. Maybe it wasn't the right time or place, but I had to tell her. Jennifer has to do something to protect her daughter.

Jennifer listened calmly. She said that she had thought the same thing herself. She said she'd asked Lilly, and Lilly said, "No!"

I felt like Jennifer pulled away. She was distant from me the rest of the night. I know this might be in my own mind, but I felt like Jennifer brought the curtain down on my interaction with Lilly. I have a sad feeling that Jennifer is not going to exert any effort to bring us together. Maybe I made a mistake by saying something.

Susy commented that she didn't recognize me at first, maybe because my hair was windblown. I drove with the top down on my car, and I had my hair pinned on top of my head.

Susy looked great. She looks very comfortable being pregnant. Some women look like they are carrying the weight of the world when they are pregnant; Susy looked natural and strong. I know Susy will be a great mother. Susy is real.

That is why I am so drawn to Carol. She is real.

It's something I am striving for, but I always seem to fall short. Maybe it's because I was raised by impostors. Laurel came up for the party tonight. All the way from St. George. She brought her boys, and they are staying with me. Laurel and I can talk about everything, almost. We chatted about literature and our favorite works. Then the conversation wandered to Laurel's young children and her future plans. Laurel wants to be a counselor. Laurel said, "I've been helped so much; I want to do the same for others." We were talking about the history of eating disorders in her family. I didn't even come close to telling her it was something I was currently battling; she'd be so disappointed. I know better than this. I talked with Karen about my "purging" yesterday. I have been out of control for a couple of weeks now. I can deceive myself easily with this addiction of mine.

In January of this year, I stopped being bulimic. I went to Hawaii and controlled my eating. I felt victorious. I believed that I was cured. But the reality is I've just been in the "control" phase of my addiction. Even though I was not "acting out," it was still an obsession. I thought about it enough to take me away from thinking about my core issues. Just because I wasn't eating and purging doesn't mean it went away. It reminds me a little of my parents and their binge alcoholism. They can go for months without taking a drink. Then *bam!* They get drunk. Over the years the binges have gone from an evening out on the town to a full weekend, even a three-day weekend. Then they will be sober for months. They are still alcoholics. It does get worse; and if left untreated, they will die.

My addiction is food, and I am out of control right now. I am kidding myself to say it's not a problem. I sat there with Laurel, my close friend for years, and talked about her struggles with her family and all their pain—and I didn't even think of myself. I didn't come close to relating the conversation to myself! The scariest part is that I can hide so well from myself.

Lorraine was there. She is beautiful. I felt shy, uncomfortable. I put on a big smile, and I don't think she could tell how anxious I was. I don't know why I was so uncomfortable. Maybe because I haven't seen her in such a long time. Maybe it's just my intimacy stuff. I still have a hard time reaching out to others. So many emotions, Lorraine Scott deeply touched my life.

Later:

Growth involves loss, and sometimes you lose some good people—at least that's what Karen says.

I don't think I'm growing, just losing. Losing and acting like I'm gaining. I'm worried I'll lose Lilly. Well, I'm gaining "stuff," material stuff. But I don't know how to fill the hole in my soul. Why am I still purging? Why can't I stop? Why am I so out of control? Why do I feel so out of control of my own life right now? *Stop Stop Stop!* Stop it, stop hurting yourself and feel your hurt.

July 21, 1989

I am just waking up, and I am tired.

I had an emotional day yesterday. I was on appointments all day, and my dad was running around being an irrational, explosive, controlling beast. He never sees anything positive, especially in me. He has moments where he is pathetic. It doesn't matter if the boat is launched. My life is about beauty and love and happiness. I wrote him this letter, and dropped it in his mailbox on my way up to East Canyon:

Dear Dad,

Each and every day we are one step closer to our own deaths. Each and every day we are one step closer to meeting our Maker.

As for me, I have decided to live my life with as much beauty, goodness, peace and love as I possibly can. Part of the joy of our existence is the pain. And we all experience tremendous pain, whether we recognize it or not, because we all inevitably have sufficient pain. I have chosen not to create any more in my own life.

I have decided to stop trying to be perfect and to be happy instead.

For me that's as good as it gets. That process entails growth and productivity and discipline and responsibility and pain and joy and laughter and love and happiness.

And hopefully, on that day I meet my Maker, I will gaze up and say, "No, I wasn't perfect. I had many imperfections—but I always tried. I brought a great deal of goodness to myself and to those around me."

Dad, sometimes I feel you have a lot of anger towards me. And, well oh well, I wish you only love and peace and happiness. I have chosen not to worry about your anger anymore. I only care about your joy and happiness.

I expect you to treat me with dignity and respect because that is how I have chosen to treat myself. And if I'm ever around anyone who doesn't treat me with dignity and respect, I will simply remove myself from that situation. For me life is too short to subject myself to anything less.

Well, I just wanted to let you know about me and how I have chosen to create my own wonderful, beautiful life.

Love,
April

July 25, 1989

I want to let go of my feelings of loss—and sadness from the past. Sometimes things don't work out.

July 26, 1989

I was down last night. Since last February I have been in a flurry of activity, and I need to settle down and get control of my own life again. I want to work and think and relax. I am burnt out. I want some solitude. I want to write. I want some time to think.

Last night there was a big fire up Emigration Canyon. This canyon is close to the city. I sat in my living room and watched the flames. It's sobering to watch such destruction. Maybe that's why I was so sad. It will take a long time for the mountains to be green again. This morning the hills are charcoal black—just ashes. The sky is hazy from the smoke, like an inversion.

I hate those damn inversions every January. They make me think that in my hometown even healthy people are getting sick and coughing up phlegm and spitting on the ground. It freezes. Polite ones simply swallow. I don't want to think about the scum lining my lungs. I can see the gray flats, synthesized to the smog until guided above the mountains. Crisp blue sky, fresh snow beckons me to play warm in the yellow sun, bright, not blocked by human exhaust.

When I was up at Carol's for the shower, I felt above the pollution. Not just in a physical way but in a psychological way. Now I'm "down"—in the city, in the exhaust.

Later:

I just sent flowers to Lorraine—I feel better. They were yellow. I hope they were bright enough.

July 30, 1989

I have been sleeping so much lately. This weekend I slept twelve hours per night. I'm exhausted.

Maybe I'm finally resting. I went to Hawaii twice and traveled all over on the road. Now I'm collapsing.

"An addiction is answering a spiritual calling at the wrong address." Karen Fisher wrote that on a card for me. She asked me if I knew what my spiritual calling was. With great sarcasm I said, "It beats the hell out of me."

Karen smiled and said, "I think it's the same for all of us. April, I think our spiritual calling is to love ourselves. And when we are full of shame and fear we try to escape those feelings by numbing ourselves out—with food or booze or drugs or work or whatever. But it only helps for the moment. And until we do the real work—inside—we will pack around the pain and the addiction forever."

I think I'm addicted to food. I have stopped eating compulsively—for the last couple of weeks—now I am just sad.

Karen asked me to pick up a book, *Fat is a Feminist Issue*. I got it and have been avidly reading it since I got home. There is one part that really struck a nerve. It is about fat being a layer of protection. I don't know why, but every time I date someone, and it gets to the point of any physical touching or intimacy, I gain weight. I put on weight to deter them or to have an excuse for why I'm not comfortable being touched.

I can track this pattern with every relationship. I can't believe I didn't notice it sooner.

Every time I feel out of control, I get bulimic. I eat a ton and then purge. I never get skinny though. Just bulimic—and tired—and stressed.

Right now, I miss Lilly. She is growing and changing every day. I miss her.

August 19, 1989

It is 5:00 a.m.—yes, five in the morning. I was awakened at four by a booming storm.

I feel cozy and comfortable being safe and warm and inside during a storm.

I feel good. I am listening to the stereo, drinking a cup of mocha, and watching the storm.

I've thought a great deal about being alone. I enjoy it. There is freedom in waking up at 4:00 a.m., turning on the light, and listening to the stereo. Interrupting no one.

But I also love children. I love their questions and their excitement, their joy at the beauty of nature and the wonder of life.

September 7, 1989

Laurel is visiting with the boys. Burton is almost six and Parker recently turned four. Every waking moment Parker wears his cowboy boots. Sometimes he tries to put them back on after his bath. Laurel doesn't let him wear them with his pajamas, but first thing in the morning, those boots are back on! It's the cutest thing I've ever seen.

Burton and Parker have a tendency to wrestle. Laurel says that they follow her around the house, like a giant tumbleweed. Every time she turns around, she sees arms and legs flailing in the air. The boots have become a bit of a problem because Parker has kicked his older brother. When Burton gets kicked—even if it is a complete accident as professed so earnestly by the younger, Parker— it hurts.

Laurel set an ultimatum to Parker: "I'll give you three chances. If you kick your brother three more times with those cowboy boots on, I'm going to take them away and throw them in the garbage."

Parker looked terrified. His mom meant business. Parker was so good. He didn't mess up once and accidentally kick his older brother all day. Then they went to the zoo, and there was one incident by the elephant house. I'm sure it was all the excitement being close to those big, playful elephants. Parker was simply trying to get Burton's attention, but his mom saw it. One kick down. His mother warned him. Then there was another side kick at the playground by the train.

Laurel stopped everything, put Parker right on the picnic table in front of her and said, "Parker, I warned you. You kick Burton one more time with those cowboy boots on, and I'm going to take them off and throw them in the garbage. It hurts when you kick him. Do you understand?"

Parker's big blue eyes misted over, and he nodded, "Yes." Laurel didn't let him down until Parker said, "Yes mom, I understand. I won't kick Burton again."

The rest of the visit to the zoo was glorious. The boys were in absolute boy heaven. The only thing missing was the dinosaurs. I let Laurel handle the explanation of why their favorite animal, a dinosaur, was missing from Hogle Zoo. Laurel was quite remarkable actually; it's not easy to explain "extinct" to a couple of preschoolers.

We parked the car in the back garage. We were all walking back to the house, the boys tumbling behind us, and I heard it. Laurel saw it. With military precision,

Laurel picked up four-year-old Parker, sat him down and removed Parker's very favorite cowboy boots. Parker started crying. Laurel said, "Parker, I told you that it hurts Burton when you kick with those boots. I gave you three warnings, and the last time you kicked him, I told you I'd take them and throw them in the trash if you did it again."

Parker wailed.

Burton was smug.

Laurel was adamant. She kissed her young son's head as she walked to the trash and threw them out.

In my trash. At my house. I couldn't bear to hear Parker's sobs.

Laurel relaxed, settled into her book, and told the boys to go play. Parker flung himself onto the couch and cried himself to sleep. Burton took out his book and started reading too.

As for me, when no one was looking, I fished the boots out of the trash. I knew that right then Laurel would never relent to her little boy's tears, but maybe she would later for me.

After a couple of hours, Parker woke up from his nap. He climbed onto his mommy's lap and told her he was sorry. Laurel hugged her little boy and explained that actions have consequences. Parker's eyes welled again, but he didn't cry. Laurel kissed him on the cheek, then Parker looked over at Burton and told him that he was really sorry. Burton smiled and said, "It's alright, wanna spar?" Soon the boys were having a sword fight with branches out on the lawn, laughing. Laurel was making them something to eat, and I slithered into the kitchen with the boots hidden behind me.

"Please ... ?"

"April, you are not helping."

"Please, he's heartbroken!"

Laurel's lips slammed shut as her shoulders automatically squared back. I knew she wasn't ready to relent. I turned and walked out of the kitchen. I wrapped Parker's boots in tissue and slid them into a brown grocery bag. Before the boys came back inside, I grabbed an armchair, slid it up by my highest shelf and hid the boots behind my books.

Dinner followed with yummy hamburgers, hotdogs, salad and milk to drink. The discussion was lively. I quickly got up to speed about the latest "Teenage Mutant Ninja Turtles" episode. When asked which one was my favorite, I quickly glanced at Laurel. She mouthed the words, "Leonardo." Da Vinci has always been one of my favorites from the Renaissance, I blurted out "Da Vinci." The boys looked at me as if I'd transformed into a rock. I didn't realize they were on a first name basis.

Laurel saved me by telling the boys that I hadn't watched the show. The boys proceeded to try to explain the TV show. Their explanation was quite hard to follow; however, once they were satisfied I was up to date, my face hurt from smiling and laughing.

Dinner quickly ended when Laurel reminded each boy to eat at least three bites of their green salad. Three seems to be the number of motherhood. Burton extracted a trace of green on his fork and popped it into his mouth. There was a debate about the actual size of a bite. When Laurel wasn't looking, Parker brought his empty fork to his mouth three times. Laurel witnessed the charade with eyes in the back of her head and told him that he had to have some visible salad on his fork for it to count.

I quickly interjected that we could play the "guessing game" and "snore-some-more" after their baths and story. The boys surrendered the fight on the veggies and raced to the tub.

The next morning, when the boot incident seemed long forgotten, I gingerly broached the subject again with Laurel. Exasperated, Laurel said, "I am not going to raise a serial killer!" After our laughter died down, I raised my eyebrows and plead, "Please, he was so sad. I don't think I've ever seen Parker without his boots on."

With determination and a tone of finality Laurel said, "Maybe after he gets married."

So be it. I tucked those boots away, and I'll keep them in case she relents—after Parker gets married.

Carol

APRIL TOOK ME TO HER apartment in one of those old, wonderful houses on the Avenues today. Her grandfather, she calls him Gramps, lives downstairs, but the upstairs is all hers. The rooms are April down to the last soap dish, the ribbon holding a picture, every pillow. It is totally feminine, like being in a pink and green flower garden.

She did all the design and work herself, the wallpapering, sewing, everything. I understand how the rooms are a revelation of herself and a sanctuary not open to everyone. I was touched she'd invited me.

She and I had lunch at Oceans a few months ago. She didn't have much time because of work, so each of us barely touched our lunch. Something reminded her of Tom's funeral. I think she asked how Lorraine was. That made her think of Hank at the funeral.

What did I do when April mentioned Hank? I squeezed lemon into my Diet Coke without a tremor.

But I know what I was thinking. Hank. I don't want to hear that name. I don't want to be connected to him. I don't want even April to think of him as my son-in-law. If I met him in a grocery store, what would I do? If a grocery-store clerk smiles at Lorraine and says, "Have a good day," she can't help crying. She says it's that way when anyone's nice to her. She cries.

I can't tell April yet. Not anyone yet. April is talking about Hank being a pall bearer. The children. I have to protect the children.

Did you know Hank and Lorraine are divorced, April?"

Then she said the strangest thing. I can still remember the words, "No, he never touched me."

Everything intensified—the pink of the linen napkins, the conversation from other tables, the waitress's stain on her crisp, white apron, my too-loud words. Inside me a voice was thundering, "Ask her, ask her." But I couldn't. Not only because of the grandchildren but because she adored her brother Tom and everything surrounding him. Maybe that even includes Hank, how do I know?

I can't talk to her yet, but maybe sometime. Why did she make that strange, strange statement? Like a bomb out of nowhere. There's no way she could know. Then why?

April

LAST NIGHT I HAD THE most disturbing dream. It was horrible. I can't even think about it without crying. *I was in a record store and there were a bunch of guys that worked there and some of their friends were all gathered together talking. As I leafed through various music selections, I couldn't help but overhear their enthusiastic conversation. They were boasting about how a few of them had nailed this girl.*

They were laughing about how she squealed and screamed and how she acted like she didn't want it, but how she really did want it.

One guy was the leader. He was so proud that he screwed her three times and one time up her tight little ass. His eyes twinkled, "She loved it. She was in such ecstasy that she was crying."

I stayed in the record store, still, I remained very still. I could feel my blood racing through my entire body. I was enraged.

Then I walked over to this group of guys and with venom said, "If a girl says no, she means no. And if she's crying, it's because she's hurt."

They all laughed.

Somehow I knew I owned this record store with a couple of these guys. I wasn't shopping. I was an owner of the store.

These guys proceeded to tell me that if I wasn't so frigid, I'd know what a good time she had with them. One guy, the leader, leaned over and put his hand right on my breast and told me "You only need a good lay." He then told me the other girl's name. She was my closest friend. I loved her—I knew she didn't have a good time with them. I knew she was really hurt.

I ran from the store to find my friend. I couldn't find her anywhere. My friend had vanished. I searched everywhere. I wanted to protect her. I knew those guys were coming after her again.

They were coming after me as well. They didn't want me to find her. They wanted to do it to her again and again and again. I was terrified as I raced after her. I asked everyone where she might be—but she was gone.

The more I searched, the easier it was for these guys to trace her. The people I asked would go directly to my pursuers and tell them where I had been and where I was going.

I finally went into a house-a very familiar house, and I knew she was there. I sprinted up the stairs and looked down the hall. The door was closed to the bedroom at the end of the hall. I started screaming for help. I yelled, "He's in there raping her." No one believed me. All these people were in the kitchen, and they looked over like "stop bothering us." No one believed me. He was a well-known, wealthy man. I knew he was a rapist ... and he was in that room, at that very moment, raping my friend.

The door opened, and he walked out. He had a smirk on his face. He said, "She loved it." I lunged at him. I knocked him on his back. I started choking him. He got a hard on, and it ripped through his pants. I reached down and grabbed his penis with my right hand. I was going to rip it off. Suddenly, his penis turned black, like a snake. I thought it was a trick, so I held on tighter.

Then the head of his penis divided into eight parts. Each part turned into a black snake. The snakes wrapped around my hand, and I couldn't get away. I was trapped.

I screamed and started to cry. He sat up with a laugh. He had an evil, lusty laugh. He said, "I'm going to fuck you to death. I'm going to go inside of you, and my snakes are going to eat your heart out."

I sobbed hysterically.

Quietly, my friend walked up to him. She looked a lot like me, only prettier and thinner. She walked very seductively and put her hand on his shoulder. She was wearing my white running bra and my white running shorts. She was very calm and very determined. Tears streamed down my cheeks as I watched her lead him down the hall. She was sacrificing herself for me, like an innocent lamb. Right before the door closed he looked at me and said, "See, she loves it."

I woke up.

I am still rattled. I don't know why this dream has upset me so. I can't seem to stop crying.

October 2, 1989

I just got back from my session with Karen, and I'm all upset. For over a month now, she has asked me to pick up a book called *My Father's House*. I've been avoiding it. But every week when I go into Karen's, she asks if I've done my assignment. So finally, yesterday I went to the bookstore and picked it up. I read the first nineteen pages, and I was absolutely furious with Karen. How could she ask me to read such a horrible book? I'm not saying that it wasn't well written. I'm talking about the content. It's about an adult woman who tells her story of incest with her father. It made me sick.

I walked into Karen's office, really pissed off at her. I told her. I told her that I was done working on my parents' alcoholism issues. I had my bulimia fairly under control, and I had been in therapy for over three years. It was time to end it.

Karen was very gentle. She validated the fact that any sensitive individual would be ill at ease with that book, but she felt that my reaction was stronger than usual. Then I started crying. I couldn't stop.

Karen looked at me and said, "What's all this emotion about?" I was crying so hard, the silent kind of tears that pour down my face when I've really lost it. I couldn't answer her.

Finally, I said, "I don't know."

Then Karen said, "Will you at least stay to work on your eating disorder?"

I nodded, "Yes."

I was still crying as she walked me to the door. I asked her if I could go out the other door so that the people in the waiting room wouldn't see me. She let me out, and I lost it even more as I walked to my car. So here I am—crying—without the faintest idea of why I feel so wounded.

October 3, 1989

I feel so wounded. It's almost like somebody punched me in the stomach. I don't know who or when. I feel like I'm hunched over struggling to get my breath back. That feeling when you are at the bottom of the swimming pool and you run out of air. Those brief seconds while you race to the surface to get a breath. You are focusing only on one thing: getting to the top to get some air. I don't know where the surface is.

Late at night:

I can't sleep. My mind is racing. I don't know where it is going. Maybe I'm losing my mind. I keep having these black and white flashes; when I was little, we had a black and white television. We didn't get a color one until I was in first grade. Maybe that's where I'm getting these black and white flashes. Some people, I've heard, dream in black and white. I never have before, but maybe I am now. Maybe my dream the other night was so traumatic that I'm softening my dreams by taking the color out. Only I don't feel like these flashes are dreams. I think they are real. I don't know where they are coming from. I feel like I'm going crazy.

I was little and naked and crying. They were peeing on me. I was crouched down in the corner crying. My tears were wet and sticky and so was their pee. I remember looking down at my legs and seeing red blotches. Blotches like when my mommy hit me. I thought the pee was making the red marks on my legs and chest and arms. Now I know they were hives ... I had hives all over my body.

"Don't pee in my pee-pee hole!" I cried. And he laughed and peed between my legs. I didn't want to have a baby, and I was scared that I'd have one because they kept peeing in my pee-pee hole. I knew that's where babies came from, from boys peeing in girl's holes. I was not even five, and I didn't want to have a baby. The other girls in my neighborhood didn't have babies. I knew if I had one they'd know. Everyone would know about the pee. I wanted to go to school and go to kindergarten. If I had a baby, I'd have to stay home and be a mommy. Mommies were always sick and yelled all the time. And hit their kids with a switch. I didn't want to be a mommy. I wanted to be a nanny like Mary Poppins and leap over sidewalks and go to different worlds. I wanted someone to give me a spoonful of sugar and sing me to sleep. I wanted Mary Poppins to take me away ... I didn't want

to be a mommy. Or be around my mommy. Or have him peeing in my pee-pee hole. He told me my husband would love me because I knew how to fuck. The boys watched us and played with their peanuts until the white stuff spurted up. Sometimes it looked like they hurt themselves when the white stuff came up. They cried and even yelled. Sometimes it scared me. And I was glad when it was over. I didn't like the mess it made. Or when they pushed so hard I bled. I liked it better when they pushed into my assy hole. I knew we weren't fucking then. I knew I couldn't have a baby where my assy came out. I'd turn around and they'd put their big thing in me, their peanuts, and it was like fucking only it wasn't. Sometimes they'd get my poo-poo on it ... they'd make me lick it off. I hated that. I hated having to lick poo-poo off their peanuts.

> *Star light, star bright,*
> *first star I see tonight,*
> *I wish I may, I wish I might,*
> *have this wish, I wish tonight.*

Then, I'd close my eyes and say, "I wished I'd stop being so nasty." And I'd pray, "Heavenly Father, I'm sorry for being so bad. I'm sorry for being so nasty. I won't fuck anymore. Please help me stop."

I meant it. I knew that if I wished on the first star every night and never looked at that star again that my wish would come true. That I'd stop fucking. I wanted to go to school. I didn't want to have a baby. Besides I didn't have boobies to feed the baby, and it would die. I didn't want my baby to die. I wanted to die. I wanted to be in a white lacy coffin. It would have pillows and lace all over it. And I would be dead. I could sleep as long as I wanted. They couldn't wake me up and scare me. They told me the devil would get me if I told. That I'd have Satan's baby because Satan did not have a body. If I didn't let them do it, they'd let Satan get me pregnant. I'd cry, and they'd put my feather pillow over my face. Sometimes I couldn't breathe, and feathers went up my nose. He'd hold it over my face until I "Shut the fuck-up." I usually shut up when he started to fuck because if I didn't ...

So I wanted a lacy coffin. To be dead and never wake up. I'd look pretty in the coffin, and they'd all be sorry for what they did. I wanted to die before I was eight because then I could still go to heaven. If I died before I was baptized, I'd be forgiven for all the fucking, sucking and being nasty. I wanted to go to heaven. I wanted to die and never wake up.

I don't want to tell Karen about this because I think she'll put me away. But if I really am crazy—maybe an institution is the best place for me.

In the neighbor's basement. The next door neighbors. They were an older couple, not as old as Gramps and Grandma, but really old. A lot older than my mommy and daddy. They had two sons in college, and they'd come home from college for a couple of months in the summer. They had a little red car that the top would come down, and they'd take me for rides. Rides. Rides up Emigration Canyon after we'd been in their basement. I can even remember the layout of their basement. We'd go in through their garage and then through their laundry room. They had a family room. We'd walk past that down the hall to the oldest brother's bedroom. He had playing cards with naked ladies on them. We'd go into his room with both of them and me. They had big peanuts. I'd be naked, looking at the cards. They'd be looking at the cards, and they'd rub their big things between my legs. Sometimes they put lotion all over me so I didn't get red spots. It was scary and exciting and fun. It felt good with the lotion on. Sometimes they'd ask me to squeeze my legs together really tight. They'd put their peanuts between my legs and rub back and forth really hard. If I kept my legs together until the white stuff spurted out, they'd give me a ride up the canyon. That was the best part. They called me their little princess. They said I was pretty. Sometimes I'd sit on one of their laps and he'd put his fingers up me. He said he was going to put his big thing up me, and he wanted to make sure I was ready. We'd just drive up the canyon with the top down, and he'd get my pee-pee hole ready for his big thing. It was okay as long as his fingernails didn't pinch me.

I am insane. Did this really happen? Yes, it did. These flashes really happened to me. At least it feels like it right now. Maybe, maybe I was just a really messed up little girl, and I got those big boys to touch me. I can't believe I'm writing this, and I can't believe I'm sitting here as an adult woman feeling the same feelings I did as a little girl. I am excited and scared. I can feel the sun on my face in the canyon, and I know I can't tell anyone about this. I know I'm being a nasty little girl. I hate it, and I like it. I feel like I'm going insane.

I feel so emotional. Why can't I stop crying? And why would I let them do that to me? Why did I keep going back? Why was I so nasty? This wasn't just kids playing I'll show you mine if you'll show me yours. This was two college-age boys fingering me and getting themselves off between my legs. And I let them. For a ride in the canyon, and because he held me in his lap.

October 4, 1989

I still feel as if it is yesterday. It's late at night. I'm having trouble sleeping. Trouble isn't really the appropriate adjective. I can't sleep. Every time I start to fall asleep, I jerk awake. Sometimes in my past dreams, I fell down the stairs or off a cliff, but I always woke up with a jerk before I hit the ground. Tonight, I hit the ground and splattered all over. I walked around my apartment for a while and then dozed off again. I dreamt that I was being chased by a madman. He followed me up to my parents' neighborhood. I hid in the excavation pipe under the road. When I thought he was gone, I crawled up from under the street and started to run across the street to my parents' house. Out of nowhere a car revved up the street and hit me. I fell down, and the back tires ran right over my hips. They were crushed, and I was bleeding profusely. Blood was all over the street. The madman had been driving the car, and I could hear him laughing. I just lay in the road and waited to die.

Now I don't want to sleep. I am afraid of it. I am afraid of my own mind. I don't know what do to.

Later:

I remember something horrible. I remember the Fuller boy. *He took me down in the excavation pipe and raped me. I say it was rape because it hurt, and I didn't want him to do it. I had just been baptized, and I didn't want to be nasty anymore. I knew that two months before, on my eighth birthday, all of my sins had been washed away.*

I'll never forget the Saturday I was baptized. I was out in my backyard playing on the swing set. Alone. I didn't want to play with anyone again. I didn't want to be unworthy of my baptism—then it wouldn't count. I wanted it to count so much. I always knew what a bad girl I was, but now was my chance to be good. I was never going to fuck anyone again. I was going to return to my Heavenly Father washed clean. I was so happy! Now was my chance for repentance and forgiveness. I was never going to sin again.

And I hadn't. I wasn't nasty for two months. Then I wandered over to the Fuller's house. Their mom was really crabby. They had a crab apple tree in their yard, and I thought it made Mrs. Fuller crabby. Anyway, because she was such a crab, Davy said we should go play in the creek. The creek was not running, and it made sense to play in there to be away from the crab. We went in the creek and played for a while. He was about ten years older, so he knew a lot of fun games. Then we followed the creek bed up under the road. He pulled down his pants to show me how big his peanuts was. I told him that I didn't play nasty anymore. He told me that he was a priest and that made it okay. He said that sex was really a sacred thing, and Heavenly Father only wanted it for special people. He said that our parents could do it because they were married. Then I added, "Ya, and my dad's an elder." He said, "And we can do it because I'm a priest." So I pulled down my panties and let him put his peanuts up me. It didn't go very far, and when he tried to wiggle around, I almost fell down. So he turned me around and put it up my bottom. I had to brace myself against the metal walls of the pipes as he pushed harder. Then it hurt—and I started to cry. I believed him that he was a priest because I saw him with the sacrament every Sunday in church. But I still felt bad and nasty. I knew that my baptism didn't count anymore. I started to cry. The pipe echoed, and he hissed at me to "shut up." I knew what that meant. So I cried, silently, as he pushed his big peanuts up my bottom."

Of course I had the nightmare. I know this really happened to me. But I can't understand why I forgot about it. I really didn't know, but now that I've remembered, I can't believe I forgot something as traumatic as this. What else have I conveniently "forgotten?" How will I know? How can I trust myself? I am a mess.

October 5, 1989

Today I woke up, and I remembered when I was little, and our house was burglarized. *I was down the street, about four houses down the street. I had to walk past a vacant lot, that had red ant piles and that was scary. I was gone for a long time. We were playing nasty with three of my brother's friends. All in high school like my brothers. This time, we played nasty with an older girl. She was a really big girl, but she did not have a big thing but had all this black curly hair around her pee-pee hole. The boys took my panties off, and we compared pee-pee holes. Then they made me lick their sister's.*

Then I got scared. I don't know why, but something really scared me. I wanted to run away. But one of the boys held me down and rubbed himself against me. I don't know what the others were doing. I was scared. But I learned how dangerous it was to cry. I knew that I wanted to get home. It took a long time. He was older and a lot stronger. The younger boy tried to help me cuz I was crying. He got yelled at. Sometimes the younger brother was nice, but he couldn't help me.

Finally, I walked up the big street to my house. I walked past the vacant lot with the red ants. I didn't care about the ants that hurt when they bite. I got home and a police car was parked in front. I knew I was in trouble for what I had done. They were going to arrest me for being so nasty. I was always a bad girl. I started crying, "Mommy, Mommy, help me!" My mom was talking to the policeman. Mrs. Fuller came out of her house and told me that a thief had been in our home. I guess my mom had to go somewhere and couldn't find me, so she just left. She had only been gone a couple of hours, and we had been burglarized. I was happy that the police weren't there to arrest me. I was also glad that I didn't come home early. The burglar would have been there. He sounded like he would hurt me really bad...

I was scared about burglars for a long time.

Later:

I have been trying to reach Karen. I haven't told her what's been happening to me. I left a message with her answering service that I must talk to her. I am panic-stricken. I need her help. My mind is spinning, and I can't figure out what's what.

October 6, 1989

Karen called me at the office. I got up and closed my door. Then I told her I'd been having a flood of memories about being sexually abused as a child.

She asked me how I was doing, and I replied, "Well, uh, I don't know what to say—I guess not very well—not very well at all. I haven't slept in a long time, and I go on random crying jags." Karen asked me to write my memories down. I told her that I have been. My next appointment is Monday at 11:00 a.m. She told me to call her whenever I needed to. I wasn't convinced that a phone call would be sufficient until Monday. I didn't really know what to say to her anyway. I am just a frazzled, confused, emotional mess. But I promised to call her if I felt overwhelmed. I don't know what I'd do without her. She is my only salvation.

October 7, 1989

I am in St. George, and I'm staying with Laurel. Only I have to be alone.

I keep seeing my nightmare—that image of my friend. I have to be alone. There are a ton of people down here. The entire town is buzzing because of the marathon. And I've got to be alone.

I rode my mountain bike to the finish line of the race, and I couldn't even wait for the first finisher. I just pedaled off to the red desert hills. I rode for a long time.

I kept seeing that image of my friend as she walked back into the bedroom with that horrid man to have sex with him.

She did it for me. She looks like me. I think that my friend, the one I care about so deeply, was me. I think that I am my friend in the dream.

I have to be alone.

Later in the afternoon:

I took Burton and Parker over to the school. It's the elementary school about two blocks from Laurel's house. They rode their bikes and their trusty yellow lab followed close behind. I took my camera and took several pictures of both boys high in the air with glorious smiles as they pumped higher and higher. I hope one of the pics turns out. I think Laurel would love it for Christmas. Their yellow lab stayed at the side of the swing sets and watched their every move. He is Laurel's sentry, and I can tell that dog takes his responsibilities very seriously regarding those boys. It's simply adorable.

Then the boys rode their bikes to the edge of the playground where Burton professed there were crystals and treasures. The boys spent many minutes digging through the dirt and the rocks and finally Burton held up his prize.

"Look Aunt April, it sparkles in the sunshine!" He ran over and handed it to me. Sure enough, this brown rock did sparkle in the sunshine.

When I handed it back to him, Burton shrugged his shoulders and said, "I got that for you. You've been sad, and you need the sparkles."

He instantly ran off in pursuit of the tricky bars. I put that rock in my pocket, and I'm positive I'll keep it forever.

I walked a bit ahead of the boys on our way home. They stopped constantly in search of treasures. I never knew so many treasures could be found in a two-block stretch of suburbia. I got in the house first and Laurel was in the kitchen. From the kitchen window, Laurel looked out and we could see the boys pedaling their bikes with their big yellow lab following behind.

Laurel smiled turned to me and said, "Look at my boys!" Her eyes were a little watery with joy. The sky was golden with the setting sun. It was such a picturesque scene-Laurel watching her boys pedal into the driveway with their trusty yellow lab trotting behind. I'll never forget that scene. I couldn't have captured it on camera. It's in my heart.

I don't have memories like that of my childhood. In fact, until recently I didn't have any memories of my childhood. None. It was almost like I started life at thirteen. I have seen the old pictures from my childhood, but I don't have any memories of my own. I wonder if I ever had pleasant memories with my brothers hunting for rocks or riding bikes. I was so much younger than they are, so I kind of doubt it.

Children are so great. They're so honest. They really tell it like it is!

If kids tell it like it is, why didn't I? Why didn't I tell anyone? Or did I? Could I have told my mother and she didn't do anything about it? Where was she anyway?

Everything I know about my mother. She's wonderful and intelligent and an alcoholic. That's a disease, like diabetes. If she doesn't manage her disease, she's out of control. How long has she been drinking? She says only a few years. I know better. She's been drinking all of my life.

My brothers, Tom and Byron, used to sneak into our parents' bedroom and steal their mini bottles of vodka and take them to Boy Scout camp. They are roughly seven years older than I am. Boy Scouts would have been around twelve. That puts me at five. I know that my parents were sneaking around with their drinking before I was five.

Tom and Byron also found in their bedroom the "porno" photographs that my parents created of themselves. I've stumbled onto a few of those pictures myself. They make me sick.

Where was my mother when I was being sexually abused by boys in the neighborhood? Perhaps she was drunk.

The story has it that my mother had a nervous breakdown when I was born. My mother calls it "a severe case of postpartum depression." She didn't leave the house until I started kindergarten. In pictures of me at various ages and birthdays, my mother wears her pajamas and robe. My mother was always sick. She had rheumatoid arthritis. I always had to be quiet and not disturb my mommy. I wanted my mommy to get better. I tried to be a good little girl. Usually that meant going outside.

I don't know what to think. I'm feeling overwhelmed. Where was I? Didn't my parents care? Was my mother really that sick? Why doesn't she have arthritis now? Isn't arthritis something you have for the rest of your life? Where was she?

The story also goes that Byron essentially raised me. I followed him everywhere. He called me a leech. Where was Tom? Tom was only a year older than Byron. Where was Tom? I remember Byron being mean to me. He pushed me and wiped his boogers on me. *He used to pee on me. He used to pee on me. He used to pee on me.*

I remember ... Byron used to pee on me. He took out his peanuts and squirted me like a squirt gun. Only it was sticky, and I couldn't get away. I was trapped. I was naked, and he'd pee on me. I always cried. I hated it when they peed on me. Who are "they?" *It was Byron and all of his friends.*

Who else was there? I don't know. I'm starting to panic now. I must stop writing.

October 8, 1989

I was going along fairly smoothly. My career is going well; I live in a beautiful place. I make a lot of money; I've basically let go of my sick behavior around my parents' alcoholism and I've exceeded every goal that I set out to accomplish when I graduated from college.

Am I making this abuse up just to create a crisis? Karen says children of alcoholism make up crisis.

My uncle committed suicide a few years ago. He was schizophrenic. He was brilliant, and he was severely mentally ill. Once, Karen Fisher said that schizophrenics often are creative and intelligent individuals. Like me. Am I merely fabricating this? Is it in my genes to be schizophrenic? Am I making this all up because I need a crisis in my life? This is something I must know.

I am going to talk to Karen about every one of these things. At this stage of the game, she needs to have all the information possible. She's going to need all the help she can get.

DESPAIR

"This is the Hour of Lead—
Remembered, if outlived,
As Freezing persons, recollect the snow—
First—Chill—Then Stupor—then the letting go—

—Emily Dickinson From *After Great Pain*

April

I HAD A NIGHTMARE THAT Karen was killed in an automobile accident. The dream was so real that I'm afraid it really happened. I'm scared. Of course, I'm scared about everything right now. I have my session today, and if she's dead I think I'll die.

Later:

Karen is not dead.

I couldn't even talk in our session today. I just sat there and cried. I handed Karen my little journal, and she read.

I made her hold our session in the back office because I felt too exposed in her big front office. Her office has French doors, and I was afraid that someone could hear us. So we went to the back. I sat on the couch and cried, and she read. When she finished I said, "Pretty boring, huh?" She looked up and said, "That's just another example of you trying to minimize yourself. Anything that makes me sick to my stomach does not qualify as boring." I started crying again.

Karen asked if I had a doctor. She wants me to call him and get a prescription for an anti-depressant and something to help me sleep. With the history of addiction in my family, I can't do it. I'll get addicted. We talked about how it would be non-addictive; the physician and she would help monitor it. I agreed to try and call him. I hope he will just listen to me and then give me the prescription over the phone.

As I was leaving, I told Karen to drive carefully. She smiled.

Later:

I just had another flash, about Hank, Tom's friend who married Lorraine. *Getting peed on. I always hated that the most. I'd do anything rather than have them pee on me. It wasn't just Byron. I remember, one time in the basement at our next door neighbor's house, a group of them was there: the college boys, my brother Byron, Hank, my cousin Charles, and his older friend. I don't know his name, but I know that he used to put his peanuts in Byron's bottom. He was older, about twenty-three or twenty-four. We were all in the next door neighbor's basement. I wouldn't do something they wanted me to do. I was naked, and they all started peeing on me. I was little and hunched over in the corner. I couldn't get away. They all just laughed and teased me and peed on me.*

I remembered another time with Hank. We went in our little trailer. It was parked right in our driveway. We'd go in there and look at "Playboys." He told me that is what

I'd look like one day. Sometimes we'd take our clothes off, and I'd help him rub really hard to get the white stuff to spurt up. Other times he'd rub his big thing in between my legs, and it would squirt out in front of me. He always tried to put it in my rear end, and if it couldn't fit then he'd rub around until it came out the front. It looked like he was coming out of me. Hank was always nicer when we were alone, but when he was with his friends he'd show off how tough he was. Then he'd usually put it up me, even if it hurt. Even if it hurt really bad and I cried.

October 10, 1989

I went running this morning, and as I was running, I had a flash of Hank. *Hank was holding me down, and he said that if I ever told I'd talk like his little sister. I didn't have any clothes on, and I was scared. Hank's little sister was my age, and she couldn't talk right. Hank told me that he made her talk funny because she told. I promised to never tell because I didn't want to talk like her. She was in my second-grade class, and she had to leave every morning to have speech lessons. I was seven.*

I think about Hank, and I feel such a sadness. He was a pall bearer at Tom's funeral. I remember Hank bringing Tom ice cream at the hospital. Tom had taken a turn for the worse and no one was allowed into the Intensive Care Unit. I remember Hank stood in the hallway outside of ICU. Hank brought ice cream in a plastic bag filled with ice. The ice started to melt, and a drop of water fell to the tiled floor. I looked up at Hank and he didn't notice. His face was frozen like the bag of ice he was holding.

Now I am seriously doubting this memory about Hank. I know there have been allegations involving Hank in Willow Creek. I wasn't surprised. To hear the news that one of my dead brother's friends is accused of sexually abusing children, why wasn't I surprised? When did I hear? Let's see... I heard that Hank was getting divorced. But I didn't even know why—mm, that day at the restaurant with Carol? Carol asked if I knew about the divorce. That's all she said. No, Carol never told me. Who told me?

I can't remember who told me.

I don't think anyone ever told me. I just knew. And I forgot it. No one ever told me that Hank abused children. I've always known.

Later:

I'm sitting here in the front bedroom looking at the bullet hole. The police took the bullet out of the wall after they found his body. They didn't repair the hole.

It's been seven years, and the tiny hole is still there. My little finger fits in the hole. I've sanded around it, and I'm ready to fill it in.

He put the .22 in front of his chest and pulled the trigger. The bullet went through his heart, went straight through his back, and then exited his body. Landing in the wall.

Gramps found him. He was my mother's younger brother. My mom said that I couldn't skip any grades in school because my uncle did. He skipped a grade and couldn't adjust socially. He was smart enough to skip a grade, but emotionally he never adjusted. My fifth-grade teacher suggested that I skip a couple of grades—go straight into seventh grade. My mom wouldn't let me. She wanted me to have a normal childhood.

My uncle was sick. I always remember him being sick. He was schizophrenic. A paranoid schizophrenic. I never knew him to be normal. He was my crazy uncle.

When I was little, I remember him buying things and then getting a hammer and breaking them in the garage. He bought a brand-new tennis racquet and smashed it to smithereens in the garage. He didn't play tennis.

My schizophrenic uncle outlived my brother Tom. He lived longer than his mother. And here is the hole from the bullet that pierced his heart. I have my spackle and I'm going to fill the hole. Paint over it as well. Disguise it. But I'll always know where the bullet landed after he pulled the trigger.

I've pulled the trigger on my memories. Am I self-destructing?

Later:

Now I'm waiting for the spackle to dry. John Bradshaw talks about shame-based people having a "hole in their souls." I wish I could fill the hole in my soul with a little putty knife and spackle.

I've been thinking about my other uncles and aunts. Besides my uncle's schizophrenia, my mom's family has a couple of alcoholics.

My dad's family has as much dysfunction. My dad had four brothers. All five of the Daniels brothers married sick women. Really sick women: one with cancer, one had a stroke, one had a hip replacement, one had emphysema, and my mother had all sorts of problems.

She had a nervous breakdown when she was thirty-two years old—after the birth of her baby daughter. She was bedridden for six years. She had arthritis. Then she had "female problems." Her menstrual periods were so severe she went through three extra-large Kotex in under an hour. She never went to the doctor for this problem. It continued for over fifteen years. When she was fifty-five, she finally had a hysterectomy.

After that her high blood pressure flared up, and now she takes two pills with every meal. This is still a family conversation topic. Add to all this that she and her husband are both raging alcoholics. They drink all the time, sometimes to the point of unconsciousness for three- and four-day weekends.

I wonder what was happening in the closed confines of the other Daniels' homes. My mother tells of visiting one of my aunts and finding her in the bathroom face down in a pool of her own blood. I wonder about the sickness, the pain, and the blood.

One of my uncles died a couple of years ago. His wife is not sick anymore. She's out gardening. She wins awards for the crossbreeding of special flowers.

Everyone at work assumes now I'm sick, and being sick is an appropriate response for Daniels women. Well, I'm sick all right, sick inside. I am exhausted and spend hours flat on my back looking up at the ceiling. My mind is being flooded with memories, and I can't stop them. I'm not physically sick, but I feel awful. Right now, I feel like putting on my running shoes and going for a run. Maybe running will help siphon off a tiny layer of pain. Maybe remove a tiny piece of my jigsaw puzzle of pain.

This is a jigsaw puzzle. All the pieces are scattered throughout the years of my life, and I have them in various compartments of my mind. I hope the pieces will eventually form a picture. I have a feeling it won't resemble a Norman Rockwell print.

October 11, 1989

Karen's right. I am on the jagged edge. I haven't slept in such a long time that I can't think straight. I am questioning if I ever had the capacity to think straight.

I left a message for my doctor to call me. I feel so ashamed. But I need help. I can't sleep, and I feel like I'm spiraling down to some bottomless pit. In AA meetings they always say, "One has to hit bottom." I'm beginning to wonder if there is such a thing. It seems like I've fallen into a huge, black, bottomless pit. I keep falling.

If some available medication can help me, I'll take it. I've heard my mother say hundreds of times, "I hit rock bottom." I've seen her hit various bottoms in a vast array of ways. I guess, watching her, I've learned that there is no such thing as rock bottom. She has professed, "This is it; I almost died." "This is it; I almost lost my mind." I don't know, I don't know a lot, but I do know one thing: I don't want to be like my mother.

I am not my mother, and I'm vowing not to do the same things she has done. If this doesn't get better, and I have no idea how long it will take, but if this doesn't get better—I am outta here. I mean it. I'm going to kill myself.

This is so shitty, so painful, why should I hang around for more? I'm not going to be like my mother and put a Band-aid on my pain and call it healed. Then be totally flabbergasted when another serious, life-threatening situation develops. I'm not into Band-aids. My mom's rudimentary first aid simply won't cut it for me. I know that sleeping pills and anti-depressants won't heal me. But I am hurt. I need a crutch. I needed crutches after I had knee surgery. I had them for a few months, but I don't walk with them now. I run six to ten miles a day.

I will contact my doctor to obtain some professional help. Those "home remedies," particularly coming from my home, are simply not sufficient. I'll need some help until I am able to stand on my own two feet. Until I gain my own sense of balance.

"Balance"—what a nice word.

October 12, 1989

I've been writing with my left hand. I am right-handed, and writing with my left hand brings the memories up with such clarity; it is almost a motion picture rolling across my mind. It's like I have this big ball of threads, and some of the lines are crisscrossed and tangled. I find one loose thread of a memory, a flash, or something inconsistent that I've never really questioned before—and I track that thread. It's easier to track it with my left hand. I don't know why. Maybe it has to do with the fact that my handwriting looks similar to when I was a little kid. Maybe it has to do with tapping into my subconscious mind. The logical and conscious half of my brain doesn't discount or edit my memories. I haven't had a memory yet whose reality I could deny. After I place the pen down with my left hand, I know they are true. Once a memory breaks out of its slumber, I can remember it with such detail and clarity. I remember the little dress I was wearing with green and black plaid. I remember what happened with my first pair of penny loafers. I put pennies in both tops. Once I ran away from a scary abuse situation, and the penny in my left shoe fell out.

I have a dozen memories like this. The details are unbelievable. I had forgotten that I had a green and black plaid dress during the first grade. I had forgotten a red and black plaid exactly like the green one. I forgot how lonely I was when I came home from school. I usually got on my little Stingray bicycle and rode around the street in front of my house. My bike was a boy's bike, and I was always self-conscious about that. When I instigate the memories with my left hand, I feel like I have more control. I am unnerved when I am out in public and smell a particular smell, and my mind flashes back to my childhood.

This happened to me yesterday in the grocery store. I smelled some man's Brut cologne. The scent has always gagged me. I felt the blood drain from my face, and my heart was racing so fast I must have been in shock. I couldn't walk for a few moments. I stood in the produce section, immobilized, right in front of the carrots. I stood there until I remembered that Hank wore this cologne. *Sometimes after he spilled the white stuff all over my chest, he would make me wipe myself off and then put some of the cologne on—so that I didn't smell like the white stuff. I hate the smell of that stuff.*

I also hate the smell of Old Spice. That's what my dad used to wear. I never liked it. I don't know why. Probably because of my experience with Hank and cologne.

I know that Tom always wore English Leather. I liked that smell the best. I guess I could place my pen in my left hand and think about Tom's cologne, but I don't want to tonight. I'm really tired. I pray for sleep. I think these smells will lead me to more memories.

I am afraid to have a memory. It's hard work, and when the trauma of one simmers down, it's only a little relief to have the truth out.

It took years and years and years for this damage to happen, and it's going to take a long time to heal. I'm giving myself time, or I'm not going to make it. I'm not strong enough to do this all at once.

My sister-in-law, Deborah, called me today and wanted me to go down to some dating service that videotapes people. You can go and pick out someone you'd like to date. Deborah is such an odd duck. I was as nice as I could be, but what a ludicrous idea. She proceeded to tell me that it was strictly a church dating service and that her mother had done it. Her mother—thanks for the reference.

"I don't have any trouble getting asked out. Right now, I'm going through a difficult time, and I'd rather not date," I told her. I really wanted to tell her that I'd rather have twenty root canals before I went to the church dating services to get a date. She told me that if I'm having a hard time, I should go down to the temple and take out my endowments! She said that if I'm having a hard time, I should take the opportunity of the blessings of the temple. I was literally speechless. That's not a difficult state for me to be in these days anyway, but I just told her it was something to think about and got off the phone. Something to think about. Actually, to think about how off track my sister-in-law really is and my entire family for that matter.

Like dating a "nice" religious man would make me feel better. And then the blessings of the temple taking away my "difficult time." As if she even had a scrap of an idea what degree of pain I am struggling with. Shit, she'd die if she knew what her husband did to me when he was a teenager. It's an interesting situation because Deborah was sexually abused as a child as well. She has some huge scars that have not yet healed.

I know that Byron was a little boy when the responsibility of a baby sister was thrust upon him. I know that he resented me horribly because in his mind his already unstable world literally fell apart when I came along. I understand, but it doesn't change what he did to me. I don't think even Byron understands fully why he did what he did. I don't believe he understands the pain he inflicted upon me.

I stopped writing tonight because Karen called me back. I am so tired. Maybe that is why I can't stop crying. I am exhausted because of these memories. They keep pouring out, and I don't know when they will hit or what they will be. It's like the gate is open and the flood has begun. In all of this I am crying floods of tears.

Karen said that she would try to call my doctor. That would help. I don't want to talk to him.

Later:

As I grow, I reflect on past experiences with a different perspective. Right now, I am thinking of Tom's death. Tom died when I was 16. For my high school English class, I wrote a paper describing how I never told Tom I loved him.

The last time I saw Tom, he was lying in the intensive care unit with all the tubes coming out of his body. His lungs had collapsed, and they were trying to drain this orangey fluid out from around his lungs. I saw him on a Sunday afternoon. He had almost died a couple of hours earlier. He wanted to see me. I was scared, and I didn't want to see him. I stood there on that Sunday afternoon and looked at my handsome brother. He looked so sick, but he smiled at me.

The last thing that Tom said to me was, "April, I love you." There was a pause, a long pause, and I didn't say the words back. I just stood there.

I have felt guilty for not returning those simple words for years now. He died. I was right there, and I couldn't say those words. I wrote a paper about it, and my English teacher wrote that it was "a touchingly beautiful story ... about a beautiful relationship between brother and sister." He submitted it to a national magazine, and it was published. I vowed to always express my love to those whom I love. And I have tried to love as openly and as generously as I possibly can as long as I ever can.

Why haven't I expressed that love to my family then? It's like a flaw in my character, a glitch in my belief system. Sometimes on holidays I'll try to give my dad a hug. It's been almost an annual event. He pushes me away. Always. I grit my teeth, try to hug my dad and he stiff arms me—literally. I thought that I had bad timing, or I was unhuggable, unworthy, bad. Or lately that it had to do with his drinking. When he gets particularly mean, my sister calls him a "dry drunk." I usually can't tell when he is clean, sober, drunk, dry, or what. He is consistently isolated.

While I was in college, I wrote another paper about Tom's death. I quoted all of my journal entries describing the days before his death and my immediate reaction after his death. It was very vivid and painful. I told about the night he died, how I tried to run away but couldn't get out of the hospital. I told about silently crying in the back of the car. I told about how I was shaking and threw up all over the shower door. I missed the toilet. After these details of pain I wrote, "And I didn't even come close to bleeding from every pore." My paper was about the atonement of Christ and the nature of suffering in the world. It was a good paper.

Now I'm questioning my perception of Tom's death: my inability to talk about love and about pain and suffering. Tom's death: love and pain.

There was a Billy Joel song out when I was in college, *Only the Good Die Young*. Whenever I heard that song I thought of Tom. He was so good that Heavenly Father called him home. When the chaos of my parents' alcoholism escalated, I felt Tom was blessed to escape. Now I've learned Tom knew all about my parents' drinking. Melinda told me that Tom even went to the bishop about the drinking. The bishop told him that people repent when they are ready to repent. He would only become involved if my parents came to him.

Tom was not innocent. Why did he wait to die for two hours until I could get there? Above all else, while all of Tom's friends were abusing me, where was Tom? I'm scared that he was involved. And I'm scared that because Tom is dead, I might blame him for what others—including Byron—did to me. Oh, I'm confused and scared and don't know.

Carol

APRIL AND I WENT TO LUNCH today at the Bistro.

She told me what she's been going through, remembering the sexual abuse she endured as a child. I am outraged. Like it's another violation of me. I'm sick of this hell where people steal other people's lives, other people's souls. She told me about Hank's sister—how Hank threatened April by saying he had caused his younger sister's speech impediment.

Now I could tell April about Hank. About the grandchildren. Of course, Hank was in on all of her old neighborhood filth. Why wouldn't he have been? It all made perfect sense. When I think of the kids from her neighborhood, Jake's and Susy's friends some of them, it makes me physically ill. Six kids dead. Three of them suicides. Three in and out of institutions. Five with eating disorders or drug abuse. Every single one of those kids was involved in the atrocity April is remembering. I think of their parents, agonizing over what went wrong, blaming themselves, but never finding any answers.

It is a perfect parallel to what happened to us in Willow Creek.

I told April. Told her the story I don't believe myself, in the wild hope that perhaps she can believe and bring some sense to me. And she keeps telling me her story, hoping I can bring some sense to her.

I never believed that a rainbow promises no more deluge. Even when I was little, I used to picture Zeus throwing thunderbolts at silhouetted mortals. For some reason they were in long dark capes, hood-covered, faceless, bent against the storm, trying to find a pine tree or boulder to hide behind while His wrath bellowed forth, not just Zeus's but God's.

Still, those people were Others. I didn't know them. They didn't draw hopscotches on their driveways or take the bus to piano lessons. They weren't little girls like me (by then an older me), buying pink taffeta, strapless formals, and going to dances with no makeup except fuchsia lipstick bright and heavily applied. They weren't housewives (later still), piling baskets full of Gerber's strained carrots and wearing canvas Keds and polyester pants. The Others had worn dark medieval capes.

So when I was electrocuted I didn't believe it, still don't. I watched me climbing up the slick washbowl sides of sanity again and again. On automatic. Effective. Doing what was necessary, holding things together. I've watched lots of firebugs washing down the drain and climbing out again, and it always takes longer than you'd think.

No one wants to hear this story. Not even April. I don't want to tell it. But if I open my mouth (it's been closed for four years), it comes out. I want to be in the recovery room again, but instead I am here now, telling my story.

It is February 14, 1986. Cold outside but not snowing. Kids can ring doorbells and run and hide if they want to, but they don't do that much anymore. Now they put their Valentines in a shoe box they've covered at home with white Kleenex and red crepe paper. Where it's Elmer-glued, the crepe paper is all squashed and blobby. They line the boxes up on the school room worktable. The boys don't care how full their boxes are, but the little girls wait until they go home and then count the cards over and over sitting on the floor by their beds after they've pulled off the candy hearts and suckers. My grandchildren took their boxes to school yesterday.

This February 14 I am sitting in a therapist's office waiting. My two oldest grandchildren, Timothy and Isabel, are watching the fish in an aquarium whose glass is so smudged with little fingerprints it's not pleasant to look at the fish. I'm here because at the last-minute Lorraine's baby fell and cut his chin and she had to take him in for stitches. She should be here any minute now. That's what I've been telling myself for fifteen minutes.

I had never been in this waiting room until three weeks ago. Now it's where I seem to live.

I don't much like the people here in this waiting room.

One-man fidgets so much you think he must have a disease. A woman pretends to read *Parents Magazine*, but she doesn't turn any pages. Little kids play with and fight over the blocks and stuffed animals. The woman next to me is fat and worn, and she isn't changing her smelly baby. She keeps trying to talk to me. She says awful things, and she won't shut up. She says her little girl ripped the head off her new doll and stuck burning matches in the cloth body. She says her husband thinks the child should have to pay for the doll, teach her to take care of property.

I don't want to hear these stories. I don't want to sit in this office. I'm not one of these people in their capes. I keep saying over and over in my head, "Please, God, please." These people are the Others.

The therapist takes Isabel into her office. I read Timothy a book called *No More Secrets for Me*. Why doesn't Lorraine get here? Why am I here?

A few months ago, a psychologist at Lorraine's church gave a lesson about symptoms of sexual abuse. Afterwards a mother of a little boy who plays with Timothy took her child to the psychologist because she caught him sticking marbles up his little sister's bottom. He's seven, like Timothy. Not an unusual story in this waiting room, I would suppose. One victim led to another—and another—and another. To an older teenage sister, to another teenager, to a father. More children were taken to therapists. More babysitters were named. The psychologist thinks only a few of the children's stories would hold up in court.

The neighborhood parents held a meeting with the psychologist and talked about their helplessness, their rage, their legal alternatives, their collapsing families.

Lorraine heard about all of it. The police knew it all but were waiting for more from the kids before they charged anyone. The bishop of the ward said he didn't know what to do. These were good and righteous families being named. Hank's in the bishopric with him. Hank said the bishop was calling in higher Mormon authorities.

Every day Lorraine called me and cried. Two of the girls were in her young women's church class. Then one of the children named Lorraine's babysitter. My son Jake, eighteen months younger than Lorraine, lives a couple of miles from her. Jake and Sara have used the same sitter even though Lorraine objected because it was a pain to find a sitter and she was an exceptionally conscientious girl, dependable and unusually available for a 16-year-old.

Because this babysitter has been named, Lorraine and Jake have had my five oldest grandchildren ranging in age from 3-7 interviewed by therapists in this agency. All Lorraine's and Jake's kids except for Lorraine's baby. The therapists took each child into a room alone. Separately, with no knowledge of what their siblings and cousins were saying, they told what Geraldine and her boyfriends did to them. The telling took many appointments. Lots of Play-Doh, finger paint, doll house people, anatomical dolls—this agency has the works. The therapists say the telling usually takes a long time. It comes out centimeter by centimeter, mixed in with all kinds of other stuff. One therapist said it's like squeezing a toothpaste tube after it's all flattened and used up. It is too unbelievable for anyone to fathom.

Ten days ago, two of Lorraine's children told about the family two houses down from Jake's. When Jake's wife Sara had her gallbladder out, the mother of the family volunteered to tend her children all day for three days. We couldn't believe how nice she was. It meant I didn't have to take time off work. The mother has two little girls of her own, and she said they all had so much fun playing together that they weren't any trouble at all. This mother, this neighbor of Jake and Lorraine's, is a daughter of a general authority in the Mormon church, a daughter of one of the Twelve Apostles. Her husband is in the bishopric with Hank.

Our grandchildren told about the "touching parties" at her house. About what the dad did to his two little girls and ours while the mom gave out Popsicles and cookies and took videos. About how she used some of the Junior Sunday School visual aids for backgrounds in the videos. She's Junior Sunday School chorister. She got double use out of the Easter Bunnies and posters she made.

At first, I wanted desperately to believe my grandchildren were making it up, but none of them have had access to the sexual information they're giving. Their mothers don't even let them watch TV except on Sesame Street level, and no TV show contains the things they are describing.

The detail from each matches what the others have said. Cynthia said, "He showed us the deer antlers and said he'd poke them up us if we told." Isabel said, "We were scared he'd hurt us with the deer horns." There is no way they are not telling the truth, and there is no way my mind can believe it.

After the children had three of four "telling appointments," after they'd talked about the babysitter and her boyfriends, we had a Heroes' Party: Norton and I, Lorraine and Hank, Jake and Sara, the five children, and the baby asleep in my bedroom. We all drew pictures of ugly babysitters hurting children and tore them up and burned them in our fireplace. We gave the children Hero Medals and told them they were protecting other children by talking. Hank pounded an old slipper and said he was pretending it was the babysitter. We talked about starting a Heroes' Day for children all across the country who'd been brave enough to tell on bad people about the bad things.

We sang songs, making words up about heroes. We played games with prizes. Every hero child got to have as many toppings on ice cream as they could get in the dish. Somehow, unitedly, we were going to get through this.

Lorraine let the police interview the oldest children, but she already had decided she would not let them testify. The summer before we had read daily newspaper reports of what happened to the children who testified about similar nightmares in Lehi, Utah.

Lorraine and Sara looked dreadful. They weren't sleeping, their houses were in chaos and their children had started waking with screaming dreams. Some panicked parents in the neighborhood were calling Lorraine, knowing something terrible was happening, wondering if their children should be interviewed. But most of the neighbors were trying to stay calm. After all their children had no symptoms, no one wanted hysteria, and no one wanted falling property values. Lorraine told one neighbor that Timothy had seen a child psychologist just two months before this all came out. The school was considering having him skip second grade, and Lorraine wanted an evaluation. The psychologist told Lorraine she had "seldom seen such a healthy child." "Sometimes the symptoms don't show," Lorraine told her neighbor. The neighbor didn't hear Lorraine. No one heard. No one could believe any of it about the people who'd been named. This was an upper-class, educated neighborhood. Parents of the babysitters were threatening legal action. Everyone was saying the therapists must have planted all of it in the children's minds: "You know children's fantasies and how they pick up on suggestion." At worst, they said, the children had misunderstood. Lorraine and Hank started looking for property somewhere else and listed their house. Jake and Sara are thinking of moving too.

The therapist who just took Isabel into her office kept saying there was more. She knew there was more. She was calling reputable people in her field all over the country, people who knew about child group sexual abuse. Scarcely anyone had published much about it then.

Isabel is six. Her photographs look like me at that age. Lorraine says Isabel reminds her of me. Yesterday Lorraine was driving her kids to after school music lessons, and Isabel casually asked her mother, "Why are the things the babysitters and the bad people do to us bad, and the lessons Daddy gives us are okay?" Lorraine had called me hysterical. I'd told her Isabel must be confused. Hank wouldn't hurt anyone much less his kids. He is a good man. But Lorraine had insisted Isabel was not mixed up, Timothy was upset about Hank too, even Leah; Lorraine demanded today's therapy appointment.

Now I am sitting in this office waiting. Waiting for Isabel to explain what she meant. Wondering how many mothers have sat in this chair thinking it is impossible. There has to be some other explanation. It all has to be some terrible mistake. Please, God, please.

Lorraine has not come. She must be dying. When she confronted Hank last night, he raced out of the house without his coat yelling he couldn't believe he was hearing this. She thinks he slept at his office. The therapist is back, asking me to please come into her office. "Isabel needs a little moral support, and I'd like you to hear whatever she says." I leave Timothy to take care of his three-year-old sister Leah, who is playing by the aquarium.

The therapist and I are sitting on the floor with Isabel while she practices singing "Two Little Speckled Frogs" into the tape recorder. We play it back so she can hear herself. She giggles when she hears herself "eating some most delicious worms" and sings "yum, yum" with the recording. The therapist asks Isabel if it's all right to tell what happened into the tape recorder and to have me listen. Isabel guesses so. For a moment she sits in my lap and plays with the brass necklace I got in Crete. My kids all liked that necklace when they were little. Some of them teethed on it. There is a snake twisting around a woman embossed on the bronze.

The therapist asks Isabel about the lessons Daddy gave. Isabel is rolling two little yellow cars back and forth on the rug while she talks.

"So you can have babies," she says, "To help you when you're married." She looks up. "Everyone has to know what to do when they get married."

"You mean Daddy helps you learn how to cook and clean and things like that?"

Isabel gives the therapist a withering look. "Sometimes we do things like that with Daddy, but not in the marriage lessons."

"So, what do you do in the marriage lessons?"

Isabel is coloring now. The therapist asks her two or three times.

"We learn how our bodies are made. Where babies come from and stuff like that."

Of course, I think, Lorraine and Hank have always believed in being open about sex education. She's just all mixed-up because everything has been so confusing. Of course. Dear God, please.

The therapist is good. She knows what it takes to have the children tell the story. Releasing the horrific secrets and helping the children realize it's not their fault is essential to the therapeutic process. Talking is also important to begin the hope for healing.

I sit quietly, my left leg cramping, longing to reach out and gather Isabel into my lap. When she talks about seeing her Daddy kissing the babysitter, I ask her where they were.

"In the front of the living room—where the rug meets the dining room tile."

"I don't get that, Isabel," I say nonchalantly. "How can you see in there from upstairs?" If she's wrong on this little thing, I pray, maybe it's all crazy. Please, Isabel, tell me you can't see from up there.

"You have to put your head down by the railing. Over by Timothy's room. I'll show you." She doesn't need to. I can visualize it.

For two hours we listen to Isabel. She is tired. She's crying. The therapist quietly says, "Isabel, I'm only going to ask you one more question. You've done so well. You've worked so hard and told us lots of important things. Now tell me, what did Daddy's penis feel like when he put it on your baby hole?"

Isabel screams, "I hate you!" She runs around the room throwing toys everywhere. She kicks the doll house over, and then she stamps and stamps on the anatomical doll that is the Daddy. I hold her on the floor and rock her for a long, long time while the therapist goes to find Timothy and Leah and their mother.

This is all I've told April this time. We were both crying, and I'll tell the rest later.

I didn't tell her how the therapist called the police while I called Norton and told him to bring Hank to the agency. When Timothy found out Isabel had told he told the same story but nothing about Daddy kissing the babysitter. He kept saying he wanted to hurry up and get through so he could deliver his Valentines. He was terribly scared. Lorraine, the baby and I waited in a small office for Norton and Hank. Lorraine tried to nurse the baby, but he just fussed and cried. I looked out the cracks of the blinds at the parking lot. Finally, the baby went to sleep.

I whispered to Lorraine, that I still had hope for her family. I gazed at the baby. Lorraine's eyes glazed over, yet I continued that I thought for the children's sake, she should work to preserve her temple marriage. At that point in shock that's what I believed. I wish I'd told April how much I regretted believing that and how deeply I regretted saying that to Lorraine.

When Norton brought Hank into the office; The therapist stepped out. Hank and Lorraine, Norton and I sat waiting for her. I told Hank what Isabel and Timothy had said. I couldn't concentrate on Hank's words, but he kept saying he couldn't remember any of it. He also said his children didn't lie. He was shaking. I remember saying, "Suicide is not an acceptable option. If you care anything about your children—you will fix this."

I don't remember what Norton said. Lorraine had bitten her hands, and they were bleeding. She was too hysterical to make any sense. I don't remember how she got her children home, what she said to Hank. The children never did get to deliver their Valentines. But I remember, or think I do, every word of what Isabel told the therapist on that Valentine's Day, 1986.

April

MY MOM SAYS THAT I never played with dolls. So why is there an entire doll collection of mine stored in a beautiful glass china cabinet up in my mother's front hallway? I love those dolls. I received the first doll when I was in fourth grade and our family went to Paris. A lovely lady made dinner and gave me an exquisite doll. Ever since I have been collecting them. When I go anywhere, if I find a beautiful doll, I buy it.

I have a collection of Barbie dolls. One year for Christmas, Santa Claus brings me a car for Barbie and Ken and another time I get a house for them. I remember playing with them. I always take all of their clothes off and have them play nasty. Sometimes I turn 'em upside down and put 'em together. They play nasty all the time, just like me. The boy up the street has GI Joe, and we'd have GI Joe and Barbie play nasty. Sometimes GI Joe sucks Ken.

I remember showing a new girl in the neighborhood how to play with Barbies. One day my brother Byron told me I couldn't play nasty with the dolls in front of her. I could only do that at home. My brothers thought it was really funny watching Ken and Barbie. They didn't have the same white stuff, so it was just pretend. My brothers and their friends would play Barbies with me. And sometimes they'd do things to me just like the dolls did. I wished that they didn't have big things. I wished that they were like Ken. Then it wouldn't have hurt. And they couldn't have squirted me with the white stuff. I always had to clean it up before anyone saw it. Sometimes I would just throw my panties away. I'd wipe myself off with my panties, and I'd just throw 'em away.

Later:

Tonight, I remembered the rabbit cage.

There was a large field in back of the Fuller's house. I remember the boys in the neighborhood made me and another little girl strip down naked, and they played nasty with us and then locked us in the cage. Two of the boys, one of them was Byron, peed on us through the wire in the cage. They were laughing that they were hosing down the animals. They said we were as horny as rabbits and that's where we were going to be for the rest of our lives. They told us that we could only get out when we fucked...

I started to cry, and the other little girl told me to never cry. That is the only way they would get us, if we cried. She started to laugh at them, like it didn't even bug her. The boys finally got bored and let us out.

I remember another time, Davy Fuller locked me and another little boy in the rabbit cage. He peed on us and told us we had to do what he wanted, or he wouldn't let us out. The little boy started to cry. I started to cry. Davy Fuller left. I don't remember when he came back.

I hate rabbits. Well, I like them when they are out and free. I think they are soft and cute. But I hate them in their cages. They look so dirty.

October 15, 1989

I have had more memories. I'm starting to dread the term, "I remember." If I fall asleep at night—if—if I sleep, I wake up dripping from my own perspiration and tears. Sometimes my night shirt and sheets cling to me. Because I'm so wet, I am freezing and shaking. This must be "cold sweats." My mother has told me about that, "April, I woke up in a cold sweat—" I know what causes me to wake up in that state of utmost anxiety. I wonder what rolls through my mother's dreams.

October 16, 1989

It is a beautiful fall day, sunny, cool and crisp. I am sitting at my brunch table watching the morning unfold. It's amazing how I can be a voyeur to such morning splendor and feel such despair inside. It's as if my insides have been ripped out, and there is nothing there. I think of my soul, and I think of endless echoes of sadness.

My feelings are crazy. I feel scared and vulnerable and victimized and excited and powerful. Above all else right now, I feel like I am going to die if all the memories come out. I believe that if all the secrets are known, even to myself, I will die.

Later:

I'll try writing down more memories. It is work. When I have the memories, it's not like a memory; it's really happening. I am going to try and write it down:

I remember going over to the Architect's house. He told me my lips were pretty. He said that they were the kind of lips boys like to kiss. Both lips.

The Architect worked out of his house. He had an office in his basement. Sometimes I would go over there all by myself. Most of the time I took the boy up the street or the other little girl.

He would draw us. We were always naked. He moved us around so we were posed in the right position. Sometimes he drew my pee-pee hole.

He also had Playboys. *We'd look at them. He told me that one day I could be in that magazine.*

I remember playing in the sand at his house. He was building something, some concrete stairs or something, and he had a big pile of sand. We'd play in the sand for hours. We'd do a big pile, shape it with a point on top and then put an acorn in the center. The first time the Architect showed us how to do it, I thought he was making a mountain or a volcano. He did two of them, and they'd be boobs. He taught us a lot. We'd get some grass for a pussy. I wondered why he always called it a pussy and not a kitty. I called it a kitty, and he laughed. I really knew it was just grass, and we were pretending it was a kitty.

October 17, 1989

I remember playing strip poker with my cousin Charles, his friend and my brothers. I never won. I was always naked.

Even after I was totally naked, I still had to play. If I lost, I'd have to suck their peanuts. Sometimes until they were really big. Charles made me rub his peanuts until the white stuff came out. If I got tired, he'd put it between my legs. Or rub it on my body.

We played a lot of games. And the loser always had to do something the others wanted them to do. I don't think I ever won. I always lost.

One of the scariest games we played was with a Ouija board. That's where we'd talk to the devil.

I knew I was nasty because I never cheated or moved it on my own—but it always told me to fuck. Whenever I played, the Ouija board would spell out F-U-C-K. I knew that if I didn't do it Satan would get my body. Sometimes I had trouble sleeping because I thought the devil was waiting for me at the side of my bed.

I had nightmares that the devil would be trying to get inside of me. I'd cry and scream. Then he'd put a pillow over my face. I had a feather pillow. Sometimes feathers went up my nose. I didn't want to have the devil's baby. I didn't want him coming in my room late at night. I tried to move my chest of drawers in front of my door. I didn't want him coming in. I threw all of my clothes on the floor. That way, if he came in, he'd trip and fall over my clothes. My dad always got mad at me because my room was such a mess.

Later:

Yesterday was the first time I remembered my brother Tom was there. He and Byron were there when the neighbor boys or the other boys abused me. They watched.

Later:

When I started puberty, I remember showing Tom and Byron my developing body. Sometimes they both came in my room, sometimes just one of them.

Byron taught me all about the bleeding and how when my blood was mixed together with sperm, it made a baby. He told me not to let anyone fuck me when I started to bleed. But it was okay if I wasn't bleeding.

Tom always rubbed my nipples. He said they were just like little mosquito bites. They itched like it too. The hardness in my nipples got bigger and bigger, and Tom loved to feel them.

He also liked to see where my hair was growing. He couldn't believe how blond it was. Tom was always nice. Sometimes he'd kiss me.

Was this abuse? It seemed more like they were teaching me. Sort of an educational process. Tom was very curious about my body, and he taught me all about it.

Despair

I had my appointment with Karen today. I couldn't talk until we went to the back office. I handed her my journal and cried as she read. I can't stop the motion picture rolling across my mind. Only it's not a movie. It's real. I can't believe I forgot. Why does a mind do that? I can remember dates and times and numbers, and I rarely forget a face. When I was in college, I took organic chemistry. It was easy for me to memorize a chart of over four hundred reactions. But I've forgotten half of my life. It doesn't make sense. Not much makes sense.

After Karen finished reading, she told me that she had talked with my doctor. He seemed to be a caring, sensitive man. She told him that I was an incest victim. When she said the word "incest," I started to cry. The word alone had violated me.

Karen asked me to check in daily and to start coming twice a week. I nodded. Then I think she asked if anyone else was involved. I told her I wasn't sure about my father. *The tile in the little shower is pink. It always smells funny in there. I don't like it very much. I like the big bathroom better. It's little and dark. I don't have any place to go, and his big peanuts is in my face. He is cleaning my crack and up my holes. He says little girls are always dirty—especially down there. The soap burns inside of me. I start to cry. He tells me not to cry, or he'll give me something to cry about. I shut right up. He must have had soap up his big thing too because all of a sudden it came out of his big thing. He wiped it all over me. It didn't burn this time. He rinsed me off with the shower. I started crying because I wanted to go outside and play. It was the middle of the afternoon, and I didn't want to go to bed.*

After I recalled this memory, the room was silent for a long time. I was crying just like when I was there, and it happened.

Karen said, "Cry, April. That's what's going to help you heal. You're feeling all the betrayal and fear and pain of that moment with your father. It was the ultimate betrayal, April. Your father was supposed to protect you and keep you safe, and he took that little three-year-old body and that three-year-old spirit and that innocent trust and violated it all."

As a 30-year-old adult woman recalling the event, I brought back the three-year-old's feelings. I was sitting in her office, crying like a baby. I couldn't stop. I felt as helpless and terrorized as a child. I walked out of Karen's office dressed in my crushed silk dress, sat down in my Mercedes Benz 450SL and gazed at myself in the rear-view mirror. I felt like a fragile piece of Dresden or maybe a delicate, hollow Lladró figurine. Something beautiful, hollow and empty. A piece molded and created by others. I would break if I wasn't handled with extreme care. I wanted to be packaged carefully and protected—instead of Styrofoam packing maybe I could be wrapped in silky lace and laid in a coffin.

October 19, 1989

I saw my doctor today. He wouldn't prescribe anything without seeing me first. He said, "I thought you had the world by its tail." And I started to cry. I can't remember what he said, but he prescribed a drug called Prozac, an anti-depressant. I filled the prescription and took one. I don't feel any better.

October 20, 1989

I went to see Karen today. We added up my perpetrators. Counting my brothers and their friends, there are close to twenty. We didn't count kids my age. The others were about seven years older. I am shattered. I kept thinking a half dozen or so. Karen doesn't think this is all.

Why did I keep going back? That is the question that keeps running through my mind: Why did I keep going back? Why did I let them do that to me? I feel so ashamed.

Karen said, "April, just imagine with me for a moment. Imagine yourself at four. Think of how little a four-year-old is. Think of how often a little child needs love and hugs and cuddling, being held in a lap, rocked and sung to. How often did that happen to you?"

"I don't know. I don't remember it happening."

"Do you remember feeling frightened—hurt—confused—even terrified?"

"Yes. Almost always. At least one of those feelings all the time."

"And did you go to your mom and tell her? Or did she come to you and say, "April honey, what's wrong? You seem so sad. Here come sit on my lap and tell me about it."

I laughed, "No, no. I can't even imagine it. My mother wasn't there. Just not there. I felt invisible to her."

"And how about your dad?"

"Are you kidding?"

Karen said, "No, April, I'm not kidding."

"Well, no, of course not," I said, "not my Dad."

"Well then," she said, "Who is left? Where were you to go to know you weren't invisible, that some human being on this planet knew you existed? To feel connection to a person, any person, to affirm you were alive?"

I need to calm down. I can't think straight.

October 21, 1989

Something is wrong with my right shoulder. I can't lift my arm. Pain shoots from the back of my head through the right side of my neck and down my arm.

Maybe the Prozac is causing some weird side effect. I can barely move. I have tried to call my doctor, but I could only leave a message. I tried to call Karen as well. Meanwhile, I'm taking a long hot bath.

Later:

Karen called this evening. I couldn't pick up the phone with my right hand. Maybe I pinched a nerve or something. But I haven't done anything to injure it. The only difference is the Prozac.

Karen said Prozac shouldn't cause this reaction, but I'm going to talk to my doctor anyway. Karen said it could be a "body memory." I didn't know what she was talking about. She said that sometimes our bodies store the memory of a trauma away, and now that I am recalling all of these memories, it is possible for my body to recall the pain. I can't think of anything causing my neck and shoulder to hurt. I did recall feeling aroused at some of my memories to the point of getting wet. I told Karen, and she said this was also common. I felt sick telling her I was aroused at thoughts of such sick behavior inflicted upon a child.

Karen repeated what she said previously about bringing the feelings up at the same time the memory is recalled. The pain is easier to accept than the arousal feelings. I feel slutty. I feel sick.

October 22, 1989

It's early in the morning. I can't sleep. The right side of my body is killing me. I'm going to stop taking the Prozac until my doctor calls.

I am writing with my left hand because my right side hurts so bad.

My neck. I feel like I have whip lash, only I've never had it before. When did my head get snapped back? When I was seven my neck snapped back ... *he thrust his peanuts to the back of my throat. My head snapped back, and I fell on my right side. My arm couldn't support me and him. He thrust his peanuts to the back of my throat. I thought he was going to knock my head off my shoulders. I cried. He called me a horse. My mouth and jaw hurt. My teeth were numb, and he held both of my ears so I couldn't spit out the peanuts. I couldn't get away. I think I blacked out. I woke up in my little yellow room with blood on my pillow. I told my mommy I got a bloody nose. My teeth were loose. I couldn't eat anything, or my teeth would fall out. I had already lost my baby teeth. These were my permanent teeth. Maybe I could grow more.*

I told my mommy that my permanent teeth were loose. I was seven years old. She called the dentist, and he came over in the middle of the night. My dentist kept asking me what happened. I was afraid he could tell what a horse I had been. I was terrified that he knew about the peanuts in the back of my throat.

The next morning my mommy stood behind me at the bathroom counter to take my little pink sponge curlers out. She started crying. She cried so hard that she made noise. I had never seen her cry like that. She was scared that she'd lose her teeth. No, she was scared that I'd lose my teeth. I was scared because she was so afraid. I decided that it was because my hair didn't turn out right. My mommy told me not to tell anyone at school about how Mommy was crying. I was certain that it had to do with my hair. She gave me a thermos full of soup for my lunch and sent me off to school. Again, making me promise not to tell anyone about how upset Mommy was...

A few months ago, I went into my dentist. The same man after all these years. He told me I must stop clenching my teeth. He put a little mirror in my mouth to let me see what was happening. I was shocked to see I had been gnawing away at the inside of my mouth. As a result of my determined habit of gnashing my teeth, I had cracked and shattered some of them. Four of my back molars have caps on them. Two of them died and had to have root canals. I have damaged my own teeth by my adamant refusal to open my mouth—especially in my sleep.

Later:

I have so many questions. I am going to write them all down so they aren't swimming around in my mind. This is an ongoing list. The more I unravel, the more questions I have.

What is real? Regardless of the exterior props and accolades, what really happened? My entire concept of reality has been blown away. I was raised in a nice middle-class home. By Salt Lake standards it was in an affluent neighborhood. My dad was a respectable businessman who took over his father's bank and made it flourish. He worked long, hard hours to make it a huge success. My mother is a brilliant woman who was raised by immigrant parents who came to 'The Land of Zion" for a better life. My mother knows several languages and is a graduate of the university. After World War II she married my father, got pregnant with their first born, Melinda, and then completed her final year of school.

My parents and their baby lived in the apartment that I am living in now. There are stories about my mother being so thin and so weak after the birth of her baby that she only weighed 90 pounds. My dad brought her a Snelgrove's malt every night when he came home from the bank.

The story continues that she was very ill when she had to take her final exams at the university. She persevered in front of a big board of men and graduated.

A few years after Melinda was born, five and a half to be precise, my mother gave birth to a boy, Tom. Then to her complete surprise, as she had not resumed her menstrual cycle, she got pregnant again. Ten months after Tom was born, my mother gave birth to another boy, Byron.

They moved to the benches of the city, to a neighborhood with a name, Federal Heights. My mother was planning to go back to graduate school after Byron started first grade—and *bam*—she got pregnant again. This time she had a "beautiful, smiling, baby girl." Which is me. Evidently my mother had such severe postpartum depression after I was born that she had a "nervous breakdown." The story is that Byron was absolutely drawn to me, and he wouldn't let anyone else even touch me. He spent hours hovered over my crib watching me sleep. Evidently, he was the one who raised me. A first-grade boy in charge of an infant girl. What's wrong with this picture? I was told, and believed until recently, that nothing was wrong. A picture of a devoted little boy loving his baby sister.

When I turned eight my sister was married in the temple. My parents were so proud. Melinda always did the right thing. She got married in the temple and then continued with her education. She graduated from BYU with honors in finance. She started working with my dad at the bank. She is a very organized, structured person. She didn't want to have children; she only wanted to further her career. Her husband insisted on having children. He would have divorced her if she had not consented to a child. She relented and got pregnant. She is not an emotional person. She is very serious and devotes hours and hours to the bank. Her husband spends more time with their daughter, I guess. Melinda never talks about it. Only about money and investments. She is good at what she does.

When my mother tells the story of Melinda's wedding, she always adds that I almost lost my permanent teeth that same year. My front permanent teeth were alarmingly loose. I had only liquids for about six months. I carried my little thermos to school every day. Luckily my permanent teeth survived, and I have perfect, straight teeth.

My mother also says that I was never any problem. When my uncle was doing his doctorate thesis in education, he gave me an IQ test. I was extremely intelligent; "gifted" was the term. I tested out with the highest IQ in the family. And I was determined. My fifth-grade elementary school teacher told my mom that she had to stand at the door and keep me from taking my books home. I was already past the sixth-grade level in math, and they didn't have educational materials past the seventh grade. The elementary school teacher suggested I skip to the seventh grade. My mother strongly objected to skipping grades. Why? Because she wanted her little girl to have a normal social life with friends her own age. My mother's brother skipped a grade in elementary school and was never the same.

So, I stayed in the fifth grade. I nervously plucked out my eyelashes and my eyebrows. Sometimes I threw up before I went to school. For some strange reason all of my friends at school turned on me. I didn't have any friends.

When I got into the eighth grade, I started competitive running. Within a few short months I was a champion. One of the best the region has ever seen. People said I was "poetry in motion." My parents were very proud. I was a loner and put every ounce of my energy into running.

My brothers, Tom and Byron, went into the National Guard to avoid Vietnam and then went on LDS or Mormon missions. Tom went to Scotland and Byron to New York. The family looked very good. A thriving business. The oldest daughter married in the temple, a mother and a college graduate—working in her father's business. The two middle sons both serving religious missions, and the baby daughter an Olympic hopeful.

The boys came home when I was in the ninth grade. Tom got married shortly after he came home from his mission. Then he died. The story of this perfect family goes on and on.

I went to Utah State University. Byron graduated from the University of Utah at the same time. He got a double degree in accounting and finance. After a year of college, I went to Israel. I came home, continued at USU, and then transferred to the University of Utah. I graduated in English. Byron got his master's degree. He met Deborah and got married within three months. I worked at a health club. Byron started working for our dad in the banking profession.

I left the health club and took a few months to decide if I was going to enter the family business. My father didn't really want me around. I entered the business anyway, and the whole family worked together. The business thrived.

That's the synopsis. Perfect picture of a beautiful, successful, all-American family. The hardest part-I believed it. I'm a tall, slender blond—with a striking face, a beautiful smile, an hourglass figure, blah, blah, blah. Supposedly I am independent and very private. Actually, I was terrified that I would be found out. I lived a secret, shame-filled conspiracy. I am a fraud. An imposter. A great imitator. An actress.

My friend Jennifer is an actress in New York performing on the stage. She is talented. I am envious. She knows lines, can recognize roles, a script and her characters. I can't. My roles blur into one. I play myself; I am a character devised by others. "Does art emulate life or life imitate art?" I imitate. An enduring performance, not a matinee or an evening. A life.

October 23, 1989

I've been thinking about what a nervous kid I was, and how I used to throw up in the morning before I went to school. I remember driving in the car with my mom. She'd drop me off on her way to work. I was always sleeping in late, and I was always late to school. I never ate breakfast because I was sick in the morning and exhausted. It was a family joke that "April has never been a morning person."

Why was I so tired in the morning? Why was I so anxious? Was I disturbed in the night?

Why did I wear tampons all the time? I started my period when I was eighteen. But from the time I was twelve, I wore tampons. I told myself that it would be too humiliating to start my period and be caught off guard. I started to run competitively when I was thirteen. I hid the tampons from my teammates. I ran with them each day, and they didn't know I wore a tampon every day of my life.

The only time I remember having someone ask about it was in college. A couple of my roommates noticed, and they were concerned that something was wrong. I told them that my period was erratic, and I didn't want to be caught off guard. For the first couple of years of my college life, there were a lot of rumors about rape on campus. Occasionally my roommates and I would talk about it. We talked about what we would do—fight, try to talk your way out of it, whatever. I said, "Well, that's one of the reasons I wear tampons all the time. It will deter him from raping me."

Until that moment I had never consciously thought that. But I knew it was true. I knew that I wore tampons because I was afraid of getting raped. In one of these same conversations with my roommates, I said, "Well, if I couldn't fight, if he absolutely pinned me down and I was going to get it, I'd just pee on him." My roommates and I all hooted with laughter. From that moment on I never went to the bathroom before I walked anywhere. I always waited until I got home or reached my destination.

Later:

Karen gave me a book called *The Courage to Heal.* I've only been able to read the introduction. It says that most perpetrators are abuse victims themselves. That makes sense. I must ask myself the question: "Are you a perpetrator?" I know I am a victim; I know I have been sexually abused, and I know that I have a terrific denial system. I do not want to have done that to another. But I must face the fact that I might have. What if I did?

More than anything, I don't want to have been an abuser. I want to have been different. I know how painful it is being a victim. I can't imagine the additional layers of pain of being an abuser.

Pain, suffering and blood. He bled from every pore. Will Christ's blood wash over them? Or did it just run down my little legs? I wonder how much of Christ's blood was theirs?

RAGE

"It is not the prince at all,
but my father
drunkenly bent over my bed,
circling the abyss like a shark,
my father thick upon me
like some sleeping jellyfish."

—Anne Sexton from *Briar Rose*

April

I WENT RUNNING TODAY. I was weak and tired at first. The sun was shining, and a man, sort of yuppie looking, ran by me and said, "You have beautiful legs." I couldn't breathe for a minute or two. Then I thought to myself, "He meant you no harm. Relax. He's gone now." I continued my run and started to get mad. I mean really mad. I don't know what triggered this anger. I was furious. I ran faster and faster, and I couldn't get rid of my rage. I made fists, raised them in the air, and screamed.

I continued running. I can't control this rage much longer. What if I hurt someone? I thought of the guy in California walking into McDonald's and gunning people down. I was scared to be thinking of this guy. What if I hurt someone or hurt myself?

I slammed the apartment door when I got back. I punched the light switch so hard I practically embedded it two inches into the wall. I was furious.

October 25, 1989

I called Karen and told her about the anger. She said, "April, your rage is so good—so healthy. You needn't be afraid or ashamed of it. Feelings aren't moral or immoral—good or bad. They are natural consequences of our human experience. All the hurt and betrayal and fear has to go someplace. We want your feelings to come out clean and healthy, like your rage, not turned against yourself in shame or bulimia or running from those who love you. I facilitate a group for adult victims, April. They talk about their fear of hurting others—or themselves. Not one of them has in a moment of rage physically hurt someone else. One woman has hurt herself though."

My eyes watered. I was silent.

Karen said, "What's going on in there, April?"

I had fantasies of cutting myself with a knife, but I had never done it. I did punish myself with bulimia. We have worked on the bulimia for a long time, and I know it has to do with control. Controlling what goes in and out of my body. Since I've started having all of these memories, I haven't had the least thought of purging. I don't have the energy.

I want to die. I wish I could be invisible and vanish into thin air. I wish I had never been born.

I want to be lacy and white and comfortable. Somewhere, where I would be safe. Where I could sleep and never wake up. Never be woken up. Never be scared. A place where I could rest. I was always so tired and sleepy. Ornery. Yes, I am always cranky and tired. I want to die. I always wanted to die. Then they'd be sorry. They'd be sorry that they didn't treat me better. They'd be sad that they hurt me so much, and they'd never get a chance to say that they were sorry. I'd be dead, and then they'd feel bad. As bad as I have felt all my life.

I remember seeing my mommy crying. I think she cried for President Kennedy when he died. Maybe if I was dead, then maybe my mommy would cry for me.

My mommy had a nervous breakdown when I was born. Maybe if I had never been born. Maybe everything would be better. I wish I hadn't been born. I wish I was dead. I wish I was invisible. I wish I didn't exist.

October 26, 1989

I am still battling this rage. My emptiness is filled with anger. I have this picture of what is happening inside of me. A huge, ugly, black monster, asleep for years inside a cave in my soul, has been awakened by an earthquake. His cozy little cave has been disfigured, and he can't sleep. He's mad. He rams his head on the doorway of the cave. He is growling and gnarling over the crevasses of my soul, looking for a place to slumber. But I have no place for him. He must leave, but I don't know how to get him out of my body. So right now, he is battering about, raging inside of me. God, I loathe him.

October 27, 1989

I went to see Karen yesterday, and she told me about a woman who went to the Deseret Industries Thrift Shop and bought stacks of old glass plates. She waited until she was alone, took the plates into the garage, and locked the door. She threw plates everywhere. She thought of her father. It took her almost thirty minutes to break every plate. Then she got a big broom and swept the mess away. Karen said that she had a great time.

Karen also told me about clients getting punching bags and wailing on them. I don't know if I'm into that. Oh, how do I know what I'd feel?

Maybe it's the old scenario: "Too sick to go to the doctor." Karen asked if I knew how much energy it took to hold it all in. I really want to let it go. I just don't know how.

I'll write. I feel better getting it down on paper. But I'd be ashamed if anybody read this.

I have mobility in my arm again. It is still a little sore, like lactic acid has built up in my arm and neck, but it's working its way out. My body was trying to tell me, "Remember!" When I remembered, the pain began to dissipate. What a strange thing.

I remember in my freshman psychology class, Psych 101, I read about some studies with individuals who had been hypnotized. The hypnotist told them they were being touched with a hot coal, and then the hypnotist touched their arm with a finger. The hypnotized individual immediately got a red dot, like a burn. Eventually the mark would blister. A blister formed by the touch of a finger, by an individual in a hypnotic state utilizing the unconscious mind. Unconscious mind, where all of my memories are stored.

I'm relieved that Karen does not hypnotize. Sometimes I tape our sessions. I'm so upset right now, that it helps me to remember. About repressing memories, Karen said, "These horribly damaging experiences have been blocked from your consciousness the same way the body goes into shock to shield us from excruciating physical pain. Blocking or repressing is a natural psychological safety device to protect us until we are strong enough to do the work necessary to heal."

Karen told me that remembering was not the problem for me. She said, "You are having such a flood of flashbacks—smells, tastes, visual cues—that pull up a memory or feelings associated with the incest. Our challenge is to create a place of safety to help you feel protected while we build the skills to allow you to process the memories and heal the pain."

As I reread the memory about my teeth, I can't recall who "he" was. I have a few, very powerful memories with "him." I get a knot in my stomach just wondering about it.

I am exhausted. I am stumbling around in a complete daze. I guess that I am finally adjusting to the Prozac because I can't seem to wake up. I slept last night and I can't wake up.

From this book, *The Courage to Heal,* I've learned that I am in the emergency stage of my memories. It's where the first recollection of sexual abuse is accepted. Now that I think about it, I have had intimations off and on throughout my life. I remember when I was in the seventh grade, and I went to one of my young women's church classes—I was twelve. My instructor gave a lesson on chastity straight out of the church-issued manual. She held up a beautiful yellow daisy. Then she said, "Girls, this flower represents your virtue. See how perfect and beautiful this flower is? Now, look what happens if even just one petal is plucked off."

Then she plucked off a petal, leaving the flower disfigured. "That is what you will be like if you date before you are sixteen."

She pulled another petal off and said, "You lose another petal of your beauty if you let a boy kiss you before you are sixteen."

Another petal was ripped off with the words: "And this is what happens if you let a boy kiss you with his mouth open."

Then another petal removed with the play-by-play commentary, "This is what you will look like if you let a boy pet with you."

Another petal, with another virtue violation, and another petal, with the warning, and another and another and another—until the only thing left on the flower was a bare bulb. "And this is what happens if you lose your virginity. The beautiful flower is not even a flower anymore. No one would ever want this flower, for it has lost all its beauty."

I didn't know all the meanings for her words, like "chastity," "virtue" and "petting," But I got the gist of the lesson. I knew that my beauty was gone. I knew I could never be restored. I knew that I was nothing more than a bare bulb. I never went back.

I was in seventh grade. I knew that something was terribly wrong with me. Something that I have sensed my whole life.

Two years ago, I visited my friend Laurel in St. George. Laurel was a Sunday school teacher in her ward. Laurel was team teaching with another woman. I went to church with Laurel, and guess what lesson the other woman was teaching? "Chastity." I was so upset. I walked out of there and said to Laurel, "What about the incest victims? There are kids right here in this ward who are being victimized right now. There were over twenty girls in that class. I'm certain that a couple of them just had their hearts wrung through a wringer." Laurel stared at me. She commented that she had never thought of it that way before. I don't think I had thought of it in that way before either.

Now I'm looking around at my redecorated apartment. Flowers everywhere. I even have them hanging from the ceiling. I wear flowers. I love to smell them, and I surround myself with them. I love flowers. I love yellow daisies, pure white lilies, and tender violets. I wonder if my passion for flowers has anything to do with watching a beautiful flower stripped of its petals with every chastity infraction? How can anyone pull apart a flower?

October 31, 1989

I am zonked. The phone rings, and I never pick it up. I used to at least pick it up occasionally if I knew the person or felt like talking. Now the phone rings and I feel violated. Why can't people leave me alone? I go to the grocery store, and men approach me. I know once that was flattering. Now I feel raped. I've started shopping only late at night. I can't bear to be seen or approached. Even if I wear baggy sweats without any make-up, I get approached. Why? I feel like I have a big neon sign flashing over my head that says, "Approach me. Violate me."

The only person I pick up the phone for is Karen. At least with her I can be real. I can let her know how shitty I feel. Sometimes I don't need to talk. I can just listen to her and cry.

I have infections in my eyes, sties from my glands getting clogged with tears. I cry myself to sleep, and I wake up in the middle of the night crying, and I wake up in the morning crying. I've never been this out of control. I go to work, and my heart races wondering what might seep out of the deep dark wells of my own mind. Sometimes I have to get up and just go into the bathroom. I usually wash my face. It feels like I am cleansing myself of the memories. I look into the mirror. I only see the scar lines across my face. My dad said I slipped through the shower door when I was three. Fifty-seven stitches.

Sometimes it takes me a minute to recognize myself. This attractive woman in the mirror is not me. Then it dawns on me. "Oh, there you are. That's me." I don't feel as helpless when I make that connection with the adult woman in the mirror.

I deal with important clients every day. What would my clients think if they knew that I stand in front of the mirror trying to recognize myself? I've had it in my mind that incest victims come from scuzzy families. I guess mine was scuzzy only we had such an attractive smoke screen.

November 1, 1989

I'm in a full-fledged depression. I feel hurt in every fiber of my being. Even the stuff holding my cells together is hurting. I wonder when I will completely fall apart. I think things have gotten worse. I'm taking my Prozac, and I don't think it's doing any good. I wish I could just die. Well, I'm not sure about that. What if I take this pain with me?

I have my session with Karen today. I wonder if I'll stop crying enough to drive to her office. I wrote down some questions for her: What is my religion all about? Am I a fraud? Hibernation from men? Pointless anger? Good memories from my childhood—are they true? Am I clinging to them or making them more than they really were? What is love?

Later:

I have never been a child. There is all this talk about "Healing the Child Within," and I was never a child. When I was little, I would lie in bed and cry. I remember wishing that my mommy would come in and hold me and make the tears go away. But she never did. I've never been held until I stopped crying.

Today I sat in Karen's office crying. Again. I would have lashed out at her if she had tried to approach me. She has only gently rubbed my hand once. It was right after my mother and father had a relapse. The "slip" they had six months after my mom got out of the hospital—for alcohol treatment. I was so disappointed and upset. I called the paramedics and watched them revive my mother while my father hid naked in the bathroom.

I wanted them to be clean and sober so desperately. After this happened, I was crying in Karen's office. As I was leaving Karen gently rubbed my right hand. That's the only time she's touched me. It's not that she is a cold person. I am. I just don't know what to do with touching. It terrifies me. Touching means pain and abuse.

This morning Karen and I talked about my pointless anger.

Karen tries to convince me, "Anger is the natural and normal emotional response to pain and loss. And in no way is it pointless." She says, "April, respect your anger. See how big it is? See how it fills you up until you feel ready to explode with it?"

"That's how it feels," I whispered.

"Well," Karen said, "that's how big the pain was—the betrayal, the shame, the humiliation—in a little tiny child who could do nothing but bury it. It's been in there a long, long time, April. The loss to that child is almost unfathomable—the pain and rage equally big—and it has to come out. It is the storm before the calm."

As soon as we started talking about how mad I was and what I had a right to be mad about, I started crying. I can't even feel the right emotion. I'm sad, so I get mad at the light switch.

Memories remind me of when I throw up. Everything is all jumbled together in a big stinky lump. I've thrown up my memories, and they are jumbled all together. The memories happened one at a time, just like eating one bite at a time. But when you throw up, everything comes up any way it damn well pleases. I have memories that are jumbled all over the place. What a stinky mess. I wish that I could just flush the toilet, but it's not that simple. I don't believe that if I died, I'd be rid of all this puke. I think it's with me. And if I don't deal with it, at my own pace, it will just keep coming up again and again and again. At least this time I can slowly go through this pile of undigested crap and do something with it besides just swallowing it again. Maybe I'll be able to give some of it back. You know, "Return to sender." Maybe some of it will evaporate into the atmosphere. I'll have to find appropriate places for the other stuff. But before it goes anywhere, I want to make sure I know what it is. I deserve to know.

Carol

THE MAY AFTER THE CHILDREN talked, I hated spring. People commented that the Hawthorne blossoms were especially full and brilliant that year. I blocked them out of my vision the same way I always had the billboards on the freeway. Always before, my eyes had searched for tender greens catching spring's light, but now I preferred looking at cinderblocks faced with ugly green artificial rock.

The last week of March Norton went to Paris on business, and I went with him. We drove through some of the Loire country, and the man-made beauty was bearable. I could look at the chateaux, although I remember nothing of them now except the images I've seen in travel posters.

One afternoon in Paris, I found myself alone in the L'Orangerie, alone in the rooms which display only the huge panels of Monet's "Water Lillies." I sat surrounded by them, in the center of the room, encircled by mauves and soft violets, blues and grays, all that amazing light. I wept. For the first time since February 14, I wept. Something broke inside me, some iron clot too deep to seek its own awareness.

I tried to tell April the rest of what we found out about the grandchildren.

On February 16, Lorraine and I took her children to our condo in Coronado by San Diego. We had to get out of Salt Lake to get the children away from the settings of their abuse. Hank voluntarily committed himself to in-patient psychiatric care, still claiming he could remember nothing.

None of my great psychological methods of "opening people up" were necessary with the children. Timothy, Isabel, and Leah erupted. We couldn't have turned them off had we tried. In the middle of the night, one of them would come screaming to our beds with a new horror.

In between the telling times, they would run and run on the wet sand, their little bodies bent into the wind. The sand was wonderful for them. They would throw it and kick it and dig tunnels that went on forever.

How can I give anyone the sense of the horror of their telling? I showed April the letter Lorraine wrote to her stake president a year after the children had talked. It gives the facts. Here it is:

Dear President Schmied,

You have asked me to advise you of my current circumstances surrounding my divorce from Hank Carstensen.

I married Hank Carstensen in the Salt Lake City Temple in 1976. I believed at that time that Hank was a righteous man and for 10 years I tried to make a celestial marriage. I had four children who, after living in true hell, finally "told" in January and February 1986, the actual nightmare that our "perfect," temple-going, family-night, daily family-prayers family was living: their father was a child abuser who had been sexually molesting them for years. The case was immediately reported to the police who eventually said they could not prosecute without my children's public court testimony. A major reason for the inaction of the criminal system has been my unwillingness to make a media circus of my children.

Ecclesiastical inaction is more difficult to understand in view of the Lord's teachings on sexual morality and His clear warning to those who teach evil to the innocent. Why hasn't Hank been disciplined by his church? My children remain available to you for questioning, as do other child witnesses including my brother's children, if corroboration of these facts is necessary.

There is not a way to describe the agony my children and I have traversed. We have all been seeing a therapist weekly for a year; you are welcome to call these doctors to verify the truthfulness of my children's story.

My children have told how Hank took them and one of my nieces to his mother's home and let her and other relatives molest these little children and to watch as Hank had sexual intercourse with others including his own mother.

Hank also networked with a child abuse ring in his neighborhood. They had orgies of abuse which they videotaped. I assume the tapes were traded to other pedophiles or sold for money.

The abusers threatened and terrified them. They killed a kitten in front of the children and told them this would happen to them if they told. They gave them injections of drugs (the children say so it wouldn't hurt so much and to make them sleepy), showed them films of all sorts of sadisms. Finally, my children reached the point where what they actually were experiencing became as frightening as the threats of what would happen if they told.

Hank was admitted to an out-of-state sexual offenders' program for eight weeks where Hank admitted his crimes. If Hank is not a pedophile and a threat to children, he should volunteer these records to clear his name since he has told you he is innocent.

Hank mailed an invitation to my children for his remarriage which took place last month. The children have not seen him since February 1986. He originally agreed to no visitation with them unless their psychiatrist deemed it to be in their best interest. As soon as he realized he wasn't being prosecuted, he initiated legal action requesting not only visitation but custody. It has taken incredible effort and legal costs to keep my children safe from him. When the children were told of his marriage and the fact that he now has two little stepdaughters, they cried and told me I had to stop him because now he would have more kids to abuse. The fact that he is active in the church may have been a factor in his ability to find another wife. They were married in the temple. The safety of unborn children, and for that matter any available children, is in the hands of those of us who know the truth. You President Schmied know the truth. If we are silent, we betray them.

I hope for Hank's excommunication, mainly as a warning to others Hank may contact but also because my children are in a fragile place.

When our new primary president told the story of *Daniel and the Lions' Den* and concluded by stating that if small children would pray, God would help them when they were in trouble, my eleven-year-old raised his hand and angrily informed the sister that this was not true. My nine-year-old refuses to pray. She describes looking at the pictures of Jesus holding the children, which had always been hanging in her room, and how she'd pray and pray, begging that if the abuse had to continue that at least Heavenly Father would make it so it didn't hurt so bad. But it always hurt just as bad. My four-year-old is still confused over right and wrong. She was constantly told Jesus wanted her to do these things and that I wanted her to have these "marriage lessons." For weeks after she'd told, she kept expressing her astonishment. "They didn't kill me yet, Mommy. But Heavenly Father wants me to be killed for telling."

Hank is aware of the sodium pentothal interview and the lie detector tests administered to him at the hospital. Since he found out he was not to be criminally prosecuted, he has recanted on his past statements and is now asserting his complete innocence. The church records should reflect that Hank is a pedophile. If allowed access to children in the church, the church may be held morally and legally responsible for its failure to protect innocent victims from an extremely disturbed child abuser. Documentation regarding the above statements is available at your request.

Lorraine Scott

After I showed the letter to April, she asked me what happened with the church. Nothing ever happened in the church. The bishop did come and talk to Lorraine one night. He said that if his own wife had to choose between believing him or their children, he knew she would trust him. The bishop advised Lorraine that she should think very carefully before breaking up her family. Lorraine moved. She did not see him again.

No one from the church interviewed the children or asked more questions, except the stake president who talked with one of the children's therapists. The stake president told us he believed it. There has never been an excommunication trial. We think we know why, but there is no way to be sure. Lorraine's neighbors, the ones who had the "touching parties," are the daughter and son-in-law of an apostle in the Mormon church. I used to have fantasies about reporting that to the *National Enquirer.* What Utah police official, what church authority is going to deal with that? Or what neighbor for that matter? All Lorraine and Jake could do was get their families out of there.

I told April people are always suggesting that therapists plant sexual abuse allegations in children's minds. There's no question children sometimes lie (although the most recent research indicates they do so less than adults), that teenagers make allegations against adults they hate which may not be true and that in child custody cases children are sometimes "coached" by one parent against another. The best studies, however, indicate that unfounded allegations account for a tiny percentage of the number of child sexual abuse cases now being reported in every state in America. A teenager's lie is usually detected early in investigation. Custody battles seem to go on forever and mothers' who raise allegations of child sexual abuse are more likely to lose custody of their children than those who don't. Most defense attorneys in the average child abuse case attack the credibility of the therapist.

Few people seem to understand that certainly in pre-internet times children simply did not have access to the sexual detail they reveal unless they have experienced or witnessed the described behavior. Nor do children generally maintain their stories over time if the experience is not real. Nor do they show the emotional effect of their "telling." Nor can they fake the explosion of their emotions after disclosure. No one could coach kids into these maintained emotional displays.

From their point of view, most children have everything to lose by revealing the abuse. Whatever the threat, be it ever so subtle, which has kept them silent—it is absolutely valid in their minds. The threat can be terrorizing such as a death threat, it can be the breaking up of the family, it can be a threat to someone dear to them, it can be their own shame which will be revealed, it can be fear of the police, or it can simply be the loss of the perpetrator's love and attention. When an adult like April recovers memories, the same feelings that originally kept the child silent emerge. This reaction occurs in little children too, but they do not have the accumulation of years of silence to deal with. They do not think they are crazy. What they do think is that they are powerless.

One of the children in Lorraine's neighborhood who was named as being at the "touching parties" developed a staph infection and nearly died. The doctors could not figure out how she could have contracted it. Did she ever drink contaminated stream water, they asked? My grandchildren had described being forced to drink the abuser's bodily waste. Another child, whose parents never took her to a therapist, later pulled out all her eyelashes and every hair on her head. Now in therapy at last, she remembers nothing.

These are factual details, but they can't convey the way it was, the telling. April understands. The drawings, for instance. Dozens of pictures from Timothy and Isabel with a line down the middle of the paper and "Daddy" on each side, labeled "Good Daddy" and "Bad Daddy." Leah's stick-like pictures of Daddy with a big line between his legs going almost to his feet. Isabel screaming at her mother, "If you divorce Daddy, you're worse than all the bad people put together!" Their stories about Daddies who were sick and then got better and everybody lived happily ever after.

That is what I had childishly hoped for too.

Timothy's guilt when he talks about how he didn't protect his baby brother. Isabel's pictures over and over, brightly colored of an abstract creature in pink ballet shoes. She labeled it "The Telling Mouse" (herself). Pictures of Geraldine with long red hair, big circles for breasts, and red pubic hair that they would scribble out with black crayon. Pictures of their daddy with huge scissors cutting off his penis and hands.

Isabel wrote: "I want to say to Grandma: You big brat. You get off this entire whole world. I want to say to Geraldine: You're a big poo. You're gross. You're awful wicked. Meaner than anyone in the world. I want to say to Daddy: I hate you Daddy, bad Daddy. Inside the good Daddy. You bug me. You hurt very bad. What you've done to us is as sharp as a thumb tack."

One effective method to help children disclose is to have them draw a floor plan. Creating the physical environment helps memories get verbalized. Abreaction. I asked Timothy to draw me a picture of his house as if he were on the ceiling looking down and could put the furniture and things where they go. He started drawing, and it looked nothing like his home. Finally, I asked him, "I don't understand Timothy. How come the front door's over there?" Timothy looked up at me, totally startled. "But it's Grandma's house. I meant to draw ours, but it's Grandma's." This is how the whole story about how they were taken to Hank's mother's started pouring out.

"There was Grandma and a couple of her lady friends and sometimes some of the cousins. We would all sit in a circle on the floor and go around, and they'd tell us what to do, like in spin-the-bottle. The ladies liked us to suck on their boobs and pretend we were babies. Then Daddy would do things to the ladies, especially Grandma. Sometimes he would lie on her and put his big thing up her. Mostly the ladies kept their clothes on, but we were naked. They always had good treats. On the way home Daddy would say, 'Wasn't that fun? You did real good. You're learning the lessons real well, but you mustn't tell Mommy or she will feel bad she can't come, and then you can't come to the parties anymore.'"

Lorraine took the sobbing Timothy into her bedroom, and I called Isabel into mine.

"Timothy's told me about Grandma's."

That's all it took. Same story, same details. Identical. Even three-year-old Leah told it, uncoached, described her daddy having sex with his mother.

Afterwards they made Play-doh Grandmas and stuck pins in them and smashed them and ground them up in the disposal. They laughed and laughed. Timothy said they couldn't call her "Grandma" anymore. She wasn't their Grandma anymore. They competed to think of the most terrible names for her. Finally, they settled on Germy-sour-throw-up. To this day that's how they refer to her, if she is ever mentioned.

In the middle of the night of that same day, Timothy came to my room. "I have to tell you something awful," he said. "It's too awful to tell. I was bad. But they made me."

"Who?" I asked in the calm, hopefully comforting voice I was trying to master.

"Grandma and the ladies. I can't tell it. Everyone will think I'm bad. You can't tell anybody, not even Mommy."

"If you can't tell it, maybe you can write it. I won't tell unless you say so."

Timothy wrote in his second-grade printing, "They made us drink kofey."

Then he started to cry. As I held him and stroked his hair, he said, "They said if we told anyone about the parties, they'd tell how we drank coffee. And I didn't even fight that hard not to drink it. But it was nasty."

While I held Timothy and tried to explain about coffee, something way deep and from way long ago inside me snapped. It has still not come back together. My old, old issues about hypocrisy, priorities and claims to exclusive truth. I wanted to burn every church manual I'd ever taught from about evil coffee-drinking people, and I wanted to kill Germy-sour-throw-up. I think of all the horrors the children told, that one broke my heart the most that Timothy was taught coffee was wrong but not sex abuse.

I've told April this. She gets it. She cries.

April

I CAN'T WRITE EVERYTHING DOWN. It is too hard. I came to St. George on business. I am staying with my friend Laurel.

I want to tell her to never let her children out of her sight. You never know who can hurt them. You never know who has been damaged and broken and wants to fill the hole in their own soul by acting out on innocent little children. I want her to guard her children with her life. Someone needs to protect them. People are not what they appear.

Laurel is making Burton's and Parker's Halloween costumes right now. I wonder if Lilly gets to Trick or Treat in New York? It's almost dark, and the Trick or Treaters are starting to ring the bell.

Later:

I went to the store to get milk for breakfast, and smashed pumpkins were all over the road. I hope that Laurel's boys don't see the mess tomorrow morning. I think it's so stupid and senseless. Why did they have to do that?

November 3, 1989

I went to the convention today and set up our exhibition booth. I had on my most fraudulent smile and handed out business packets and chocolate candy to many governmental employees in the state. I felt so empty that I thought if a big gust of wind came up, I'd blow away.

It seems apropos that I am the "Marketing Director" for this family business. I'm the one to project the image for the business and the family. And I'm all smiles about it.

November 4, 1989

My mom and dad showed up to help me with the booth. I don't even know what to say.

November 5, 1989

Karen and I had a session on the telephone this afternoon. I told her about the boys peeing on me. While we were on the phone, I remembered being in the next-door neighbor's basement with those two college boys, Byron, Hank, David Fuller, my cousin Charles, and Charles's friend. I *wouldn't do something that they wanted me to do. I can't remember exactly what, and they took out their peanuts and squirted me. I was naked, and I huddled in a corner, and they just kept peeing on me and laughing. I was crying. I was crying really hard. I don't remember how it stopped or when or even how I got home.*

Karen said something about my mother, and I replied that my mom never knew. Then Karen said, "How could she not smell the urine?" That question went straight through my body like a bolt of lightning. Where was my mother, and how come she didn't smell the urine? Who did my laundry? My mother did, every Wednesday.

The thing is, I don't feel anything about this. I almost feel apathetic that my mother didn't notice the urine scent reeking from me—or from my laundry. I don't expect her to notice. I guess I haven't realized that I deserve to have a mother who notices.

November 6, 1989

I spent the day with Laurel and her boys yesterday. They were all so cute, but I wasn't exactly my perky self. Laurel is very concerned and cares about me. I gave her the book, *My Father's House*. That's the one that really triggered my memories. I haven't been able to pick it up since. Laurel is gentle, strong and open about it all. She has such grace.

She asked me if her husband could give me a blessing. It really scared me. I called Karen on the phone. It's Sunday morning, and I called Karen's answering service and told them it was an emergency. I felt a little dramatic, but it really sent me into a tailspin. I know that Laurel loves me, and her husband would never do me any harm. But the thought of being in a submissive position under a male frightens me. I can't do it. I can't be under a man's hands, even if it's for a blessing.

Karen helped me on what to say to Laurel. That I really appreciate her concern, but I'm a little too vulnerable for that particular physical position. After I told Laurel she understood. I was touched that she had offered.

November 7, 1989

I'm back in Salt Lake. I had a rough night—jolting myself awake every few minutes.

I went to work, and my darling little three-year-old nephew was there. He came into my office and crawled into my lap. I wrapped my arms around him and held him tight.

He was mellow and gentle. We sat there behind my desk for a long time. I'm not exactly sure who was holding whom. He is so young. I can't believe what happened to me at his age. He is innocent and trusting and young. I love him so much. I think I'd kill anybody who did something to him—like what happened to me.

My eyes teared as I held him, and he looked up at me and told me to go back to bed. I guess he thought I was just yawning and had watery eyes. He is precious; so was I.

November 8, 1989

I read in John Bradshaw that many victims of childhood sexual abuse have a more severe trauma than the adults in Nazi concentration camps. He was going on the premise that the adults already had developed their own sense of themselves—children who are sexually abused are robbed (I like to say raped) of their ability to develop their sense of themselves. They do not have themselves.

I grew up in the LDS church, and it's very complicated for me. The church teaches of love and forgiveness and growth. But my particular experience with it has been that I just plain don't fit. I know a lot of good people in the church, and I know many that merely use the church as a front. Books have been written on the subject, and I could probably write one, but as concisely as I can state it: I believe that the church has many beautiful teachings, and many good individuals are striving to better themselves in the church—I don't fit into the mold. I gain so much more on my own. Or am I just running?

Karen used to be a Sunday school teacher. I wanted to know her opinion on the church. Being the good therapist that she is, she isn't going to tell me. As a matter of fact, she never tells me her belief systems. She only questions me about mine to help me discover myself.

I was concerned because the church teaches of an "opposition in all things." I buy into that belief because of what I am going through right now. I have experienced the hell of sex, and I want to believe that the opposite of my experience is heaven. I want to hope, to believe that sex is not an atrocity.

When I was young Byron told me that sex was the most God-like act humans could perform. It was sacred because it could create life. I believed him. I must have been split at the time because I didn't even bring up the acts that occurred between us. I was in the sixth grade; Byron had made his big transformation. He used to be a "D" student and almost flunked out of school. He hung around with a bunch of kids who sluffed school and went out by the wall and smoked. When he got to be a senior in high school, he went through this saint-like transformation, like Saul becoming Paul. Instead of coming into my room to abuse me, he came in and we talked about religion. I remember he read from the Sermon on the Mount: "But I say unto you, Love your enemies, bless them that curse you, do good to them that hate you, and pray for them which despitefully use you, and persecute you."

Now I think the scripture was about Byron. At the time I thought it was about the kids at school. I was ostracized by all the kids in my sixth-grade class. Why?

The kids picked on me. Last year in the spring, all of my friends and I went into the girls' lavatory and hid behind the yellow tiled wall that led to the outside. Huddled in a tight circle, I told them all about fucking, boners, pussies, blow jobs, "69," how not to get pregnant, and periods. I told them exactly how it was ... entirely based on everything I knew. My friends went home and told their parents about what they learned in the lavatory from the Daniels' girl. The parents told them to never play with me again. I didn't have any friends because I was foul and dirty.

Twenty years later I am wondering why none of those righteous mothers asked, "Why does April know so much pornographic information?" Why didn't one mother investigate? Why didn't anyone ask my parents?

My mother who didn't smell the urine on me. Maybe one of the PTA moms did approach my mother. Maybe—and maybe my mother just buried her head in the sand.

I didn't have any friends in sixth grade. I didn't have any friends until I became a "hot" runner. Then I was popular again—-that was my identity. But I knew that if anyone got too close again, they'd turn on me.

I didn't trust anyone. Not until I was desperate after Tom died in my sophomore year in high school. Then I reached out. And I was lucky. Now I have some real friends.

November 9, 1989

I must make a presentation today. I have tried to get this account for a couple of years, but I haven't been successful. I believe that it is rigged. The bid specifications are tailored for only one investment banker. The secretary said that their current banker designed the specs, so it looks rigged.

To make a long story short, I "low balled" our proposal. I wanted to wake them up.

I am nervous. I must leave soon and drive all the way up the canyon. I'm feeling a little sick. This is what I do for a living. Yet I am more nervous today than I have ever been—even my first presentation wasn't like this. I knew I could speak in front of a crowd. Now with hundreds of such meetings behind me, I'm anxious. I feel like dying. I want to scream. My heart is racing so fast, I feel like a rib is broken from the inside.

Later:

I just got home from the Board of Directors' meeting. I am floating on air.

On the way up the canyon I stopped at a 7-Eleven store and tried to call Karen, but she was in a session. Then I got a Diet Coke and promptly threw it out. As I was driving up the canyon, I had fantasies of driving off the road and dying. I stayed on the road. I kept going. I made the presentation. I even confronted the chairperson and the current banker. I wasn't as sharp as I have been in the past. In

75

fact, I was really "off." But I wanted to die on the way to the meeting, and I lived and made a presentation. I feel like I just sold a five-million-dollar account.

Maybe I am going crazy—I am so happy—and I didn't even get the sale. I came in $12,000 less than the incumbent with a better plan, and I didn't even make the sale. I can't walk into the bank right now this blissful and tell them I didn't get the sale. I'm just glad it's over, and I'm glad I showed up. Victory!

Later:

Karen finally phoned me tonight. I guess I do have a huge victory under my belt.

I told her about the meeting. She asked me about the chairperson. He was an older man, retired, and definitely the decision maker. The other members of the board would never question his authority. They were younger, much younger than the chairperson, probably in their thirties.

The current banker was there. He was also older. He didn't know much about fiduciary bonds. The chairperson wasn't even going to let me speak. He made a motion that since Mountain View Bank did not meet the bid specifications, our bid was ineligible. He scolded me and told me to follow the specs before I came back. And I challenged him.

I'm smiling as I write this. I told him that the bid specifications were tailor-made to fit only one bank in the state. In front of the board, I asked him who wrote the specs. He replied, "The current banker."

I said, "My proposal offers you broader benefits utilizing stronger carriers, and you are going to throw out our proposal based on one small technicality? You might wonder whether the bid specifications were designed by someone specializing in bonding. I am not suggesting that you have us write your specifications. But I am recommending that you get an objective source to evaluate the specifications and these proposals."

I know that some of the members on the board heard me because they asked questions. But the chairperson decided that there was not enough time this year, and they would postpone any decisions. After the meeting a couple of the board members asked me for my card. They still had a lot of questions.

Karen asked me if there were any women on the board. Not one. The chairperson was an overbearing, illogical man. And the younger sheep—I mean men—seemed to be afraid of the chair and quietly acquiesced to the chair's commands. But I spoke my piece and knew I was right.

This reminds me of abuse in my childhood. One dominant man with several submissive men around him. I don't think I could have put myself in a more vulnerable situation. I stood up for myself. I expressed myself. Karen helped me see that this was a huge victory.

Later:

I am so exhausted. I feel like I am trying to hold a memory back. Since I began remembering I am struggling with power. There were times when I was the center of attention, and I liked it. As a thirty-year-old woman writing this, I despise myself. Maybe today was about showing up, feeling empowered and then not getting what I deserved, expected, wanted or planned on. Maybe it had to do with getting "short changed." That's what the abuse situations were like. I went to get attention and love, to be heard. I got attention, but I didn't get what I wanted. I couldn't explain why. I thought I was a nasty little girl, and I got what I wanted. That's why I kept going back, and that's why I never stopped them. Such theories were all I could come up with.

I feel like a super ball propelled by hydroelectric force into a wall, a wall in a racquetball court. I'm bouncing from wall to wall to wall. My speed is not dissipating. I hit a wall and gain momentum which flings me with even greater force into the next wall.

November 10, 1989

I've been thinking about my hair. Laurel says I have great hair. I've never done much with it. It's basically wash and wear hair—blond with natural curl, down past my shoulders. My hair. My long blond hair. I used to have long blond hair to my waist. I should write with my left hand. I'm afraid, and my rational right hand wants to stop me.

I'm writing with my left hand. I used to have long blond hair. My mommy would wash it once a week and brush it in the sunshine. Sometimes she put lemon on it to get the tangles out. Sometimes, sometimes it was nice to stand on our balcony with my mommy as the sun warmed and dried my hair.

Sometimes it wasn't so nice. Sometimes she would hurt my head and snap it back. She'd get mad at the snarls and at me. Sometimes she cut my hair. Sometimes if I wiggled around she would hit me with the brush. Sometimes I'd stand there and cry; then the sun dried my tears and my hair…

I loved my long blond hair. I wanted to be like Cinderella or the Good Witch of the West in the Wizard of Oz.

My hair, my hair.

"Tickle my dick with your long blond hair," he said. He tangled my hair, and I was afraid that my mommy would get mad and cut my hair or hit me with the brush. He peed in my hair. He peed up the white stuff. It's the same itchy white stuff that kept coming out of my hole. He'd put it up there with his big thing, and then it burned when I went tinkle. He peed in my hair, and I didn't want my hair to itch or be stinky and white. So I cut my hair. The girl across the street was playing with a gray cat on the neighbor's lawn. She asked me why I cut my hair. I told her that it was dirty. I meant that it was nasty, but she didn't understand. She didn't understand that you were dirty when you were nasty. My hair was nasty and dirty so I cut it. Then my mommy wouldn't tug at my tangles until I cried, and he wouldn't jerk my head around his peanuts. I cut my hair with the scissors in the front hall by the wrapping paper. The girl across the street let me pet the cat, and she didn't make fun of me… the other kids did when they saw me.

But there is more. There is something more I'm not remembering.

Rage

November 11, 1989

I ran by the cemetery today, and I was envious of those lucky dead people. Imagine lying there in a silk, cushy coffin. Better than sleeping—my dreams haunt me. Maybe death is the final resting place or a place for me to rest. I am so tired. Then again, I have no guarantee that I'd be able to rest. Maybe my death would be haunting. Maybe it would be worse than living, and I'd just be trapped in my coffin. I feel trapped in my body. My body. It seems like other people have been in it more than I have.

Tonight, I took my notebook and walked over to the cemetery again. I live right by it. I'm not sure I'd call this living. Maybe I am already dead. I don't feel anything. I'm just walking around in this beautiful casket that most people call a body.

I sit on the wall of the cemetery and watch the view. Clear tonight. The twinkling lights of the city add dimension to the tombstones before me.

I sit here and write:

the f poem
of life
futile, fragile, fun
and fucked
frame it up
so it fits
my therapist
says
her name even
starts with f
so there it is
futility leading
the list
and fun because
it is so fucked
and fragile
and fatal
funny how all
the f's fit
within my framework

Karen says that the memories come in an ebb and flow. So does the pain. Right now, the waves are crashing thunderously to the jagged shore.

November 12, 1989

Are we held together by anything more than scar tissue? On Friday I walked into Byron's office. We worked efficiently through the budget and the financial capacities and liabilities, and then I stood up to leave. Slowly I turned around and looked at my brother. He was concentrating on a scrap of paper until he felt my gaze. He raised his eyes and said, "Did we forget something?"

I gazed at him for a moment and remembered all that I had remembered. My gentle brother. Yet he was such a mean teenager, and now his voice is a solemn monotone. He must be exerting all of his energy to hold back his feelings, his emotions, himself. He hardly ever smiles or laughs, and he didn't even cry when Tom died. Where does his pain go?

As I looked down into my brother's brown eyes, I thought of how much I loved him. Then I wondered if what I was feeling was love or pity or what. We do have a bond, an incredible bond that I have always felt was love. Now I don't know what it is. Maybe it's scar tissue. Maybe we are all held together by scar tissue.

November 13, 1989

I woke up this morning with such a gnawing ache. I wasn't fully awake yet, and I felt like deep inside of myself a pain had transcended my physical body and gripped my soul. I feel imprisoned by pain. It has engulfed my essence and permeated my spirit.

My mind does not offer solace. I think the neurological connectors between my brain cells have been damaged, and the only impulse transmitted is one of pain a contraction between intermolecular synapses of my soul, squeezing out through the cells to tissues and organs transmitting pain—not sweating blood, only tears— secreted by lacrimal glands of my vision glistening like diamonds on my face.

My mind has betrayed me. I created a world, and it was more illusion than the box in my living room conducting the images of television. only I can't turn the images off.

I created a family, the perfect "All American" family. We were living out the "American Dream." Now I can't edit out the ugly parts for the audience. The most avid patron of the performance was me.

I'm lying on my floor in an exhausted heap. The entire picture of my life is unfolding for me. There are no gaps and inconsistencies—everything is making sense. The pain is making my body throb.

I am relieved that things make sense, but I am so sad about my life.

I feel utter sorrow when I think of my mother and the fictitious illusion she created herself to be—and I longed for her to be. I am saddened by her eloquent words of love and the reality of a vacant person. I am saddened by the thoughts of my brothers and sister. My sister was independent and lived an adventurous, exciting life—apart from the family. My first brother Tom I made into a sensitive saint not capable of handling the horrors of living—so he died. And the other brother I made my little parent, my strong protector.

All of them were damaged and hurt. They all exhibited behaviors manifesting the deep victimization of our lives. They were not "independent," "saints" or "strong." They coped.

November 14, 1989

I question if life is worth living. Yesterday Karen said, "You have to realize, you've already survived."

I don't feel like a survivor. I feel like a steamroller ran over me. Karen said that she believes people don't remember until they are ready to remember. She said, "You may not feel like it right now, but you are strong enough." I just cried, always silent tears. I wonder if I hold back the noise when I cry, or do others add noise?

Karen went on. "You are a survivor. Other victims are unavailable." I wasn't comprehending her words, so she continued, "The others are either dead or institutionalized. You and those like you are the only type we can really work with. For whatever reasons you are strong enough to be here. The others are essentially unavailable."

"I don't feel very strong."

"You are, you might not feel that you are, but you are. Trust me on that one."

I nodded but thought to myself, "I don't have much choice but to trust her."

Now I'm sitting in my cozy little apartment staring. I've been thinking about those comatose patients in institutions. Maybe they are the strong ones. This is such an internal battle. Maybe they are more courageous for giving up the external world and retreating inward to battle their pain.

Maybe not. Maybe they aren't feeling anything. Maybe they have chosen to shut down their minds; their bodies are merely functioning involuntarily.

Involuntary. My body functions involuntarily. I am here and write as the tissues of my heart automatically contract and send blood pulsating through my arteries and veins. I remember other times my body has worked on its own.

I was little, just starting kindergarten. Tom came up to my bedroom to say good-night. He did that a lot. Sometimes he would tickle me. He asked me to take off my pajamas so he could really tickle me. Sometimes I laughed until I cried. Sometimes I was quiet.

Sometimes he took out his peanuts and tickled himself, and he'd trickle around my pee-pee hole with his fingers. I was really ticklish there. It felt good. He'd tickle me until I tingled down my legs and up through my arms. He'd tickle me until I tingled all over. Sometimes I'd jerk because of the warm tingling all over my body.

November 15, 1989

Today for the first time, I went back and read through my journal for the last six weeks. Reading about the first dream, the one in the record store with the gang rape, and then remembering "my friend." The friend I loved looked like me and was wearing my clothes. I can't believe I didn't recognize her. I cry when I think about it. I cry when I think of the rapist's penis turning black in my hand, dividing into an eight-headed snake which wrapped around my right hand and trapped me. I feel like the snake is inside of me and has grown to an enormous size. The snake is the monster of my rage.

Shakespeare said the world is a stage. I've heard of actresses and actors collapsing after a performance. I come home from work every day and nearly collapse. I am tired because I am acting.

Every day I walk into work and face my perpetrators. I play the part of the little sister with all the brains and, worst of all, the looks. I'm the little sister my family resents. They say I was spoiled and "given it all." I know now they resent me because I remind them of their own pain.

I am exhausted by my performance. But it is all I know. If I let go of my pretense, who will I be? Nothing? I am nothing but a hollow shell. At least I have a shell.

I keep asking myself, "Why did I go back?" I knew I was being hurt. Why did I go back? I think now I understand. It was something. It was horrible. But it was something. My existence was acknowledged.

Now I face my perpetrators and am a fraud every day of my life. I act as if we are the happy family running a multi-million-dollar bank. I continue. This is all I know.

November 16, 1989

I've been reading about sexual abuse. I may be intellectualizing, but I'm not running from my feelings by throwing myself into some fantasy relationship taking drugs, gorging then purging food, gambling, or some other addictive activity. I am searching for hope. Insight. Can these painful chains be broken? I don't want to be merely the sum total of my earthly experiences. If that is the case, I am outta here. I have to know if there is hope of creating my own life. I don't want to involuntarily or subconsciously respond to my life. I want to break the chain and transcend our archaic socialization.

I watch my little nephews, and they learn by imitating. If we have unhealthy models, how do we learn? And if our learning process started as infants before we had language, can we go back and relearn? Can we identify those warped perceptions which are powerfully present yet latent in our unconscious minds? And how do we bring forth the knowledge in our minds? An emulsifier? After it emerges, if it is warped, how do we reprogram our beliefs for a better life?

I believe thought precedes action. I want to intellectually understand my patterns. Then I can begin to change my behaviors and theoretically change my life. I'll give this my best shot. Because this life is fucked. I feel like I have literally been so fucked that I see the world as fucked. And now I'm taking the enormous challenge of altering my deep-seated views of a fucked world.

My concept of life being worth living is much like my concept of communism. Sounds great on paper, but the practical aspects of it are not beautiful. The theory is great, but people mess up the beauty of the concept. That's how I feel about life being worth living. Theoretically it sounds great, but people mess it up. Based on historical events and based on experience communism does not work. And based on my personal history and based on my experience life does not work.

I am rereading a book by John Bradshaw. I read it before to help me understand my parents' alcoholism and my co-dependence. Now it is like a new book. This morning I read, "Spirituality is the essence of the human existence. We are not material beings on a spiritual journey; we are spiritual beings who need an earthly journey to become fully spiritual."

April, a spiritual entity on an earthly journey, a journey to become fully spiritual. I want to shed the layers of environmental dysfunction I have carried from my childhood. I want my spirit to be free. I want to be free.

Carol

THREE MONTHS AFTER THE CHILDREN talked, I quit my job. I finished out the quarter, but then I had to quit. I can't teach people how to deal with emotional pain when I have so much myself. I'm still seeing a few private clients, but gradually I will help them make the transition to a new therapist. One of the hardest things for me has been my feeling that I am abandoning my clients because abandonment is such a central issue for most people. Leaving a job I had loved is a huge loss too; but I simply could not continue to spread myself so thin nor could I continue to be the big "expert" in psychology. Sometimes I feel like I don't know one thing about the nature of human behavior.

At least I have time to see April. I have told her most of the grandchildren's revelations.

After a week Lorraine took her children home, and Jake and Sara brought theirs to Coronado. It was the same thing over again except this time there was less emphasis on Hank and more on Lorraine's neighbors, the apostle's daughter and son-in-law. Five-year-old Cynthia named the teenage boys who were involved Mustardface and Tinklemouth. Later she picked these two boys out of the high school yearbook, and sure enough they were friends of their babysitter. The police apparently were not impressed.

Claire, Jake's three-year-old, kept saying that if Cynthia or her cousin Isabel touched her then they were really bad even if someone made them. At three she was obsessed with guilt. Claire said the apostle's daughter was "pretty nice. Once she put me in the sink to wash the blood off. The warm water felt real good, and she didn't hurt me."

Cynthia asked, "If Uncle Hank's bad, how do you know if you'll marry someone wicked?" She maintained she loved Hank and "He wasn't like the others." She wondered if she was bad to still love him. Cynthia wanted to know too if she and Isabel would have babies right away.

Cynthia said the apostle's daughter told them, "I'll run over your mommy and daddy with my truck if you tell," and "When I drive carpool, I'll drop Claire in the road going to preschool, and she'll get lost or run over." Cynthia and Claire watched as the apostle's son-in-law strangled a baby kitten. They made the children help bury it. "We can do this to Claire," they told Cynthia. "We'll bury her right here by the kitty if you ever tell."

The touching parties followed a set pattern: first they would show pornographic videos of children, explaining to their audience that "all children learn
these things." Then they would play "touching games." "First one with their clothes
off gets an extra treat." Everyone would "touch," as though they were performing
at a recital. This part would be filmed and then played back. Then everyone would
dress, and they would have refreshments. The whole "party" took less than an hour.
Usually about seven children, a couple of teenagers, and three or four adults were
there. Sometimes there were costumes and props, and sometimes the children were
given injections, "especially if it was going to hurt." We gathered this meant if
partial penetration was attempted. Professionals refer to this kind of group adult/
child sex as a "sex ring." The production of pornography is usually a major purpose.

Cynthia and Claire described a show the adults put on for the children. It
sounded like a strip show. Hank would have all his clothes off except the top of
his garments. Cynthia said he "looked sort of dumb trying to dance around 'cause
he wasn't a very good dancer." They described how Geraldine held them while
the boys "put something tickly up there." They just thought it was funny." Claire
described how they would tape treats on the baby's penis, so the kids would like to
suck them off. Claire said, "I thought that was sort of funny and sort of sad. The
boys made our bottoms bleed. I don't want to talk about it anymore."

Cynthia made up several variations of a same story, where the bad people are
locked in a castle and somebody good comes and "melts them down," or everybody
is made suddenly good and they all make popcorn and are happy together. Cynthia
drew a picture of different colored hearts: "My heart and the bad ones. The sun's
over them for a test to see if they can feel the sun. There are flowers under my heart
because I can see the flowers and they can't. Tinklemouth and Mustardface have
black hearts, and Hank has a blue heart. The black heart is crueler. My heart is
pink. They're not going to pass the test, but I am. The bad ones have hearts so bad
'cause they had bad mommies and daddies."

She drew pictures of Hank running away and bullets coming at him from
all directions. There was another picture of a snake biting the neighbor: "The
rattlesnake has him in his mouth; now he's going to jail with all the naughty people." Cynthia called Hank "poo-poo brain, pervert, non-Mormon and liar." She
said Hank told them Aunt Lorraine wanted them to have the lessons, but their
mommy and daddy would hate them if they knew. Cynthia wrote when I asked
about her feelings: "I'm mad the people touched us. I want to ask Heavenly Father
why did they choose to do bad things. I want to ask him why Aunt Lorraine married Uncle Hank. Why was Uncle Hank up on the stand in church?"

I wrote down what they said and have used their words.

One of the saddest things for me is that I don't see how my children, Jake
and Lorraine, can ever be close again. Sara keeps saying, "Where was Lorraine?"
Lorraine will ask herself that same question every day for the rest of her life I suppose. When I ask the children, "Where was Mommy?" I get answers like "grocery
shopping" or "to lunch" or "teaching her young women's Beehive class" or "doing

dishes when Daddy gave us our baths." Where was Lorraine? How does denial work? For that matter where was Sara? Jake? Norton? And where was I? Why didn't I know something? I have a graduate degree in psychology and still I saw no symptoms. How could we all have been such idiots?

Anyone hearing this story would ask how the mothers could have missed physical symptoms with the children later talking about "blood" and so on. The literature on child sexual abuse helps explain. In less than five percent of substantiated cases of reported abuse does medical evidence survive. Perpetrators generally seduce gradually and gently over time. Doctors say the anus can be stretched gradually and leave no medical evidence. In the case of our children, there was never complete vaginal penetration, only partial and mostly with objects. Claire had a number of urinary tract infections, but the pediatrician told Sara not to be concerned. They are not uncommon in small girls. The main reason for no suspicion, however, remains the total denial system all of us had. How could we suspect what never entered our heads as the remotest of possibilities?

Norton says it's mainly the world we live in. To be looking for sexual abuse ten, twenty years ago would be like expecting a nineteenth century person to be looking for cars, he says. It didn't exist. Certainly not among people like us. Our family and church values reinforced this blindness. In our family you held the marriage together at all costs. In the church not only do you support the family, but the father presides. Neighbors in good church standing are worthy people per se, people to be trusted, to share with you the roles of child-rearing. Such attitudes make for secure and safe childhoods when the rules are obeyed. It's just that nobody talks about the other side of the coin: the side that can be "bad." No neighborhood could be a better set-up for a child abuser than one where everyone is and has to be perfect, and no one who attends church diligently has admissible problems. I can't blame the church. I totally bought into the perfectionism and denial. I do blame church leaders now if they don't deal with problems when they know about them. The bishop told Lorraine she should believe Hank because he held the priesthood. Just as the priest had told April.

Two images flash through my mind when I ask myself why I didn't know. Leah was two, and I was tending, preparing to give her a bath before bed. When I carried her to the bathtub, she kicked and raged hysterically in intense fear. I finally just sponged her off. I thought she must have had her head under water somehow and been terrified of the water. When I told Lorraine about it, she didn't know what I was talking about and said Leah had never done that. All I can assume is that Leah thought I would do what baby tenders do.

Lorraine remembered later, after the children had told, that Leah had gone through a time when she screamed and screamed when Lorraine tried to clean her after a dirty diaper. Lorraine thought she might have an infection and took her to her pediatrician. Leah made such a fuss that the doctor didn't examine her and told Lorraine to stop using soap in her bath. Apparently doctors also have denial systems.

My other image is of Cynthia, Jake's daughter, at age five. We were sitting by the fire at Jake's house, and Cynthia came running out naked from her bath. She wanted to be by the warmth of the fire for a moment. Then she did a momentary wiggly bump-and-grind-like dance. I thought, "Where did she learn that?" She ran back to get her pajamas on, the conversation switched and the sight of her doing that dance totally left my mind. I never mentioned it to Jake or Sara. It only flashed back after the children talked about the abuse. Now I can see her in front of me. How do our minds do such things? Block out what they cannot accept?

April repressed her abuse for more than fifteen years. How does this thing which therapists refer to as a "time bomb set for the future" work? No book, no psychiatrist can explain how our minds act for our survival, how they split, repress or dissociate. The process is both wonderful and terrible. April and many, many others like her know how terrible.

April

I HAVE BEEN THINKING ABOUT human aggression. I am questioning whether it is a predominately male issue, and if so, why? I learned in psychology that men commit crimes of violence far more frequently than do women. Even to the point of self-destruction. When men commit suicide, they typically "blow their heads off," "hang themselves," "slit their wrists," and so forth. Women typically take sleeping pills or asphyxiate themselves.

Why is this? Why are men so much more aggressive? Is it biological? Or has our socialization programmed males to respond in this fashion? Or are men less evolved than women and rely on more traditional animalistic ways of coping? I would like to believe this is a socialization problem; then it can be changed.

The Courage to Heal says that most perpetrators are men; and nearly all male perpetrators were abused as children. The research indicates that men who are perpetrators and who were not abused as children are a rarity. They don't even receive a full percentage point.

As a general rule then, a man who sexually abuses a child was himself abused.

Typically, females sexually abused as children do not become adults who abuse. Heterosexual males account for ninety percent of abuse. The remaining ten percent is divided between women and gay men.

What do abused little girls do? They turn against themselves. They develop eating disorders, become suicidal, cling to various addictions such as drugs, alcohol, sex, work, exercise, over-achieving, and so forth. Males tend to act out, and females act in. Why? Socialization? I'm betting on it. But maybe it's just that men have their genitals hanging out, so they act out, and women's genitals go in—so they take their pain inside.

November 18, 1989

Karen called me at the office. She asked me how I was doing, and I replied, "Fine, except that I want to cut off all the penises in the world and burn them." She laughed. I did say it with lightness in my voice.

My sense of humor has sustained me in my despair.

At times I have laughed instead of cried. I have laughed at completely inappropriate times. For example, I laughed at Tom's viewing. His pregnant bride, said, "Tom would just die if he knew I had an open casket for him." I laughed. She didn't realize what she was saying. Others did not laugh, but I did. Sometimes laughter and tears are so very close. Sometimes my feelings get all mixed up. Sometimes I don't know what I feel.

I hope someday I will be real. I want to cry when I am sad and laugh when I am happy. I don't want to laugh because I feel so stupid and confused. If I have to guess at an emotion, laughter is usually a good bet. One day I want to laugh when something is funny or feels good, not to hide my pain.

Later:

I just returned from my parents' anniversary dinner. Today is their forty-seventh wedding anniversary.

I had never heard of the restaurant where we were to meet. It's on State Street, where the teenagers cruise up and down and the prostitutes hang out. It was their anniversary. I assumed the restaurant would be nice.

I walked in and almost walked right back out. My eyes were burning as I looked through the smoke for my family. Could I have the wrong location? Then my three-year-old nephew came running up to me. I couldn't believe anyone would bring a child here, I couldn't believe that my family was at this gross place, and I couldn't believe that I was here. At best the place is a low-class truck stop. I bet the motorcycle cops and my family were the only ones in the place who had bathed that day.

I can't believe that my mother consented to coming here. My dad said the food was excellent. "Okay, that's the ticket. I'm okay with that."

I cut into my rubberized turkey with instant mashed potatoes sopping with instant gravy while my dad was consuming his Salisbury steak. I had to wonder if my father's taste buds had been destroyed by the alcohol. I imagined my parents landing in this greasy twenty-four-hour coffee shop, having a piece of dry bread and coffee to sober up before they came to their beautiful home. I thought of the nights my parents would drive away after we had gone to bed. They said they went to the bank. Now I wonder how many times they landed in a place like this. I looked up at my mother, and she smiled. A resigned smile of "oh well." I pictured a little girl and a preteen and a teenager watching her parents driving away. Hatred seeped up my throat like bile as I thought of them leaving me. "They were sleeping, so we left for the bank after the kids had gone to bed," my mother would always say. I did sleep, but I woke up frequently, waiting for them to stumble home. They were always so tired in the morning from all of their "hard work." I resented the bank, and I resented them for leaving me.

So here I was in an all-night coffee shop with pumpkin-colored wallpaper, paper napkins, linoleum tables, a dirty floor, and scratches all over the plastic glasses.

I am sad realizing how strangely appropriate that place was for my family. With so much noise and confusion, we couldn't talk. We had to gag down imitation nourishment.

And my beautiful, intelligent, well-educated mother. My mother who professed her love of literature and art. She was celebrating her anniversary here. Had she been that desensitized? Or was she just a fraud with all her talk of aesthetics and culture? Or had her life just broken her down to the point that this was where she was?

As I drove home, I wondered if my core was as scuzzy as that coffee shop. I wondered if my Mercedes was just a sugar coating. I turned on my stereo to Mozart.

Now I'm home. Am I a fraud? I didn't decorate this beautiful apartment as a smoke screen to others. This apartment is me. I only let a few people in here because it exposes so much about myself.

My mother adores this place. But my father adamantly refuses to set foot in here. He refuses to write down my phone number. Frequently he is downstairs to visit Gramps. I have asked him to walk up the stairs to see my apartment. He refuses.

I am taking comfort now that his presence has never polluted this ambiance. I feel peaceful and safe here. I have a place of my own.

November 19, 1989

So sad. I am so sad for the little girl once I was, the one who was not wanted and couldn't make anyone want her. They only wanted her to relieve themselves.

I couldn't make them love her or hear her. Her cries fell on deaf ears, muted by pain.

I want to hold the little girl, once I was: my desk sits under your picture. The phone rings. Rarely does the receiver leave my shoulder. A place for you to rest your head when you are tired. Now I hear echoes of risk management, self-insured retentions and fiduciary capacities. I pause and smile at your photograph; the sun warms my back, laughing, as you tumble and surf to the shore. With sand in your suit you run to prepare for another tumble with the beach. Then you run for the water where I am waiting, but not there. I am letting you discover and grow on your own. I am here—but there, always there, when you need me. For now I place the plastic to my ear and say, "Good Morning!" much like you say it. My heart leaps at the phrase and the part of you that has become a part of me. And while you are growing and discovering—remember even though you may not see me, I am here.

November 21, 1989

I saw "The Tomb of the Unknown Soldier" in the summer of 1983. It was a hot, August day. Soldiers, boys about my age, were guarding the tomb.

Anyone from any war could be buried there, a son or daughter or husband or lover. It could be anyone.

I gazed at my face in the mirror this morning. I'm not sure why I thought of "The Tomb of the Unknown Soldier." Maybe it makes me think of myself. My body is the tomb of my soul, and I could be anybody. Something inside of me is "Missing in Action." I could be anybody. Sexual abuse has no limits. I could be your friend or your wife or husband or lover. I could be the one smiling at you each day at your office or the downcast one in the file room. I could be driving a Porsche or sleeping in the streets. I could know that I was abused or I could not know. I could be anyone.

When I was student teaching, I taught a unit based on Arthur Miller's *The Crucible*, a play about the Salem witch trials. I related the Salem events to Nazi Germany. Social fear pushes people to betray their values. I told my students about an SS Officer who was ordered to execute hundreds of naked women and children. The officer who initiated the order carefully watched the subordinate officer to see if he could handle it. The subordinate followed the orders exactly. Later at the Nuremberg trials, many officers like this man would claim, "I was following orders."

When I lived in Jerusalem, I spent an afternoon at the Jewish memorial for those slaughtered in Nazi Germany. I spent three hours walking through the building. The atrocity, the horror and the human capacity to inflict pain is beyond comprehension. The human capacity for suffering is limitless too.

When I went over my unit plan about the Salem witch trials, Nazi Germany and the Milgram experiments with my professor, he told me he was a reporter at the Nuremberg trials. He believes we have evidence everywhere of how unable humans are to take responsibility for their own actions.

I don't understand how these evil acts can be committed in the name of following orders. I also don't understand how individuals can commit evil acts because they fear being socially unacceptable. Peer pressure increased the sadism of my abusers.

For all the intellectual capacities of the human brain, are we no more intelligent than sheep? Or maybe less: I don't know of too many case studies of sheep recreationally slaughtering one another.

November 22, 1989

I have been thinking about Nazi Germany. In the movie *Sophie's Choice*, Sophie was working in the home of the SS officer running the concentration camp. The officer's home was a short distance from the camp, and his home looked like any other. They had flowers in the garden. The children played just as "normal" children do. The mother ran the household and always had nutritious meals on the kitchen table. Daddy came home from work, kissed his wife and embraced his children.

Only Daddy was running a concentration camp. He was responsible for exterminating millions of lives. What did this family think was happening? Didn't they have any indications of what was going on right by their home? Didn't they wonder what happened to the servants who left their home? They had prisoners right in their home, human beings living like animals in their basement. What did the mother of this family think? Or did she just not think at all?

He comes home, "How was work dear?" "Daddy's home, give him a kiss, and here's your dinner, honey. Sit down and relax. I hope your day went well." ("Sweetheart, you smell like decomposed bodies and burnt human flesh, take a shower honey, and freshen up a bit before dinner.")

November 24, 1989

What am I fighting? Who is the enemy? I'm fighting for myself. But I don't know who I am. How do you build a life—except on how you want it to be?

"... a wise man, which built his house upon a rock: And it fell not ... a foolish man, which built his house upon the sand ... and the rain descended, and the floods came, and the winds blew, and beat upon that house; and it fell: and great was the fall of it."

My house was built on quicksand.

November 25, 1989

Amid the thorns I saw a bud emerge—tightly protecting itself, not ready to open and to bloom, nurturing the potential beauty that could overcome the thorns. Caught in an unexpected frost, the bud died. And the thorns, they survived the frost.

Why did Karen make me promise not to kill myself? I feel like I've gone to pieces and "all the king's soldiers and all the king's men won't be able to put Humpty Dumpty back together again."

November 26, 1989

I wonder what I was like as a baby. Do I have any good memories? I shudder at "I remember."

Rock-A-Bye baby on the treetop ... and down will come baby, cradle and all."

Did my mother ever sing this song to me? Such pretty, soothing music and such horrible words.

November 27, 1989

I woke in a cold sweat. In my dream a madman kept stabbing me. I watched the blood spurt from my body with every penetration of his knife. His knife sliced me to shreds, breaking my inside heart. My blood was lubrication for a moment—easing my torment—giving him courage to advance and rip my soul in pieces which kept falling in the toilet. He penetrated, raping me of all feeling.

I am little and see the blood in the toilet. My mommy says that I am too young to men straight. But men do put things up me and cause me to bleed. Sometimes pieces of my hole fall out in the toilet. Mommy says I don't men straight. I just bleed after they put things up my hole.

CONFRONTATION

I will do such things—What they are yet I know not,
But they shall be the terrors of the earth. You think I'll weep:
No, I shall not weep. I have full cause of weeping, but this heart
Shall break into a hundred thousand flaws Or ere I'll weep.

—William Shakespeare from *King Lear*

April

MY BROTHER BYRON'S CAR IS in the shop. This morning I give him a ride to work. We have been in a flurry of business activity and have not talked in weeks. This morning I promised myself that I would talk with my big brother.

After I got back from Hawaii, we had gone on a business trip together. We had a long drive, so we had some time to talk. Byron had told me what a hard time he was having dealing with his shame. When he was four years old, my cousin took Byron into a field and stripped him. Byron said that a group of teenage girls stood there and laughed at him. How shaming that was. He realized he would be shame based for the rest of his life. I had asked Byron if he ever remembered me being sexually abused. He said that he did not.

This morning I reminded him of this conversation. Then I said, "I don't know if you consciously remember this, but I was sexually abused as a child, and you were there."

I was getting off the freeway, and I didn't crash. Byron said, "I need to pick some things up at the store. Could you swing by Price Savers?" I pulled into the parking lot. It wasn't open yet. Then Byron asked me if we could pick up his mail at the post office. It was on the way to work, so I agreed. Byron went into the post office and didn't come out for over forty minutes. I watched quite a few people go in and out before he emerged. Byron walked out carrying his mail. He didn't offer any excuses. I continued to drive to the bank.

When we pulled into the bank parking lot, Byron said, "You know, I remember when you asked me that this spring. I also remember some very inappropriate events that happened. But I didn't want to bring them up because you didn't remember."

"Byron, I remember."

I parked the car in silence. I didn't know what to say, and his face was ashen white. There was part of me that wished I had never said anything to him. And another part of me wanted him to feel my pain; or at least feel some pain.

Finally, Byron opened the door and said, "Let's go to work."

94

November 29, 1989

I haven't slept at all tonight. I am on red alert. I am upset because I know Byron is upset. His face was white. He married a woman who was sexually abused as a child. What if she found out that Byron was involved in my abuse? She would probably kill him. Deborah has a horrible temper. Byron and I have both told her that she is a "rage-aholic."

Maybe I shouldn't have said anything. I am troubled that I had to tell him. Secretly I wanted him to feel bad. I feel bad for being so cruel. I can't imagine his pain.

It's almost five. I think I'll get my polypropylene underwear on and go for a run. It is a dark morning. A dark mourning.

November 30, 1989

Today is Thanksgiving. I can't think of a worse "holiday" than sitting around a table with my family and gorging myself. It fits that I'll sit around stuffing my face just like I've stuffed my emotions all my life.

The only reason that I'm going up to my mother's is to see my nephews.

December 1, 1989

I am not going to send my dad a birthday card. I guess I'll give him a call. And say what? I hope I get his answering machine—maybe they'll be drunk. I can't believe that I just wrote that.

Later:

Laurel came to Salt Lake to Christmas shop. At a gift shop Laurel walked to a corner shelf in the back of the store. She found this lovely paper doll. The doll was a curly-headed blond girl cut out of cardboard. She had about ten different little paper outfits. Laurel was trying a pink ballerina outfit on the doll.

I exclaimed, "Oh, she's beautiful! I love paper dolls." Laurel looked up with such a startled expression. I was wondering if I had spoken a different language. She said, "I didn't know you liked dolls, especially paper dolls." I didn't know what to say.

There's a phrase, "it's on the tip of my tongue," which describes this feeling. You know that you know, but you can't remember what you know. I hadn't known that I loved paper dolls. I was on the verge of a memory, but nothing ever came. Finally, I asked Laurel, "What do you mean?"

"Paper dolls seem too flimsy for you. You have this thing about buying quality products." She cast a quick look at what I was wearing. I had on very expensive clothes. I was wearing a cream silk blouse with black leather pants. Expensive things last longer. Why such an affinity for a doll made of paper? I laughed with her.

Now I'm sitting by the fireplace. Why that paper doll? What have I forgotten? It didn't give me an awful feeling, but something's stuffed away. The fire just snapped. A paper doll could burn so easily. I still want to go back and buy the doll.

December 3, 1989

Right now, I am struggling with money. What good is it? Carol has a lot of stuff, and it didn't buy her immunity from heartache. Stuff is just a layer to cover the shame, or money can be used as a weapon. Why does our society value it so much? Just because it's on the outside and easy to see?

When I was in high school, my English teacher told us about the value system of the Hindus. He said the individuals most highly regarded in that society were the ones needing the least. My teacher laughed. "Imagine how low we'd be on their value scale with our big houses and cars! In India the highest individuals are those carrying the least on their backs. We'd collapse under our materialism." The comment has stayed with me. I don't know if it is true or not, but I know I have all this stuff and I know how I feel—maybe the Hindus have something with this one.

Money ... money ... money ... "Cheer up, April, here's forty bucks." I am six. I am crying. He tells me to quit crying or he'll give me something to cry about. He gives me forty dollars, and I can't stop crying. He takes me to the store, and we buy a bike. It's a boy's bike. I ride around and around and around. I want to ride away. Sometimes I cry as I ride around. Sometimes it hurts to sit on the seat. He tried to put his big thing up my hole, and it hurts to sit on my bicycle seat. It's a boy's bike. Maybe if I was a boy, it wouldn't hurt.

December 4, 1989

Sad. I don't want to think. I have a session with Karen today. I have to know if she has known about me all along. If she knew, why she didn't tell me? I feel stupid wondering if she has known this about me all this time. I have been seeing her for three years. She must have known, and why didn't she tell me?

Later:

I asked Karen if she knew. She said, "Every time I asked you about your childhood, you said that you didn't remember." Yes, she had asked me about my childhood, and I could remember very little. My few memories were totally unrelated. Maybe that's why I remembered them.

Karen said, "April, I felt certain there was some abuse." I laughed. "Remember when you first came, you said you were concerned about a friend with problems. So protective of your pain—your injuries."

"I had to trust you enough to tell you about my parents' alcoholism."

"The first big secret," she continued. "We spent over a year working on your co-dependency with them. You developed strength to let go of your parents' self-destructive lifestyle. You learned to get yourself out of the middle of that mess."

I remembered back to how good it felt to finally realize I couldn't control and wasn't responsible for my parents' alcoholism. "By then I trusted you enough to let you know the next secret," I said. "My binging and purging."

"Yes, and we began to explore your difficulty with intimacy. But the more we identified the need to help you with issues around emotional and physical intimacy, the more resistant you got. Remember? You started talking about taking time out from therapy. One of the most important rules of therapy, April, is never rip away a person's mask until you have helped her build a face to replace it with. I still remember vividly the day I said to you, 'April, I really think we have to spend time getting into your sexual history.' You started crying on the spot. You told me how scared you were. You didn't have to tell me. In that moment you looked exactly like a terrified little girl. Twenty-five years fell away, and I could see a five-year-old—alone, panic stricken, and ready to bolt. I told you we would go very, very slowly, and it would be okay."

I have two lives—my life before memories and my life after memories.

How could I have forgotten?

I am threatened by my own mind. My mind betrayed me by forgetting and now it is betraying me by remembering.

There is a quote: "Once a mind is stretched to a new idea it can never go back to where it was." What if the new idea is mental illness? Can I go back to normal? Whatever that is. Some of us have more damage than others; some of us are in more pain. My damage was severe. Maybe those of us with a lot of damage are forced to have many options on how to appear. Maybe I chose to be an imitator and an imposter. Like my parents, like my family—maybe we are more mentally ill than the people down by the shopping malls begging for money. At least they are not pretending to be happy.

I went to Trolley Square yesterday. The day was cold, but the sky was clear blue. I pulled into the parking lot, and a guy walked right up to me and said, "Could I please have some change so that I could get something to eat?" He looked like he could use a shower, some shampoo, a comb, and something to eat. I gave him a dollar. As I handed it to him, I looked into his brown eyes and said, "Take care." He is more honest than I.

December 5, 1989

I went to see a movie tonight with my mother. We saw *Dead Poets Society*. I can't think of anything but that movie. I cried. My mother's eyes were dry.

In one scene a teenage boy hears that his friend has died. He stumbles out of bed and walks into a winter morning. It is just before dawn, and the boy says, "God, it is so beautiful." Then he bends over and throws up.

I threw up the night Tom died.

I can't believe my mother did not shed a tear. Maybe she doesn't have any tears left.

December 6, 1989

Our sewer backed up last night. This morning I went downstairs and stepped in six inches of human waste. I called my insurance company, and they sent "Utah

Disaster Kleen-up." They are down there now with their pumps, vacuums, and machines. It stinks.

This is an old home, my mother's childhood home. I've made it beautiful. And the sewer backs up. Maybe it just got too full. All the shit for all these years. At least three generations of shit. No matter how much wallpaper, paint, and flowers, the sewer backed up.

It's too much for me to clean up. The professionals have to do it. I wouldn't want their job. I wouldn't want Karen's job either. She's a professional with a job of cleaning up years and years of excrement.

Excrement, money, shame, me, my dad, ownership, control, power, sugar coating, sewer backing up.

My dad. Is there any possible way to get through to him? Carol tells stories to her grandchildren. Could my dad get a story? Like this one:

A man once lived in a time of plenty when things were easily obtained and discarded. This man wanted more. He collected money and toys and jewelry and trinkets and more. He believed that the more he had the more he was.

The man had heard of van Gogh's *Portrait of Dr. Gachet* selling for $80 million. The man longed for a painting such as this, framed and protected by sophisticated laser security, hanging in his home.

Thirty years before the man was given an even more valuable work of art. The work was created by the greatest artist of all. It was life itself.

The man who always wanted more failed to see the beauty framed in the female body. Determined to make his mark, the man defecated upon the creator's art worth infinitely more than van Gogh's painting.

The original work of the creator was almost beyond recognition. But life has its own power. From the wreckage of the man, this woman escaped. Professionals began the arduous process of restoration. The layers of excrement were removed from the woman, and she became free.

The woman is not fully restored, and neither is the glory of God. But the process of recovery and healing has begun.

The man, well, the man still doesn't know he has it all.

And he has nothing. He yearns for trophies to call his own and he already has so much more. The man doesn't understand that beauty can never be owned.

The beauty he yearns for lies within the silent chambers of his heart. But his heart is layered with so much excess, he has never found the beauty. One day the man with so much desire to conquer and destroy will meet the One with the ultimate power to create. The Creator will destroy the destruction. With the touch of the Creator, the man will begin to rebuild his shattered soul.

The woman continues to discover her innermost beauty. She discovers the grace of God within her soul and the glory of God surrounding her. There is no place where she may go and not see God's face, not know that she is God's creation, God's self unfolding and God's own.

December 7, 1989

Today is the anniversary of the bombing of Pearl Harbor.

Gramps says that war is insanity. I agree. War represents the dysfunction of our society. It's about power and possession and slavery. War reminds me of sexual abuse. It is insanity. If we have the ability to arbitrarily blow up the world with our sophisticated nuclear weapons, why wouldn't we overpower, abuse and murder the soul of an innocent child?

Gramps has been on this planet for 90 years. He has seen more changes than any other generation throughout history. Or have we changed? We have more stuff, more technological changes, but has the world changed? No, I don't think so. The manner of our slaughtering one another has changed but not the nature of murder.

I wonder when the sewer of our society will back up?

The sewer of my mind has backed up, and I feel like I'm drowning in shit.

December 8, 1989

I have been bulimic as long as I can remember. It was my secret ritual. The secret power game I played with myself. I wanted to purge myself of what I swallowed. I wanted to throw up until there was nothing left. I vomited until I had the "dry heaves." Then a white foamy liquid came up.

It was like the white stuff they made me swallow.

I heaved until only the white stuff was exhumed from my gnashing stomach and the empty resources of my soul. I know I was trying to purge the damage of sexual violation. I tried for years and years and years to get it out. Bulimia was my way of control. Controlling what went in my body and what went out.

December 9, 1989

The Courage to Heal talks about "coping mechanisms." I do them all. Eating and purging is right at the top of my list. I also rationalize, forget, leave my body, disassociate, avoid intimacy, stay busy, minimize, and I'm sarcastic. I am a mess. How am I ever going to clean all this up? I don't know who I am.

I am a frightened little girl with all this grown-up stuff around me. I have a grown-up body, a grown up education, an adult job with adult responsibilities. I am big. I can swoop down and pick up my nephews without missing a beat. Only I am little, deep inside my adulthood. I am a little girl who wants to be swept up in someone's arms and held without being violated. Sexual contact seems to seep up with every human touch. I sexualize everything. Is it just me? Or does everyone sexualize everything?

I tried to watch TV today. I watched a cola commercial, and I saw close-ups of legs, breasts, and butts. Isn't there anything else to give us meaning or thrill us? Sex seems like the ultimate fraud. A cheap thrill for a dysfunctional society. Using our bodies and shutting off our hearts.

There are many emotions associated with sex: power, control and instant gratification. The same emotions I have when I'm bulimic. I don't know what love is, but I don't believe it has anything to do with sex.

I'm only doing this because I love you. Doesn't that feel good? The boys are going to love you when you get older. Spread your legs a little and let me make love to you. That's a good girl. I love you. This is what Mommy and Daddy do to have a baby. You're so special that's why I want to teach you how to love. It will only hurt for a second. Hold on honey. You're doing real good. Here just a little bit further. Sometimes I scream because it feels so good. Go ahead and scream and let Daddy know that it feels good ... oh baby ... you were so good. You'll always be Daddy's little girl. Don't tell Mommy or she will feel bad. Don't tell her that you know how to make love better than she does. Don't tell her that Daddy loves you more...

December 10, 1989

Gramps and I got our picture taken today for Christmas. I am uncomfortable in front of a camera lens. I always look a lot more relaxed and comfortable than I feel. I am surprised at how well the photographs turned out.

December 11, 1989

Karen pursued the subject of photos:

I found pictures of my Mommy and Daddy. They were nasty pictures and they were taken with my Daddy's Polaroid camera. My daddy took pictures of me too.

December 12, 1989

I can tell now when I'm going to have a memory. It is a strange sensation. I can push it away if I want, or if I really relax, the memory comes. Sometimes the trigger is a flash of something like posing for pictures this weekend.

I am doubting my vision of my father. Maybe I was wrong about my memories. Maybe one of my perpetrators called himself "Daddy." I've heard many women talk about their "Sugar Daddy" or their "Old Man."

No, my brother Byron told me he found Polaroid pictures. He called them "self-made porno." I also found some when I was a teenager. I have never repressed that memory. It made me sick. Later in college I took "Human Sexuality." I don't remember much about the class. I hardly ever went, only for the tests. But I got an A. I've always been good at taking tests. I remember from this class: "Anything is appropriate between two consenting adults." When I heard that line, I thought about my parents and the pictures I found. I made a mental note that I would never consent to self-made pornography. Thinking of those pictures still makes my stomach turn.

Maybe I am crazy. Maybe that experience of finding the pictures of my parents was so traumatic that I made up the other memory of my dad. I was abused by my brothers, the neighbor kids, older adults, but not my father. Then I found the Polaroids. Maybe I am just mixing traumatic events together.

My heart is racing. I must go for a run. I have to clear out my mind. I am in a panic.

December 13, 1989

It is snowing. I wish it wasn't cold. I dreamt that I woke up in a field of flowers, yellow, blue, and colors of the rainbow. But no rainbow for I was at the end. My hair, gold, with grass tickling the skin on my back. My eyes closed. On my lash a drop of rain. I felt God above me, a soft breath upon my ear—a breath I did not have. I was rigid. A body with no life. I dreamt but never awoke. Life betrayed me, gone from me. The lawn was the lace of my coffin. The rain God's tears saying goodbye and the flowers brought by mortal obligation on the holiday for remembering graves, for the dead. Memorial Day I think, but I can't remember.

December 14, 1989

I remember getting car sick. I was seven and in the back of the station wagon. We went up through the canyon because my cousin had a farewell in his ward. He was 19 years old, and he had been drafted into the army. He was going to Vietnam. He talked about the war. He might get killed. I didn't know where Vietnam was, but I wanted to go there. My second-grade class made cookies for the boys in Vietnam. We popped popcorn to pack around the cookies, so they wouldn't break in the box. That's all I knew about Vietnam. It's a place where you went to die, and kids sent you cookies packed in popcorn.

I got sick on the way home. I was in the back of the station wagon. The part near the door that swung open like a gate. I was back there with my cousin, Charles. He was in high school. He put the car blanket over his legs and pushed my head down in his lap. We were really quiet, and he made me suck his peanuts. My dad was driving, my mom was in front also. Tom and Byron were in the middle seat. Charles nudged Tom, so he would turn around and watch. They laughed. They asked my dad to turn on the radio. They wanted to hear the Beatles on KCPX. My dad turned it on KSL, the Tabernacle Choir. As we listened to Richard L. Evans and "The Spoken Word," I licked my cousin and my missionary bound brothers watched.

I got car sick, and I threw up. I had never been car sick before. My mom thought it was because we were in the winding canyon, and I was in the back. From then on, I got car sick. I always had to ride up front, sitting between my mom and dad.

December 16, 1989

We sponsored a ballet tonight. Mountain View Bank paid a few thousand dollars to Ballet West to sponsor a night of the ballet.

My entire family was there, my sister, my mom and dad, my brother and his wife, and me. During the intermission my sister-in-law said that one of my nephews accidentally knocked his front tooth loose on the bedpost. She had to rush him to the dentist because she was afraid that he would lose his tooth. My mother started in on the famous "April's loose front teeth story."

My mom, the dentist, and I all stood in the entry way of the house. He did not come in. I don't even remember him taking his coat off. He gently put his finger against my front teeth. They were my permanent teeth, and they were loose. He asked me what happened, and I didn't know. But I knew, and I was afraid he would be able to tell. I didn't want the dentist to know. I didn't have any bruises or marks. I didn't fall down or hit anything, and I knew it. I told him that I didn't fall down and that I didn't know how my teeth were knocked loose. The dentist wanted to see me the very next day. I couldn't eat solid foods for six months. I quietly carried my thermos full of soup and strawberry instant breakfast to the lunchroom every day. I never told, and soon I even forgot why my front teeth were jarred loose.

Twenty-three years later as I sat in my black silk dress at the performance of the ballet we sponsored, my mother told the infamous story of April's teeth. I gritted my teeth and felt streams of sweat pouring from under my arms. I wanted to scream. Here we were in a sold-out performance of *The Nutcracker,* and I wanted to stand up and scream! I didn't scream. But my heart was beating like a drum roll. With my jaw still locked, I turned and looked at my mother. She was saying, "We never did figure out what happened to April's teeth. It must have been a virus or something." My eyes did not flicker as I said, "I know exactly what happened to my teeth." No one said a word. I was waiting for them to ask me what happened to my teeth in the second grade. Not one person in my family asked. Everyone was silent, and no one broke the silence.

I was ready to tell them. No one asked. No one moved until the Utah Symphony started playing. The theater lights were dimmed, and the curtain went up. I sat in the theater for the entire second portion of *The Nutcracker*, and I don't remember any of it. I was enraged with my mother. To this day she gives an eloquent oration about the mystery of April's beautiful teeth. She feels so blessed that I didn't lose them.

December 17, 1989

I keep thinking about my mother. I am so sad. I cry when I think about her. What was life like for her? It must have been overwhelming. She must have known. She must have had some indication of what was happening with her children. Maybe that is why she had a nervous breakdown after I was born. Maybe she couldn't handle the thoughts of protecting her baby girl. She didn't name me for six weeks. She must have been barely able to survive.

Her generation was different than ours. Divorce was unthinkable, and women did not have the means to financially survive. So she stayed, and the longer she stayed the more broken she became. I wish I could do something for her. I wish I could make her life better. I wonder, if I had not been born, would her life have been better?

I wrote about my mother today. I cried the whole time. I decided to write a poem about her. It ends with the lines, "no longer able to enable the empty chime even for a time."

December 20, 1989

I feel as if I am crawling my way back to a sane reality. And crawl I will.

Later:

One of my memories does involve my daddy in the shower. I was little. Maybe three or four. I know now it was my daddy. Some people had an imaginary friend when they were little. I had an imaginary self born by a phantom father. Pretending and make believe were my forte. I escaped swirling down the shower drain with his semen into the sewer of shame. I pretended to be a princess, perfect and loved. His placebos sugarcoated my shame, leaving the phantom raging inside of me, rising like bile and undigested acid. I spit the secrets down the drain of despair.

December 21, 1989

It's almost Christmas. I don't feel very festive. I try not to think about anything. I hope that something will make this all go away. Maybe I really am crazy.

December 22, 1989

I went shopping for a present for Lilly today even though it will get to New York late. A special toy—*Sometimes I got toys from the man across the street. I used to call him the "Toy Box Man." He had a shoe box under his bed, and after we played nasty, he would give me a toy. I always got to pick which one I wanted. I remember one time he gave me two toys. He let me pick before we played nasty. I picked out a top, and then he put the point up me. I was used to that. I suggested it. After he put the top up me, I rolled over on the blanket, and he rubbed himself on my bottom. He didn't try to go in my assy hole like the others did. And he gave me another toy after his peanuts spit up on my back. He was nice. He gave me toys, and he didn't make me cry. I went back a lot. He had two little sisters. They were both older than me. Their brother was old. He wasn't a daddy, but he was old.*

Sometimes after I got my toy from the "Toy Box Man," I would play with his little sisters. One of them had a red cash register, and I would pretend to pay for my toy.

Even though I had already paid for it.

December 23, 1989

I believe in Heaven, not because I've been there. I believe in warmth and cold, darkness and light, winter and spring. I know opposites. I haven't been to Heaven, but I know of Hell.

December 24, 1989

I bought my nephews an aquarium for Christmas. I have a room in my house just for them, and that is where we are going to keep the fish. We went to the pet store, and I told them they each could pick out any freshwater fish they wanted. We walked away with two goldfish.

I bought a 20-gallon tank, and they wanted only two little goldfish. They clutched the plastic bags holding their fish. One named his fish "Peetree" and the other named his fish "Cards." When we got home, we placed the plastic bags in the tank for a while before we let the fish out.

The oldest one wanted to put his fish in the bathtub. I smiled and told him that the aquarium was the best place for it. He adamantly disagreed. He felt that his fish needed more freedom than that. He looked up at me and said, "How would you feel if you had the whole world to play in and then you could only swim around in circles?"

I could see his point. Children know the obvious. I thought of me, running in circles around the track. Hours and hours of circles.

Running in those circles is what got me out of my childhood prison. I don't remember this story, but everyone in my family does. My dad has never forgiven me for it. Evidently, he tried to put his arm around me while we stood on the grass by the awards stand at a track meet. I pushed my father away and hissed, "Don't you ever touch me again." Several people saw it. My dad was embarrassed. I don't remember.

My mother must have been very angry, upset. She must have confronted him with something. My dad still refers to this as the time he almost divorced my mother. He blames me. He wanted a divorce because of how I said it, my tone of voice. Venom. I spit out the words, "Don't you ever touch me again." He thinks I was an ungrateful, spoiled brat. I wasn't very grateful for what he gave me. He claims, "I gave April everything she ever wanted and then some."

And then some.

December 25, 1989

Karen says all this was too traumatic to deal with as a child. I didn't have the skills or tools to cope. Who does? Some adults still can't cope. They are the ones in institutions, dead or unavailable.

I saw one of Byron's close high school friends downtown. He is a street person now. He was a beautiful, quiet, sensitive teenage boy. He got mixed up with the wrong crowd. He was friends with both of my brothers. He grew up a few houses away from Hank. He was involved with the abuse. I guess he just couldn't handle the pain he was inflicting on others; he checked out. He burned his brains on drugs.

I wonder what has happened to the others? The other perpetrators, the other victims?

Tom is dead. I think somewhere deep in Tom's mind, my brother knew he couldn't handle himself with children. Four months after his wife got pregnant, he was diagnosed with cancer. Four months after that, he was dead. One month later, his wife gave birth. I think Tom was far more noble than Hank. Hank acted it out.

I am more courageous than any of them. I'm trying to heal, trying to break the chain. I'm trying to stay alive. I'm beginning to believe that life is worth living.

Later:

I went by my parents' house today. My whole family was up there for Christmas. I walked in, took a deep breath, and said to myself, "Welcome to the dysfunctional family reunion." Why did I take such a deep breath? It's not like I don't ever see my family. Every time I set foot in that bank; I am faced with one of my perpetrators.

I tried not to check out. I sat down and tried to observe the interactions. We are all intelligent, well-educated individuals, and we don't have anything real to say to one another. Our shallowness is a comfort zone. Things are too messy for us, and discussing anything meaningful might lead to some shameful family secret. We shuffle gift certificates around, gleefully smile, and tell each other "Merry Christmas." No one ever hugs. My family never touches each other.

I stared at my father. He never meets my eye, so I knew I was safe in staring at him for a minute. He looked so sad. When he is not ordering people around or smiling, his countenance is one of pain. He is 60-plus years old, and he looks like a forlorn little boy. He is. Despite the agonizing pain he has inflicted upon so many people, I feel sorry for him. He must be miserable, lonely and unbelievably sad. I cannot begin to conceive of his pain. I don't know his story, but I think he was sexually abused as a little boy. Since my cousins on his side of the family have abused me, it's a pretty safe bet that something was happening in my father's family.

I can't even comprehend the pain that he must feel. He has layers and layers of pain added to the unhealed wounds of his childhood. I'm surprised he can even walk.

When I went home, since it was Christmas, I decided to open my Bible and read a few chapters about Jesus. I turned to the section where Jesus was on the cross and He cried out, "Father, why hast thou forsaken me?"

I understand that cry.

December 27, 1989

I have a picture of myself when I was little. I am sitting on Santa's lap. I look very pensive. I have always been leery of people sneaking into people's houses when they are sleeping. Even though Santa brought me toys, I didn't trust him.

December 30, 1989

A memory is a contraction, uncontrollable from my womb. Shaking pain reverberates. Labor, giving birth to the soul inside. I am blinded by blood shed from wars handed down by murdered souls for generations. I have scars that won't heal until dissected and disinfected of contamination. It is painful labor and blood, giving birth to myself.

December 31, 1989

It's New Year's Eve. Who cares? I'm in a time warp anyway.

January 1, 1990

The attic in Gramps' and my house is jammed with stuff. I can't open the door. I am going to try to work on this mess.

January 2, 1990

I am going through the attic, and I can't believe the useless crap that has accumulated. Miniature soap from motels, burnt out Christmas lights, tattered pillows, scraps of paper, expired gift certificates. This is going to take me forever.

Since I am the youngest in my family, I believe that I have been storing up all the family junk for years. Finally, I couldn't close the door anymore. And my memories started tumbling out.

Later:

I tended my nephews tonight. Byron picked them up and held the smallest one. I walked them out. In the entry way, he asked me about my plans for the house. I told him I was planning on restoring it. "What a horrendous task," he said as his son slept on his shoulder. I looked up at the ceiling, years of layered wallpaper and paint in the house where our mother grew up, our grandfather's house. Now the wallpaper is cracking, paint is peeling, the layers need to be stripped. "Yes, it is horrendous." I gazed at my brother. We've shared horrendous things. We've removed some layers. Healing has begun. I looked up again at the seemingly endless layers that will be peeled away to get to the authentic, antique home. The walls will still be crooked. Uneven walls can add to its charm. This will never be a perfect house, but it will be beautiful and so will we.

January 5, 1990

I'm still doing a great deal of staring. I am empty inside.

I started my period today. I have been thinking about blood, tears and salt water. They are all about the same. It seems like I learned something in biology about blood and salt water being very close on the evolutionary scale. Tears and salt water are close. Both tastes salty. So does blood.

Women are good at removing blood from underwear and sheets and themselves with cold water and "Shout." I like to scream and shout it out. I wonder if pink is feminine because it is red washed out? Some have said pink is an angry color with all the shouting and scrubbing. I guess so.

January 6, 1990

My sister and my father barge into my office all the time. No one in my family has learned how to knock. We don't have any concept of boundaries. I walked into my brother's office, and I noticed that he had all this stuff on his chairs. "Nobody can sit down," I said. He looked up, "Exactly." I smiled.

I thought of him as a boy. He built barricades around his bedroom. You had to crawl through the doorway to get in. Then he had rigged a bright spotlight in your face. He didn't want anyone sneaking up on him.

January 7, 1990

I am mad. I have been mad at all of this before, but I am really mad now. Sometimes I am so sad that I can barely move. Right now, I am mad.

I have been thinking about my mother the night of the ballet. I am furious! "We never did figure out what happened to her teeth. It must have been a virus or something." Ugh!

Where was my mother during all of this?

January 8, 1990

I try to concentrate on memories for a half an hour each day. It's hard. I can't separate out any particular time for it. I am just living it. Karen and I talk about the coping mechanisms of children and why suddenly I am remembering. I know all these theories, but I struggle believing they apply to me.

I keep spacing out. Maybe I'm trying to hold something back. Something big. But not a memory. It's something big though.

January 9, 1990

I am struggling. I don't want to do this memory stuff anymore. I have accepted what Karen says about deserving to know everything about my life. But now I am struggling with it.

I know I was sexually abused.

This healing process reminds me of the Middle Ages when they would put leeches on sick people—to draw out the "bad" blood. If the sick person didn't die from the illness, then they'd die from the bleeders.

Is there another way? In a hundred years will they look back on this "treatment" as archaic?

January 10, 1990

I feel haunted.

Who is She?

I keep asking myself that over and over again. She didn't look like anyone in the neighborhood. She resembled me. Only older. Who could She be? She terrifies me.

I can't stop crying. She was really hurt. I don't know who She is.

January 11, 1990

Who is She? I know She belongs in my special little journal for these memories. I guard it with my life. I hide it in my purse when I take it to Karen's. Karen reads it and makes a copy for my file.

I drove straight to work after my session today. I don't want anyone to accidentally see this journal. What if I was on the phone and one of my siblings needed my keys? I would be horrified if they impatiently rifled through my purse. To be extra careful I grabbed my keys then stuffed my purse under my seat.

A couple of hours later one of my secretaries burst into my office, "The front windshield of your car has been shattered. There is glass all over."

I raced outside.

Someone stole my purse. They stole my journal. All of those gross, explicit details. I am sick.

I feel raped of my rape.

January 12, 1990

I called Karen to tell her about my journal. I am devastated. I'm not writing anymore.

Karen says we have copies.

Some person is reading my journal.

I want to quit therapy.

January 18, 1990

I told Karen I was quitting therapy. She closed her eyes and rolled her head back on the couch.

I said, "Are you mad at me?"

She replied, "No, just frustrated."

I asked her why, and she said something about my potential. I wasn't listening.

She said, "I don't think this has anything to do with your journal. I think this has to do with me bringing up your overdue balance."

I was mad. It had everything to do with my journal.

It's true. My balance is high. Therapy is expensive.

I'm overloaded. And now I really want to quit therapy, so I can save some money to pay her off.

I told my sister-in-law, Deborah, that I quit therapy, and she said she was proud of me. She told me to use the money I save to go on a vacation. A little rest and relaxation would be good for me.

January 29, 1990

I had lunch with Carol Scott today. I asked her if I could heal without professional therapy.

She said, "I don't think so." But she was so startled she put Sweet and Low in her Diet Coke.

Carol told me the story that I have always known. Her nightmare. It relates to mine. I have to get back into therapy. She said that it's too huge to do on my own. I know she's right. I hate this. I hate my life. I am afraid.

Rage tingles down my arm as my fingers shift the car. I am alert to loss, angry at everything passing by. The glass shields the wind. I cannot feel anything real. I brake at the intersection and turn without signaling onto an unmarked street not on my map. Accelerating, I speed to a canyon fresh growing and green. Slowly I stop the vehicle, set foot on the ground, gaze back to my mobile casket and walk away.

February 1, 1990

I bought a new journal today. I'm going to work on it for half an hour a day. Then I'm going to pack it to Karen's in an armored truck.

Carol

THE "TELLING" WENT ON FOR months. All of the children were in weekly therapy. You would be having a sandwich with one of them and suddenly, "Mustardface said he liked my boobs better than Geraldine's. Are little boobs better?" and so on. We adults trained ourselves to respond. Sometimes you shrugged; sometimes you said, "Tell me about it"; sometimes you said, "Yuck!" and held the little ones tight and asked if they wanted to draw their feelings. You try to be calm and steady and tell them over and over how brave they are. It will be all right.

You never sleep. You wonder if you'll ever sleep again. If you do doze, you jerk awake and your jaw is locked so tight it aches. Every night is full of nightmares that repeat. A volcano is sending ash everywhere. I must hide all these people from the ash. We are in a jungle with nowhere to hide. The ash will cover and choke the world. A dam breaks, and I am in a farmhouse with the children. If I can hold the door shut, the flood won't come in. But through the window I can see the titanic wave coming at us, and I know the door will not hold. A little boy is disappearing in quicksand. I am on the edge, but there is nothing to hold out to him. Helplessly I watch him sink. Even after he disappears, his cries continue.

The other bad part of the nights: sex. Sometimes physiologically necessary, but just something I did, take it or leave it. The images would roar through my head the whole time. I could barely remember the intimacy and playfulness Norton and I once had.

Yet I was only their grandmother. I don't know how their parents coped. Sara wouldn't take sleeping pills, and she would sleep only a few hours for weeks at a time. How do our brain cells know when it's appropriate to go crazy? Those first months, Lorraine went crazy, except she couldn't. The needs of her children wouldn't allow her that luxury. That critical time seemed the hardest on Lorraine's baby. He sensed every vibration she was feeling. I remember driving with Lorraine and the baby in his car seat. He was screaming, screaming, screaming. Refusing to be distracted, comforted or nursed. For hours on end it seemed he screamed out loud Lorraine's silent scream.

In the fall Norton became critically depressed. Like most of the rest of us, he eventually started psychotherapy and Prozac. He would sit for hours in his office, staring from his 10th floor window at the flat, graveled tops of ancient downtown buildings.

All of his life Norton had felt pretty much in control of things. If he was doing a business deal, he worked with or confronted his associates, and results were tangible. He got the business, or he didn't. He persuaded people to his point of view, or he didn't. He was always effective. At the least he could have impact; he could be heard. Now he had to face a legal system in which all of us seemed to have no credibility. Nothing happened. When he suggested the police search homes for pornographic videos, they called the alleged perpetrators and made appointments, explaining why they were coming. We knew we had a good legal case, and yet we could do nothing, the police said because the witnesses were children.

Then there was the Mormon Church. Norton had his share of disagreements with church policies, but he was a fervent believer and totally loyal. He had given and given to the church—time, money, energy, thought, love. We had talked about what it might be like for him to be a mission president or some equivalent. Now no one in the church would listen to him. After Lorraine moved, Norton and I went to the new bishop of her old ward. We thought that since he had moved into the neighborhood recently, he needed information. We told him everything we knew: the names of all the children who had been mentioned. We told him we knew what a difficult position he was in. He couldn't go around implicating people without positive proof. We tried to be empathetic and supportive. The bishop listened respectfully. He said he didn't see how little children could manufacture the kinds of stories we told him. He said he believed us and would pray for us. I suggested ways he could warn his ward without implicating or hurting anyone, ways he could help the children who had been named and had never seen a therapist. His response was, "I don't see that there is anything I can do. It is really not within the parameters of my office. It's in the hands of the stake president." Then he tried to say, "God bless you." I thought Norton was going to slug him. Little innocent children were to go on being sacrificed, and it was not within his jurisdiction. He was not his brother's keeper. The apostle's son-in-law would continue to sit next to the bishop on the stand in church, looking down on all the faces of the children he molested.

Norton went to his friend, a young and very effective general authority. For 30 years he and his wife had been two of our best friends. When the children told, almost the first thing Lorraine, Jake and Sara did was take their children to him for blessings. Our friend had met with Hank then too and tried to help him. He had urged Jake and Lorraine to keep in touch with him. He is a brilliant, spiritual, unselfish person, totally devoted to his calling in the church and to his fellow human beings. When the names of the apostle's daughter and son-in-law came up, however, all contact with him about our particular situation ceased almost overnight. He assured us he could do nothing. After a couple of months, he invited us to dinner at his home, but he made a point beforehand of saying that this particular subject could not be discussed. His wife was not supposed to know anything about it. Norton was furious. Hurt and furious. He felt betrayed. True to

Norton's style, he told his friend the general authority exactly how he felt. We don't see them anymore.

Then there was the fracturing within the family. Lorraine and Jake were completely estranged. That was killing all of us, and again Norton felt helpless to do anything about it.

Finally, most importantly I thought, Norton had his deep religious issues. Unlike me he had always assumed if he tried to do what he should and if he trusted in God, he and his would be protected. For the first time in his life, he faced the simplistic quality of his faith. He had to come to grips with evil. For a long time he could not pray. He went to church and wept during the hymns. He watched the "falling away" of his children as they struggled with the church.

Near Christmastime I came home with packages in my arms, and Norton helped me put them around the tree. He didn't look at me when he said, "I took my pistol to the safety deposit box today. It's better. I don't want to cop out on you."

I wanted to die for him. I wanted him to die rather than have to face the abandonment he felt from God. I could do scarcely anything, not even listen, he talked so little. Walking in a room where he sat alone was like being enveloped in a fog of despair so thick I could scarcely breathe.

Now, looking back, I think it was from that time he started to rebuild. Started from the bottom of everything with full recognition life could never be the same for him. Finally he started to fight. For himself. And against them, the abusers. He fights with legal and social action.

I'm fighting with myself because I'm afraid Susy could have been abused by Hank. Yvonne too. Was it possible? Where had I been? When they were little?

I was in a pretty bad way along with Norton. I hated seeing people casually. The only connection I wanted was to rocks. Granite, cold, sheer, formidable and unyielding. Black twisted cutting lava, habitable to black crabs and bare bleeding feet. Smooth stream-rounded pebbles, wet and sensuous, their curving indifferent to human fingers rubbing back and forth, back and forth, in a moist cupped hand.

Rocks. Black for a sun-drenched lizard. In a dark cave, pungent and sweet with nature's reeking. Stub your bare toes on rough sandstone, bleed a little. Cup the black smooth stream pebbles and rub them back and forth, back and forth, until some continuity is shaped. Forget the humans. Connect to rocks and nothing else. Rocks are real.

But I couldn't linger in that place. I had to help my children and grandchildren. Ultimately, would they have to learn to forgive? Would the perpetrators crawl on their bellies begging for forgiveness?

April

February 9, 1990

I TALKED TO CAROL TODAY. Her mother died.

I sent her flowers and this note:

I hear the sadness in your voice and through the static on the line. I listen, for someone you love is gone. And I pray for you; limitations of our humanity I cannot comfort. I only listen. I pray you understand that I understand and care. I know in your sadness is a strength where you will be comforted.

February 10, 1990

I really believed that note. Only by experiencing our feelings will we be comforted. There is no strength in denial.

February 20, 1990

Before my journal was stolen last month, I was having strange feelings about the girl in my dream. "She" was stronger and older than I was, but looks eerily similar.

I don't know who She is, but She is very important to me. I can't stop crying.

I've tried to call Karen. I can't get through to her. Please, please call back!

Who was that girl?

I feel like I'm tumbling down a dark abyss. I feel helpless.

Did She have a name?

Later:

They put a loaded gun up Her. She watched them put the bullets in it. They told Her if She moved they'd shoot Her.

I have remembered the most hellish piece of my past. It is not for anyone to hear. I am sobbing. I will say only this:

She is me.

Still Later:

Karen called. I could barely talk. I told her I thought I was schizophrenic. I told Karen about Her.

Very calmly, Karen talked to me. I muffled my cries. This doesn't mean I'm crazy. It just tells her how bad it got. So bad I split away from myself to the point I was outside my body watching. She took the worst, not me.

(double you)
tears on my lips
burning skin soft
tears sting
damp from the (w)hole
tears for tears
more than salty excretions
bleeding my soul

February 24, 1990

Karen had a special session for me today. I am desperate.

Karen helped me understand that I don't have a multiple personality disorder.

She talked about being a little girl. She had a grandmother she adored. Karen felt so much joy around her grandma that she acted a little differently with her. Karen wasn't split or anything. It was just that her grandma brought out wonderful parts of her personality. Karen said that we all do that to a certain extent. My extent was severe. The parts of my personality I labeled "Her" were trauma-induced.

Karen asked me to write down all of the characteristics I've attributed to Her: She is pretty, thin, and sexy. She is calm. She is strong. She can handle more than I can. Nothing harms Her.

My very first dream? The one about my friend being raped? The one who came to save me? That was Her—me, but not me.

She was older than I. I used Her when I was little, about seven or eight. She was in her late teens. I don't know when I stopped using Her. Maybe when I started running.

Karen said it wouldn't be uncommon for me to have such a strong identification with different parts of myself that they feel like a split. But, it's not. It's all me. She said it wasn't a multiple personality disorder. I don't really understand the difference between dissociated splits and multiple personality disorder. I just want to be whole.

I wasn't alarmed. It rang true for me. It kind of sounds like disassociation on steroids.

February 25, 1990

"April come she will ... die she must."

I remember those words from a Simon and Garfunkel Album: *Sounds of Silence.*

114

I was always silent.

She came and She died. At least She died to my conscious life. If She had not come out, I would have died.

I remember hearing that song playing as Tom abused me. In a way I was envious that that April could die. I was also sad for Her. I am sad for me. I brought Her out to take the worst of the abuse. I couldn't let myself die.

Later:

She doesn't speak. She has the "Sounds of Silence." She has so much feeling and so much pain and no words. She was the sacrificial lamb.

As Jesus cried out on the cross "Why has thou forsaken me?" She cried out for me. And I forsook Her. I retreated to the farthest corners of my mind because I could not bear to witness the sacrifice of my beloved self.

February 26, 1990

She believed in a magical world. She believed that Her sacrifice would save others' souls. She was strong enough to be crucified. She never bled from every pore—only from her cleansing and birthing orifices.

She wished on the first star every night. She prayed to her Heavenly Father to protect Her. She knew it was His wish that "thy will be done."

She came out and faced the dark forces. She would not let the devil possess my body. She let them pee on Her and in Her. She let them F-U-C-K Her, after Satan told them to do it on the Ouija board. She let them rub against Her when they played "rise table rise." The devil was always there when She came out. She protected me.

She never flinched when they held the candles under Her hands, Her arms, and Her pee-pee hole. She never cried or spoke.

February 27, 1990

Karen says I can integrate Her fully into my personality. Some characteristics have been integrated already, or I wouldn't have remembered Her. I want to be whole. I want to love Her. I want to take care of Her like She took care of me. She is a phantom, a mortally wounded phantom drifting through the empty caverns of my mind.

February 28, 1990

I have always known about my troubled sleep. I do not sleep very peacefully.

I think that if I can understand Her and what She is to me and what part of me She is, I believe that healing will begin. Real healing, even restoration. But I don't believe I will understand until I understand Her. Understand myself.

Then I believe I will understand love. I haven't believed in love for a while. I hope that understanding Her will give me the key to myself. Which will lead me to love.

Myself once removed. Listening to a phonograph in a dreary basement, songs of the 60s, clothes all over the floor. An abused word called love. I wanted more. I was left with adult monsters raging inside: birth, death, restoration, alter egos, showers of tears to drown in—or to cleanse.

March 2, 1990

I ran into Lorraine Scott today at Crossroads Mall. I look awful. She looks great. She was holding her little boy. She placed a hand on his back. I was intent on her hands; my mind flashed to Tom's funeral and Lorraine's hands. Her hands are stronger now. The last time I saw her was at Susy's shower in July last summer. She looked great then. Last July I had not remembered. I didn't know. I was uncomfortable with Lorraine. I thought it was because I knew of her pain and I felt guilty and ashamed about it.

Over three years ago I ran into Lorraine at a bookstore. We both love to read. We were gazing in the self-help books. I was clamoring for knowledge about adult children of alcoholics. I was so self-conscious. I didn't notice what books she was buying.

But I knew. She looked as if her teeth had been kicked in and were eating away at her insides. I knew what she was going through. I had heard she was getting a divorce. Rumors flew that Hank was enamored with all the money, that he was living "high off the hog" with the Scotts' money. I had heard he was having affairs with women all over the country. I knew what Hank was doing. I knew he was molesting his daughter. I knew it because I know Hank. I imagined that Lorraine probably stumbled upon them in the bathroom or something. And Lorraine divorced him. Then Lorraine was left to pick up the pieces of the destruction, mess, and havoc that Hank had inflicted upon his little girl. I imagined all of this. No one told me, but I knew. Because I know Hank. And I knew what Hank did to me as a little girl.

Hank and Tom did a lot of things to Her. They played games with me, and when it got too scary, I sent Her out. They played with the Ouija board. They told me that the devil would possess my body if they didn't "cork" my "hole." They put all sorts of things up me to stop demons from getting in. The worst was the gun.

At least Tom stopped himself. Even if he didn't consciously know what he was doing, I believe he willed himself to die. Hank tried to be righteous, even a mission for the church. But the addiction is far too deep to take care of itself with a few prayers of willpower. The damage, pain and addiction lie deep within the very fiber of our souls. One needs help from trained professionals and from the spiritual entity giving us life to heal.

March 3, 1990

Finally, a break in the clouds. I love the feeling of being on the verge of spring. I love when the trees start to blossom.

The days are quite kind. The sunshine is melting the block ice which trickles and seeps ever so slowly. Like my memory thawing a numbness—removing the tourniquet I forgot—pain bursts to my frozen limbs. The days are my friend as I discard the weeds anchored in my mind's garden and plant tender seeds for love's future bloom. The days I cherish for giving me time to heal and grow.

March 5, 1990

Wow! I went to my first survivors' group tonight. I was so nervous. I was terrified I would know someone in the group. I don't trust anyone.

I found everyone in the group felt that way. It is held at the Intermountain Sexual Abuse Treatment Center. There are two therapists facilitating the group and six adults. All women. I'm relieved about that. I'm not ready to talk to a strange man about my deepest secrets and shames.

We set some ground rules, the most important: What is said in this room stays in this room. It is hard to tell them anything. I'll bet all of us have heard, "I'll kill you if you tell." And the shame. I especially don't want to tell them about Her. They'd all get up and run. We went around the room and introduced ourselves and told a little about our history and who abused us. One woman doesn't remember who abused her. She doesn't have any memories. She knows she has been abused though, and so does her psychiatrist. After listening to her for about five minutes, I knew she was abused.

She doesn't have one memory, but I know she was abused. She is a "typical" survivor. I don't know all of the clinical terminology, but I do know that we women are all connected. We all have a range of coping mechanisms and addictions. The most common coping mechanisms are dissociation or repression. The most common addictions in my group are sex or food.

I don't feel alone in my group. It is the first time in my life that I haven't felt threatened in a group situation.

March 10, 1990

I have season tickets to The Salt Lake Acting Company. I hadn't read anything about tonight's performance, *The Ghostman*, about a man whose father died and then his memories started.

I watched my process and my pain in front of me on the stage. About half way through the play I checked out, went into "mind freeze." I watched the whole play and didn't shed a tear. I think I was the only one.

Later:

I can't sleep. I'm sure it's the play. I'm starting to cry. I don't think I can stop.

March 11, 1990

I called Karen, and she agreed to meet with me today. I went into Karen's office and sat on the floor by her fireplace and cried. I couldn't talk. I told her about the play. She has seen it. She said it was painful to watch. I said, "Good, maybe you can understand my days." I wanted her to hurt. I wanted her to feel some of my pain. I don't know why.

I'm still crying. I have been lying on my bed. Sometimes I drift in and out of consciousness. My dreams always lead to the play and my abuse. I wake myself up crying.

I wish I'd never been born.

March 13, 1990

I have lost control of my bladder. I am "wetting my pants" all the time. I feel like a little kid. I can't make it to the bathroom.

I remember them peeing on me. And I know that I vowed to pee on my attacker if I ever got raped.

I'm peeing.

March 14, 1990

A woman in my group called me tonight. I was surprised to hear from her. She knows a woman from my old neighborhood, Andrea McCall. She asked if she could let Andrea read some of my writing.

I haven't heard about Andrea in years. I don't even know what happened to her. Their family moved away when I was in high school. She married young. She's five years older than I am. I always thought she was nice. I didn't think the rest of her family was as nice as Andrea. Her brother was the "Toy Box Man."

March 16, 1990

Andrea called. I don't even know her current last name. I guess she's been married a couple of times and has had a string of relationships. Typical. Typical of a survivor. I know she is a survivor. I know she is: it's the same feeling I had about Hank. I knew he was abusing his children, and he was. I know Andrea is a survivor.

We are getting together tomorrow. I asked her what she looks like, and she said, "I'll be wearing my hair in a braid. I've seen you a few times. I'll walk right up to you."

Later:

I am rattled. Just hearing Andrea's voice sent me back to being three years old. Until this week I hadn't thought about Andrea. I thought of her family, but I didn't think of Andrea—only her brother.

Andrea was a pretty girl. I remember she was sitting on the corner lawn playing with a gray cat. I came over to say "Hi." She looked up at me alarmed.

"Why did you cut your hair off?"

With the defiance only a three-year-old can muster, I said, "My name is Daniel. I am a boy now. So I cut my hair."

Andrea did not laugh at me. She let me sit by her and play with the little gray kitty. Andrea was in second grade, and while I was sitting by her, the other kids didn't make fun of me.

DANIEL ... DANIEL ... DANIEL. I wanted to be Daniel. Daniel had a peanuts, so he wouldn't get hurt. If I cut my hair, they'd think I had a peanuts. I wanted to make myself Daniel. I believed I was Daniel. I put peanuts up me to try and grow a peanuts. My brother told me that boys have holes just like girls. Then their peanuts grow. So I put peanuts up me to try and grow a peanuts.

My Sunday School teacher told me about *Daniel and the Lion's Den*. Daniel slept in a lion's den. He made it through the night without getting hurt. I wanted to be Daniel. I prayed every night that I would make it through the lion's den. I needed Daniel's strength and his faith. I was Daniel.

After Tom died Byron and I would go on long drives and listen to music. We frequently listened to Elton John's "Daniel." We listened to it over and over again. It's saying goodbye to a brother. I thought that the song made me so sad because of Tom. Now I know that I was grieving the loss of my Daniel. My protector. I was grieving the loss of Tom, but I was also grieving the hope of Daniel.

My protector in the dark den of lions. Daniel. I grieved unknowingly when my blood brother died, a loss of familiar family. I wanted Daniel back, protecting from the pain of Tom and lions of the night.

My mom said a part of her died when Tom did. I empathized, understanding more than I understood. I knew the grief of losing a part of me when my hope of becoming Daniel was laid to rest.

I'm waiting for Andrea. I wonder if I will recognize her. I wonder what she will be like. Will she be brave? Honest? Authentic? I hope so.

I wonder how we will start this conversation. "Hi, were you sexually abused in our neighborhood? How have you survived?"

Later:

It's midnight. Andrea just left my house. We talked at the restaurant for about three hours. Then I asked her if she'd like to see my house.

I think she was a little surprised because it is so feminine. She remembers me as a tomboy trying to be Daniel. I said to her, "Really, I believe I am basically a very sane person. But after hearing your voice yesterday, I remembered about Daniel." I told her about cutting my hair and wanting to be a boy.

Andrea said she was sexually abused in the neighborhood too. We talked about some of her memories. As we were talking, I remembered some things. I know she remembers some of it but I'm not sure all.

Andrea said that after she talked to me, she remembered seeing me in the oak bushes with my panties down. A group of kids were laughing at me. They started breaking off branches. I started to cry. Andrea stopped them.

I remembered. Her words took me back to the scene:

The branch snapped. They were breaking branches off the trees. My panties were down, and I started to cry. I knew the branches were going to be used to hurt me. To put up me. Or whip me. I cried louder.

She stopped them. They argued with her for a minute and then dropped the sticks. She told me I could put my panties back on. That was hard when I was crying. I put them on backwards. I usually didn't do anything right, not even put my panties on right.

I stayed by her side. I was afraid she would go away, and they would come back. We walked to her house. I was quiet but still crying. She told me when I stopped crying we could go into her room and play. I stopped crying. We went into her room and played with dolls. Paper dolls.

She took out her pretty pink scissors and cut me a whole chain of paper dolls. I thought she was magic. She made the kids stop. Then she cut out dolls from a regular piece of paper. She got me to stop crying too. Maybe she was magic.

I told my group about Her. Then I told them about "Daniel." Over half of us in the group have remembered splits so severe that we gave them names.

I don't understand it all, but I don't feel insane.

Carol

SIX MONTHS OR SO AFTER the children talked about Hank, Norton and I went to a movie, *The Color Purple*. The movie ended and I sat alone with Norton. There's a scene in the movie when Oprah Winfrey's character, Sophie, plows through a field of corn to confront Whoopie Goldberg's character, Celie. Sophie spits out something like, "You told Harpo to beat me." Celie withers and whispers something about earth being temporary and Heaven lasting always. For the first time I dared let Lorraine's pain flood through me. I thought of my admonition to save her temple marriage. I never thought I could hurt that bad. The theater was empty. I kicked and pounded the seats in front of me and cried and swore like a mad woman. I knew that Lorraine could not save her temple marriage. I was ashamed of my naïve advice. I knew then that eventually I would have to exorcise Hank from my system.

All of us had fantasies about driving over him, sending him to jail and so on. Norton imagined that if the divorce court granted Hank visitation with his children, Norton would walk into Hank's office, shoot a nine-millimeter bullet into his brains, call the police and then tell the story to the world. If it weren't for the rest of us, Norton said he'd be willing to pay the price.

My colleague told me of a place in Massachusetts where they do Gestalt therapy, psychodrama, yoga, guided imagery and so on. Having confidence in him, I decided to try it. A year after the abuse was reported, I went to a five-day retreat in the beautiful woods around Lexington.

On the third day about 50 people gathered in a large room, working in twos or threes on "old, bad stuff." We could ask a leader to work with us if we wished. I started almost a pretend sort of crying, but then what the leader said about breathing worked, and I was sobbing for real and moaning deep from my abdomen. Images of Lorraine, Sara, Jake, Claire, Leah, Cynthia, Isabel, Timothy, Susie and Yvonne, and the other little children in the neighborhood mixed all together. Someone said to scream, but when I tried I couldn't get sound into my vocal cords. Finally, I heard this scream-moan I was making. Like an animal. The leader handed me a "Hank" pillow. I saw Hank's hands. Filling the space. Smothering a child. Fingers always moving, eyes blank with a vacant, blind, inhuman stare. I saw his huge hands on Claire. I smashed and hit his face, but mostly I clawed. The pillow was Hank's face. I didn't want to kill him. I wanted to claw his eyes and face. I scratched the pillow almost to pieces—long, deep, bloody scratches down his putrid, white cheeks. I experienced a time-lapse—a trance. When I quit, exhausted, after what I thought was maybe 10 minutes, my leader said I'd been scratching the pillow for nearly an hour. I lay still on the rug for a while, while he stroked my hair and told me to take deep breaths. Then I went to the restroom and threw up, dry heaves over and over for a long time. It was the single most healing thing I've ever done. When I remember it now, I can feel the scratching in my fingertips. They tingle with the release of pure, clean hate.

Healing happens. The human spirit is unendingly resilient. All things being equal, I believe time is always on the side of healing.

In our family there are changes. Susy has a husband, a career and a baby, all of them life affirming. Jake and Sara have a new baby, new life. Norton is better, at least a little better. He listens to Mozart a lot. Lorraine is a more whole person than she has ever been, doing things she never dared before. Yvonne is working hard in her therapy. Susy is starting to deal with the abuse Hank inflicted upon her. She's in hell. She's too strong to stay there. Susy is paying now. I remember when she was little. She's watching her dog, Helga. She's wearing her Mexican blouse with blue embroidery. Her bare tummy shows above her shorts. Her long hair is all tangled. She will not leave Helga until she's ready to go. I am too impatient and leave her sitting in the bushes but Helga will protect her. She has a yellow bunny suit on for Halloween. Cutest child that ever lived. I thought no one could receive more love. In kindergarten, I sent her to another school because her teacher was so mean. How could anyone be mean to her? Where is she now?

No reparations can ever be paid her—by anyone. All we can do is help her break the silence.

The little children have done an amazing job of putting their demons to rest and getting on with growth.

Timothy has a shelf full of trophies from swimming and soccer. He won the state spelling bee. When the reporter for his elementary school newspaper asked him what he was most proud of, he said, "I'm most proud of what I've learned from losing. Even if I didn't get a trophy for it."

And yet. War veterans who've saved others' lives are awarded medals, and heaven knows they've earned them. Just being there in that horror without ever raising a gun merits a medal in my opinion. Almost all these heroes, at least from Vietnam, have Post-Traumatic Stress Syndrome. I've met women who should get medals too—mothers alone raising families, women battling in courts to save a child and the adult survivors of childhood abuse. Their diagnosis is also post-traumatic stress.

I don't think anyone—a psychiatrist, a criminologist, anyone—understands how violating a child's body can kill that child's soul. Abuse is everywhere in our country. The latest estimates are that one in five women and one in six men will be abused before age 18. With so many victims, why should it be such a big deal? "In some cultures," people say, "child abuse is the norm." How do these people presume to know what abuse does? How can they not recognize the price? In some cultures, murder is the norm.

Our bodies are who we are. Children, especially, cannot separate their bodies from their sense of self. I have known adults who had schizophrenic mothers or alcoholic fathers or abusive parents—and the paying goes on forever.

They say that child abuse is not about sex but power. Possession. Slavery. It has been about silence, but the world is full of hero-mothers and hero-women. Women are no longer silenced: April is talking.

So is Yvonne. Talking and dreaming. She could write a book of her dreams. A rival to Stephen King's. So could Susy. There was Yvonne's dream about the blender. Parts of people grinding up in the blender. She has told me another. She and Susy are under water in the ocean. There is a shark. The shark is circling coming closer and closer. It has a huge red penis. They cannot help each other. There is blood. Terror. Helplessness. I cannot convey her dream, but when she told it to me somehow I knew it, how it was. There is no conveying it.

April

I'M GAINING AN APPRECIATION FOR Her, and for Daniel. It is a lot calmer for me right now. I'm learning to accept the reality of what I needed to do to survive.

I am gaining respect for human survival. I go to my group, and I cannot believe what these women have endured.

After group I usually come home and put on some classical music and ponder what I have just experienced. I hear the most tragic stories, and I am inspired by the courage. I want to write about these courageous women, but I agreed that what is said in that room stays in that room.

I want to give them all an award for surviving and give them the world for their miraculous growth and healing. Occasionally I am so moved I cannot speak.

Other times I get mad at their comfort with their pain. Sometimes I want to scream, "If you're so miserable, then do something about it!" I want to hit them on their heads. Easier said than done, and no one knows more than I how hard it is to break out of our patterns.

I am almost done with my therapy workbook. Karen said that I'm the first client she's had who has completed the entire thing. I did it one half hour every day. I cry a lot.

I feel better. It is spring, and the tulips are in full bloom in my yard. I feed the birds every morning. Then the cat from next door comes over and watches the birds. Both of my dogs bark. It's a chain reaction.

On Saturday Gramps and I cleaned up the yard. I was on my hands and knees pulling up weeds while Gramps sat in his chair and watched. He works a lot, but today he wanted to drink his Diet Coke.

I had dirt all over my hands as I looked up at him. I felt the warm sun on my back, and I thought, "It doesn't get much better than this."

May 23, 1990

I am feeling better. I am not "Pollyanna" or anything, but I am feeling better.

But I don't feel good at work. I am like an imposter merely going through the motions. I enjoy the work, but my interactions with my family are trite and meaningless.

I cannot be me around them. I guess that is an obvious statement, but I haven't known who I am. I am gaining a better sense of myself, but I lose it around my family.

June 19, 1990

I am so sick. I can't even talk. I have laryngitis and a sore throat. I've been in bed all day.

I can't go to work.

It's weird having laryngitis in the summer.

June 23, 1990

I still don't have a voice. I'm starting to think this might have something to do with "not talking." I have a book that says laryngitis is "fear of talking, fear of expressing yourself."

Who am I afraid to talk to?

June 25, 1990

I still don't have my voice back. I was lying in bed this morning. Like a lightning bolt I thought: "You have got to tell your family. You are making yourself sick by not talking."

Karen's happy for my decision. She said, "You are finally to a place where you can have yourself. I think you're ready for a family workshop." Karen and another therapist will facilitate it.

I replied, "Whatever. I have got to tell. I'm not strong enough to carry this around anymore."

"You're strong enough to finally tell," was Karen's calm reply.

June 26, 1990

I have my voice back.

June 27, 1990

Today my dad was at the bank. I walked out of my office and said, "Dad, could I talk to you for a minute?" He replied, "Sure." He just stood there, so I walked into his office and sat down on the couch. He followed.

I said, "Dad, as you know, I've been in therapy for a long time. I've reached a stage in my therapy where I would like to share some information about me with my family. Because you are the head of this family, I'd like you to be there."

"No." He stood and started to walk out.

I said, "Dad, this isn't a meeting about your alcoholism. It's about me. Please. This is as important to me as *anything* in my life. If I were getting married or I died, wouldn't you attend my wedding or my funeral?"

He said, "Funerals are for the survivors."

"Exactly."

He had been shaking his head no the entire time I'd been talking. Then he said, "You know we support you. Talk to your mother. She'll go." Then he walked out of the office. He left the building.

I slowly got up and walked into my sister's office. Melinda looked up from her desk and said, "What was that all about?" I didn't realize that my dad had been yelling. He had slammed the door on his way out. I began the whole story again about being in therapy for a long time and reaching a place where I wanted to share some things with my family.

Without flinching Melinda said she would be there. She didn't even ask what it was about. She's coming.

I walked down the hall to Byron's office. Same story. Byron said his wife had been planning a party, and he'd have to talk to her. I emphasized that I only wanted him. Byron looked a little startled and said, "I'll still need to talk to her."

So it's set. Melinda and my mom for sure. Possibly Byron. And a definite "no" from my dad.

June 28, 1990

Byron talked to his wife. She wants Byron to go. Byron stood in my office and said, "April, I have to tell you I've had a pretty strong reaction to all of this. I'm the only one who knows what you're planning to share."

He was right. He knew. He had told Deborah, who had started working on her own childhood sexual abuse issues. Byron didn't know how much I had remembered about him. I could tell by the way he was standing in front of my desk.

"April, I'm having some problems with this. I've always been placed in the role as your 'little parent.' And I'm worried. I want to protect you. What if it doesn't go well for you? I don't want you to be hurt anymore. I'm worried. I don't want to be there and hear all this and not be able to protect you."

I knew what he was saying. He was terrified. I said, "Byron, don't worry. No matter what happens, it won't be as bad as it was when we were children. We are adults now."

Humbly my brother said, "I'll be there."

After he left my office, my eyes misted over as I gazed out the window. I thought about what painful lives we have led. I thought of Byron as a six-year-old taking the point of a compass and poking it into his stomach. Naively he thought that would kill him.

I wish I could protect him from his pain. I know the only way to alleviate this pain is to identify it—put it all on the table—and deal with it. We can't hide it or stuff it inside anymore. It festers and grows. I don't want to hurt my family or "salt their wounds." I am going to do this because I know it is the only way for them to clean out their wounds and heal.

July 12, 1990

Tonight was the first night. The other therapist is a man named William. He facilitates family groups all the time. He works mostly with families trapped with substance abuse.

This is an addiction which goes one layer deeper. I believe that the alcohol in my home was a direct result of the incest.

Tonight's session was primarily to establish a comfort zone for all of us. I knew what we were going to do. We mapped out my mother's family of origin and my father's. I had traced it back before, but I'd never seen it on paper. I sat on the big soft couch and looked up at the marker board. It was all there in black and white. Generations of addictions and dysfunction handed down with the valuable heirlooms. Seeing it so clearly reinforced my commitment to tell. Somehow, some way, we have to make this stop.

July 13, 1990

Byron loved last night's session. He walked into the bank this morning and approached my dad.

Byron said, "Dad, this is great. It's going to be healing for all of us. Latecomers are welcome. Please come."

My dad refused.

I swallowed hard when I heard them conversing in the hallway. I am afraid of tonight. Every time I tell, I feel like I am going to die. I know that goes back to my basic programming. "If you tell, you're dead." Although I know that threat is irrational, it automatically flashes through my head.

I want my dad to be there—and I don't. What if he tries to hurt me? My brother will protect me. Maybe he won't. He didn't before. I am terrified.

Later:

It is eight o'clock in the evening. Laurel drove up from St. George to be with me when I returned home tonight.

I walked in the door, and she was stunned. She looked up and said, "What are you doing here? I thought you'd be gone until one or two in the morning."

I am traumatized. Stunned. I don't know what to say.

The meeting started with what they call "Face offs." You sit in a chair directly across from the person you are confronting. You sit knee to knee. You can hold hands if you want. The two therapists sit on either side of you, right where your knees are touching. One person starts. The format is like this:

"I resent you for …
I love and appreciate you …
I apologize for …
I commit to you …"

I started. Byron and I sat across from each other. I looked up at him and said, "I resent you for … " Then I stopped. My words wouldn't come. Only silent tears.

Karen rubbed my left arm and gave me a tissue.

I paused and then looked into my brother's eyes and said, "I resent you for sexually abusing me when I was little."

My brother nodded.

I told him some incidents I remembered. I didn't express graphic details.

I said, "I love and appreciate you for trying to be my little parent. I understand what a tough position you were put in—you were a little boy yourself. I love and appreciate you for all that we have shared as adults. I love and appreciate you for being here."

Then I went to: "I apologize for being born." I sobbed. I have felt his world was turned inside out when I was born. I don't believe he would have been put through so much pain if I had never been born. I apologized. For being around for him to "act out" on. I apologized for being such a well-trained abuse victim that sometimes I initiated it. I apologized for enjoying it. I explained how I had come to terms with the events that had destroyed my life.

I committed to him that if he had the courage to take the same steps, to walk through his pain, he could come to terms with it also. I committed to him that I would always be there to support his healing process. I committed to him that I would always be real and express myself for who I am. I committed to him that I would not bear any more secrets. No matter how ugly things were, I promised not to hide them.

This whole process took me about an hour. My words were broken between my tears. When I finished, there was a knock on Karen's large French doors.

Karen looked a little startled and then excused herself. She came back in and said, "Byron, there is an emergency phone call for you."

A few minutes later Byron returned, "You don't know this, but Deborah is pregnant. Right now she is having a miscarriage."

We adjourned the meeting. We agreed to meet again at 6:00 the next morning. Byron left.

Then we were all sitting there. I was shell-shocked. My mother said, "I just have one thing to say. Do you mind if I say this one thing?"

We all looked at her.

My mother said, "April, I know exactly how you feel."

My heart rose. I was certain she was going to say that she had been abused as well. She continued: "When I was twelve, I was babysitting. The father of the house came home early. I started to get up to leave, but he asked me to sit down and talk. I sat on the couch with him. He moved a little closer to me and then he put his hand on my knee. I was so scared I got up and ran away. I know what it feels like to be attacked."

I was speechless. The room was silent. I had just sobbed for an hour, dredging up my most shameful past. She talked about a hand on her knee. I talked about oral sex and Ouija boards. Did she hear me? I wasn't talking about playing doctor with my brother. I spoke of incest.

Karen said to my mom, "Do you know what just happened here? My mom said, "Well, yes."

Karen said, "I'm not sure you do. Do you see April's pain?"

My mother looked at me and then away, quickly and in a hesitant voice replied, "Yes."

Karen said, "Mrs. Daniels, your daughter just sat knee to knee with your son and divulged a childhood of sexual abuse. Her pain fills the room. Can you start to try and feel her pain?"

My mom just sat and stared at Karen with an expression completely void of comprehension.

Karen said, "You know, Mrs. Daniels, one of the ways *you've* survived through all these years is denial. You just used it here. April's pain was so pervasive and so huge that you got it down to some kind of size you could manage by denying its reality by telling yourself it was like something you had experienced that was—oh, let's say, unsettling. Well, you must begin to accept that April's experience was not like your experience. You have got to begin to connect with your daughter's pain."

My mother just sat and looked blank. My mother, who never smelled the urine, saw the blood, understood the loose teeth, just sat and stared blankly.

I tuned out. I wanted to run from the room. Karen finally said, "I don't think we should pursue this without Byron. Let's start exactly at this point tomorrow morning."

So, I came home. Laurel is here. I don't know what to say. I wonder what Byron is thinking? He was white when he left.

I just got back from our session. I am euphoric. I could write and write and write about this.

We started the session with what happened last night. Deborah lost the baby in the middle of the night. But she is all right.

Then we talked about what happened with us after Byron left last night. My mother retold the story. Then I said, "Mom, what happened to you doesn't even come close to what happened to me." My mother said, "I know, I know—but—"

Then my mother went on a long, drawn-out, rambling story about when she was at the university. One of her professors tried to kiss her.

Again I said, "Mom, that doesn't even come close to what happened to me." My mom didn't hear me. She started to say something about how she knows what it feels like to be attacked. William, the facilitating therapist, said, "April, say it again."

I said, "Mom, that doesn't have anything to do with what happened to me. It isn't even close."

My mother started to say something else about her school days. I felt the fingernails of my clinched fist dig into the palm of my hand. Suddenly Karen slammed her hand on the table. She said, "Mrs. Daniels, get in this room!"

We all jumped. I have never seen Karen do anything like that. The room was silent.

Karen said, "We have to stay on the core issues of incest—not on tangents of past school-day frights. In this moment we are talking about incest. We are not talking about you! We are talking about your daughter's incest." Karen was angry. She pulled her eyes from my mother and back to me. Her face softened and she said, "Okay April. Go ahead."

Byron and I continued our face-off. He told me he resented me for all the material things my parents gave me.

He was correct. I got all of the stuff. And I knew why. He resented me for looking to him as my parent and my protector. He resented me for taking away part of his childhood and making him my parent.

He loved and appreciated me for everything I had been through and for commandeering this family healing process.

He apologized for abusing me.

He committed to always strive to be open and real. He committed to continue his healing process.

I cried. We embraced.

Then Melinda and I did our face-off. I resented her for not protecting me. I resented her for not being my big sister. I resented her for having such horrible friends. I resented her for not knowing that her boyfriends were abusing me.

I loved her for showing up.

I apologized for underestimating her. She was "showing up" at this session more than I ever imagined. She has always played it safe, "laid low." But now that the truth was out, she was really present. I was thrilled.

I committed to never underestimate her again. I committed to let her know who I am. I committed to continue my healing process and communicate to her about it.

Melinda resented me for not acting like a little sister. She said she always wanted me, and I wouldn't even play with her. I didn't let her be a part of my life.

I sobbed.

She loves me.

She apologized for her friends and for not knowing.

She committed to always be open and real with me. She wants to be my sister. We cried. We embraced.

Then Byron and Melinda did their face-off. I watched my two siblings reveal their innermost secrets and feelings about one another. I continued to cry.

Then Melinda and my mom went. Melinda cried. I've only seen her cry one other time. She bore her soul to my mother about her deepest pain. My mother nodded. My mother never shed a tear.

I cried continuously. The things my sister said were true for me also.

Then Byron went with my mother. He told of all his hurt and the betrayal he felt as a boy. He cried. I cried. My mother did not.

My mother's words were, well, eloquent and appropriately vacant. She always says the right thing. She is a master of our language.

Then my mother and I did our face-off. The first thing I said to her was: "I resent you because I don't believe you are getting any of this."

She nodded.

I told her that I resented her denial system. I resented her words of love and her abandoning behaviors. I resented her more than anything else for never coming clean with herself and taking care of herself. I resented her for not knowing. I resented her for being so submissive to my father. I resented her for not protecting me and being my mother. I read her my poem:

is there a time
to be friends
or make amends?
the moment has passed
at long last
with a cost
a token ... death awoke end.
no longer able
to enable
the empty chime
even for a time.

I carefully explained it to her. How I didn't want to enable her—to participate in her eloquent, empty words. How I didn't know if we could make amends because she wasn't real, and how sad I was about that. How sad I was to watch her live her life, continually discounting herself and giving herself away—and then professing that she is not. Professing that she is spiritually growing and enlightened.

I said to her, "I love and appreciate you for being here. You have suffered so much. You are incredible for surviving all these years and years of abuse."

I paused. With a muffled moan I said, "I apologize for being born." It took me a long time to continue. I was shaking and sobbing.

"I ruined your life, Mom. You had a breakdown after I was born. You didn't leave the house until I started school. I'm sorry I was born."

My mom just stared at me. She never cried.

Then I said, "I commit to you to live. I was born, and there is nothing I can do but make the best of it. I commit to you to live the best possible life I can. To be fully human, to feel my own pain and my own joy. I promise to share my joy in living with you."

Karen and William were both crying.

My mother's response was hollow. I don't know if she experienced any feeling. I know that when I heard her words, an empty chime rang through my soul.

I cried. I cried for the life she was missing. I cried for the person she might have been, if only she'd had the courage. The courage to see herself in a different light. The courage to see she is worth more, much more.

This is my wish, my prayer, my dream and my hope for all of those afraid to see themselves for who they really are:

reflections:
you will hear your voice
in the wind
echoing love through
the canyons of your soul
dancing colors of light arch
across the blue morning sky
remember the promise
(even after strife)
reflections we see and we'll be.
you'll know always know
what is
past the light speed of present
future presence now
presents of more.
you see everything beautiful
mountain treasures rainbows
sunsets ocean glories

waterfalls powerful infinite
and yes
knowing you are more
much more.

August 3, 1990

It's been two weeks since the family meeting. I have felt like the weight of the world was lifted off my shoulders. The majority of my excess baggage is gone. I have felt hopeful—until today.

My dad came up to my house today. He was a flurry of activity. He began changing the locks on my doors. I told him that I didn't want him to do that. I said that he was violating my boundaries.

I started to cry.

He was yelling. He wanted me out. He said that he almost divorced my mother when I was fourteen. He said I am a selfish, spoiled brat.

I tried to call Karen. I was afraid he was going to physically hurt me. I was sobbing. Karen was in a session with a client.

I called Laurel. I asked her to stay on the line until my dad left. I was afraid.

My dad said, "I don't ever want to see you again. Don't ever come around my house or the bank again. I am disowning you. You are disowned, disinherited, and fired."

I cried, "You can't disown me because you've never owned me."

Laurel was silent on the phone for a long time. She heard every word. I'm glad. I was so emotional. I can't possibly remember it all. Laurel talked to me afterwards. She wants me to come down to St. George. I might.

Right after I hung up the phone, Karen called. I told her the story. She was upset, and she understood. Karen thinks it would be a good idea to get away for the weekend.

I was sitting here and my mother knocked on the door. She was going to a meeting and decided to skip it because of what happened. She listened to me for a long time. I know that my mother doesn't give me everything I deserve, but I was glad she was here to listen to me.

I would really like to give her the benefit of the doubt. Maybe she was so shell-shocked at the family meeting that she couldn't cry. Sometimes my mother does try. It's not as much as I would give to my daughter or anyone I care about who is in pain—but she tries. I feel bad for her. I was the one disowned, and I feel bad for her.

August 5, 1990

I'm in St. George. I'm lying by the pool watching the boys swim. I love their lives and their happy childhood.

Later:

I am a little surprised at my strong reaction to this last conflict with my father. I am so sad. I wish things were different. I have lost so much. I hoped that my healing would bring us together.

My hope is like razor blades I swallow, descending internally with no way out. Restrained by reality, manifest in a sadness, gripping me in the darkness. To cry for a love I will never feel. My hope turns inward, dissecting the silent chambers of my heart.

September 5, 1990

I don't know if I will ever adjust to being disowned and disinherited. I didn't lose my job though. Melinda and Byron told my dad that if he fires me, they are leaving as well. Besides, they need me. Every now and again they make noises that they really don't need me. But deep inside they know they do. I think that it would be very threatening for all of them if I left. So I'm back at work. It is very tense when my dad is around. He walks out the door when I walk in. I wanted so desperately for the end result to be different. I wanted to be accepted. I wanted to be understood. I wanted something from my dad. I wanted something from my mom. I think that my family got scared with this last explosion between me and my father.

Melinda came into my office and said, "You really hurt Dad when you were fourteen." I looked up at her and I was stunned.

I said, "How did I do that?"

Melinda replied, "When you were at the track meet and Dad tried to put his arm around you, and you told him to never touch you again."

"Think, Melinda. Think. Why would I tell him not to touch me again?"

My sister and I locked eyes for a moment. She did not respond.

"You have a fourteen-year-old daughter. Is there anything in this world she could possibly say to you that would cause you to hate her for the rest of her life? If your teenage daughter said to you, 'Fuck off and die,' would you hate her forever? I am a thirty-one-year-old woman. Our father still will not forgive me for something I said over sixteen years ago. He says I almost ruined his marriage when I said, 'Don't touch me again.' Think, Melinda. I was fourteen years old, and I probably said those words with all the hatred I could muster. Why do you think Dad is still so upset by those words?"

Melinda did not know what to say. She stood by the doorway to my office for a long time. Then she said, "No, there is nothing that my beautiful, wonderful fourteen-year-old could say to me right now that would be unforgivable. She's fourteen. It's what teenagers do. All kids say things to their parents sometimes. It comes with the territory of having kids."

I think she got it. But it showed me that no matter how great the family meeting was our family patterns are deeply entrenched. Was it all in vain? I am going to be the scapegoat role for a long, long time.

Even though things didn't end "happily ever after," I am glad I told the family secret. I'm glad that I have done what I have done. Otherwise, I wouldn't have a life. I have a chance for a life now.

Today is Karen's birthday. I wrote a poem thanking her for her whisperings of freedom.

September 7, 1990

Karen and I met today.

Karen said to me, "April, I think one of the greatest gifts you could give other survivors would be to gather your journal entries and other writings, package them up and publish them.

I resisted. My journals and writing were so personal. They were rough and illogical.

Karen continued, "I would like to write portions, as your therapist, to explain what was happening therapeutically. No one has ever done this before, and it would show the healing process from beginning to end."

I felt exposed and certainly not healed. I balked.

Karen asked: "Do you know how extraordinary you are? There are a myriad of different manners you could have acted out instead of taking this path to healing, to freedom.

I told her that I didn't feel like I had a choice. She looked directly into my eyes and said, "You had a choice. Think of all the kids from your old neighborhood. Think of the untimely deaths: the suicides, the drug addicts or those who have lapsed into the abyss of mental illness.

There are so many paths of dysfunction and pain that adult survivors of sexual abuse chose. You are one in a million."

I knew better than to argue with her because I had a long history of minimizing myself, and she'd call me on that. I'm going to try to absorb the concept that I have done so much solid healing work and that I'm in a place to build my own beautiful life and I am free. (I'm still not sure about the one in a million bit). Then I thought about how valuable it would have been for me to have such a resource from another survivor when I was in crisis.

I told her that I'd get all my writings together. She could then write the therapeutic portions to tie it all together.

Karen said that this would be an important gift for other survivors. That would be nice.

ACCEPTANCE

"In the midst of winter, I finally learned
that there was in me an invincible summer."

—Albert Camus from *Actuelles*

April

I WENT TO CAROL'S TONIGHT. I dropped in for a visit. Carol and Norton were passing through the doorway to their study at exactly the same time. Carol reached over and pinched Norton's side. Their eyes met, and they smiled. I almost felt like an intruder. I saw a moment of genuine love. There wasn't an embrace or a lingering look—it was brief and concise.

I was touched by something I saw and felt, an intruder on a moment of intimacy. Ashamed of feeling, as I watched, my eyes watered and I wondered, "Can it be?" I've only seen imitations performed for others—and here and now I saw love. A place I fear to go. One I doubt I will ever know.

September 25, 1990

My sister-in-law, Deborah, has started having a lot of memories. Byron asked me what he could do to help, and I replied, "Get her into therapy."

Instead he bought her a copy of the workbook. I do the workbook religiously, but it is not enough. There has to be a professional facilitating the pain and suffering. It is too much to handle on a "do-it-yourself" basis.

Oh well, maybe it is a beginning for her. There is a section of the workbook that asks the survivor to get a letter of encouragement from another survivor who is further along in the healing process. Deborah asked me to write her a letter. Here it is:

> Dear Deborah,
>
> When I first remembered the overwhelming incidents of sexual abuse last October, I felt I had gone insane. I thought I had lost my mind. I was terrified and frightened of everything and everyone. I was afraid of myself. How could I have forgotten half of my life? My perceptions and my reality seemed such a fraud. I couldn't trust. I had a picture in my mind of the Hotel Newhouse crumbling—my reality was that I was left amid the rubble to build a new life. It seemed impossible. I knew I had to have help. I still do. I had to trust.

138

When I teach children to swim, it takes a great deal of coaxing to get them to jump to me. I will not drop them. I never have. And after I catch them a few times, they learn they can trust me. When I remembered, I felt like a young child clinging to the side of the wall. Carol and Karen were in the pool saying, "Jump to me." I was terrified because I have jumped before and I have been dropped. Dropped and thrown so traumatically that I had to forget about the entire experience. But, Deborah, in this last year I have reached out, and I have jumped. I have leaped into the arms of love. There are people out there that will catch us—and teach us how to swim and love and splash joyously in the sunlight.

Deborah, you don't have to let go of the edge of the pool. You can cling to the side and shiver. Please don't. Reach out. Let go. Trust me—there is nothing as exalting and as joyous as feeling the water caress your body and gently floating with the waves. There is nothing like having someone hold you until you are comfortable to swim on your own. There is nothing as wonderful as saying, "I'm tired of swimming now. I'm getting out to dry off, and I'll swim again, joyfully, on another day."

Don't cling to the side. You can do it. I know you can.

There is nothing I would trade for finally, finally having myself: for feeling my pain and sorrow and truly laughing at the simple beauty of my life. I love the smell of the flowers in the morning. I love watching my dogs chase a ball. I love your sons' excitement as they feed the birds—I love discovering and feeling and understanding for the first time in my life.

Please trust me. It's worth it. There is nothing as beautiful or as wonderful as our own souls. Push through your pain and you will have yourself.

Love,
April

Carol

CYNTHIA IS HAVING A HARD time right now. She doesn't want to go back to therapy.

"It's dumb," she says. "I'm sick of talking."

"Cynthia, pretend you're a littler girl than you are. Pretend you're a little girl named Pearl."

"Is this a story?" Cynthia likes to play story games with me.

"Of course, it's a story. Pearl is eight years old. Her mother thinks she's very pretty, and her teacher thinks she's very smart. Her grandfather says she's so good at math he will have her do his bookkeeping soon. Her soccer coach says—what, Cynthia?"

"He says she better not miss the game." Cynthia laughs.

"Okay. So Pearl is a lucky little girl. And besides, she has two goldfish named Swimmy and Goldie. She always remembers to feed them."

"Whoops!" says Cynthia.

"The only trouble is that Pearl's stomach hurts all the time. Her mother took her to the doctor, but he couldn't find anything wrong. The doctor asked her all about what she eats and how often she goes to the bathroom."

"Oh, noooo! How embarrassing," Cynthia says, but she is giggling.

"Anyhow, the doctor says if she doesn't get better, he'll have to do all these tests. Pearl doesn't want that, so she pretends she's just fine. But Pearl still feels sick. Finally, her mother takes her back to the doctor, and they give her a shot and stick this little camera down her stomach and take pictures of it. The doctor still can't find anything wrong in her stomach. So, he asks her what it feels like. Pearl says it feels like—what?"

"Like a piece of rotten fruit is in there. Like you want to throw up, but you can't. Like it's all hard, but it moves around and hurts different places."

"Oh, that's great, Cynthia. Pearl tells the doctor that, and he says the old rotten fruit is poisoning her and making her hurt. He says a little bit of the poison seeps out all the time. He says they have to get the poison out. Then what happens?"

"The doctor says he can cut her open," Cynthia continues. "Pearl says, 'No Way!' Then what?"

"The doctor says this hurt is invisible, but she can get rid of it the same way your body gets rid of other things—like when you breathe, you get rid of carbon dioxide, when your nose runs, you get rid of mucous; when you throw up, you get rid of bad food; and when you go to the bathroom, you get rid of that stuff."

"This is getting yucky," Cynthia says.

"Too bad. We have to finish it now. The doctor says they will shrink Pearl's bad fruit. He has her take deep breaths and let them out, and then he says he can smell the bad fruit. He has her punch an old pillow and pretend it's something she's mad at. She gets all sweaty doing that. He has her scribble as hard as she can on a big piece of paper. Sometimes they talk about something so sickening that Pearl has to throw up. Then little tiny pieces of slimy, green, rotten fruit come out. The doctor says that's good. Sometimes they try and tell jokes and laugh and laugh. The doctor says that's a good way, too. Then he says, 'Bad stuff can come out when you cry. Think of something real sad.' What does she think of?"

"Her sister's dog got run over. That was saddest of all."

"Pearl tells the doctor about the dog. He says, 'Does your stomach feel better now?' 'Maybe,' says Pearl. It's hard to tell. She thinks her stomach feels better, but she's thinking about it more, so in one way it seems like it hurts more. She cries all the time. Even when she isn't with the nice doctor. She gets sick of crying all the time."

"Yeah," says Cynthia.

"One day the doctor says, 'The bad fruit is all gone, Pearl. You've breathed it out and sweat it out and yelled it out and cried it out. But the tiny seed in the middle of the fruit will always be in your stomach. It's hard and solid. It won't hurt you though because it's rubbed smooth and clean like a stone in a river, like a pearl. You're better.'"

"Is that the end?" asks Cynthia.

"Almost. When Pearl tells her mother about the fruit, her mother says, 'Pearl, I'm glad you're smart, and I'm glad you're pretty. But most of all I'm glad now you've got a good tummy.' That sounds so funny that Pearl and her mother start to laugh and laugh and laugh."

"That's the end," says Cynthia. "I know how they make pearls. I saw it at SeaWorld."

Cynthia went back to therapy.

Therapy is helpful. However, I know better than most that therapists don't have all the answers in dealing with sexual abuse. Take Freud. When his "hysterical" patients described childhood molestations, at first he believed them and declared child sexual abuse to be the main cause of hysteria. His colleagues were outraged. To save his prestige in the scientific community, he came up with a total about-face; the Oedipus complex in which the child desires the parent and therefore fantasizes sexual acts from an adult. I wonder if people understand that maybe Freud copped out and in doing so changed the entire history of psychoanalysis.

Victims may not be called hysterical now, but they are everywhere. All ages, both sexes. Does anyone see how their abuse translates into welfare, job dysfunction, crime, prison costs, prostitution and violence? Do they get that over eighty percent of people with eating disorders are child sexual abuse victims, and that more people in the United States currently die from anorexia than from AIDS?

April

KAREN HAS CANCER. I AM so worried. What if she dies? Will I make it?
Later:
I just got back from the hospital. Karen has had major surgery, and her prognosis looks good. I'm still worried. Karen was lying in the hospital bed, and she reached over and touched my hand and said, "Just because this happened, you don't need to fall apart. You are strong, April." The corners of my lips curled up slightly. I wanted to smile to reassure her that I wouldn't fall apart—but I wasn't exactly sure that I wouldn't. I've fallen apart so many times, what's one more? Besides, I've learned that eventually I get the pieces back together again. I am not Humpty Dumpty.

Karen placed her hand over mine and said, "April, I don't think I'll be able to write the therapeutic perspective for your journal entries, but I still think you should publish them. It's important. You could call your friend, Carol. She might be interested in writing the therapeutic commentary."

I had gathered everything together and with her analysis, it could be a good book to help other survivors. I know Carol has the therapeutic background to tie it all together, but I don't know if she'll be interested. It's just my dumb little story.

Before I left the hospital room, Karen made me promise to contact Carol.

I called Carol and explained the idea that Karen had about my journal and other writings. I told her how raw and illogical they are and that they really need a therapeutic perspective. I told her that Karen was going to do that portion, to bring some sense to my crazy words. Then I told her that Karen had cancer. I broke down before I could tell her that Karen made me promise to call her.

Carol agreed that it would be an important work for other survivors. She didn't agree to anything until she read what I had written. She asked me to bring everything to her. Carol knew what I had been going through, but to have her read it in such raw form unnerved me. I rambled on about how rough they were. She assured me that she didn't care; she just wanted to see them before she made any decisions. Before I lost my nerve, I grabbed my box of writings and drove them to her house.

At least I kept my promise to Karen. I know Carol will say no. They are just too crazy and discombobulated.

I'm going to lunch with Carol today. She called yesterday and said she wanted to talk to me about my writings and the project to help other survivors. She didn't give me any feedback on the phone. I know she asked me to lunch to let me down easy. My writings are scattered and jarring. I was only writing to try to figure out what was going on inside my head with this explosion of traumatic memories surfacing. I know they don't make sense because they didn't make sense to me. They do now, actually, they make a lot of sense. A lot of therapy helped me understand that.

Oh well, at least I can tell Karen I tried. And, it will be good to see Carol. She really is the closest thing to a mother I've ever had.

Later:

I'm stunned. Carol not only wants to write, but she wants to write her story. To tell of how Hank's abuse almost demolished their entire family. She wants to tell how she had all this knowledge and perspective, and it was difficult for her to see the signs in her own grandchildren.

I asked about how rough my writings are, and she said that with some editing, it should be fine. She said, "It's not like the general public will read this, probably the only people reading this will be therapists, who will get exactly what's happening, or other survivors dealing with their own abuse issues."

That rang true for me. Probably the only people who read it will be therapists or women already be in therapy. No therapeutic commentary will be necessary.

This could be an amazing story. Truth is definitely stranger than fiction on this one. Our stories collide with a common perpetrator, Hank.

I've been doing a lot of self-evaluation. I think a year ago I would have died without Karen. I think I'm strong enough now to make it.

Last night in my group, a woman had a horrible memory. It was very moving to be there. A part of me was grateful not to be in such pain. Another part of me was humbled. I thought of Karen watching and guiding me through my pain. I thought of her gentle questions.

I watched like an archaeologist observing, and I pondered progress: excruciating pain questioning life. I was too acquainted with the pain. The black struggle subsided, invisible. No more a part of me. A part Karen watched and helped me question. Afraid no one would challenge the sickness, when Karen got sick, I learned manners of questions that heal whole my soul.

When things get hard now, I step back and try to think of the questions Karen would ask in the particular situation. Trying to ask the questions she would ask has really helped me.

I feel so alone. Karen says when you grow, you lose some good people along the way. I guess you lose some not so good people as well. I'm grieving my losses right now.

I got a card from Lilly. Ever since I talked to her mom about my fears, I haven't seen Lilly. When I first started having my memories, I decided that it was probably my fear that Lilly was being abused. Lilly is exactly the same age that I was when I was abused, so I wondered if I was displacing fear about my own abuse onto Lilly. It is strange. Jennifer hasn't made any effort for us to get together. She doesn't return phone calls. Maybe she is too busy. Maybe it is the fact that we live so far apart. Then again, maybe I hit a nerve. I guess I'll never know.

I've learned about the prevalence of sexual abuse. I wouldn't be surprised if Lilly is being sexually abused. It is everywhere and no one talks about it. I'm not going to abandon Lilly. Somehow, I am going to stay connected; and when the time is right, I'll help her.

I don't believe that the majority of people in our society have acknowledged sexual abuse as a problem. It baffles me. How can we be shocked at the violence on the streets, the drugs and other manifestations of dysfunction in our civilized society—when aberrations are occurring in the most basic unit of our society? Within the family unit, individuals are damaging and violating one another. It has a ripple effect: war, violence, crime, drugs and other insane actions do make more sense when it is recognized that these horrors are committed in the quiet confines of a home.

Is it possible to break the chain of dysfunction? Every individual who heals brings light into a dark world.

Halfway through the month, half of the moon lights the December sky. I shiver and wonder, "How light would it be with a full moon?" I know I remember the illumination of the whole. And I hope when things are not as bright as I want them to be, I'll pause, remember the moon—and the light permeating the darkness with only a sliver of the moon—and know the fullness will come.

It's Christmas Eve. It's 10 below and even my dogs with heavy coats come inside. I gaze out the window and watch hundreds of tiny sparrows feed and sing songs of springtime. Where do they go from the cold? Delicate and beautiful, they are stronger than frozen ice.

I took my nephews out to feed the birds. Now they are plopped down on my floor watching *Roger Rabbit,* their favorite. They've got to have a wonderful childhood.

January 3, 1991

My family has slowly gone back to where they have always been.

I watch some of the women in my group and other friends. It's the same story: lots of tears, lots of talk, no action. They cling to their denial systems and their warm addictions like security blankets. Only their blankets are smothering them.

Healing takes legitimate suffering. It is not about molding yourself to please your therapist. It is a process in which a trained professional reflects reality in order for you to take the journey inward.

January 13, 1991

I talked to Hank's stake president. Carol Scott had asked me to. I want to. I hope that the truth can be heard in as many places as possible. He asked me if I would be willing to talk to a general authority, and I agreed to do so.

January 14, 1991

I met with a couple of general authorities. They seemed to be very caring, compassionate men. I told them everything. I told them about my family, the neighbors and Hank.

I told the general authorities about the children from my neighborhood. The deaths, the suicides, psychiatric hospitalization. About the perpetrators. The ones I grew up with.

We all came from well-educated, upper-class, righteous homes. We grew up in a nice neighborhood. Over half of us have had incomprehensible pain throughout our lives because of the sexual abuse that happened to us as children. Some are bouncing in and out of therapy, and some are perpetuating the cycle; they are acting out. Like Hank.

I think the general authorities believed me. They asked me if I would be willing to speak at a council.

I told them I believed that the support of the church could help the perpetrators get into professional counseling.

One of the general authorities said, "This council might help push them into therapy."

Another one asked, "Can you forgive your dad? Can you forgive the others?" I smiled. That has been quite a discussion in my therapy. Forgiveness.

I told them it depends on the definition of forgiveness. I said, "If you mean reaching an understanding of how sick they are and a small degree of their pain, and if you mean realizing that it is never okay it happened—but knowing you can heal and get on with your life—then yes, I can forgive my dad and the others."

Carol

HOW MANY CHILDREN HAS HANK abused by now? I know of nineteen. These do not include children in his new life: his two stepdaughters and a whole new neighborhood.

After four years and many requests, the church canceled Lorraine's temple marriage binding her to Hank. However, the church letter said her children would remain sealed to Hank. Lorraine didn't tell the children that part.

April has gone to Hank's stake president and a general authority higher in the church and told her story. They said that they believed her. But now, they say, there is too much legal liability for the church to take disciplinary action. Excommunication probably wouldn't do any good anyway, except to warn his neighbors. Perhaps the church is afraid of the publicity. I have no right to judge. They know they can't think of Hank as simply a monster—much as I wish to, much as I wish revenge.

How many more victims is Hank likely to abuse? One recent article stated that the average pedophile in prison admits to at least one hundred. That Boy Scout leader caught in Utah acknowledged having about 400 victims. Our society hasn't recognized what an appalling problem sexual abuse is. Nobody likes to think about it, and I don't blame them. Neither did I once upon a time. Neither did Susy or Yvonne.

April

I GUESS IT'S TIME TO go out and look for a new job. I've always known I couldn't stay at the bank forever. I guess telling the church authorities has expedited my process of departure.

I'm going to lose a lot of money. I'd rather lose money than lose myself again.

I had such an unusual experience today. I went to a special seminar on investments and current market trends. At lunch I ended up sitting by one of the speakers. We started talking.

We were talking about the Iraq situation, and he said, "I'll move to Canada if my son is drafted." He proceeded to tell me that he served in Vietnam, and he has an 18-year-old. He said that he would rather go to jail than have his son go to war.

We talked for a long time. His feelings about war are as strong as mine about sexual abuse.

Our conversation wandered a bit, and we talked about books. He has read almost everything written by Joseph Campbell. I've read some of his work as well. Campbell writes that there must be a "recurrence of birth." He calls it *Palingenesia*.

Talking with the speaker today made me think about Iraq.

The U.S. bombed Iraq last Wednesday. I thought of all my meetings, all my therapy and all the people I know with their sophisticated denial systems. I imagined making a TV movie:

> The tall, cherry wood shelves lining his study are filled with books on the nature of man. I sit motionless, my back against the couch. There is a candle flickering by the pane glass. Drops, like tears, slowly run down the window. A circle of fog brought by the heat of the candle appears. It is black outside.
>
> He sits still digesting the news.
> "No, I don't believe it," he says.
> "What?" I whisper.

"I don't believe it. Maybe there's a problem over there, but not a bloody war. It's all media sensationalized. Publicity, media hype and nothing more. If they don't have any news, they'll create a good story. There's probably a problem over there, a personality clash, and the media blows it up to be torturous slaughter."

I ask, "What about the pictures—the actual film coverage of the bombs in Baghdad?"

"Merely trick photography, my dear. It looked more like a fireworks display to me."

"The President of the United States spoke to the entire nation stating that indeed we had bombed Iraq. How can you not believe this?"

"That speech was the most watched broadcast in television history. Don't you think a politician like Mr. Bush loves to be the center of attention of such a frenzied media blitz?"

"How can you even say this? The evidence for the war is everywhere. Everyone knows about it!"

"That's just it. No one does. Have you been to Iraq in the last two to three months? Have you actually seen this war?"

"No, but it's all over the news. I'm sure I could track down somebody who is an 'eye witness.'"

"How can you be sure, especially of strangers? How can you be sure they are not part of the conspiracy or even brainwashed?"

"I can't believe you're denying reality. Saddam Hussein has an insatiable appetite for power. He has no regard for human life. When he was testing Iraq's chemical weapons, he tried it on his own villages. He just plowed down his own people!"

"I've heard that story myself. Have you ever heard of folklore or urban legends?"

"What do you mean?" I ask, dumbfounded.

"It's like the fisherman who caught 'the big one.' The fish gets bigger the more times the story is told. The United States could also be accused of trying out weapons on its own people. Many people in Utah have suffered and died of cancer because of nuclear 'testing' forty years ago. Maybe Hussein was doing the same type of thing, and it just turned into a big fish story."

I sit speechlessly.

"As I'm sure you know, many businesses and ambitious individuals make a great deal of money on war. These stories, these reports, this documentation, it's all a conspiracy. The media throws out propaganda portraying Iraq's evil to justify this military fiasco. This spoof generates a great deal of attention and monetary benefits for everyone involved."

I am stunned. Can the human species be so paranoid and gullible? A log in the fire pops, and I stare at it.

He continues, "You see, humans are not capable of being so ruthlessly cruel to one another. We have evolved beyond that. We are civilized. These gruesome, macabre acts you hear about cannot be true. Human beings have an intelligence which raises us above all the other species. Humans cannot run fast. We do not have sharp claws or savage teeth. We cannot even blend with the environment surrounding us. We have survived, we are 'the fittest' because of our intelligence. When we were merely gatherers and hunters, we learned to function in groups. The rudimentary basis for our society started when we learned how to work together. It is against our nature, or at least our intelligence, to destroy one another. This so-called 'war' is quite simply an illogical fallacy. To believe humans are capable of being so ruthlessly cruel to one another, all in the name of power, is insanity."

I reply in a subdued tone, "Well, there's one thing we agree on—insanity. I believe humans have a great capacity to be cruel and destructive. You deny our macabre acts, and I can understand why because I want to as well. It would be nice not to acknowledge war, incest, suffering, torture, neglect or even death. But it's real. Just as intelligence, love, joy, nurturing, beauty and life are real. Humans are capable of colossal destruction, and humans have a capacity for infinite love. To ignore that is to never understand the great power in our humanity."

He is silent. The candle has brought more steam to the window. "It is cold," I say, "but in order to see I must go outside."

January 30, 1991

I showed my mother my script. I said, "Mom, I use a lot of metaphors when I write. This isn't about Iraq. It's about incest."

She replied, "You misspelled torturous, monotonously, monetary, fictitious, and you split your infinitive—otherwise, very nice."

No one could accuse my mother of not reading my work about incest. I asked, "What do you mean I 'split my infinitive'?"

She replied, "You wrote 'to never understand'; it should be 'never to understand." That's for sure. I split my infinitive "to understand" after I split my personality, the verb "to be."

February 14, 1991

Today is traditional for lovers. Carol's grandchildren first talked about Hank on Valentine's Day. In the past I have felt like a misfit on this day. Now I am loving this day. Why? Because I have myself. I am learning to love myself, and that is the most intimate relationship one possesses.

Various individuals may come into my life and enhance it. My life is good. It is not perfect. I am in the process—and that is good.

One day a few months ago I was running, and I was screaming. I literally was running down 11th Avenue screaming. I ran for a long time. Then I thought to myself, "I'm screaming so loud. Even if God was trying to talk to me, I wouldn't be able to hear it."

I stopped running and looked down at the cemetery. I gazed at the graves I had envied for years. Those buried in the cemetery are dead; a small realization for some, but it was a huge "ah-ha" for me. My hand moves. My heart beats. I cry. I laugh. I am alive.

What is the life force? What caused the whole evolutionary process to start in motion? Love? Love—if I scream, I can't hear it. If I hate, I can't feel it. I do both. It comes out when I draw.

Lightly I sketch the lines. With space proportional and connections of limitless beauty. Intricate details alone—merely a lash or enamel—together a creation of the highest I AM. A physical manifestation beyond the finite. A glimmer illuminating our spiritual pinnacle of omniscience.

March 11, 1991

Everything is not perfect, but I have a lot more good days than bad. Relatively speaking even my bad days aren't that bad—not as bad as the abuse itself or the emergency stage of the memories.

I have been out looking for a job. Friday, I received a nice offer from a well-known bank headquartered in Salt Lake, but my sales territory will be out of state. I accepted. It is going to be hard to move, but I am excited also.

Here is my letter of resignation:

To my beautiful sister and my gentle brother,

These words are to you from your little sister. The sister who was born many years after you and born very happy. Very happy to be alive. The sister whose happiness was squelched by a traumatic childhood. The sister who became the family scapegoat. Your sister who was locked naked in a rabbit cage for hours on a hot afternoon, your sister who was peed upon, anally raped in the excavation pipe under the road, and could only have liquids during half of the seventh year of her life—because her teeth had been knocked loose by the penis of the most important man in her life.

The pretty sister with all the problems. The one who tagged along and was a "cry baby" when she was "ditched." The sister you resented and the one who wished she had never been born. Your beautiful sister who fantasized about her comfy coffin lined with lace, a fantasy she had as long as she can remember.

These words come to you from your sister who believes in the power of loving and coming back from the dead because it has happened to her. This letter is written by the sister who knows she can only be writing this letter because of the grace of God.

This letter is written by one who brought to this planet a strength to survive. This letter comes to you as a promise—a promise of peace and hope and love.

A promise that was probably made between us before we ever descended to this earth. A sacred promise covenanted between eternal brothers and eternal sisters. I promise to support and love you forever. I promise not to rob you of your right to be fully human.

And I promise to always strive to be genuine and real and fully human. I will always be grateful for our eternal relationship and our enlightening, endless, fulfilling lives.

With great trepidation, I am leaving our shared day-to-day work environment. But I am not abandoning you. I am your sister, and I will be forever.

I love you,
April

March 17, 1991

Last year on this very day, I met Andrea. We both remembered going back to her house to play with paper dolls.

Paper dolls have always meant something wonderful to me. The most important thing they represent is a little girl who stopped a group of kids from hurting me. She was brave. She was only a little bit bigger than I was and she stood up to them. She is a heroine in my life.

Today I finished cleaning out the attic at the top of the house. I found so much old stuff up there. And then I found her:

A tear could have washed her away. In the attic, underneath layers of dust, I found her. Carefully I brushed the dirt from her face. She was water colored by my grandmother's hand. Evidently for my mother, when she was a little girl. The floor creaked as I walked past some tarnished brass. I took her away from the dark attic. Only then could I see her beauty.

An antique paper doll, salvaged from a hundred-year-old home. Her hair is blond and her eyes hazel—like my mother's. Like mine. I am a thirty-two-year-old woman now, living in the home where my mother was raised. I am as old as my mother was when she bore me. I wonder, if my mother had kept this doll, would things have been different for her?

I'll keep her. My life is different. She's fragile, mere paper and watercolors. Forgotten in a dusty attic for decades. I am going to display her, protected, under glass. I want to display her resilience. Somewhere, where I can always see her. To remind me, to never forget.

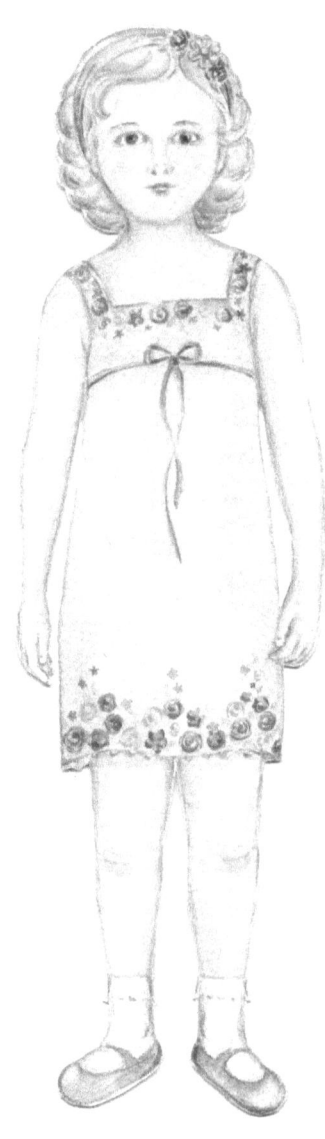

EVOLVE

"We delight in the beauty of the butterfly, but rarely admit the changes it has gone through to achieve that beauty."

—Maya Angelou

Carol

WE ARE HEALING. THERE ARE white scar lines, scar tissue too, rough and purple, but the skin is tough. There are still wounds stinking of gangrene.

Susy is healing too in her own way. All day she sits in the hammock in the glowing green garden where the new ducklings are hatching. She pushes the hammock with one long leg. She weeps.

She reads *Nausea* and *The Brothers Karamazov.* She weeps. The ducklings peep. She protects them. She weeps. When she reads *Hamlet* she changes the words to "Break my heart, for must I hold my tongue?" The iris change to peonies. She pushes the hammock. She weeps. She looks at her reflection in the pool. The ripples distort it, and she cannot make it out. She sits on the hammock in the glowing green garden, and the shadows stretch long across the lawn. She weeps.

It's strange how crisis forces us to relearn ourselves and our world view. Human beings seem to have to say, "I can take suffering if someone will just explain it to me. Just make it serve some purpose."

"The rain falleth upon the just and upon the unjust." I have always known that. When I encountered sorrow, I asked, "Why me?" But not very loud because I had always thought, "Why not me?"

"Why not me?" I asked once in Egypt. A begging woman about my age, belly swollen to seven or eight months, was holding a child. Our eyes met. For a few seconds I was her in her despair. I know there are floods, plagues, famine. Suffering beyond any knowing. But the evil of humans to each other is of a different category; it eludes the cosmology of nature. How do we find meaning in the holocaust, in the Khmer Rouge's killing of one in four Cambodians, in the individual horrors that daily fill the pages of every newspaper in America?

My first coherent image of myself after learning of the sexual abuse: I am shaking my fist in outrage at the universe, me against the Gods. I was smitten in the place I had spent my life trying to defend: my children. Over and over I said in my head, "My God, why hast thou forsaken me?" Then I would say, "Survive. We will survive."

During these months of turmoil, all of us were helped by therapy but it was slow going. Eventually, we all quit going to church. Norton became a member of the National Committee for the Prevention of Child Abuse and did a lot of public speaking and fund raising for them. I made presentations at the Sunstone Symposium on the subject and wrote articles about sex abuse for local news magazines. We went to national conferences of the Linkup organization and tried to make our small impact in a national way. Two adult victims of Hank's abuse who were children in his old neighborhood came to us for financial help to pay for their therapy. We tried to help out with Lorraine's children and Jake's too. The happiest way of doing this was taking them on trips to Coronado. Best of all, several grand-babies were added to our family. Still, the pain and chaos our entire family endured felt like being in a war zone.

April

I STARTED MY NEW JOB today. It's a strong bank with lots of commercial opportunities. They don't have any markets for the higher-level investment bonds. Their markets dried up a few years ago. I'm going to have to go at this with standard markets, until I can design a program and get some markets to back it. Exciting! I can't wait.

Everyone at the new bank is very cautious around me. I came from one of their biggest rivals, and they know me. Sometimes I hear the secretaries whispering and as I approach, they stop talking. Even the other investment bankers, the sales guys like me, are cautious. I'll work hard and really smart to prove myself.

June 4, 1991

My nephew's fifth birthday party was today. I went and felt like I'd crashed the party. It was awkward with my sister-in-law. My little nephew was in the pool when I rounded the corner. He was so excited to see me, he jumped out of the pool and ran into my arms sopping wet. I didn't mind a bit. My clothes can dry. I told him that simply because I had a new job, I would always, always be there for him.

He looked over at his mom and said, "See, I told you she'd come."

Deborah looked down and away.

Karen Fisher always told me that I would be teaching my nephews good boundaries, and how to take care of yourself, by leaving unhealthy situations. I know that he doesn't understand it now, but I hope one day he does.

Before I left, I held my nephew tight.

When I got home tonight there was a message on my answering machine from my nephew. He was so cute, he thanked me for coming to his party. He ended the message in his tender little voice whispering, "I love you forever and ever!"

June 6, 1991

I had a barbecue for the women in my survivors' group, and a few of my close friends. Some that I ran track with, some that I met in college, and some who have been like family to me. Jennifer came; and Laurel came up with her new baby boy,

Paul. Paul was truly the hit of the party! Even Karen Fisher came. It's one of the only times I've seen her outside of the confines of her therapeutic offices.

It was a rather odd mix of people. As I looked around, I knew that this entire group of people loved me. I told them all that I had been sexually abused as a child, and that I'd had an incredible therapeutic session with my family. I talked with the General Authorities of the Church; and with the guidance of my therapist and Carol Scott, my journal entries were going to be combined with some therapeutic commentary and we were possibly going to publish it.

Karen Fisher stood up and asked that everyone try to protect my anonymity. This was simply a gift to other survivors to know that they, too, could heal and learn to live happy and fulfilling lives. Every single person there commended me and vowed to protect my anonymity. Someone asked Karen if she was going to be writing the therapeutic portion of the book. She said that she really considered it, but cancer took away too much of her energy. She said that we found someone even better: Carol Scott.

Carol's children were extremely popular and well known in high school. Everyone knew how cool the Scotts' mom was. The women in my therapy group also knew of her reputation in therapeutic circles. Over and over, people commented that having my story published with Carol Scott would be a beautiful gift for other survivors of sexual abuse: a gift of hope.

I knew that if I published my writings anonymously, and even if I changed the identifying details, the people at this barbecue knew me well enough to know it was me. I told them that the shame of being sexually abused is so tangible, it's hard to discard. I told them that the decision to possibly have my writings published was not an easy one. I didn't always want to be known as a Sexual Abuse Survivor, but Karen Fisher had convinced me that this gift would help others who were struggling with the same issues.

I glanced at the women in my group, and I knew that they all related. Then, as I glanced at my longtime friends—the ones who had sustained me and provided lifelines to me all these years—I knew I could trust them. I knew they would never violate my trust. I knew that I would never be known as merely as a Sexual Abuse Survivor. I knew they loved me.

June 7, 1991

Jennifer's father heard about my abuse and called me early this morning. Jennifer's dad is a fun-loving, charismatic guy. Everyone outside of their family calls him "Boss." Anyway, Boss asked me to lunch. Boss was a Prisoner of War in Germany during WWII. He was a fighter pilot and spent most of the war in a POW camp. He rarely talks about it.

For two hours today, I listened to him. He talked about his time as a Prisoner of War. He almost died there. He built a bond with the other American Prisoners that is unbreakable. They still get together. That's the only time he talks about it—until now. He showed me large scrapbook of all his medals, notes, and photos from the War. He told me to always live my life to the fullest and have fun every day. One page of his book had a single scrap of paper, barely legible:

dum spiro, spero.

I placed my finger slightly below the scrap of paper. Reverently he whispered, "While I breathe, I hope."

The prisoners would whisper that phrase, in Latin, to one another. Sometimes, if a prisoner woke up from a horrible nightmare to realize awakening was a worse nightmare, they would slide this tiny scrap of paper to him. Boss had it when they were liberated. His eyes brimmed with tears when he said, "I almost lost hope."

He told me to never lose hope. To remember that it's over. When things come up that remind me of the past, to simply say to myself that I already survived it. They can't hurt me anymore. Then, he said, "Try to do something fun." He said, "If you can't do something fun right then, start thinking about planning a time to have some fun." Boss is the best skier and water skier I know. When he was in that German POW camp, he vowed that if he made it out alive, that he would live. He said, "And now, I'm telling you: live. Enjoy your life. Remember: it's over. They can never hurt you again. You are strong. Enjoy your life: dum spiro, spero, April."

July 1, 1991

The "stake president" who failed to do anything to protect Carol's grandchildren works at this bank. He's still the stake president in Willow Creek. Many of the other producer's joke that he conducts his stake president's duties here at the bank. Other's scoff that he's vying to become a General Authority. I see him in the monthly sales meetings when all the investment bankers are brought into town. I doubt I'll have much interaction with him.

July 15, 1991

I came to town for a sales meeting. I met with Karen while I was here. Apparently, Karen had quite a few telephone calls from my sister, my mother and my father. My meetings with the General Authorities resulted in my father getting called into his bishop's office last week.

When Karen spoke with my father, he accused Karen of sending me to meet with the General Authorities. Karen corrected him and said that they called me into their offices. I was called in to tell the General Authorities about the abuse that Hank inflicted upon me when I was a child and he was a teenager.

My experience meeting with the General Authorities was quite remarkable. After I met with them and told them everything, they asked me if I would be willing to speak at a council. I hesitated. Possibly I don't understand that whole repentance process, but I know that "nature abhors a vacuum." If these perpetrators are stripped of their membership in the Church, I am worried that it would cause more harm than good. I'm worried that their addiction will escalate, and they will hurt more children. On a rainy day in January, both the General Authorities that I met with told me that a Church Court could help push these individuals into therapy.

Later, when I met with two other General Authorities, they told me that they were humbled and honored to be in my presence. They believed me. I think that they are loving leaders who deeply want to make a difference. They want to help people and they are devoted to making this world a better place.

Now, several months after I met with the General Authorities, my father was called in to see his bishop. I guess he's blaming Karen. Karen and I talked about how I'll probably be asked to meet with my father's bishop, and that I should just show up and tell the truth.

Karen looked good. She's resting more and taking better care of herself. I see her about once a month and talk to her on the phone weekly. I think all will be well.

August 1, 1991

I've been on the road so much; my territory is out of state. I'm trying to visit all the main prospects in my new territory. You have to be in front of them. One of the guys I work with calls it "windshield time." You just get in front of them.

It's been good, though. I'm away. Nothing beats hard work. I spend most of my days in front of prospects, or traveling to get in front of them, and the nights are in some motel. I finished designing the custom program for the higher end investment markets in June. I sent it out to three markets, and all three markets are interested. If I can land one other bond market to back my exclusive program, I'll guarantee my longevity at my job. They didn't even have a market for this; now they have three huge markets vying to back it. Once the backing is in place, I can really sell. There won't be much competition, and the rates will be incredible to generate a lot of new biz.

August 3, 1991

My sister, Melinda, and I are going to meet with my father's bishop. I am nervous. I am relieved that Melinda decided to go with me. I called my brother, Byron, and asked if he would go. He declined. I don't know what Byron is thinking or what is happening with him. His five-year-old son called me in June and told me he couldn't call me anymore. My cute nephew's words: "It's not okay with my dad."

Byron is the one who wept, thanking me for championing the family healing process. He knew I was called into the General Authorities' offices. Maybe he was called into his bishop's office too. I wonder…

Melinda and I met with my father's bishop. The bishop was very kind. In almost newsreel fashion, I told him what had happened.

Then Melinda stunned me. She told me that when she was a senior in high school, I told her what Daddy was doing. Melinda said that we were at the pool, and I told her I didn't want to go home because of Daddy. She said that she wrapped me in my towel, she knelt down in front of me and asked. I told her.

Melinda said that at that moment her entire world turned upside down. She said she didn't know what to do. She was larger than life to me, but she was only a teenager. What teenager can cope with this type of disclosure? She said that she began working long hours as a checker at a grocery store, studied constantly, hung out with her friends and was never home.

I had never heard this from her.

She said that she basically "checked out" of the family because she couldn't cope with it. She knew my parents were drinking. She started drinking too. She joined a sorority at the U, worked and studied all the time, then spent the rest of her time at the Sorority house on campus.

I never remember her being home. I vaguely remember hearing her car pull in the driveway late at night. She seemed like a distant aunt to me. She was always the cool one but never home.

She cried in front of the bishop. She apologized to me.

We told the bishop what Byron had revealed at the family meeting. That both of my brothers had confessed to their bishop about what they had done prior to their missions. Both bishops had forgiven them and let them go on Missions.

The bishop got tears in his eyes. He took notes about everything. He said, "Well, I never knew. I always thought your dad was a tough ol' bird, but I never knew. He's a good man in so many ways; this is hard to believe."

We both agreed with the bishop. I told him that I've had people walk up to me and thank me for all the wonderful things my father has done for them. He hired his older sister to do typing so she could help feed her family. He employed my mentally ill uncle for decades. My father still cries when he thinks of my uncle's suicide. Gramps still works for him. In many ways, my father has a good heart.

People are not black and white. My father certainly isn't. Although, my interactions with him have certainly been "all or nothing."

I told Melinda and the bishop one of my most poignant memories I had now recalled about my father. I was a little girl, and the entire family was gathered around the dinner table. My brothers were learning about World War II in school. My dad didn't want to talk about it. My brothers were getting frustrated because my dad was a Ranger in the war. He was a tough guy.

I looked up at my dad and asked, "Daddy, did you ever kill anyone?"

The table went silent. My dad looked down and whispered, "I hope not."

He got up and left the table.

Melinda remembered that day. I don't remember her ever being home for dinner. Melinda continued my story. My mother told us to never talk about the war. Melinda said that she knew he was in some treacherous situations. He was an Army Ranger sergeant and was part of the troops who took back Guadalcanal. I know that he saved two soldiers' lives. They had to swim down a river in the middle of the jungle with all their gear on their backs and keep their guns dry. Two of his men couldn't swim. My father went back to get each man, twice, and carried them and all their gear down the river. For some reason, I wanted the bishop to know that my father had been a war hero. I pray he never killed anyone either. I want to remember him as the Army Ranger who swam back and saved two other men. I don't want him kicked out of the Church to which he has devoted his life.

We ended the meeting in prayer. We all knelt. Melinda said the prayer and asked the Lord to forgive her for not protecting me. Her voice broke when she said it. She prayed that our family could heal and forgive and again live in the Lord's shining light.

When she finished all three of us were crying.

My father's bishop gets it.

August 20, 1991

My heart is wrenched. My nephew, Byron's son, turned eight years old. My nephew called and said, "Aunt April, I just wanted to call and tell you that I wanted to invite you to my baptism, but I couldn't."

I exclaimed, "Oh honey, congratulations! You got baptized!" My nephew said, "I really wanted to invite you, but my dad said I couldn't." My heart sunk, but I listened and exclaimed, "Oh darling, congratulations! It's wonderful you got baptized!" He continued, "It wasn't as good without you. I feel bad that I couldn't invite you, but I just wanted to let you know why."

I said, "Honey, I would have loved to have been there. Please remember that you can always count on me. Please keep my numbers handy. If you ever need anything, call me."

He whispered, "Hang on, I think someone is pulling in the driveway."

I heard his feet padding on his kitchen floor. Breathlessly he came back on the phone. "My parents are home. I hafta go. I love you Aunt April."

"I love you too, honey. Call me anytime."

"I'll try."

Click.

My darling nephew was scared to call me, and he obviously couldn't call if his parents were home. I watched those kids three to four days a week. Once Gramps said, "I know you love those boys, but I think Byron is taking advantage of you. You need to build your own life."

Now, I'd do anything for more time with them. I don't know if I can build my own life without them being a part of it.

My mind keeps returning to my nephew's breathless little voice and his rapid plea, "My parents are home, I hafta go." He was nervous that he'd be caught calling me. He'd been told not to call me again. His little brother called in June to tell me he couldn't call anymore.

There is a song from *Les Misérables* that I listen to over and over. I think of those two little guys, whenever I hear these words, "God on high, hear my prayer..."

Oh please, dear Lord, let them be okay. I can't stop crying. I feel like my heart is bruised tonight. My nephew's words are entombed in my heart.

August 23, 1991

It's Parker's birthday today. He turned six years old. I am in Twin Falls, Idaho. I pulled into a gas station to call him. We talked for over 20 minutes. I heard about his adventures, his party and his new basketball hoop. As I was listening to his adventures, I looked up to see a gorgeous Bald Eagle dip down into the Snake River. I have no idea if the Bald Eagle caught a fish or not. It was spectacular. I told Parker about it. He yelled to his mom that I saw "a eagle" for him. I heard Laurel in the background say, "An eagle, son."

The gas station had a rack of postcards. Sure enough, there was a picture of a spectacular Bald Eagle. I sent the postcard to Parker.

As I was driving back to my motel, it started to drizzle, a slight rain. Suddenly, the sun blasted through the clouds. A huge rainbow arched above the mountains. It took my breath away. Life is wonderful.

September 15, 1991

I sold five new accounts this week. It's not the volume I wanted but selling five new accounts feels good. Once we get the custom program finalized, all the seeds I'm planting right now will come to fruition.

September 29, 1991

Laurel called yesterday to tell me that my sister-in-law, Deborah, called her and told her a bunch of lies about me. In the mail today, I received a card without a return address. It was one of those cards that can be printed at a Hallmark Store on a machine that lets customers enter their own messages. This card had a cartoon picture of Humphrey Bogart, and it was inscribed: "Here's to your new name, your new job and your new life. Hope it's worth it." There was no signature. On the back, in tiny letters, was a notation that said, "A custom Hallmark Card by Deborah Daniels."

I called my brother's house and my sister-in-law answered the phone. I said, "What's with the card?"

She was quite surprised I'd called and said that I must be mistaken. She added, "As you are about a lot of things."

I paused. She wasn't part of the family meeting. She refused to go to therapy after Karen Fisher and my brother strongly encouraged her to do so. She had revealed that her uncle sexually abused her, but claimed, "I'm fine and I don't want to live in the past." After I wrote her my letter of encouragement, I didn't get any response from her. Listening to her terse denials on the phone, I slowly counted to myself, to calm my heart, then I read the entire card to her including the credits with her full name on the back.

She exploded. She yelled, "April, you are trying to destroy the entire family! Especially my family! Byron has lost so much business since you left! You took all that business from us; we are really struggling here!"

"Deborah, you are wrong. I'm not even marketing in the same state that Mountain View Bank has clients."

She sneered, "You are just a vindictive bitch! We are all sick of your pity party about your tragic childhood!"

And then she hung up on me.

I called my father. My dad answered the phone, and I said, "Dad, please don't hand the phone to Mom. I would really like to talk to you."

I didn't hear anything until my mother said hello. I repeated what had just transpired with my sister-in-law. My mother said, "Well, April, you really didn't expect going to the general authorities would have no ramifications, did you?"

I tried to find out what had happened. My mother told me that the bank had lost a lot of business since I'd left. She just read about the new accounts I sold. I told her that my business was several states away. She said, "How do you explain all your accounts leaving us?"

I didn't know that any of my accounts had left them. I told my mother that I hadn't contacted any of my accounts. She didn't believe me.

With steel in her voice she said, "That doesn't make any sense. They've been with us for years and suddenly they leave when you do?" She hung up.

I'm gazing at the phone in shock.

I can hear Gramps in his kitchen. The kettle is boiling. I'm sure he's making some oatmeal. He loves a cup of warm oatmeal when it gets chilly. I think I'll wait to take the dogs out. He's old but he can tell when I'm upset. I don't want to talk about this with him, and I don't want to worry him needlessly. I haven't felt like this since junior high.

October 7, 1991

I had a session with Karen today. I took the card in that my sister-in-law sent. Karen read the card. Then held it in front of her and said, "A grown woman with three children acting like a malicious 13-year-old is sick."

Point taken. My sister-in-law is sick.

Karen and I discussed my nephews for the remainder of time. I'm struggling with my worry and sadness. Karen said, "April, those boys will come back to you one day. Possibly when they are older and aren't under their parents' direct influence."

I hope so. I have to believe that they are learning to set healthy boundaries. My heart aches when I think of them. I pray they are okay.

October 16, 1991

I started remembering two years ago this month. The life I had built for myself, my known reality, ceased to exist as those memories surfaced. At least I understand now how all the pieces fit together. I don't understand others' reactions or why my sister-in-law, Deborah, did what she did. Her childhood abuse was even reported to the police. My brother told me there is a record of it. She professes that because she told her mom and reported it to the police that she dealt with it. Telling or reporting of abuse isn't necessarily dealing with it. Telling can be a beginning to healing. However, it still takes a lot of therapy, support, reframing of reality, letting go of denial, and much more. The only way I know to heal from sexual abuse is via professional therapy.

After her strange card and even stranger behavior on the telephone, I'm not so sure she has dealt with it. My brother calls her a "rage-a-holic." I've heard her rage filled screams.

I have to continue healing my own soul. The best way is in therapy and practicing what I've learned in my therapy with action. It takes practice for me to alter my behavior, perceptions and interactions.

In one of my Al-A-Non meetings, a man shared one of his "aha" moments. This man was an avid skier. His "aha" moment was that he realized that if he read a book about skiing, he would have learned all about the fundamentals of skiing. However, until he got up on the slopes and actually tried to ski he really wouldn't know how to ski.

I have read a lot. I have had a lot of therapy, and I know the beliefs and actions I need to eliminate. Theoretically, I know how to continue building my own, balanced, healthy life. I know what a healthy, loving, productive life looks like—but I have to continue cultivating and living it.

Carol

WHAT ABOUT YVONNE? YVONNE, MY baby. Why haven't I realized how at risk she was? She's only five years older than Timothy. She knew Hank when Lorraine was first dating him. I paid him to drive her to dance lessons.

Yvonne, my youngest child, back in kindergarten singing, "Who has new shoes, pretty new shoes, Who has new shoes on today? Yvonne skip around and play." When she was six they asked her to be Mary in the Christmas pageant in Sunday school. I made her a royal blue dress and she wore my light blue chiffon scarf over her blond curls. At the Mother's Day program, she sang a solo in church: "Mother, I love you, Mother, I do. Thanks for all the things you do". She licked the microphone before she began and sent a rasping noise through the chapel. Then she sang, right on tune, loudly, bravely. When she was seven, she broke her leg jumping on the trampoline, but she'd still go out and play on it, cast and all.

What was Hank doing to her beautiful little body back then? Will she go through her own hell, like April is doing now? April and all the others out there, all the prematurely grown-up five year-olds?

Back then she was Mary. My Mary.

Now I know about my youngest child Yvonne. All through those terrible years of her eating disorder and depression and even with all the therapy she had, she too had no memory of Hank's abuse until his own children began to talk. Over and over again I've asked myself how I could not have suspected. When my grandchildren revealed his acts, the spinning record in my brain never stopped. "If he touched Yvonne, I'll kill him." But I haven't. I'm not killing him even now. How totally amazing.

But the why, why, why will never stop.

April

CAROL AND I MET WITH some publishers this past week. I don't think much will come of this.

November 1, 1991

Gramps told me today that my brother, Byron, is having a big celebration for Gramps' 90th birthday. He's rented a conference room at Little America. For Gramps' 85 birthday, we had an open house here. I haven't heard from either of my nephews in months. Maybe I'll get to see them at this party.

November 21, 1991

I'm not invited to the party. Gramps says I'm going anyway. I don't know what to do. I tried to call my brother and Melinda. They aren't returning my calls. I saw my mother the other day. She told me that she was sure it was an oversight. I'm not so sure.

November 28, 1991

Today is Thanksgiving. I went skiing with Andrea, my childhood friend who saved me from the boys by the school. She was only in 5th or 6th grade at the time, and she stopped them. She took me back to her house and taught me how to cut paper dolls. Maybe that could be the title of the book Carol and I are putting together. We are all connected, like the cut-out dolls from the single pieces of paper of long ago.

Carol and I are connected in our suffering, our wounds and our battle to heal. I feel like I'm connected to all who have suffered. I'm connected to those who symbolically extend a hand and say, "I can't make it better for you, but I give you, my hand."

Carol and I are also connected by a common perpetrator. We have an unbreakable bond. If my journal entries and other writing combined with Carol's story go nowhere, at least I know I have one person in this world who understands, one

166

other person besides Karen who understands. One person who knows how prominent individuals can inflict such evil.

Paperdolls is a nice title. We are all connected.

December 5, 1991

My cousin from California flew in for Gramps's 90th birthday celebration. He's staying with my brother. My cousin wanted to see me. He told me that Byron expressed sadness that I wasn't in his life anymore. Then my cousin told me that Byron said he grieves the death of two siblings: Tom and me.

I am not dead.

December 7, 1991

Today is my grandfather's 90th birthday. Fifty years ago today, the Japanese attacked Pearl Harbor. My mother and her brothers were in Sunday School. When my mom walked up the sidewalk, her father greeted her on the front porch. They huddled around the radio the rest of the day—listening to the news.

My grandparents immigrated from Norway. The Nazis took over Norway a year and-a-half prior to the attacks on Pearl Harbor. During the German occupation in Norway, my grandparents didn't hear a word from their families. Gramps said that when the Japanese attacked Pearl Harbor, he felt that the world was ending. My grandparents thought it was Armageddon.

Gramps still has a picture of Franklin Delano Roosevelt in our front hallway. FDR is our savior. My grandfather has seen much in his life. In 1914, my grandfather watched as electricity was first installed in his home. When his father switched on the first light in their house, Gramps' mother made all the children gather around as she prayed, thanking the Lord for the miracle of electricity.

My grandfather has seen so much in his 90 years: two world wars, the Korean War, Vietnam and the Great Depression. He remembers the miracles: electricity, indoor plumbing, toilets, automobiles, airplanes, and telephones in every home. He married the only girl he had ever kissed—and he's missed her ever since her death in 1982. Now today, he celebrates his 90th year, and he's refusing to attend the party unless I go.

I don't want to cause a problem. Even my mother suggested that it would be best if I don't go.

I don't want a scene on this day, this day for him. My sister-in-law was so inappropriate the last time I talked to her. I don't know if the Church held any disciplinary hearings or if they are just mad because I'm starting to experience some success in my new job. I don't think I'll go—but it hurts. I'm tired of making sacrifices for this rigidly wrong family of mine. I could just go and let the chips fall where they may but based on my sister in law's sick card and hysterical rage last summer—I fear Gramps would get hit by an inappropriate and utterly toxic rage. I will take Gramps to a special dinner, just us.

After I decided not to go, I tried to explain my decision to Gramps. He didn't understand, and he was still threatening not to go. My mother came to pick him up, and he wasn't ready. My mom came upstairs. I was secretly hoping that she'd ask me to go. Then Gramps would go. My mother asked me to talk to Gramps again and tell him that I didn't really want to go. She asked me to beg him to go. She said, "April, there are all these people here, some have flown in from great distances. Gramps has to show up."

I went downstairs and knocked on Gramps' living room door. He didn't answer at first, until I said, "Hey birthday boy, it's April!" He smiled and answered the door. I told him that I loved him more than anything in the world, and that I promised I'd make it up to him, but I just couldn't go to this party. I didn't take the tactic of saying, "I wasn't invited." Instead, I told him that everyone would be very uncomfortable with me there, including myself. That was true.

I told him that I'd take him out for a really nice dinner and we'd go up the canyon to see the mountains. He made me promise that I really didn't want to go. I told him that I would be very uncomfortable. He went. My mother smiled as she closed the door behind him. Tears slipped out.

Later:

My cousin just left. He brought his wife and daughter for a short visit. They are on their way to the airport. Their daughter is the same age as Byron's oldest son; she's eight. She asked me how the goldfish were doing. My nephew's goldfish. I let her feed the fish, and she told me she was going to let my nephews know that I'm taking really good care of 'em. I smiled.

This is my maternal cousin. His father is an alcoholic also, so he's aware of some of the family dysfunction. We all sat in the living room and chatted for a while. Gramps wanted my cousin to know that he doesn't believe in God. Gramps said, "Religion is based on man's insecurities." I've heard my grandfather's thoughts about this many times. Gramps continued, "Religion is about power and money. Almost every war in our history has been fought over religion."

My cousin smiled and said, "Gramps, you won't get any argument from me."

I think my grandfather was genuinely disappointed. He loves to argue about religion. Gramps smiled and said, "Well, then that's settled." Gramps continued with his advice regarding money: "Take good care of your money, and your money will take good care of you."

My cousin's eyes lit up, "Now that's good advice, Gramps!" The conversation meandered about for an enjoyable afternoon. Then my cousin had to bid his farewell. He's an attorney in California. He is building his practice and works long hours. His eyes glistened over as he said goodbye to Gramps. I'm pretty sure that will be the last time my cousin sees Gramps. It was a good farewell. My cousin gave me a tight hug, thanked me for taking such good care of Gramps, and then said, "I hope you feel better soon."

Confused, I looked over at Gramps as my cousin closed the front door.

Gramps said, "Your mother told everyone that you had the flu. I walked away when anyone would ask. They shouldn't have lied. They are the ones who didn't invite you. I still think you should have gone. It's my birthday celebration."

As I hugged him, I said, "Happy Birthday, Gramps. I love you."

December 14, 1991

A celebration: We signed the deal for the new program-backing yesterday. I took Gramps to dinner in Park City at Stein Erickson's Lodge.

My company officially has an exclusive market now. We'll be able to sell a powerful program at incredible rates. The Chief Executive Officer and the Chief Financial Officer sent me roses.

Dinner with Gramps was fabulous. The mountains remind him of Norway. I took him up to Deer Valley and to Stein Erikson's Lodge. Stein Erikson is a champion skier from Norway, and Gramps was thrilled with the Norwegian décor, the flags, the food and the ambiance. There were a pair of long wooden skis mounted on the wall. Gramps told our waiter that he skied on a pair like that in Norway. As we were leaving, they gave him a special Norwegian package and card signed by Stein Erikson.

December 24, 1991

I went running on the road above the cemetery today. I looked to my left and saw Karen Fisher and her daughter putting a Christmas Wreath on a grave. I think Karen's mother is buried there. One time Karen told me that her mother will always have a sacred part of her heart. Karen said that occasionally she goes into that sacred place and sheds a few tears. That's how I feel about Karen. She will always have a sacred part of my heart.

December 25, 1991

Skiing on Christmas has been a tradition for years. I used to meet Melinda and her whole family up there. Today I was alone. Later in the day, I rode the chair lift with a man about my age. He was from Chicago. As we were talking, I found out that his wife recently died and this is his first Christmas without her.

We skied the remainder of the day together. He talked about his wife constantly on the chair lift. I merely listened. I felt so much for this grief-stricken man.

Later: Gramps and I are sitting by the fire, drinking Christmas cocoa. We are both quiet gazing at the flames. I recall a poem by J. R. R. Tolkien about sitting by the fire and reflecting. My brother loved Tolkien's trilogies. He loved the battles and the wars. I loved the lyrics and the poetry. "I sit beside the fire and think...." I wonder what gramps is remembering. Of all that he has seen: Christmas's long ago with my grandmother singing carols? A Christmas in the early 1940s when the Nazi's overtook Norway and they didn't know what had happened to their family? I wonder about my family. A culprit as dark as war has overtaken them.

Carol

AFTER HANK'S REMARRIAGE, SUSY DECIDED she had to do something to inform parents in his new neighborhood of the children's vulnerability. One dark night at midnight, she and I drove to his home and while I cowered in my car, she spray painted "Child Molester" and "Perpetrator" in huge letters all over the front of his house. As we were escaping at full speed, we agonized as to whether Susy's act would hurt his stepchildren but felt sure it was worth it to warn everyone including them.

Later, Susy and Yvonne decided to sue Hank civilly for their abuse. Hank, although an attorney himself, never defended himself or answered the complaint. The girls were awarded a no-contest judgment of two and a half million dollars, but it was hard to collect the few dollars monthly the judge thought Hank's financial condition enabled him to spare. For a few months they received a hundred twenty-five dollars each. Before the judgment, Hank called and asked Norton what our girls wanted since they knew he had no money. Yvonne called him back (while we listened on the extension) and informed him that if he would admit what he had done and get in therapy with a qualified therapist who would send progress reports to them, they would drop all charges. Hank said nothing. His wife got on the phone and screamed that her little girls were terrified of Susy and Yvonne and our whole family who were trying to ruin their lives. His payments soon ceased altogether.

There was a magic incantation I tried to chant during those awful years. I closed my eyes and tensed my body and said in one breath: "Hold on to who I am. Nobody can have me. Hold on to who I am. Nobody can have me. Hold on to who...." After the magic it occurred to me how much easier it was for Jesus Christ to take the sins than for God the Father to be the Judge. I'd known for a very long time I had to forgive God, but I never knew before we had to pity Him. "Have mercy on God's soul," I added to my incantation.

April

ONE OF THE GENERAL AUTHORITIES I met with last summer called a couple of weeks ago. He asked if I would be willing to meet with Hank's current stake president and Bishop. I wasn't doing cartwheels about it. Reluctantly, I agreed.

I met with them tonight. They asked me many sincere and heartfelt questions. I know they believed me. The stake president asked if I would be willing to testify at a Church Court against Hank.

My mind flashed to my father's tirade against Karen Fisher, after he'd been called into his Bishop's office. This is serious. Non-Mormons might scoff at it, but for those in the faith, this is as serious as it gets. I answered honestly, with I'd rather not, but I will if they deem it important.

I conveyed what I'd said to the General Authorities. My go to motto about addiction and such. "Nature abhors a vacuum." I also told them that the General Authorities told me that a church court might help Hank get into therapy.

I swallowed and agreed.

As I was leaving, they asked me if I was the one who plastered Hank's neighborhood with signs that Hank was a pedophile and to keep the children safe. That's the first I'd heard of that. I told them that typically pedophiles have many victims. Some estimate in hundreds. It could have been any of those past victims.

They told me that they'd let me know when I'd been asked to testify in the church court.

I called Laurel later that night. She's really upset with my "Nature abhors a vacuum" motto. She said that isn't how repentance works. She said if Hank is to have a chance, he must have a church court.

I think I've made a mistake. Not having a church court gives these perps a cover that everything is okay.

I'm sick. I am wrong. I'll be sure to express my egregious mistake when I testify at his church court.

Carol and I have been reviewing our writing. I have learned much by reading Carol's portion. Carol is about the same age as my own mother. Carol's pain, fight and dedication to her children and grandchildren is courageous. I wish my own mother had fought for me as Carol has fought and continues to fight for her children. Who am I kidding? I only wish my mother could really see me. I wish she could at least acknowledge me for who I am. I think it's too painful for her to see me. To see all that she didn't do or refused to see. My mother is incredibly bright and sees the most intricate details. However, she gets lost in the minutia especially regarding me. It's almost like I'm a blind spot for her. She can't see me.

My father and brother getting called into their own bishops' offices has caused this gigantic rift with my family. Melinda went with me to talk to my father's bishop. I doubt she told my father about it. Melinda is a wimp. She molds to whatever the situation. Even when we were working together Melinda went along with whomever said the last thing. Spineless. She figures out who has the most power and goes along with them.

I think of Judas' betrayal for 30 pieces of silver.

February 1, 1992

The goal is to have *Paperdolls* published in April in honor of Child Abuse Prevention Month. Karen Fisher read the manuscript and wants me to change it more.

Karen said, "April, I still have hope for your siblings. They are simply afraid. Afraid to deal with their pain and afraid of all the changes they'll have to make. You can understand that, can't you?"

I grudgingly agreed.

Karen continued, "The details need to change more. Change the dates, some genders, and possibly your profession. If they get identified, I fear they'll get backed into a corner and never have the courage to heal and to be free."

I don't feel like changing it. This book probably won't even do anything, so what will it matter? To appease Karen, I'll change the details more.

March 15, 1992

I went to the laundromat today. As I was folding the hot blankets, I heard a woman's voice reading parts of my journal. I glanced up to see two women huddled together reading the *Utah Holiday* magazine preview of *Paperdolls*. One was reading parts aloud. I watched as one wiped tears from her eyes. I quietly left. I sat in my car for a long time before I could turn the key to the ignition.

April 2, 1992

KTVX, a local television news channel in Salt Lake leads its evening news with a story about *Paperdolls* tonight. The story lead, "Shockwaves blast through the Salt Lake Valley as a new book...." Shock waves? Like this is an earthquake. I'm

173

speechless. The book has already been delivered to local bookstores and starts selling tomorrow.

April 3, 1992

I walked up to The Waking Owl, a quaint bookstore by the University, and bought a copy of *Paperdolls*. There was a line to buy my book. A man in front of me bought six copies. I bought one. I walked home and put it on the shelf. I doubt I'll ever take it down. It's done. It's here. It's part of my house like it's a part of me, but it's on the shelf.

April 14, 1992

The book has sold out. They had to do a reprint. I'm stunned. This whole thing is surreal. Carol and I have done interviews on every television station and quite a few radio shows in Salt Lake. Neither of us let the cameras show our faces. Carol wants to protect her children and grandchildren. I want to protect me. I don't want to be known for this. I'm so much more than just a survivor of sexual abuse. We are going to go to St. George tomorrow for two radio interviews. I can't wait to see Laurel and the boys.

May 2, 1992

I've received about 30 letters from other survivors of sexual abuse. I started reading them. My heart is breaking. There are many who have suffered much more than I have. I'm not sure how to respond.

Karen's been on vacation. She called me from a beach house she's renting after she received a call from a television reporter. Karen reminded me to protect myself. She said that it might feel good to finally get some validation, but she said that others might not be so welcoming of this message.

We chatted briefly about all the letters I've received. She's going to help me craft an appropriate and kind response.

I miss Karen. She is taking more time for herself. She's recovering from her surgeries and radiation. She's taking a couple of months to relax on the beach in California somewhere.

May 15, 1992

Greg Schmeid, the stake president in Carol's portion of *Paperdolls* works for the same bank as I do. Several of the women in the office are all abuzz because Schmeid's secretary spent a good portion of the afternoon standing at the copy machine making photocopies of *Paperdolls*. I feel sick.

May 16, 1992

I called Carol and told her about the secretary making copies. She gets how threatening this is for me. She tried to lighten the mood. She told me that if the stake president comes after me to threaten him with copyright infringement. I am still laughing. She knows how to lift my spirits. Humor is a wonderful tool.

May 19, 1992

The stake president called me into his office today. Schmeid's office at the bank. He said he'd heard great things about the new program and how hard I'd been working. Then he said, "You have to quit talking about that book you wrote with Carol Scott."

I felt like the walls on his office were caving in.

He continued, "I know you wrote *Paperdolls* with Carol Scott. I'm the stake president who presided in her stake when all these allegations surfaced. We investigated thoroughly. We called in the General Authorities. One of them said to me, 'Where there's this much smoke, there's fire.' But we couldn't prove it. We couldn't expose the Church to that much liability."

I told him I'd never talked about any book I'd read, let alone written, with anyone at work. He raised his eyebrows as if he highly doubted that. I felt the hair on the back of my neck raise. Lightning is about to strike.

June 16, 1992

Wendy Hammond, the woman who wrote *The Ghostman* is in Park City for Writers-at-Work. She's teaching a class on playwriting. More importantly, she did a reading this afternoon of one of her plays.

Before Wendy began her reading, she said something like this: "As a writer and as a human being, I am obsessed with evil and what causes evil to become evil. For example, I don't believe that Saddam Hussein was just born that way. For these plays, I've used the family backdrop as a canvas, and I played with the ground rules of reality to the absurd." Wendy then introduced three actors, who read these works with her, entitled "Three Brutal Comedies." They were brutal. They were funny. They were tragic. They were amazing.

I went into the lavatory after the reading. Several women were also in there crying and drying their eyes.

Carol sent word to Wendy that we wanted to meet her. Somehow Carol arranged for us to have dinner with her tomorrow. I'm kind of nervous but also excited. I am in awe of her talent and ambition. She's grappling with evil and what causes it.

My goals are much simpler. I'm trying to learn to shower with my eyes closed.

I'm trying to work through simple scars and childhood wounds that still bind me. I'll leave understanding evil and battling the war on pedophilia to those incredibly valiant souls like Carol, Wendy Hammond and Oprah.

I had my annual employment review today. The "stake president" attended my review with my boss. I got glorious reviews for the new program in place and the markets I've opened, tremendous work ethic and successful sales for the first year. My boss was extremely pleased with my work. Then he cut my pay by $10,000 a year. And now, as if it couldn't get any worse, I'll be reporting directly to the Greg Schmeid, the infamous stake president.

I haven't slept at all. I don't know what I'm going to do. I have quite a few potential accounts coming up in the next 90 days. I hope I can close them.

I'm in Sandpoint, Idaho. I have several clients here. I just hung up the phone with Karen. I can't breathe. The doctors found six small tumors on her lungs. The prognosis is terminal. She's been given six months to six years. She's hoping for six years. She asked me to believe in her. There's no one I believe in more.

She told me that when I get back into town, we need to meet and make a transition to another therapist. She said that she recently bumped into a woman who is very warm, loving and smart. A doctor. I told her that I didn't want to go to a shrink. Karen gave me her number and asked me to call her. Karen said, "After you meet with her, come in and we'll talk about it."

Blinking back tears I muttered that I loved her. She said that she loved me too, She ended with her signature ending, "Now go out there and do good."

I walked along the chilly beach of Lake Pend Oreille for a long time. I came back and wrote this:

> i listen and wait
> occasionally the sand shakes
> as a train rumbles by
> i hear the clang of masts
> on the sailboats in the harbor.
> the wind chills the barren beach
> on tiny waves the sun's reflection shimmers.
> my face tingles from the cold
> and the loneliness of this vacant shore.
> six years you said: i need you to believe
> in me. there's no one on this planet i believe
> in more. six years is a lifetime. i've
> known you six years, a lifetime. the time
> of my life began six years ago. and now
> it may be the time of yours. six years
> ago i never would have foreseen me crying
> on this empty shore. i wouldn't have

felt the wind upon my hair or felt
peace with the harvest moon or believed
in the solitude of the seagulls' screeching
communion before the tranquil setting sun.

October 1, 1992

The "stake president" called me into his office today and fired me. He said that the markets dried up; and if I didn't have a product to sell, they couldn't afford to pay me anymore. I have a three-month severance package, and he's giving me a positive letter of recommendation.

I called my main contact with the company financially backing the exclusive program we developed. He is as stunned as I am. The market, the financing and the program is still in place. Greg Schmeid lied.

October 15, 1992

No one I know has ever been fired. I've built a solid market with a customized program in place. Next year it will boom. Utah is an "at will" state. That means that an employer can fire an employee at will. Basically, an employee can be fire for sneezing wrong. This means I could never sue for wrongful termination. Carol thinks I should take some classes at the U. I don't know what to do.

October 21, 1992

I met with a new therapist this week. Karen's right, she's really kind. When I first called her, she said she wasn't taking any new clients. Then I told her that Karen Fisher suggested I call because she's too sick to see me, I wrote a book called *Paperdolls*, lost my family and just lost my job. She told me she'd make room for me.

October 27, 1992

I'm in St. George right now with Laurel and the boys. I'm trying to be the fun Auntie, but I think they can tell I'm down. As I was putting my makeup on this morning Parker came running downstairs with a one-dollar bill in his hand. He reached up and said, "Here Aunt April, my mom told me you lost your job and I want you to have this." He had a huge smile on his face. He kissed me on the cheek and ran upstairs. I am going to keep that dollar forever.

November 15, 1992

I've had my résumé out everywhere. I have such specialized experience and skills and the job market is very narrow. I'm worried.

Carol

A FEW DAYS AGO, I was at Sara and Jake's. Claire was cutting out paper dolls.

"I just learned how to make them in a string," she said proudly.

"Can I see them? Are you going to color them?"

She handed them to me. "Be careful," she said. "I want them to hold hands. They tear easy."

Every moment children are being torn apart easily.

Yesterday April brought a friend to see me. She too has started to remember Hank's abuse. It is the same. It begins all over again. She was Susy's friend too. When this girl was little, she spent almost as much time in our house as in her own. I remembered the never-ending phone calls, what a mess the kitchen was after they'd cooked, the huts they made in the oak brush outside our yard, the plays they'd put on for us. Now her story is the same. I listened to her.

After they left I sat on the couch, numb, almost indifferent. In front of me on the coffee table was a Picasso book. The eyes Picasso paints. Sometimes three or four in a broken face. In those eyes—the pain, the terror, the comprehension.

April

MY MOTHER CALLED. MELINDA'S FOUR-YEAR-OLD son, Jared, is in a psychiatric hospital. My nephew tried to burn his house down screaming that he was going to kill his parents. My mother told me that she doesn't understand it. Melinda and her husband recently went out-of-town, my mother exclaimed, "Jared was fine the entire time he stayed with us."

I can't believe that Melinda let Jared stay with them. At the family meeting my brother asked about my father's access to the grandchildren. Karen said that it was fine, but to never leave the children with him unattended.

I called Melinda at work. She started crying. She said that it's probably something in Jared's biology (he's adopted). I was quiet and said, "Melinda, do you really believe that? Why did you let Mom and Dad take care of him for so long? You know what Karen Fisher said."

She said that Mom was with the kids all the time. Besides, my dad has changed. He's too old now.

I'm pacing the floor. I have lost everything in order to protect my nieces and nephews. My actions were in vain.

I called my therapist. She told me to call the hospital. She gave me the name of the lead doctor at that hospital. My therapist warned me that he won't tell me anything. She told me exactly what to say.

"Hello, my name is April Daniels. I'm Jared's aunt. I know that you can't say anything to me regarding my nephew's condition. I wanted you to be aware of the history of sexual abuse in my family of origin. I wrote a book about it called *Paperdolls*. I know that my nephew stayed at my parents' house, with my father, for two weeks last month. I do not know if Jared has been sexually abused or not; I wanted you to be aware of the family history."

The doctor listened and said, "April, you are correct. I can't say anything. Thank you so much for calling. This information is extremely helpful to us. Thank you very much for calling." The doctor sounded sincere.

I called Melinda's ex-husband and told him that I called Jared's doctor. He was so relieved I'd called. He was contemplating calling himself. He shares two beautiful daughters with Melinda. Immediately after the family meeting, Melinda called him and told him everything. He wasn't surprised. In fact, he told me today that he'd been suspicious about it for years. After Melinda's call, he put his daughters in therapy. They are in junior high and high school now. I hope they are okay.

November 25, 1992

My mother left a message on my answering machine today. She was spitting mad. She told me that I'd completely "muddied the waters" by preventing my nephew from getting the help he needs. Melinda pulled my nephew out of the hospital and all therapy.

I called my mom back. She told me that I had no idea about my nephew's condition, and I'd impaired the hospital from making an accurate diagnosis. Therefore, it was a waste of money to keep him there.

I told her that I didn't state my nephew had been sexually abused, but there was sexual abuse in the family. She told me that has absolutely no bearing on this situation.

November 26, 1992

It's Thanksgiving. My mom pulled in front of the house to get Gramps. I walked him down to the car. My mom wouldn't look at me. When Gramps sat down in the car, he looked up at me and said, "Why don't you join us April?"

My mother flinched. I gently closed the car door. I slowly walked up to my house.

December 12, 1992

I sent Byron's sons a Christmas card. I received it back today, unopened. My sister-in-law's handwriting scratched across the envelope, "Return to sender."

December 24, 1992

I took a small Christmas present over to Karen Fisher's house. I gave her a card with the poem I wrote her in September. She was sitting by her fireplace. She put her book down when I came in. She smiled, and I bent over to give her a hug. She blinked heavily as she read the poem. I told her that in the next edition, I was dedicating the book to her. She took a long time to respond. Finally with a broken voice she whispered, "Thank you."

She asked about Byron's sons. She asked if I'd heard anything about them. My eyes welled and I told her no. She said, "You'll get them back. There's too much love there."

I nodded. I didn't tell her about Melinda's son. That was too much. She smiled and said, "April, the greatest gift you could give this world would be for you to have two, maybe three children. You are so wonderful with kids, and you have so much love to give." I gave a gift to survivors by writing *Paperdolls* and lost everything. I love kids, but I really don't have much to give now. I smiled and said, "Maybe one day."

Her house was so warm. It smelled of cinnamon and Christmas spice. Soft Christmas music was playing in the background. I will always remember her sitting by the fire with her red and white Christmas quilt wrapped around her legs.

January 9, 1993

Wendy Hammond is in town. Dr. Crane, a professor and playwright at the U. held an open house for her. Wendy invited me. Wendy took me aside and wanted to know how I was doing. I told her about the "stake president" firing me, I told her about Karen's prognosis, and I told her I still hadn't figured out what I was going to do.

Wendy said that I reminded her of shattered glass.

January 10, 1993

We've had a mammoth snowstorm. It's been snowing continuously for three days in a row.

I took a long, hot bath after I tried to shovel the snow. As I was soaking in the tub, I watched more snow fall. I think the snow was a metaphor for my life right now. It just keeps on dumping: my family betrayed me again, my boss (the "stake president") at my new job blatantly lied to me then fired me, and now Karen is so sick she can't see me anymore. Her prognosis is terminal. I'm still hoping for six years rather than six months.

I submerged my head. When I surfaced, I took a deep breath and said out loud, "April get over yourself. The snow is falling on everyone, not just you. Everyone has losses. Everyone has been betrayed. Get over yourself. You don't have a corner on the market on pain and loss. You are an adult now. You haven't lost everything."

I laughed at myself, dried off and immediately grabbed a pen and paper and wrote down everything that I had: Gramps, Laurel and her boys, a house, a keen mind, a healthy body, a strong work ethic, awareness of my whole life and self and a strong desire to continue healing and to grow. And last I wrote: "hope."

I have hope. I have hope that I will truly find joy and be able to dance in the light.

February 26, 1993

I talked to Wendy Hammond tonight. She's in New York and the World Trade Center was bombed. The bomb was in the basement. The city is in shock. She said everyone is hyper-vigilant, on edge, waiting for another blast.

I said, "That's the modus operandi for kids in abusive homes, waiting for another bomb."

My new therapist is kind, loving and very supportive, but it's not the same. I don't feel like I can be as vulnerable.

A national publisher picked up the book and they want Carol and I to write an Epilogue. I've struggled with it. I finally wrote something that I believe is authentic. I didn't write that I was so out of balance I felt like putting on my old ball and chain again, but I did write about the analogy. I think the *Epilogue* rings true for me. Here it is:

"The month before *Paperdolls* was released in Utah, *Utah Holiday* Magazine published several excerpts from the book. One day, as I was standing at the laundromat sorting my socks, I noticed two women walk in with a basketful of laundry and a copy of the magazine. My heart jumped.

"They threw their whites into a washer, then sat down and read the magazine out loud to each other. They were reading my journal entries. I didn't stop folding, but I listened to every word. Pretty soon another young man was listening as well. One woman started crying. She mumbled something about her best friend having exactly this same thing happen to her. My eyes watered, and I opened my mouth like I was yawning.

"They will never know that the author was standing right by them, sorting her socks. I will never forget it. This experience gave me an indication of the response this book was to receive.

"I was unprepared for that response. I have received hundreds of letters. Most came from adult survivors of sexual abuse. Sometimes as I read the letters, I could feel the pain dripping from the pages, and I was staggered. Most thanked me for writing the book and giving another account that healing is possible. Some asked me for answers. I am not a therapist, and I can't give answers. A good therapist won't give answers for you but will ask questions and render support as you process your answers and make your own adjustments. The answers lie within you, within me, within each one of us.

"'Every time you heal a dark part of yourself, you bring more light into the world,' Stephen Paul wrote in *Illuminations*, and I agree. Recently, I had a telling experience where I witnessed the light passed on to our next generation.

"The week before Halloween, I was taking care of Laurel's sons Burton, Parker and their younger brother, Jason. Three-year-old Jason had a Halloween party at his preschool. When I picked him up, Jason was so thrilled to show me his treats and prizes that he bolted out the door. He was breathless as we sat on a bench. I was thrilled to see his joy with lollipop ghosts and crayoned witches. I noticed the woman in charge walking out of the school. She had a box full of pumpkins. When each car pulled up into the driveway, she took a pumpkin out of the box and gave it to a child as she or he got in the car. I had walked, and I felt a little awkward. I made a small sound like I was clearing my throat. The woman turned to me and said, 'Are you here for Jason?' I nodded. Her lips went tight as she said, 'Well, he doesn't get a pumpkin because he refused to do one.'

"I looked down at my three-year-old friend and said, 'Didn't you want a pumpkin?' Nonchalantly Jason said, 'We already have one.' I smiled. The woman clicked her tongue and said, 'Jason, all the other kids did one.' Jason wasn't affected. Very calmly he looked up at his teacher and said, 'We already have one.' Then Jason excitedly exclaimed, 'See my ghost?' And we walked home.

"There is hope for children like Jason, whose parents respect and listen to their voices. Jason is respected for who he is. Jason's parents are committed to breaking multi-generational chains. They are giving more light to the world.

"Our hope lies with the freeing power of healing. Jason's parents and I have healed dark parts of ourselves. My way of sharing my healing process has been *Paperdolls.*

"When I first began my healing process, years before I even started having memories, Karen Fisher told me the story about prisoners back in the 1800s who were shackled with a ball and chain. Of course, most of the prisoners complained about their ball and chain, but they didn't even realize how accustomed to the cumbersome object they had become—until they were released from prison. When the prisoners tried to move without their balls and chains, they lost their balance and fell. The astounding fact about this story is that most prisoners asked for their balls and chains back. It sounds ludicrous, but it's true. It was too scary to persevere through that imbalanced period of wobbly uncertainty.

"Maybe this is part of human nature; we become accustomed to the familiar and despite how ludicrous or painful it is, we cling to it. How many of us know of someone who stays in an abusive situation—even when that individual acknowledges it is abusive? How many of us do that ourselves? I certainly have.

"For a long time, I didn't realize that I had a ball and chain. I thought it was more of a support system like all humans had. Then I started switching balls and chains—going from one person to another, or one addiction to another. Finally, I settled on making the best of my ball and chain. I decorated it. I bought diamonds and accessorized it. For a ball and chain, it was beautiful. Ultimately, I realized that no matter how beautiful it appeared, it was still a ball and chain. So, I removed it. *Paperdolls* chronicles my process of letting go.

"I have had some wobbly moments. Now I'm gaining my equilibrium. I don't ever want chains back because I am free. I don't want to sound Pollyanna-ish or say I'm living happily ever after because I do have problems. But I have a sense of knowingness or a confidence that I have never known before. When a problem comes up, I have the tools to work through it. If the problem is reminiscent of the abuse or something triggers some 'old stuff' for me, I know what to do with it. If I start to feel overwhelmed, I have a gauge for myself. For example, I say to myself: 'This is painful, but not nearly as painful as remembering the abuse.' If something is painful, I might need to say to myself: 'This is horrible, but it's not as bad as the abuse itself—if you can survive that you can survive anything.'

"I'm actively working on myself with therapy and a support group, but sexual abuse is not the focus of my life. I remember when I was in the emergency stage of the memories—I couldn't conceive of a time when my mind wouldn't be obsessed with the subject. It was as if I had lost control of my mind, and my memories took over my life. It's not that way now. I have a full life and a stronger sense of self. I'm excited by the prospects of continually discovering myself and discovering the joy of life.

"Before *Paperdolls* was even published, I was nervous about telling such a personal story. Now I've realized that it is a personal experience for the reader as well. Anais Nin wrote: 'We don't see things as they are, we see them as we are.' The responses I've read are as vastly different and as touching as the individual experience the reader brings with them. For example, one person might get angry with the legal system; one might be furious with Hank; one might feel despair every time a connection is made with my voice as an innocent little girl; one might be frustrated with my mother; one might identify with Karen; and one might deny it or anything like it.

"Amidst our differences, there is an intricate weaving of the universality of the human spirit. I have a deep respect for the human capacity for suffering. I am astounded at the unending resilience of the human soul. I am in awe of the human capacity for love.

Carol

THE NIGHT OUR DOG HELGA died we were alone, Yvonne and I. There was a puddle of blood by the garage where Helga lay. Yvonne made the decision. She said Helga could not suffer.

I took Helga to the vet. Yvonne did not want to come. I think it was the first time I had left Yvonne alone in the house at night. I worried. On the table at the vet's, Helga looked at me as I held her trembling head. She quivered for less than a minute, for only a breath.

When Yvonne was a toddler, she'd poke her fingers in Helga's eyes and ears. Helga would lick her face all over, even her mouth. Yvonne drank her bottle lying on Helga's brown and golden hair with her fingers moving through the fur. I looked again in Helga's eyes. Helga was supposed to protect Yvonne. "I forgive you," I said. And Helga forgave me too.

I cannot breathe. I will never breathe again.

April

A MUFFLED TEAR, MY HEART. I feel the tear, and I wonder why my face is wet. I run to the bathroom gaze into the mirror. I am crying.

Karen Fisher is dead. My heart is ripped. Maybe my heart is made of paper.

Karen did not even say goodbye.

She pushed me to be so brave, to be real, and to speak my truth. Then she didn't have the courage to say goodbye. The paper heart pounding in my chest burst into flames and incinerated. I could taste the ashes in my mouth. I threw up. Hot angry tears sprang from my eyes.

I want to be April Daniels and rise from the ashes, again. The remnants of my char-colored heart stink like a dirty ash tray. The black dust tainted everything I touched.

I stop.

Enough. I've had enough.

I'd been so brave, told the truth, and as Karen said, "Be authentic and let the chips fall where they may."

I don't have any more chips.

Gramps and I went to the mortuary this evening. Karen loved Gramps. When they met, Gramps told Karen about his immigration from Norway to Utah. Karen commented that his lifespan saw so many changes; she couldn't think of a generation that had such dramatic change and technological advancement.

Gramps then told the story about when electricity was first installed in his childhood home. His mother, my great-grandmother, fell on her knees and thanked her Heavenly Father for the miracle of electricity. As Gramps told the story, he smirked. He had long since left the Mormon Church and frequently proclaimed that religion was made by men to cushion man's insecurities and was used by dictators to control the ignorant masses. He said that when he was young, he was ignorant. Gramps continued his story with one I'd heard all my life. When Gramps was seventeen years old, the Church called him on a three-year mission in Norway. He didn't leave his homeland. When he completed his mission, the

186

Church gave him a one-way ticket to Zion. He was promised numerous blessings and prosperity.

Gramps paused, then looked at Karen, held up his right index finger proclaiming, "I never received one blessing! I created my own blessings!" Karen was delighted. She laughed out loud.

Gramps was dignified and respectful at Karen's viewing. I had a hard time talking and Gramps conducted himself in his typical and consistent gentlemanly ways. He said all the right things extending sympathy and polite condolences at this time of loss. He was a buffer shielding my raw emotions.

Karen's partner had heard that I was upset that Karen hadn't said goodbye. She enfolded me in her arms, held me, and said, "April, Karen didn't know she was going to die. She really thought she had several more years. Then she got so sick so fast. She struggled to even breathe. She was in so much pain. Please know you were her 'Shining Star.' She loved all her clients, but you were special. She really loved you. You have to know that."

Tears brimmed over my eyes. I mumbled that I knew. Of course I knew. How ridiculous of me to be angry when she was suffering. How selfish and myopic of me to express anything when Karen's immediate family was grieving so deeply.

Why is this so hard for me? Even in my most dire times, I only saw her once or twice a week. I haven't seen her in months.

May 16, 1993

It snowed today. Yes, in May. I have a cherry tree in the backyard blossoming. It has a hint of snow on it, like powdered sugar. I remember an A. E. Housman poem, that ends:

"To see the cherry hung with snow."

I make a fire in my 100-year-old fireplace. Instead of planting petunias on this weird day in May, I'll gaze at the fire.

May 17, 1993

Today is the Norwegian Independence Day: 17th of May. Gramps and I have the Norwegian flag displayed high on our house, hanging out the top windows of my apartment. Today also would have been my grandmother's 93rd birthday. She died 11 years ago.

Karen died six days ago.

Gramps and I walk the dogs through the cemetery. At my grandmother's grave I watch the tattooed anchor on his right hand brush the leaves from her name. My anchor. I try to concentrate on anything but Karen, the funeral and her death. My eyes keep watering. He reaches over, patting my dog's head and says in

Norwegian, "There, der Lulleba, livet går opp på. Utleie oss gå now." ("There, there little one, life goes on. Let us go now.")

He isn't addressing the dog.

I planted geraniums and petunias in the garden. Gramps sat in his chair, sipping a soda and watched. Gramps declared, "It's paradise!" I can't help but smile. He finds joy in the simple things. He is so happy; he's going to ask my mother to come up to the house and see his flowers.

Since I left my parents' bank, my mother and father haven't entered the house. My mother comes up on rare occasions to help Gramps with something. My father won't come inside. He pulls up in front and waits. I haven't spoken to him since the day I told him I was leaving the family business. A year after I left the business, *Paperdolls* was published. My older nieces have told me that their mother, Melinda, doesn't believe it, "because the dates don't add up."

Per Karen's request, the identifying details, including the dates, were drastically changed to my family.

My sister doesn't talk to me because I called the children's psych hospital and informed my four-year-old nephew's doctor about key aspects of our family history: The sexual abuse. Melinda hasn't spoken to me since.

When I was little, two of my favorite Bible stories were: *Daniel and the Lions' Den* and *Joseph and his Multi-Colored Coat*. It's obvious why I loved the story of Daniel surviving the night with the lions. As time goes on, I understand more and more why I loved the story of Joseph. He was his father's favorite, cast in a hole and sold, then triumphantly ruling when his brothers had to come to him and beg for help. I know I was the "favorite." I was despised by my siblings and betrayed by them.

Karen always said that I am much stronger than I think I am. I'm not so sure. I feel like I'm free falling to my demise. I have to snap out of this. I have to figure out what I'm going to do. If I didn't have Gramps, I don't know what I'd do. He is my anchor.

He came over here to America without knowing the language. He was promised a slew of blessings because he left his homeland and came to Utah to build up Zion. When he got here, he was ostracized for being a foreigner and taking all the Americans' jobs. He was an educated man, well spoken, thoughtful, with a lot to contribute. He was only able to obtain manual labor positions. He said that he "shoveled shit" in order to feed his family. He felt completely betrayed by the Church for promising him so much and then shunning him for coming here.

If Gramps could do it without any support in such a foreign land, so can I. I can do this. I'll shovel shit if I must. I refuse to ask for my "ball and chain" back. I know I'm out of balance, but I believe there is a better way to live. I can build my own beautiful life. I simply must figure out how.

June 7, 1993

The new edition of *Paperdolls* was released this week nationally. I took a copy over to Karen's family. It has been hard for them—they lost their mother.

I'm not sure why this is so hard for me.

Karen often reinforced that I was to be "real" and "authentic." Then again, one of my old running coaches used to always say, "Shoot for the stars, and even if you miss, you'll end up in a pretty high place." He used to say, "Fake it 'til you make it," and one of my favorite lines was, "Act as if and soon you will become."

I think Karen would be okay with me "Acting as if until I become" right now. I don't want to be sniveling around whimpering that I've lost everything. I want to be empowered and strong. I'll act as if and hopefully soon I will become.

July 4, 1993

I walked to the cemetery and watched the fireworks tonight. I'm trying to remember a time when I wasn't so sad—and I can't. Maybe after I was baptized in 2nd grade, maybe.

Was I ever happy?

Right after the family healing meeting, I was hopeful. I thought that all the junk of our lives could be dealt with or at least released. I thought we could start fresh with a new and pure focus for our health and prosperity. My family is talented, and I thought together we could do anything. I had no idea that the forces against change would be so strong.

I am lonely, although I see. I feel. I smell. I have to have faith that I won't be as lonely, that I will find others who can see the light also.

July 22, 1993

I feel aimless. I have no purpose.

July 24, 1993

Today is the official Utah State Holiday. This is the day when the Mormon pioneers arrived in Salt Lake. Legend has it that Brigham Young stood at the mouth of the canyon overlooking the valley and declared, "This is the place."

Gramps and I planned on sitting on the front porch to watch the fireworks. I grilled a couple of hamburgers. Gramps was already sitting on his favorite chair on the porch. I walked up behind him and said, "Here you go, Gramps! Hot off the grill especially for you!" He didn't respond.

My heart sank as I touched his shoulder. He slowly looked up at me. I said, "Gramps, is everything okay?"

He said, "No, I'm lonely. I miss Mama."

He meant my grandmother. Sometimes, I think he forgets that I'm not his daughter. I knelt beside him and gave him a hug. I said, "Gramps, I know you do. I can't imagine how hard it is, especially on holidays."

He swallowed a cry and said, "I miss her every day, but especially on the holidays."

He never even kissed another girl. She was the love of his life. On Valentine's Day in 1982, my grandmother had a stroke. She died later that evening.

Gramps and I watched the fireworks in silence. After he finished his hamburger, he said he was too tired to wait for the finale. I helped him to his room. At the door, I listened until he was in bed.

August 5, 1993

I maintained a relationship with the company that backed the custom program I designed for my last job. One of their executives called me today. He was pretty upset with my employers. Apparently, my last employer purchased another rather large bank in Boise. This Boise bank was my main competition when I was developing the exclusive program for them. Now my competitors will be selling the product I developed.

I know for sure that the stake president manipulated my exit. I bet he was too uncomfortable having me around to remind him of his cowardice. I represent everything he didn't do when the Scotts were going through their hell.

On a more positive note, my contact said that he might have a good lead for a job for me. It's an up-and-coming bank in Oregon. He said that he met with them last week, and they seemed really interested in receiving my resume.

August 7, 1993

The bank in Oregon called me today. I chatted with two managers for almost an hour. It's promising. They are going to fly me up to Oregon for an in-person interview! I'm worried about Gramps, but I must get a job. I'm going to keep my fingers crossed that there will be some way I can spend most of my time here. From the conversation I had with them today, it might be possible.

August 10, 1993

I called Laurel today and Parker answered the phone. Today, Parker politely said, "No, you may not speak with my mom because she is in time out." I tried not to laugh. I asked him what his mother had done wrong. She said a bad word, "Shoot." The boys put her in time out for 30 minutes. It's one minute for each year. She's a smidge older than 30, but that's as high as they can count.

About 45 minutes later, Laurel returned my call. She was laughing. She said that's the best punishment she's ever had. The boys set the timer, and she sat in the corner and read. They didn't leave the kitchen because they wanted to make sure she didn't get off her chair.

What a joy! I have a hunch those boys will never forget putting their mom in time-out after she said a naughty word.

August 17, 1993

Karen Fisher was my lifeline. She told me that I was pretty much done with my therapy, except for a few minor issues. Denial is such a powerful coping mechanism that I'm afraid I can easily kid myself about myself. Karen told me not to worry about that because I was so much more conscious of my pain and have healed so many of my childhood issues. I have to remember that. I have to be able to trust my instincts.

August 21, 1993

I can get myself in a focused and productive place. Frequently I'll forget and think, "I need to remember to tell Karen about that." Then my heart drops and I have to sit down. Sometimes I can't breathe until I say to myself, "She's gone, you'll be okay. Go easy on yourself. This will take time."

August 22, 1993

It's dark still. I woke up with this thought: "Those we have loved remain in our hearts." I was thinking about Karen. I think one of the struggles I've had with Karen's death is trying to justify my sadness. The questions she asked me to help me discover myself will be with me always. When I get anxious or unsure, I can ask those questions to myself. She will be in my heart always.

August 23, 1993

I have something called a sound card for this computer. I plugged a microphone into the sound card. Gramps always whistles as he putters around the house. This afternoon, I asked Gramps to come upstairs. I held the computer's microphone out and asked him to whistle one of the old Norwegian Folk songs, called *"The Nightingale's Song."* After I played it back for him, and he laughed and said, "I like that!"

September 4, 1993

Parker was baptized today. It was such a joyous event! He beamed when he came out of the water. He is such a charming and adorable boy. I'm sitting here listening to Burton and Parker discuss the day. Parker said that he could truly feel the Holy Ghost.

There are so many people who are critical of Mormons, and even critical of all religions. Gramps says, "Man-made religion out of his own insecurity." He says that more wars have been fought in the name of religion than any other cause.

Gramps might be right on the cause of war. The Christian Crusades weren't exactly Christlike. However, the Mormon religion teaches us to be Christlike; to be of service to others; be loving and kind; work hard; contribute to society; be honest in all your doings; be humble and thankful for your blessings; and so many other wonderful values that simply feel right to me.

There is goodness and joy in the world. I need to be around it more and embrace it.

September 15, 1993

The bank in Oregon offered me a job: a base salary with commission.

October 17, 1993

I love fall. The autumn air is crisp, and the mountains are so beautiful. My new work is challenging, but not daunting. I still have trouble sleeping. I feel like I have a pool of sadness deep in my soul. It's always there and I don't know what to do with it. So, I just go on. I try to be as productive as possible. Sometimes, I'm just too sad to notice the beauty in my days.

I force myself to keep moving. I make a list of things I must do; and as I complete each task, I make a large check mark by my completed task. Those check marks get me through my saddest days. Sometimes, I worry that I'll drown in it. So, I take out my list. There's a famous quote by Winston Churchill that I think of often:

"If you are going through hell, keep going."

I'll keep going.

I haven't spoken to my father or brother since I left their bank. I see my mother when she visits Gramps. She doesn't say much. We exchange greetings with as much meaning as the checkout clerk at the grocery store: "How are you today?" "Fine." "Good to hear." "Have a nice day."

November 13, 1993

I hate the sound of someone's wheels spinning. My neighbor's car was snowplowed in yesterday. They are trying to get the car out of the embankment created by all that thrown snow. The wheels are spinning and spinning. I hate that sound.

When I write, that's how I feel. I'm just spinning and spinning the same old stuff. I don't have any emotional traction to get out of this rut. I need something to hold onto so I can pull myself out.

I hate the sound of wheels spinning on the ice.

November 25, 1993

It's Thanksgiving. Laurel invited me to St. George. I should have gone there. I have to get out of this funk. Each night, I make my to-do list. Then spend the day checking off the items. I need to put on my list, be happy, find joy, reach out, or something. The only reason that I don't have any place to go for Thanksgiving dinner is simply because I chose not to go. I am responsible for where I am.

December 7, 1993

Gramps and I took our picture for our annual Christmas card picture. Brent, the guy I've been dating took the picture. Every time he'd try to get the dogs to look up, Gramps would look down at the dogs. Then, click, another shot with the dogs looking up and the top of Gramps' hat! We finally just started laughing at our comedy of errors. We burned through an entire roll of film and then ran to a one hour photo shop. Fortunately, we had one-photo that turned out adorable. Gramps looks so proud, the dogs are looking up, and I look okay. We look happy. We gave one to Gramps, and he has it on his refrigerator door.

December 18, 1993

Years ago, I read "*The Color Purple*" by Alice Walker. Today, I kept thinking of this line:

"I think it pisses God off if you walk by the color purple in a field somewhere and don't notice it." I haven't noticed the color purple or a rainbow in the sky for such a long time. The sky was golden tonight with the setting sun, and I noticed. The air was cold tonight, and I could see my breath as I walked back in the house; but my heart was warm.

I am not just going to survive. I am going to thrive. I'm not sure what will unfold for me, but I'm going to be happy, or at least strive to be happy. That will be enough.

December 25, 1993

It's early and very quiet. I can hear Gramps; he's probably making the cocoa. He invited me down for a Christmas breakfast: white toast with about an inch of butter, salami, eggs with anchovies on top. Gramps is 92, and I can't believe his arteries aren't completely clogged. He loves these Norwegian foods — the more salt the better.

After breakfast, I'm going skiing then over to a friend's for dinner. I know Karen always wanted me to be authentic. But right now, my motto is: "Fake it 'til you make it." I'm going to pretend to be happy and hopefully my heart will catch up with my actions.

February 14, 1994

Today would have been my grandparents' wedding anniversary. Gramps is quite sad. We stood in the entry of our house and looked at the many pictures of his sweetheart. Gramps has a picture of my uncle, who killed himself. Gramps found him, and my father helped clean up the room and all the blood. A few years ago, I was stripping and repainting that bedroom—and I found the bullet. Tonight, I was standing in the entryway ready to deliver Gramps' dinner. He reached up and took down my uncle's picture. He murmured something about his son. He said it so softly I couldn't quite understand it. Then he looked up at me and wiped his eyes. I touched my grandfather's shoulder.

It's ingrained in us to protect our children. My grandfather's grief filled the room. In silence, we lingered in the chilly entryway.

Eight years ago today, the Scott children began to tell of their abuse and trauma. I pray this day will bring them love and hope. I pray our efforts of writing *Paperdolls* will help peel back a small layer of denial in our society. I pray it has saved at least one life.

March 12, 1994

It's my birthday. Gramps took the bus downtown to buy me a birthday cupcake at ZCMI.

March 17, 1994

My niece, Melinda's oldest daughter, got married today. I haven't had much interaction with these nieces because Melinda divorced their father when they were quite young.

Right after *Paperdolls* came out, Melinda called me and said, "I want to talk to you about the book my daughter is reading."

"Okay," I said.

"She's reading *Paperdolls*."

"Okay," I said.

"Well, why is she reading it?"

"I have no idea. Why do you think she's reading it?"

"Did you give it to her?"

"No, Melinda."

"Well, maybe her therapist asked her to read it."

"I didn't know she was in therapy, that's great."

Silence.

"Well, if she calls, will you promise not to tell her that you wrote the book?"

"I can't promise that. But I can promise that if she calls, I'll let you know I talked to her."

My niece never called. I have no idea if she knows I wrote the book.

Later:

The wedding was beautiful. My niece came up to me and gave me a big hug and thanked me for coming. Melinda ignored me. Byron ignored me. My parents ignored me.

April 2, 1994

Work is going well. We have a slew of solid prospects and proposals out. Many municipalities and other local governments have their fiscal year ending July 1. If all goes well, this will be a nice summer. At least I can do something right.

My job involves interviewing bankers throughout the nation that have enough savvy, experience, insurance, and funding to sell our products. We have a sophisticated filtering process before we approach a potential banker. The bank must have 20 years in business, experience with bonds, millions in reserve, several layers of re-insurance, and maintain high levels of malpractice insurance.

After we identify two or three banks in each state, my job is to go out to their locations and meet with the key bankers and executives in person. Then, I narrow it down to only one or possibly two bankers per state. My bosses have been thrilled with my appointments. Maybe that's a silver lining from all my therapy, I can seem real and authentic more easily.

As a bonus, I have a profound appreciation for all that my mother and father did for us professionally. Obviously, the banking and business advancements won't make up for the abuse and alcoholism. However, the professional stage they handed to us is an extraordinary gift. We were given a rare springboard to generate lucrative and prosperous lives.

By the way, I met with my parents' company and granted them an appointment. My brother didn't attend the meeting he sent his assistant. My parents' company will be selling our products. Thank you, mom and dad.

June 1, 1994

I was on-site at a large bid opening today. Byron was there also. We were awarded the proposal. After it was announced, all these men gathered around me to congratulate me. They were all laughing and joking. Several of them will make a great deal of money with this account. Out of the corner of my eye, I watched my brother slowly shuffle out of the room. I always thought it would feel good to beat him, especially since he told his boys they couldn't ever talk to me again. I was wrong; it didn't feel very good.

We had the best year in the bank's history. The Bonding Department has almost doubled in size. My boss credits most of our growth to my marketing efforts. I'm trying not to minimize these compliments, but I know that it takes a team. One can market all day long, but if you don't have a product and service to back it up, nothing happens.

I'm down. I'm sure it's the letdown after the big push and celebration. I'm not motivated. There's not much to do right now. My boss wants me to take some time off, relax and get rejuvenated. He doesn't want me burned out. I am tired.

My boss bought a brand-new Corvette and has personalized license plates that say, "Blessed." He is. As for me, I haven't even cashed my bonus check yet. Maybe it has to do with money and my abuse.

This afternoon, Gramps and I walked up to the cemetery to my uncle's grave. It would have been his birthday. He would have been 67 years old. Gramps is 92 years old now. He wanted to walk. Gramps bent over and placed a single red rose from our garden on the grave. Silently he removed his dark glasses and wiped his eyes.

It's been five years since I remembered. I can feel now. I know why I am the way I am. I understand why I'm leery of my neighbors.

Every time I hear Gramps conversing with a neighbor my heart skips a beat. Then I swallow and remind myself that's old stuff. I doubt I'll ever sit on the porch and chat with the neighbors—but at least I know why.

I've been water coloring. It helps my anxiety to paint. After a few minutes I noticed a few tears blurring my work. Everything blurred. Sometimes that's how I feel about my life. I can't cry, or everything will blur.

October 17, 1994

My tears keep leaking out. Today I tried to go shopping for some new clothes. I am a boring and conservative dresser. The clothes racks today were filled with vivid colors. I thought of colorful, gorgeous peacocks. The most colorful ones are the males. The bland, brown peacocks are female. Color attracts attention from predators. I dress boringly so I don't attract attention from predators. I was standing right in the middle of Nordstroms, and I couldn't get my tears to stop. Will I always have latent residual effects of this childhood abuse?

October 24, 1994

I don't like my life. I have done everything I was supposed to do to heal, and I lost everything. I wish that I could die in a car accident or something; then I'd be off the hook.

I know Laurel is here for me, and it would break her heart if something happened to me. But I've been such a burden to her. I can't burden her with this last battle I'm fighting right now. I'm vacant and alone. I'm not sure life is worth living. I've fought so hard to get here and for what? I saved my pride by getting another great job—and better. I enjoy the corporate game of drumming up more business. Maybe I'm thinking too much. Then again, maybe I don't have what it takes to build a healthy and happy life.

November 7, 1994

I told my therapist how I'm feeling. I told her how easy it would be to be driving down the freeway in Idaho somewhere and careen off the road.

I'm going to go back on antidepressants. I'll be meeting with her three times a week.

November 13, 1994

My therapist asked me if there was any place I'd like to go to relax. I told her I love Carol's place in Coronado. My therapist picked up the phone, and we called Carol. I'm going to Coronado for a couple of weeks to relax.

November 21, 1994

I'm in Coronado. Norton and Carol's place is right on the ocean. My bedroom overlooks the ocean, and I was lulled to sleep listening to the waves crash against the rocky shore. The sky is gray with streaks of pink warming the new day. If anything will bring me out of my funk, it is this place. My therapist was right to call Carol.

I'm rereading *A Gift from the Sea* by Anne Marrow Lindberg. Lindberg's personal life was shattered when her son was kidnapped and tragically killed. I always thought Lindberg's time by the sea helped her heal. Maybe it will for me also.

One time when I hiked Zion's Canyon, I forgot my camera. I decided to try to take "mental pictures." I would pause and really look at the incredible views. It only took a few seconds, but I really noticed every detail I could. I said to myself, "Instill this, remember it." And I have. I still have those mental images with me.

I want to take the beauty and serenity of this place with me always. I don't want to go back and shut down all my emotions with activity and work. I want to keep this with me somehow: mental pictures.

I hate to admit that I feel so flat in such a gorgeous place. I guess it's true, what you have on the inside is what you see on the outside. Lindbergh's words are helping:

> I do not believe that sheer suffering teaches. If suffering alone taught, all the world would be wise, since everyone suffers. To suffering must be added mourning, understanding, patience, love, openness, and the willingness to remain vulnerable.
> —Anne Morrow Lindbergh, *Gift from the Sea*

I have suffered, but I am not wise. I have not grown. I am not open. I have been a human doing, not a human being. With my checklists, productivity and work, I have shut down. I have not even remotely been vulnerable. My fears have blocked my ability to even notice the simple joys of my everyday life.

I've been so afraid of loss that I haven't even noticed the simple yet profound beauty of my life.

I know being in a place like this really helps. Pausing and noticing the beauty is important. I am paying attention. Lindbergh's words have reinforced my commitment to continue healing and growing. I can be open and vulnerable again.

I have been afraid to feel anything because I thought that if I started feeling I would only feel bad. I think the positives in my life outweigh the negatives. Today is Thanksgiving. Today is a day of gratitude. I'm going focus on the positive and all that for which I have to be thankful.

I have an incredible support system: who else has close friends with a beautiful beach home where I can convalesce? Norton and Carol have been amazing to me. They care about me. Laurel and her entire family are there for me. She calls every day to check on me. Gramps is worried. He's 92 years old and would still do anything for me. I have a great job; my bosses in Oregon almost pushed me to take this time off. I have a wonderful work ethic and a desire to improve.

I think it's all my old fears and shame that is laced with my fear of loss. I have to remember Boss's advice: No one can ever hurt me like that again.

Dum spiro spero: "While I breathe, I hope."

Later:

I am on the beach. The reflection of the waning moon glistens on the quiet tide. I can feel. I intend to feel the positive.

I have always felt that there are equal portions of positive and negative in the world. Now I'm wondering if there is more positive than negative. I'm afraid of feeling the pain of the negative so much that I've shut down so much feeling. I must become aware. Notice. Maybe it's all about what one thinks about.

Not in some superficial way though. I mean what one deeply believes in their core. My core has been damaged, then I started rebuilding it, then I shut down to survive. I didn't shut down like I did when I was a kid, but I still went on autopilot. I didn't feel as much. Now I'm feeling and I'm feeling the positive also.

I do have so much to be grateful for on this blessed Thanksgiving Day.

November 26, 1994

Probably for most people, it's easier to be positive, optimistic and happy. I think for me, I must concentrate twice as hard on the positive elements in my life. I bet that because my developmental years were so damaging. It felt like at any given moment a land mine would explode. I know that most people are good, but deep in my heart, I fear.

November 27, 1994

I'm going to take positive mental pictures several times a day. It doesn't have to be a big deal, just something simple. I watched two turtles playing on the rocks this morning. I felt the sun on my face, the cool sand crunch against my toes and breathed in the fresh ocean breeze.

I know when I go home, I won't have such gloriously beautiful scenes to absorb, but I'll have some. Even if I notice the scent of an orange as I peel it. The key for me will be to pay attention. Notice. Absorb the positive in the miniscule everyday events. I think that will help sustain me and help override my nagging anxiety and sadness.

November 28, 1994

I'm ashamed that I felt so bad when Karen died. I'm ashamed that I shut down emotionally for the last year. When Karen died, I couldn't cope with it. I'm not exactly sure why because she was just my therapist. I kind of think she made a mistake by not saying goodbye to me. What if she made other mistakes? I couldn't deal with these questions. I shut down and went to work.

I'm not sure if I can deal with these questions now. It's unresolved. The therapeutic relationship is such a weird thing; I mean I hardly knew anything about her. I know nothing about the last months of her life. Maybe she did feel good enough to go to a movie in March two months before her death.

I'll never know. I'll know I've realized so much about myself—primarily because of her poignant questions and her skills. She was a good therapist; I'm here, aren't I? Many of those in my childhood neighborhood are sick, dead or worse.

I guess it's not so bad having my relationship with her unresolved. One of her frequent catch phrases for me was, "April, frame it up so it fits." I can't frame this up with anything, and it certainly doesn't fit. I don't know anyone who has had their therapist die.

Later:

I found this beautiful blue bottle at the swap meet yesterday. The guy said it was Italian. It's made of glass and has a tight lid. As cliché as this sounds, I decided to write a letter to Karen and stick it in this bottle. Then throw it over the cliffs into the sea. Here it is:

Dear Karen,

I didn't know what to do with my feelings about your death—so I stuffed them. I often quoted you and said to myself, "April, compartmentalize them and take those feelings out later."

Well, it's later. I still don't know what to do with these feelings. I don't feel like I should grieve you. You were only my therapist. You weren't my family or even a close friend. I paid you. I paid you to help me. Now why can't I let you go and continue paying someone else? Why do I have all these weird, sad feelings of loss when I think of you?

First, I don't think I'm as strong as you seemed to have thought I am. I had months to prepare for your death, and I still wasn't ready.

Next, I'm mad at you for not saying goodbye. I know, I know, you were so sick you died. I guess I can forgive you for all that, except you pushed me to be so brave. That family meeting wasn't easy, and publishing the book, sheesh I never knew so many people would be so deeply affected. I had no idea that there would be such a backlash.

You were right that I should protect my identity. Although those involved have instantly recognized me. I lost my great job because of the "stake president." If I hadn't published the book, I probably would still have that job. If I hadn't gone to the General Authorities, I might have still been at Mountain View with my family. Despite losing all that money, at least I still have my soul. It's worth much more than 30 pieces of silver.

You were right.

I'm writing as if you told me what to do. I know you didn't. You'd question me so I could figure out what was happening inside of me. But sometimes by your questions I could tell how you felt. I knew you were happy when I left Mountain View.

I guess I'm down to my most raw fear and feeling: Karen, was my case too much for you? Did it take so much of your psychic energy that it drained your ability to fight the cancer that was set lose through your body? The cancer that was diagnosed right after the family meeting.

I'm going to pretend that you'll get this letter. I'm going to pretend I know your response: "Of course not. April, you don't have that much power, and I'm in charge of me."

I know it's ludicrous. One person isn't that powerful. No matter how horrific my childhood was, it wasn't like some radioactive waste that you carelessly handled and caused your cells to replicate uncontrollably to your demise. Or was it? Did you take in more than you should have? If you did, I'm so sorry. I'm mad at you. You should have been more careful, set better boundaries. You, who was in the midst of writing a book on boundaries at your death: you knew better.

There, now that I wrote it, I know the exertion of handling my case didn't kill you. It sure would have been nice to hear it from you. I wish that you had said goodbye.

Since I'm pretending that you'll get this, I'm going to pretend that you said goodbye. I'm going to pretend what you said:

"Oh April, don't ever forget how strong you are. You've been through the hardest part. You might not have developed all the tools yet to cultivate a happy and peaceful life, but normal people spend their entire lives cultivating those skills. Remember, you are a process. As we all are. Yes, April, I made a mistake. I should have said goodbye. I wasn't as brave as you are in saying the hard things to those you love. But I didn't make a mistake about you. You are one in a million. You are strong. You are loving. You are on your way to continue cultivating a beautifully authentic life. I love you. You'll have a part of me with you always. You are not alone. Goodbye and God bless you. "

Karen, I love you too. And you are forgiven. We all make mistakes, and not saying goodbye isn't that big of a deal. I know you are here with me always.

Goodbye: God Bless you too.

I feel better. I'm nervous about going back to my routine. When I am hurt, I don't want to ignore or stuff my pain. I need to feel it, deal with it and let it dissipate. I don't want to end up right back on this suicidal edge again. I'm scared because I'm not convinced my life is worth living. I hope it is.

After the "stake president" fired me and Karen died, I hurled myself into a mindless activity pattern. When I paused, I reflected, and I felt. I couldn't process that much loss.

"And if you gaze long enough into an abyss, the abyss will gaze back into you."

—Friedrich Nietzsche

It's much better to deal with issues when they come up. If I can't right then, as soon as possible, I need to deal with my stuff. I stuffed and then couldn't cope with it all. I didn't know how to deal with it all at once. I spent far too long gazing into the abyss and the abyss almost engulfed me. I almost fell. I don't ever want to be on this edge again.

When I ski, I know that wherever I look, I will go. If I'm worried about missing some rocks, and I keep looking at them, sure enough, I'll head right towards those rocks. When I traverse a precarious cliff, I concentrate on looking ahead and not looking at the cliff. For where I look, I go. I have to concentrate on the light—the positive and beautiful aspects of my life. They are there. Everywhere. I simply cannot gaze into the abyss anymore. I am facing the light and letting the shadows fall behind me.

Karen used to always say that we learn things intellectually first, and then our feelings catch up. Years ago John Bradshaw said that emotions are "energy in motion." If that is true, possibly if I can experience some new emotions, such as joy—that life is worth living—it will embed into my psyche more positive feelings and beliefs about my life and the worth of my existence.

What brings me joy? I can't even believe I have to think about this; I simply can't beat myself up about it right now. I need to settle down, be patient with myself and ponder about what brings me joy.

Later:

I walked barefoot along the beach and occasionally the waves splashed up past my knees. As I felt the soft breeze caress my hair and the sun warm my back, I came up with this list of things that bring me joy and shift my thoughts from a negative spiral. Here's my start:

- The sunlight glistening on the dogs' coats as they romp in the yard.
- Birds singing in thanks as I feed their bird feeders.
- Gramps's smile when I finish planting the flowers.
- The hope of planting fall bulbs. I ponder the infinite beauty of the tiny brown bulbs and visualize the glorious blooms breaking up through the snow.

I think that I'm going to come up with 365 of these. Put them on some 3 x 5 index cards and read one every morning. I have to remember that the down times are temporary. The sun will rise again.

December 1, 1994

As I walked along the beach today it seemed that the waves curling to the shore were symbolic of my prior anxiety: Waves of anxiety were pulsating through my body. I'm going home this weekend. What if I can't sustain this balance and sense of peace? What if I can only be okay on a gorgeous beach in paradise? I can't make a big lifestyle change, like come and live on this beach forever. When I get back to my job with all its stressors, I can take mental breaks throughout the day and notice small joys surrounding me. I might have set an alarm or something to remind myself to take mental breaks periodically throughout the day. During those breaks, I want to notice anything nice. Even if it's something as simple as the smell of an orange as I peel it. I tend to think about things while I'm doing the simple, routine stuff. I intend to pay attention. I hope noticing these simple positive elements surrounding me becomes part of my repertoire of my beliefs and foundational feelings.

I'm okay. I'm not thinking about killing myself; I'm thinking about how to better know myself. I'm grappling with how to become more aware of my core beliefs and how to plant more positive experiences into my psyche.

Carol

SIX YEARS AFTER OUR FIRST KNOWLEDGE of Hank's abuse, Susy's husband arranged a meeting with Hank's new bishop, his stake president, Yvonne, Susy, her husband, Norton and me. We told these church leaders the complete story of the abuse of our grandchildren, of other children who had accused him, of molestations committed during his adolescence and of adult women including April who testified of his abuse when they were children. We also told him we knew he had recently been fired from the State Tax Commission for sexually harassing a young employee. They already knew that because they were helping him with his house payments due to his unemployment.

The stake president and bishop seemed to believe our story but said they would have to consult the church legal department before any action could be taken, an unusual procedure in the church court system. The bishop asked us how he should protect Hank's stepdaughters. He said, "Hank's wife is a very devout wife." They said they'd let us know what church discipline would be taken. No one ever got back to us. We believe the lack of church response was due to Hank's connection to the Apostle's daughter and son-in-law.

Ten years after my grandchildren told, Hank's brother called Jake. He'd gone to high school with Jake. He flatly stated, "Hank committed suicide last night, and I thought your family should know." He said that he, himself, was alienated from his family; and he knew Hank had serious problems. There would be only a graveside service, as the obituary in the paper confirmed. Hank's wife had appeared at Lorraine's front door that very same day and said she had to talk to Lorraine. She had only ever insulted Lorraine before; she'd fought fiercely for Hank in the many court appearances while Hank tried to get custody of Lorraine's and his kids. This wife had told Lorraine the children should be in Hank's home where the gospel was lived, and the women trusted the priesthood. Hank's wife now told Lorraine that in the spring her two oldest daughters, then ages 12 and 14, had told her that Hank was sexually abusing them. She had threatened Hank with divorce and with going to the police. He left their home. That summer Hank went to Arizona to work for three months. Her children continued their disclosures to their mother as did Hank's 3-year-old and 6-year-old. His wife again threatened Hank by phone with police action. In early fall, Hank's mother drove to Arizona to bring Hank back to Salt Lake. On the way home, they got several drug prescriptions for sedatives. Hank went to bed at his mother's home and was found by her the next morning, dead by overdose of prescription drugs. His wife kept crying to Lorraine. "What shall I do? What shall I do?"

Norton and I called her on the phone that very day. She said she thought Hank's mother knew he was going to kill himself and in a way was an accomplice. Hank's wife thought his mother was afraid she would be incriminated if Hank were arrested. Hank left a note to his stepdaughters saying he'd never hurt them and that Heavenly Father would understand. (He'd once sent a note to Timothy on his birthday saying the therapists had planted things in Timothy's brain, and Heavenly Father knew Hank was innocent).

Hank's wife told us that her kids were a mess—the oldest one spent most of her day curled in a fetal position in her room. Her girls felt very guilty for Hank's death. We told her we would pay for therapy for her children, but she never called us back. She said this oldest girl had been to the bishop and told him Hank was physically abusing her, but the bishop had never told Hank's wife of the girl's complaint, or that other adults had asserted to him that Hank was a pedophile. Norton told Hank's wife that she probably had a legal case against the church; but the church was helping her financially, and she didn't want to pursue it. We've never spoken to her since. As far as we know, nothing ever happened legally or in church action to Hank's mother or to any of the perpetrators in the child sex ring.

Hank's death was a cause of both shock and rejoicing in our family. Some of us were able to hate him considerably less. Susy and Yvonne had fewer nightmares. We agreed suicide was the best action he ever chose, even if his decision was motivated by fear of incarceration. We all felt the world was a little safer place after the morning his mother found him dead. And me? How did I react? Over and over again the words ran through my mind, "If Hank's mother had been mine, who would I be now?" And yet ... over the years I have come to believe that the radical morality advocated by Jesus Christ is the most profound and creative product humans have yet produced. To be as concerned with another's well-being as one's own, beyond the relationship of kin or friend, is hard to imagine. I believe an attempt to embrace this morality, however imperfectly, is the only thing that will save humankind from itself. Implicit in this philosophy is the exhortation to forgiveness.

After Hank's betrayal of our family, I wanted never to forgive him. I don't believe forgiveness can be given on behalf of another or that anyone should be exhorted to forgive. It comes, as it will, like a bodily response. I'm not sure it can be "worked upon." Perhaps it falls, like Portia's "gentle dew from heaven."

April

CAROL CALLED TODAY AND LEFT a message on my answering machine. Hank killed himself.

I'm shocked. During the last few weeks, the new wife's teenage daughters revealed that Hank was also abusing them. They separated. This "new wife" took their six-year-old boy up to Primary Children's Hospital. They found irrefutable evidence that this little boy had been sexually abused.

The new wife told Carol she'd screamed at Hank: "The Scotts let you off the hook ten years ago, but I'll see to it that you rot in jail for the rest of your life."

Hank killed himself. I guess he OD'd. Sounds like his mother helped him or something.

I'm stunned.

My mother came up to visit Gramps today. I ran out to the sidewalk to tell her about Hank.

She already knew. Hank had called my brother before he did it. I called my sister. She said that Hank had called Byron at the office. She didn't know the details, but my sister knew Hank was dead. I thought he was an awful coward.

I told my sister, "I believe people can change. I believe he could have changed. He could have spent the time in jail, got tons of therapy, and spent the rest of his life trying to make it up to his victims. Trying to make it up to everyone! He'll be in more hell now because there won't be any way for him to even try to make restitution!"

My sister was silent. I think she mumbled something like, "We don't know that."

I said, "Oh come on, there are tons of testimonials of those who have had after-death experiences. The most miserable souls are those who have taken their own lives."

Silence.

I called another friend who knew about Hank from high school. She had read *Paperdolls.* This dear friend is a very active member of the Church. Her husband is

206

in the bishopric, and she is the primary president. After *Paperdolls* was published, several of her high school friends stated that they had been abused by Hank. This dear, sweet friend cheered when she heard that Hank was dead. She was relieved that Hank wouldn't be able to abuse any more children.

I made more phone calls to more friends and slowly realized that I am shockingly unique in my perspective. I am the only one I know who believes Hank shouldn't have killed himself. Not all cheered, but everyone I talked to was relieved. The world is better off without him.

I called my former boss, whom I refer to as the "stake president." My call went straight to his voice mail. After the smooth "stake president's" voice ended with the standard "beep," I said, "Hi, it's April. I'm not sure you are aware of this, but Hank killed himself last night. I believe it is such a tragedy, especially since his soul was under your stewardship for so very long. Apparently, his new wife found irrefutable medical evidence that Hank was abusing their six-year-old son. She told him that she wasn't going to let him off the hook like the Scotts did ten years ago, and she was going to see to it that he went to jail. So, he killed himself."

Greg Schmeid called me back and agreed that it was a tragedy. He quoted some scripture and I envisioned someone tying something around their necks and drowning themselves. I hadn't ever heard that scripture before. He said, "Yes, it's right in the Bible. It's better to kill yourself than hurt a child."

I was silent.

Then Schmeid congratulated me on what a great job I was doing at work. He received good reports from some of his top producers about our innovative product line and the sales results.

I mumbled thanks and hung up. How can he live with himself? I don't wish the stake president dead or anything, but where is his soul? Does he even have a conscience?

I firmly believe that anyone can change. Hank could have and maybe the "stake president" will. For his sake, I hope so.

October 30, 1995

Years ago, I read Maya Angelou's *I know Why A Caged Bird Sings*. As a child, Angelou was raped. She told. The man was killed. Maya Angelou felt that her telling killed the man. She didn't speak for several years.

As a child she thought it was her fault.

Hank chose to be a coward. He chose to kill himself.

An illogical, childish fear has seeped up to my consciousness: what if I hadn't written *Paperdolls*? Would he still be alive?

I scoff at how ludicrous the question is; but in a small way, I do understand how a small child named Maya in 1930s Arkansas told, a man was killed, and the girl who told thought she was responsible.

Possibly some old fears and old programming are surfacing, "Don't tell!" "If you tell, really bad things will happen!" I told. It has nothing to do with Hank's suicide.

After Maya Angelou regained her speech, she became one of the greatest voices in America.

If all victims and survivors tell, possibly the evil sense of responsibility many victims carry for the ramifications of the perpetrators' evil actions will be alleviated. If we speak, our voices will help others heal and possibly help stop perpetrators from acting out.

I know my childhood pain does not compare to what Mayo Angelou endured, but her life and her voice gives me hope. I too know why the caged bird sings:

I know why the caged bird sings, ah me,
When his wing is bruised and his bosom sore,—
When he beats his bars and he would be free;
It is not a carol of joy or glee,
But a prayer that he sends from his heart's deep core,
But a plea, that upward to Heaven he flings —
I know why the caged bird sings!

—Paul Laurence Dunbar
(This poem inspired Maya Angelou's autobiography,
I Know Why the Caged Bird Sings.)

There is a whole group of African American women whom I admire so much: Maya Angelou, Toni Morrison, Alice Walker, even Oprah. These women have transcended incredible odds, and their voices have become a force of change in our world.

When I was in Israel, I saw the location where many believe the battle of Jericho happened. According to the bible, the walls of Jericho fell after Joshua's army surrounded the city blowing their trumpets. May all victims speak out and blow their trumpets to disintegrate the walls of denial perpetuating abuse.

Carol

I HAVE SEEN THE GRAND Canyon at dawn. The sun faintly blushes the upper rocks but the immensity is almost all purple and gray shadow. Darkness. Caverns.

Once I lay on its edge at sunrise. The world turned under me. I could feel it turning. I couldn't tell where the rough molecules of the sandstone ended and my cheek began.

Now in my head I see the path through the Kiabab forest leading to the North Rim. There are flying squirrels in the Kiabab. Those squirrels live nowhere else on earth.

Over and over I see myself walking that narrow path. The Indian paintbrush and wild columbine and bristlecone pines that are thousands of years old fringe its edges. I have to go to the rim where I will be able to know if I must step and sink into the purple shadows. There's no fear or pain in that. One step over the edge and I will be part of the huge awful shadow. That option is my biggest comfort. I must go to the very edge and look down and then decide. No one can come near me there. I can look down alone.

I play this scene over and over. It's beautiful and awesome and obsessive. Maybe irresistible.

I can stop on the edge, but I cannot turn around on the path. I try very hard to think if there can be other choices. I concentrate so hard while I look at the ever-changing light and shadow in the canyon and see tiny glimpses of a muddy ribbon river at the bottom.

The cliffs are steep, almost vertical. It's scary. One slip. But somewhere there is a path down into the deepest part. I don't know what I will do. I like not knowing. I like the power of my own control. I like the wild columbine and the purple dusk.

April

GRAMPS AND I HAVE BEEN doing a photo Christmas card for 10 years. In honor of this anniversary, I gathered all the Christmas cards Gramps and I have done over the years. I scanned them into the computer. Then, placed each one inside an ornament I drew on a Christmas tree I illustrated. Gazing at these pictures a feeling of gratitude washed over me: Gramps has always been there for me. He's so proud of me. I can see it in his expression in these photos. When he was a little boy he went down to the docks in Bergen. A sailor gave him an anchor tattoo on his hand. My great grandmother was so mad. When she saw the tattoo on her son's hand, she raced down to the docks and screamed at the sailor who placed such a permanent mark on her little son.

I can understand her anger. For me, that anchor represents the solid and consistently loving influence my grandfather has had in my life. He is my anchor.

Gramps turned 94 today and I really wanted this picture taken on his actual birthday. Gramps didn't want to go outside because of the cold so we came up to my apartment; in front of the fireplace. He is sitting, and I'm kneeling in front of him. The dogs are snuggled around my legs. I placed it at the bottom of the tree. The foundation. This picture is slightly larger than the rest. I typed the year each photo was sent to remind everyone of the year they received it.

January 31, 1996

At 3:00 a.m. I was jolted awake by a huge thud downstairs. Gramps got up to use the toilet and fell. He was conscious when I got there. As I was trying to help him up he straightened his whole body. I couldn't get him to relax. It took a long time, but I finally got him back to bed. After a few minutes his muscles relaxed, and he could bend them.

It's about 4:30 a.m. now, and I tried to call my mother. No answer. Should I call the paramedics? He seems to be resting now. His speech is good. His muscles all seem to be working. If my father were speaking to me, I'm sure he'd tell me not to call. It would cost too much money for the ambulance.

I checked on Gramps again. He's sound asleep.

February 1, 1996

I'm concerned about Gramps falling while he's bathing or in the shower. He's too embarrassed to have me help him. I talked to my mother, and we are going to get a male nurse to come in every day.

February 7, 1996

I hired a home health care company. A couple of women nurses visit, but usually a male aid helps Gramps shower and dress. He's a delight and exclaims that Gramps is a treasure. He's got that right.

February 14, 1996

It's Valentine's Day. Ten years ago, the Scott grandchildren started telling what was happening to them. I didn't know it until I read Carol's portion of *Paperdolls* but now every Valentine's Day, I retreat for a moment and pray silently for the Scotts, their grandchildren and their children.

March 1, 1996

This morning Gramps was still in his room when I checked on him. Before I opened the door, I took a deep breath, bracing for what I might find. He was sitting straight up and he exclaimed, "Did you see her? Did you see Mama?"

I told him that I didn't. He said, "She was just here! She was sitting right there on the end of the bed talking to me."

My grandfather professes to be an atheist. I moved near the corner of the bed where he was pointing. I swear it was 25 degrees warmer.

March 12, 1996

When I went down to check on Gramps this morning, he was extremely confused. He was dressed and wanted to go to work. I told him to finish his breakfast, and we'd go. I was planning to take him to see his doctor. I called my mother. Thirty minutes later, my mother knocked on the door.

We took him to the doctors.

Gramps is admitted to the hospital. He had a stroke. He struggles as he looks at me. He's trying to move his lips, but they don't work. I ask him if he's trying to tell me something. His head jerks to one side. I hold his hand and tell him it will take time. I tell him that the crocus and daffodils are blooming. His head jerks again. I ask if he wants me to bring him some flowers from our yard. His head jerks to the side again.

A nurse comes in the room. The nurse says that he's trying to nod. She says it's the most alert he's been. I help him get out of his bed. He sits in the chair. I promise he'll be home in a few days. He looks down.

My parents left when I arrive. I wonder if there has been something said without me in the room.

March 24, 1996

Gramps has been in the hospital for two weeks. He won't get out of bed now, and he still hasn't spoken. I know he can understand me. He looks out the window every time I come. I say, "You want me to take you outside?" He looks outside again. A nurse helps Gramps get in a wheelchair. We wrap extra blankets around him, and I wheel him out on a deck with an incredible view of the valley. I hold Gramps's hand and talk about the yard, the dogs, and he gives me his shorty jerky nod. He looks at me. I tell him how much he means to me, what a good life he's lived and what a strong example of truth and righteousness he's always been.

His eyes dart to me. That's a common Mormon phrase, and he hasn't gone to church in years. Our eyes locked in a moment, and I smile. I say, "When I think of you, I think of love, strength, a thirst for knowledge and a commitment to always doing the right thing. That's truth and righteousness."

I swear his eyes twinkle.

My mother is waiting for us when we come back into his room. She addresses me and says, "We are moving him to a nursing home." She speaks as if Gramps's can't hear her. Tears spring from my eyes. I tell her that I promised Gramps that I'd always take care of him. She says, "April, you simply can't care for him." Gramps is looking down. She mutters that we'd get him back home as soon as he has more strength.

April 1, 1996

The nursing home sucks. Gramps hates it. He doesn't even try to look out the window now. He met my eyes then looked down. He's giving up. He hates it. I hate it for him. Please, please, please, get stronger so I can get you home Gramps. Please.

April 12, 1996

It's 5:00 a.m., my father calls. The first time he's spoken to me in six years. He tells me that Gramps just died. I go into the bathroom and throw up.

April 14, 1996

My dad told me that he's conducting the service. My mother pulled me aside and said, "This has really changed your father. I am thrilled he's speaking to you again."

I nodded and thought, "It's more like he's dictating." My father also announced that my siblings are saying prayers. My mother and uncle are speaking. I was the primary care giver to my grandfather, and I don't have any part in the service.

I was the one who brought Gramps so much joy all these years. My siblings never came to see him. I'm feeling erased again and I'm supposed to be grateful that my father is communicating his orders to me?

Laurel is here. She totally gets it. Laurel reached for my and hand and said, "Anyone who counts knows."

April 16, 1996

The funeral was today. As planned, my father conducted, my siblings said the prayers, my mother and uncle spoke. They all did a nice job. Then, my father stood up to conclude. He was talking about how short life is and how important people are. Then he said, "... if there is anyone in this audience whom I have offended or hurt, I beg for your forgiveness ...."

I was stunned, distractedly thinking, "What is he doing? Here? Now? Are you kidding me?" I didn't hear his words that led up to this, but I was drawn back into the moment when I heard him say, "And with that said, I'd like April to come up and say a few words."

As I was walking up to the pulpit, I thought, "I'm not going to touch that whole beg for forgiveness plea, I'm going to talk about Gramps." And I did. I told about how Gramps would always call up to me. How I'd answer, and we'd laugh. When Gramps came home he would always hang his coat and hat up and say, "It's good to go out on an adventure, but it's good to be home." I ended up by saying, "Now Gramps, you've had your adventure here on Earth, it's good for you to be home in Heaven."

As I gazed at the audience, my nieces and nephews were openly crying. Afterward, Tom's daughter, my beloved niece with whom I am so close said, "I want you to speak at my funeral! You are such a good speaker. I never knew." Laurel stood close and I quietly shrugged and said, "What was my dad doing?" She steered my arm towards my father and said, "Go talk to him."

"Dad?"

He fell on one knee and said, "I need you to forgive me." I reached for his hand and said, "Dad, I forgave you years ago. You have to forgive yourself."

213

GROWTH

"Last of all…
see the sun and not mere reflections of it in the water…
see it in its own proper place and not in another;
and contemplate it as is."

—Plato, *Allegory of the Cave*

April

June 21, 1996

MY FATHER IS TRYING TO earn my forgiveness. He's here, in my home, almost every day. He decided to put electricity in my garage and install an automatic garage door opener. He's digging the electricity lines himself. He's out in the backyard, digging ditches. I went out there and placed my hand on his shovel and said, "Dad, I really appreciate this, but really, you can pay someone to do this."

He said, "I can't think of any other way to earn your forgiveness. I have to do this."

I reminded him that I forgave him years ago. He said, "This is the only way I can forgive myself. I have to do this. I can't just pay someone to help you."

I handed him back the shovel and said, "Dig away."

July 4, 1996

A couple of months ago, Microsoft® sent me an entry form for an "Activate the Internet Contest." They think we're an advertising agency or something, rather than finance. I learned some desktop publishing software to quickly get jobs ready for print.

It was easier to do the graphics myself than do the back and forth with the designers at the printing company.

Simply by entering Microsoft's contest, one received a CD with $100 worth of software. During a lunch break, I put together some photos, and added my favorite Shakespeare quotes on it. I pulled out the microphone and recorded the quotes. Wrapped it up and sent it in.

Today, I found out I won. Not only do I receive the $100 CD, but Microsoft® is offering to fly me to New York, I'll get a T-1, and two robust servers. This internet thing might be something.

Since I did the entry form on company computers, I felt like I had to disclose this to my boss. My boss runs the investment division of the bank. His office is next to mine. I told him everything. He is such a great guy. He said, "You've added millions to the bank. If we paid overtime, I'd owe you for years. Go! Go have fun!"

September 5, 1996

Gramps was neat as a pin. However, I'm overwhelmed by how much stuff I have to go through. Where did all this stuff come from? I want to simply chuck it all, but what if there is something important?

It seems like I was doing this exact same thing when I remodeled my upstairs apartment. Now I've found my uncle's old high school yearbooks; wedding pictures of couples long since divorced; letters, drawings, and old photographs of people from long ago; and a family I shall never know.

I find the telegram that my grandmother sent via the Red Cross to the Nazis in Norway during World War II. It is written in Norwegian and German. My grandmother's handwriting in English at the bottom of the page: "Please let me know if my mother, Henrickke Hoem is well, please let me know if she is alive. Please." My grandmother is begging the Nazis.

My grandmother didn't find out that her mother had died in an air raid (ironically her village was bombed out by the Allies) until 1946. I know my grandmother wasn't able to say goodbye to her own mother either.

Why am I writing "either"? Karen was not my mother. Did I transfer my stuff with my own mother to Karen? Karen was my therapist. My grandmother used to moan in her sleep. She'd cry out and sometimes scream out loud.

I understand.

September 7, 1996

I'm in New York City. I came a few days early and I was able to get tickets to the U.S. Open Women's final today. Steffi Graf won. She didn't lose a set. I didn't really come into the match with a favorite. I love her demeanor, her quiet confidence and how she is extremely consistent. I've also read that her father was quite a bully. Her father wasn't there today, and Steffi didn't seem to notice. Maybe she was relieved. And of course, that's probably why I have extra compassion for her. Her dad sounds like a jerk. If she's lucky, maybe one day he'll change. Maybe he'll be out digging trenches in her yard to make amends.

September 10, 1996

Microsoft® went all out. I decided to have the T-1 line put in my house. My boss didn't want it at the building, he wanted me to have it. I have no idea what I'm going to do with all this incredible equipment.

September 30, 1996

I had a heart to heart with my boss today. I told him I really think this internet thing is going to be something. He rolled his eyes. I asked him if I could take a short sabbatical to see if this pans out. He said, "I'll see you in 6 months."

October 5, 1996

I'm close to Tom's widow and her entire family. We decided to have a garage sale to sell all this stuff. I took truckloads over to her house. Most of it was mine. It's much easier for me to determine what to do with my own stuff rather than what belonged to my grandparents.

I swear I'm never going to buy anything again or at least be selective on what I bring into my life. At least this stuff is tangible, the emotional and psychological stuff probably takes up more energy, time, and space—and much harder to dump.

November 23, 1996

After Gramp's died, I did a webpage about Gramps' life and his death. I included information about his immigration from Norway, Ellis Island, the Depression and his love of my grandmother, music, books and art. I scanned a bunch of pictures of Gramps taken throughout his life. Before Gramps died, I had him whistle into a microphone on the computer. He whistled "The Nightingale's Song." I put the recording of Gramps's whistling on the website.

A local television reporter saw the website I did for Gramps. The reporter came to my house and interviewed me on camera. I didn't think anything would come of it, but he called this evening to let me know it would air tonight. It's Thanksgiving eve, and it was part of a special Thanksgiving story. I have so much to be grateful for. My grandparents were remarkable. My grandfather could only find hard labor jobs because he was an immigrant who came to America during the Great Depression. Typically, he worked six days a week; yet, he managed to read daily, sing in the Mormon Tabernacle Choir and put all of his children through college. My grandparents had a weekly date on Saturday nights. When they were young, they'd walk down to the Tabernacle on Temple Square and listen to the Utah Symphony or a youth group. As they aged, they'd build a fire and listen to an opera or a symphony on their record player. Although they didn't have a lot of money, they enjoyed the finer things in life.

December 7, 1996

I couldn't decide what to do for my Christmas card this year. I finally decided what to do.

After the newscast aired about the website I did for Gramps, I figured out how to make a video of it. I sent that out to everyone as my Christmas Card. That way I won't have to tell anyone that Gramps is gone, and it does have a wonderful message for the holidays.

February 21, 1997

While I was out walking the dogs, a woman from my sexual abuse group broke into my house. I felt so violated when I came home and found the pieces of my chess set scattered about the room. She used her car keys to scratch some of the woodwork on the entry way doors. She left a rather unsettling note asking why she wasn't worthy of me.

I called the police.

Before I even entered a sexual abuse support group, Karen Fisher advised me to not see any of the other members outside of the therapeutic group setting. Karen said I was one in a million. She said most who have been through what I've been through are quite dysfunctional and exhibit a myriad of inappropriate and sick behaviors.

I know Karen wasn't perfect and sometimes got it wrong; but after the crazy break-in, I think Karen was right.

I don't want to say that everyone who has been sexually abused is this needy or dysfunctional. I know some wonderful women who are healing and leading productive and meaningful lives. I'm not sure why some heal better than others. It will take someone much more patient and smarter than me to figure all that out.

March 1, 1997

My six-month sabbatical is ending. I put in a rack of modems in my house and have about 200 people paying me to dial up to the internet. I'm only charging $10/month, but that gives me a base of $2,000. Plus, I'm starting to have some interest in companies making web pages for them. And, of course, I'll do the banks. I met with my boss, and I'm officially the Marketing Consultant. I'll do the outsourcing, but I won't have to travel to all the conventions. He still wants me to handle Utah and Idaho. He asked if he could pull me in if they get in a jam.

It seems like the best possible set up for me to explore this internet thing.

April 12, 1997

Gramps has been gone for a year. Every single time I bring the dogs in, the oldest one runs into Gramps's room and looks for him. I don't think she'll ever accept that he's not here.

This afternoon I took the dogs up to the cemetery. I picked some daffodils from the yard, and we left a doggie tennis ball on the grave. When we came home, I played fetch with them in the backyard.

The female, Lulleba, is running towards me with the tennis ball in her mouth. Suddenly her back legs collapse. She can't move. I run to her. I pick her up. Holding her, I run to the car. I am crying as I drive. She looks up at me with her big brown eyes. I hold her tight. I tell her how much I love her. She gasps a guttural type cough and goes limp. I hold her as I walk into the Vets office. Her head wobbles loosely. I put her on the table. The technician checks her chest with a stethoscope and says, "She's gone."

They leave me alone for a long time. I pet Lulleba and tell her to take good care of Gramps. I remove her collar. I'll keep it forever.

April 17, 1997

Laurel sent me such a precious picture of Lulleba with Burton. Laurel took this picture at the Lakehouse a few years ago. Burton was probably only about four years old at the time. Burton had been throwing the tennis ball for Lulleba. He could only throw it a few feet, and Lulleba would patiently trot over to pick it up and bring it back to him. He giggled incessantly at the whole process. Laurel snapped this picture when he had his arms wrapped around her neck. The tennis ball was at their feet, and they are both smiling.

I sent Laurel this note back:

> *"Thanks so much for the incredible picture of Burton with my little girl! I can't believe how small they both were! When my mom came up, she was actually crying. She said the thing that got to her the most was that Gramps named her Lulleba, 'little one' in Norwegian.*
>
> *Thanks again for the picture and the flowers, and for everything. And for being my very best friend.*
>
> *Can you believe how fast time goes? Remember that first day I got her? You, Burton and Parker watched her while I was at work. After work, when I came by to pick her up, Lulleba was curled up in a little ball, sleeping under your couch."*

You know how people always say that dogs start looking like their owners? Laurel always said that Lulleba looked like me. Lulleba brought me through a lot. She was always there for me, patiently waiting for me to pull myself together. It seemed she knew me better than I knew myself. In my times of despair, she would stay close and simply watch over me like a sentry guarding my soul.

May 26, 1997

It's Tom's daughter's birthday, the daughter he never met. She's in Europe serving a mission for the church. She's loving it. She's like her father—she loves to travel; and she loves adventure. She's had a wonderful life.

I think Tom died a hero. Maybe one day I'll be able to tell his daughter. Tom confessed to the bishop and was forgiven and absolved by the ecclesiastical authorities. However, I believe he feared something toxic was still lurking inside him. Possibly, he was afraid he'd hurt his unborn child. I think our fears and our minds can be that powerful. I think his core, his love, prevented him from physically heal-ing because he was afraid of what he might do later.

That is absolutely an April theory. With no solid science or evidence whatso-ever. I chose to believe that he sacrificed himself because he didn't want to take a chance on releasing the unhealed toxic monster still latent inside his soul.

He was a young man who battled cancer when radiation was relatively new. During his treatments he got pneumonia. The radiation made his lungs less mal-leable. His lungs collapsed and couldn't inflate because the lung tissue was stiff, and he died.

If his beautiful daughter ever asks me, I will tell her both versions of her father's death.

June 7, 1997

I'm in St. George visiting Laurel and the boys. We were sitting by the pool when Parker brought up the story about the cowboy boots that his mother had thrown away. Burton took over the story about how Parker was kicking him until he was bleeding, and their mother had to save his life by taking away the boots. The story gets better with time.

Laurel and I looked at each other and smiled. They don't remember that Laurel took away Parker's boots at my house. No one but Laurel and I know that I still have them safely tucked away.

July 4, 1997

I haven't been to my parents' Lakehouse in years. My mother and I are up here this weekend. It's surreal. Everything is the same but overgrown. I started weeding and trimming the branches. It's gorgeous.

My father didn't want to come up. I think he's still a bit shy around me. It's like he doesn't know how to act. It's a new dance, a new relationship. We are both cautious with each other.

My mother is more confident. She seems to be happy just to be with me. She talks a lot. She drifts into her memories—the good ones. Occasionally, she tries to rewrite our history. So far, she hasn't tried to rewrite anything major. I'm not sure if she's dealt with anything major; maybe she has, and she just doesn't want to talk about it.

My father talks about it. Not constantly, but whenever I tell him he doesn't need to do that for me, his canned response is, "It's the only way I can try to make up to you for all that I have done." I doubt he'll ever be able to forgive himself.

October 18, 1997

I have issues with money. It's becoming more poignant since I've owned this business and becoming more successful. The Internet is taking off and there is so much demand for this commercially viable new frontier. There are only a few people doing what I do; and there is an extremely high demand. Based on simple supply and demand economics, I should be making a lot of money—like millions. I simply can't charge that much. I've justified that I'm providing a great service at a fair price. I've justified that when this tech boom levels out, my pricing is right where it should be.

The truth is I don't think I'm worth it.

January 12, 1998

My niece, Tom's daughter, sent me a letter from Europe. I am so grateful that my sister-in-law always welcomed me into her home and let me be such a part of my niece's life. Years ago, I took her to Hawaii when she was in 9th grade because she got straight A's. One evening, my niece and I were sitting on the beach watching the sunset, and I recited Robert Frost's poem "Nature's first green is gold." She played with the sand in her hand then recited a quote from "The Little Prince" by Antoine de Saint-Exupéry: "...one loves the sunset when one is so sad."

I was melancholy. I was sitting on the beach with Tom's extraordinary daughter with whom he never met. I had a private theory on why Tom let himself die for her and it made me sad.

Now, years later, she was watching the sunset behind the Swiss Alps. With her curly script, my niece wrote portions of the Robert Frost poem back to me She signed the card: Gold stays in our hearts.

March 12, 1998

Today is my birthday. I spent the morning on the slopes, and then spent the rest of the day mounting the flower boxes under all the windows.

I was hanging out of my upstairs windows when I heard my grandfather's huge metal ladder. My neighbor climbed up and finished mounting all the boxes.

He said, "Are you going to plant them?"

I smiled and said, "Of course."

He laughed and said, "Oh, your grandparents would have loved it."

I've always loved flowers it's a bonus to think that my grandparents might approve from Heaven.

May 3, 1998

My father met me at the garden center at Home Depot this morning. He knows how much I love flowers and he wants to buy all the annuals for my yard.

I've never known my father to be patient.

This morning, he stood by the carts and waited. He was diagnosed with congestive heart failure last fall, and maybe his newfound patience results from his medication. I prefer to think he's changed.

At one point, I glanced up at him. He was staring intently at me. I swear he had a tear in his eye. I simply smiled and thought, "May peace bring solace to your heart."

July 12, 1998

Burton is staying with me for the weekend. For dinner he said he only wanted mashed potatoes and gravy.

After the water was drained from the perfectly boiled potatoes, Burton looked at me and said, "Where's your mixer?" I looked at him like he was speaking an alien language. He clarified and said, "You know, to mash the potatoes." Yikes, I simply don't have one. We mashed them with a fork.

Burton asked, "It's unusual because your house is decorated so cool, your yard is impeccable, so it's not like you aren't domestic. Why don't you cook?" Since Burton is 15, I decided to tell him.

When I was growing up, the kitchen was a war zone. We had family dinners almost every night. On good days, we ate in silence. I told him I didn't want to tell him about the bad days.

Burton told me that he'd noticed my dad had changed. Burton thought my father seemed calmer and nicer.

We talked about his parents. He said that he knew he had a lot of his father's traits, but he also has his mother's traits. His plan is to take the best from each of them. I told him that was a most excellent plan.

He smiled. He told me that his favorite scripture was Ether 12:27. He quickly retrieved his scriptures: "And if men come unto me I will show unto them their weakness. I give unto men weakness that they may be humble; and my grace is sufficient for all men that humble themselves before me; for if they humble themselves before me, and have faith in me, then will I make weak things become strong unto them."

Burton looked up at me and said, "Do you think this will help your dad?" I nodded.

Later:

Burton is in his room now. I'm sure he's not asleep but probably reading. I keep thinking about how hopeful he was about my father changing. I know my father is trying. He comes over and helps me out whenever he can. He goes to his

AA meetings. I think he's even in therapy. I just don't trust him yet. I don't know if I ever will. I forgave him primarily to let the anger, resentment and the hatred go that was filling my heart. But it's not like it didn't happen.

Getting comfortable in the kitchen isn't at the top of my priority list. I can't close my eyes in the shower. Recognizing my feelings and not numbing myself out with work seems much more important. Getting comfortable with myself seems important. Not trying too hard to please everyone seems like a high priority. Trusting my neighbors and realizing that not all people are out to take advantage of others seems to be another important one. Seeing the joy in the simple things in daily life is important. Helping my father change is not even on my radar. It's his deal. It cute that darling Burton is willing to help an old man realize he can change. That's as good as it gets.

September 18, 1998

I've been reading more of Gramps's journals. I've learned so much about him: his struggles, his ability to build a good life and how he enjoyed it.

I write to keep perspective on what's what. It helps me tune in and recognize what's happening inside. I think that most sexual abuse survivors were trained to ignore feelings. Writing helps me gain objectivity and see the obvious. It's a paradox because writing is a solitary activity, but it helps me get out of myself.

Another gift Gramps gave me was the love of gardening. It's a process with consistent attention renders incredible growth and beauty. In my own small way, I'm making my world a better place. It's a bonus if others enjoy it as they pass by.

October 4, 1998

My niece, Tom's daughter, is engaged! She met him before she went to Israel last year. They are so happy, excited, and cute. Of course, they are both worried about money. Fortunately, she got her master's degree in Ed Psych. He still has a couple of years of school, but she has a fairly good job. They'll figure it out.

It looks like their wedding will be sometime next year!

October 31, 1998

Oh my goodness! My niece and her fiancé went to a Halloween Party and dressed up as Clark Kent and Lois Lane. They e-mailed me pictures of them in their costumes, and I can't quit smiling. They are the perfect Superman couple!

Laurel sent some pictures of her boys in their costumes. Burton went as "The Rock" and carried around a bunch of rocks. Parker went as Peter Parker from Spiderman. He's so athletic, but it was fun to see him dressed up as the science nerd. And the little boys were vampires.

As for me, I always get a lot of trick-or-treaters. Most of the time, the parents are standing at the bottom of the porch steps. Some of the little ones tentatively knock on the door. One little boy, dressed up like a dragon, reached into his candy sack and tried to give me a piece of candy back. I thanked him but tried to explain that it was all for him. His father laughed and said, "I guess our sharing lessons worked." Adorable.

Smiling, I closed my front door and remembered Karen Fisher's words: "Everyone deserves a happy childhood." I'm so glad that so many get that.

November 4, 1998

Well, I saw myself in pictures last night. I am fat.

Since Gramps died and I started this business, I quit running. I eat whatever I want, and whenever I want. I didn't sleep much last night. Seeing myself was disturbing. There's no excuse even when the camera adds 10 pounds, I am fat. I bet I've gained 50 pounds. Maybe 60. Since the throes of my eating disorder, I threw out my scales. I must get some scales and figure out where I am. I must get real. I am so ashamed of myself. Internally, I am screaming to myself, "Just don't eat for a week, then your stomach will shrink."

In college, I had some crazy bet with Carol's daughter Susy. We bet each other that we could go a week without eating. We could drink water, and that was it. We both did it. We both won the bet and lost a lot of weight. Susy drank bouillon. I couldn't stomach it. It was easier to starve. I can feel the shame pulsing like an electric shock going through my entire body. We both have had serious eating disorders. Obviously, I still do. Now I've ballooned out. I've ignored it for almost three years. I've literally eaten away my feelings.

I've tried so hard to focus on the positive—to work hard, to build this business and to always look for the positive aspects of my daily life. I truly do feel that if I could have survived the abuse and then dealing with the memories of the abuse, that nothing could ever be as hard. I told myself numerous times that my life is "a piece of cake" in comparison.

Unfortunately, I've eaten way too many pieces of cake. I loathe myself for it. Shame and self-hatred are innate for me. Simply being aware of something doesn't necessarily make it something that's resolved or "dealt with." Karen used to say there's a lag between our intellect and our feelings. My lag is years. I'm trying not to be "all or nothing" about it. I've got to get things in perspective. Take one day at a time. I need some help. I think I've got to get back into therapy.

The therapist that Karen recommended to me has left the state. She's in California somewhere by the ocean. She helped me through Karen's death. I've been on my own ever since. I'm doing okay with starting my business, taking care of the house, loving my Aunt April role with Laurel's boys, and being highly invested in Tom's daughter's life. I've done some good things. I need some help with this self-medicating eating deal.

225

A friend gave me the name of a therapist. I have an appointment set for next week. I hope she's good.

I met the new therapist today. One of the first things that I told her was that I wrote a book called *Paperdolls*. Before I even said the subtitle, she stopped me and said, "So, you're the one."

She had admiration and respect in her eyes. She almost took a moment and just gazed at me. I was honored. But I also felt uncomfortable. I felt foolish that I let myself get so fat, that I'm so afraid of feeling my feelings and that I've insulated and isolated myself so very much.

I wanted her to say something like, "I admire you for what you've contributed and the gift you have given other survivors. You don't have to be a role model—not here."

She didn't. She asked me why I was there. I gave my generic answer: "Therapy is like going to the dentist. You can't really see inside your own mouth. Sometimes you have to open your mouth and let someone else take a look inside." I made it sound like I just needed a check-up.

I don't feel like I need a check-up. I feel like I've ignored myself and let myself fall apart. My subconscious let me pack on the pounds to protect myself because I wasn't consciously taking care of myself.

I re-read that last paragraph. Maybe that's it. Maybe that's all I've done. Maybe I am okay, and I need to consciously be aware of myself, of my feelings and my vulnerabilities. I know I'm an adult, and I can protect myself. My subconscious doesn't need to flip into auto drive and slam the food down. I hate that I got off track. At first, I wrote that I hate that I got lost; but now I've realized what has happened, and I'm struggling to get back on track.

Today is my dad's birthday. I called him at the office and wished him a happy birthday. It's hard for me to describe how he acts around me: shy, humble, humiliated? He doesn't say much. He said, "Thank you for calling," and got off the phone quickly. I hope he enjoys his day.

I don't think he wants to carve out a new relationship with me. He's trying desperately to earn my forgiveness. It's almost like he acts like a servant around me. He is extremely respectful, quiet, and humble. At Gramps's funeral, when my father fell on one knee and begged my forgiveness, I told him that I had forgiven him years ago and that he needs to forgive himself.

When I think about it, I'm not sure he'll ever be able to forgive himself. I couldn't if I were him. I pray one day he has some level of peace with himself.

December 15, 1998

I came up with a wonderful idea for my niece's wedding present. I've gathered photos of the bride's and groom's parents, grandparents, and great-grandparents—as far back as possible. I've tried to get each couple's wedding day pictures. I have photos dating back to the 1800s. I've scanned them into the computer. I'm using Photoshop to fix and restore them. I envision that it will look like a large group photo. My niece and her fiancé will be in the front center in color. Then, I'll arrange all the photos of their parents, grandparents and ancestors posed behind them. Possibly in an antique brown or black and white.

I hope it visually offers them support. When things get tough, they'll have this visual of those who have gone before them, battled many of the same battles, suffered different pains, and persevered finding solace in this miraculous and complicated collage we call life.

Plus, it's a way for me to get my brother Tom into the picture. It's been so long now. Many of my niece's friends don't even know that her stepfather isn't her real dad.

December 26, 1998

I'm down at Laurel's house. Early this morning, Parker, Jason, Paul and I went over to their ward house and shot some hoops. I think every LDS ward house has a basketball court. Parker plays on the junior high team and practices with the high school team. He is good.

This morning we decided to scrimmage. It was Parker against the three of us. That's three against one. Parker is good. We were no match. I told the little guys to bump into him, hang onto him and tackle him. Basically, I told the little guys to play football while Parker still had to play basketball. It was a blast. They were hanging onto him, grabbing his arms, trying to tackle him—and he still beat us. Everyone was laughing and tackling Parker. He was pouring sweat while dribbling the ball, running to the hoop and laying it in with his two little brothers hanging onto him. Then he'd turn and give each of them a big bear hug, and they'd laugh and laugh. What a glorious morning.

When we came back to the house, all four of us were sitting at the kitchen table eating cereal when Laurel walked down. They joyously told her the story; of course, the story got better with each telling. And, of course, Parker always remained the champ. Then Jason said, "We would have won if I had better shoes."

Before Laurel could respond, Parker said, "Mom probably threw them away." He turned his nose in the air and said, "Scarred for life." Laurel and I looked at each other and shared a secret smile. Parker was referring to his precious cowboy boots that Laurel threw away years ago at my house. I tucked 'em away and am going to give them back to him on his wedding day. The boys have no idea that I still have 'em. What cracks me up is that at various times, the boys all still remember that Laurel threw them away! It's part of their family lore and what they bring up to remind their mom what a mean mom she is!

It's a reminder of what a great mom she is! She sets boundaries, gives them chances to learn and then follows through with love. Maybe because she did this when they were little she doesn't have to work as hard now. They know she's doing what's best for them. They've learned that their actions have consequences and not to hurt others. All sorts of great lessons wrapped into the one event with Parker kicking his older brother too many times—and Laurel taking his boots away—forever.

December 27, 1998

We all went to church today. There are many good people in Laurel's ward. I loved going, and I especially loved seeing my adorable nephews with their slicked back hair, white shirts and ties.

December 28, 1998

I took Burton driving today. We went over to the big college parking lot and practiced. He backed up and even parallel parked. I can't believe he's going to be driving soon. He's turning into such an incredible young man. He's quite tall and very strong. He towers over me. It's strange to think that the little boy I used to swoop up into my arms now looks down at me.

Burton watches over his younger brothers. He observes, interacts, listens and offers cool older brother tips. My older siblings never did that. I wonder if Burton is unique or if all the oldest siblings take that type of leadership role with their younger siblings?

Laurel is too hard on herself. She knows her own shortcomings; but from an outsider's point of view and getting a chance to see small snippets of the inside of her family, she's a wonderful mother. She loves them first and then sets boundaries that are reinforced with love. She talks to them; she listens; and she has them pretty busy with school, sports, music, church, reading, and all sorts of social things. It seems to be such a healthy, delightful, balanced family.

December 29, 1998

We all went to the mall today. Laurel took back some Christmas presents. One of the most amazing things is that these boys wrap their arms around their mom and walk around the mall. That seems unusual for teenage boys. It seems most teenage boys go through a stage never letting their mom's hug 'em or anything—especially in public. Laurel has always been so loving with her kids. One time she said, "There's nothing like just giving your son a hug to tell 'em that you like him and love him.

We spent a couple of hours at the bookstore. Laurel and her boys are avid readers. Every one of them loves to read. Sometimes she has to set limits on their reading and make them go outside and play. What a great problem for her! "Okay, you've all been reading for too long. You have to go outside now!"

Burton found a fun book called *Harry Potter and the Sorcerer's Stone*. He's reading it out loud to Jason and Paul. Laurel just walked by me and quietly said, "I might have to buy a couple more copies of this one."

December 30, 1998

I brought my computer and I've been working on the collage. Burton saw it and said that it looked like the Beatles album cover "Sgt. Pepper." I decided that everyone will be in black and white except my niece and her fiancé. They will be front and center in full color. It's starting to come together.

I've spent a lot of time looking at these young couples. My great-grandparents looked so young with hopeful eyes looking to the future. They had no idea that the Nazis would occupy their beloved homeland, and one of them would be killed in an air raid. I gaze at my great-grandparents on my father's side. Was one of these distinguished men a pedophile? Or did the devastation of fighting in WWII cause something in my father's psyche to snap? I'll never know.

I've learned that abuse and dysfunction is generational. I have heard stories about my mother's uncles and their drinking. My dad hasn't said much of his relatives. My paternal grandfather was a tyrant, and my paternal grandmother was an angel. The same adjectives numerous people have said of my own parents. I pause. Gazing at my father's young and hopeful face on his wedding day, I believe his ambitions of a good life have been achieved. He didn't get there easily, but he has changed. On his wedding day he came home a war hero. Now he is still a war hero, only this war is conquering his own demons.

December 31, 1998

We finished *Harry Potter*. I'm confident Burton could be an actor. His reading was riveting! We drank carbonated grape juice and cheered when the clock struck twelve. The little boys fell asleep on the couch. Burton and Parker each picked up one of their brothers and carried them to bed.

Then we went outside and looked at the stars.

Socially I'm becoming a loner. It's strange because I go out and work with clients, speak in front of large groups, come home and sit in front of the computer coding or designing, and then collapse into bed.

Gramps died three years ago. Brent came to the viewing, and I never saw him again. I'm sure he was waiting for me to finish grieving but not even a phone call on how I'm doing? When we were first dating, we had an understanding that after Gramps left, we'd get married. As the years progressed, we never talked about it again. He is a bit of a playboy, good looking, driving a Porsche around. He really likes the girls. I was certain that he was seeing other women. Now, he's gone. Like attracts like. I'm sure I was a good fit for him too. Not available until Gramps was gone, then when Gramps passed on, we didn't talk to each other again.

In one of my survivors' groups, a woman had a pattern of getting into abusive relationships. The woman kept exclaiming, "I can't help it, I fall instantly in love, the chemistry is powerful."

One of the counselors said, "I believe most chemistry is simply unresolved issues."

That rang true for me. During my mother's first in patient stay in rehab, I learned that adult children of alcoholics typically marry alcoholics. I was dating the love of my life. He was gorgeous, smart, a rugby player, a skier, and an alcoholic. He had a 12 pack of beer every night. Minimum. He always justified it, that he could drink so much because he was so big. When he drank, he withdrew, got quiet. Oh, how I loved him. The chemistry was right. He felt so familiar. He felt like family.

After that family session when I realized I was simply repeating a pattern, I called the love of my life and broke up with him. He was heartbroken and thought that all this family therapy changed me. It had.

The next day, I called Karen Fisher. And so, my journey began.

Since then, I've basically ignored any of my "attractions." I've had a checklist of healthy qualities for a prospective partner and forced myself to spend time with them. I've convinced myself that we are all God's children with unlimited souls and brilliant treasures within all of us. I believe that's true. However, I think my unconscious has overruled me again. I've picked out healthier, yet still emotionally unavailable men. And the old rule still applies like attracts like. I'm emotionally unavailable.

I think I am basically unlovable.

Tomorrow is my niece's wedding. Traditionally, Mormons have a wedding breakfast. It's the first meal the couple has after they are married. Many are married in the temple, earlier in the morning. My niece asked me to give a tribute at the wedding breakfast. The big group ancestral photo is all done, and this will be the perfect time to give it to them.

January 31, 1999

My niece got married yesterday. It turned out nice. Luckily, I found a nice easel and covered it before everyone came in the restaurant for the breakfast.

When I stood up to give my tribute to my niece, I told some cute stories about her. Then I got a bit serious with a smooth segue to my brother and how he died a month before my niece was born. I quoted part of Wordsworth's famous poem.

Trailing clouds of glory do they come—on earth as in heaven.

And I removed the cover. I heard a couple of gasps from the audience and even saw a few tears. It was a wonderful moment. It was my way of having my brother Tom's presence felt at his daughter's wedding.

I sat down next to my father. He embarrassedly tried to wipe the tears from his face. He leaned over, his voice broke with a whisper, "Thank you."

February 17, 1999

I miss Gramps. I'm gazing at the genealogy picture I made for my niece's wedding. He's about 19 in this picture. He was my rock. He was my pillar. He taught me how to endure. His voice is repeat clips running through my mind: "Build a good life," "Get a good education," "Work hard," "Study," "Learn," "Take good care of your money, and your money will take good care of you."

Shortly after the 1989 Earthquake in California, *Time Magazine* published an article about the heroes of that earthquake. Strangers risked their lives saving others. My repressed memories had barely started to surface. I felt like my mind was having an earthquake of its own. Gramps asked me to sit down with him at his kitchen table. He held up a copy of the *Time Magazine* article. Then he read the parts about the heroes. He read stories of brave men and women scaling teetering concrete freeways to save strangers trapped in cars. He read about onlookers running into buildings on the verge of collapse to help retrieve a wheelchair bound woman. My grandfather finished reading and said, "There are many people who take advantage, who lie, who steal, who harm others. But most of us, most humans are good."

I'm not sure how much my grandparents knew about what was happening in my childhood home. I know they tried to be there for us. My grandmother was there whenever I got sick. She was the one that made the tomato soup for me. My grandfather called my father a "hefty" man. Sometimes he called my dad a bully. My grandfather frequently added that underneath it all, my dad was a good man with a good heart.

Aren't we all?

Laurel and the boys called and sang "Happy Birthday" to me on the phone. Over the long-distance phone connection, I could hear that those guys have developed beautiful voices. Laurel has always been musical. Even as a teenager, she'd spend hours behind the piano playing simply to relax. When I was visiting last, she was at the piano with Jason figuring out the notes to one of his favorite songs and switching it to a different key. I didn't even know Laurel could do that. Jason boasted, "My mom has perfect pitch!" Here I've known her almost 30 years, and I never knew that! It makes sense. She plays numerous instruments: piano, guitar, flute and the violin. One day in college, she got a dulcimer. It's a cool looking string instrument that she plays on her lap. The boys love it when she plays. They love it when she sings. One of my favorite mental pictures I have of Laurel is sitting on the couch with one of her boys (she does this with all of them). Her son has his head in her lap, and she's singing softly to him as she combs his hair.

No wonder the boys love to sing.

Selfishly, I think I've had a vicarious "mothering" experience watching Laurel with her sons. I am in awe of what a functional, loving family looks like. It's certainly not a perfect family, and Laurel would be the very first one to scoff at my accolades. But for me, it's perfect. It's such a contrast to my family of origin.

And oh, how I love her boys. She has given them structure and boundaries so that they are free to grow. My ability to describe it is limited because I haven't experienced it. For me, if Laurel's family were like a garden, it would be a well-tended garden. She's planted the seeds of love, knowledge, courage, honor, spirituality, music, art, athletics, respect, humor, laughter and so much more. She's aggressive with the weeding and is teaching the boys how to pull the weeds that could hold them back, strangle them or harm the other glorious traits now growing within the psyche of each boys' own gardens.

Ironically, Laurel doesn't like to garden.

How funny is this? Just as I was writing the entry in my journal there was a knock at the door. Laurel sent me flowers for my birthday! Oh, what a wonderful surprise to get flowers delivered! It's an arrangement of orchids, roses, tulips and daffodil: a spring bouquet. Oh, how I love flowers.

My niece, Tom's daughter, and her newlywed husband are taking me to dinner tonight. They have absolutely no money. I'm a little worried about how they are going to pay for it, but they are insisting. It's for my birthday. At least I won't be alone tonight.

Carol published a stunning book about abuse. It's a fictional psychodrama. I couldn't put it down. Carol lays out the helpless suffering of a mother and grandmother with authenticity. The poignant pain and wounds rip wide when perpetrators run rampantly free toxically damaging everything in their wake.

When Susy and I were in college, she came to my house after their family Christmas in Coronado. She told me about the harrowing experience of saving her father and Hank from a riptide that swept them far out to sea. Without hesitation, Susy leapt into the water, swam out and saved them.

Susy's a hero, risking her own life to save others.

In this new book, Carol fictionally describes standing on the beach watching the riptide tow Norton and Hank out to sea. When suddenly Susy grabs a life preserver, a rope, and swims out to them, Susy saved them all. At the time Susy saved Hank from the riptide, his predatory pedophilia had not been exposed yet. Even if we'd known, I still admire Susy for saving him.

After Hank's suicide, my friend Jennifer cheered. I understand the Scott grandchildren finally felt safe from him. Carol and Norton were relieved. I was mad and sad. Hank was a coward. I still believe that anyone can change. It takes courage to change, and Hank was a coward.

I empathize with Carol's feelings of despair. I hope Susy doesn't regret saving him. He could have had the courage to change. Anyone can change.

November 19, 1999

Burton's high school football team won the State Championship. The city held a parade and blocked off Main Street to honor the team. Burton was in the back of a truck with a smiling a swarm of cheerleaders three years older than him. I met his eye; he smiled, shrugged, and then gave me a little wink. Burton has a calm confidence. He's quite popular but doesn't seem to notice. He's funny, responsible, and kind.

Later that evening, we were in the family room chatting. Burton was sitting by his mom and had his huge arm draped around Laurel's shoulders. It's confirmed, I'm having a vicarious mothering experience watching Laurel with her boys. My psyche and perspective has changed. It seemed like the change was at a glacial pace. Now, I realize it was much faster. These boys are wonderful. Now I know that simply by the luck of the draw, I was born into a pocket of very damaged and toxic teenage boys. Most are good and want to do the right thing. Most want to be okay.

It feels good to shed my outdated latent fears and beliefs.

January 1, 2000

I flew home today from St. George. The flight was practically empty. I guess everyone was spooked by the whole Y2K hype. I wasn't. When I booked my flight, I was pleasantly surprised at what a good rate I got on this plane fare. It would have been more expensive to drive!

It's always good to be prepared for an emergency, but people got a little extreme on this one. Legend has it when the calendar year shifted from 999 AD to 1000 AD, people were sleeping in the churches because they thought it was the end of the world. When Laurel and I went to the grocery store, I was shocked at how depleted the shelves were. People were nervous about this whole Y2K business.

I think it's good to be prepared in case of an emergency, but this did seem a bit excessive. There were hundreds, if not thousands of people camping out in the desert near St. George. Apparently, they were waiting for a spaceship to come down and pick them up.

Adults are adults, and even if I don't understand the decisions they make, if they want to dance by the fire and howl at the moon in the middle of the night in the Southern Utah desert, let 'em. But when they pull their kids out of school and society, well, it kind of bugs me. Then who am I to judge how parents raise their children? I really can't judge it, but I will judge if and when I perceive abuse being inflicted on anyone—especially a child. That's my line in the sand. Emotional, physical, or sexual, if you are an adult and you are abusing kids, animals, the elderly, the disabled—okay anyone who is an underdog—well, I will do something. I will make a phone call. I will step in. I will do something. I will not sit idly by. Otherwise, dance away by that bonfire in the desert; I'm not into kicking sand around on a cold desert night, but if that's your thing, go right ahead. And I promise I won't laugh when you slink back to work after your spaceship doesn't arrive.

January 2, 2000

A relaxing day as I contemplate this year, decade, century, and millennium: I hope our quirky little species becomes more peaceful, less dominating and violent in the next century—maybe in the next thousand years. Right now, the lingering nonsense from some of our DNA and archaic traditions are savage.

I hope that we will not destroy ourselves because of our fears.

Fear is something I've had to look at within myself. My developmental blueprint was laden with fear, and I've had to transcend it. Although I've faced many of my fears head on, occasionally I still wake up in the middle of the night with a racing heart and sweat soaked sheets. Generally, my conscious mind is at peace. My nonconscious mind still wrestles with memories of long-gone years.

March 12, 2000

I am content. I can't imagine it getting any better than this. I'm certainly not perfect but overall, I enjoy my days. My work is ever changing and exciting, and I don't have weird irrational fears randomly flaring up in my psyche. I'm okay. Everything is good. I'm loving my low-key, simple birthday.

December 9, 2000

I have been trying to figure out my Christmas card this year. Absolutely nothing noteworthy has happened this year. It's been such a wonderful year, one of my best yet, simply because all is well. Last February, we had one of those incredible pow-der dump days. The sky was vivid blue, and the snow was fluffy white. I stopped skiing and quickly snapped a picture of the hill. I'm using this picture for my card this holiday season. This is what I had printed on the card:

> *Recently, I ran into an old friend whose entire life has changed: Divorced, moved to a new city, and then remarried with a whole new family. My boring life paled in comparison. The canvas of my life is still the same. I live in the same wonderful old house, I love my work, I relish my close friends whom I consider family.*
>
> *My young nephew recently asked which season of the year was my favorite. With a chuckle, I said, "This one. Whatever season I'm in!" I love the change of the seasons. Right now, I love the sunrise glowing above the snowy mountains. And my heart leaps when I see the sun glistening on the freshly fallen snow. Everything is miraculously still the same and my heart is filled with peace and contentment.*

September 11, 2001

A deathly silence, the Twin Towers in New York fell today. Although Salt Lake is over 2,000 miles from New York, the city is darker and hushed tonight. Everyone is walking around in stunned silence.

September 25, 2001

I saw my therapist today. We talked about the towers, New York, the Pentagon, and the courageous souls on United Airlines Flight 93 that wrecked in the field. I'm quite confident that if I'd received word about what was happening, I would have done anything in my power to bring that plane down also. I reacted that way when my friends and I were attacked on the subway in Paris, I wrote *Paperdolls* to try to prevent more destruction and death (literal deaths and psychological ones).

My therapist commented that so many are on edge, waiting for another attack or another bomb to drop. Without hesitation I said, "That's exactly how children in abusive homes feel all the time."

October 7, 2001

A dark day: The U.S. began attacking Afghanistan. I take after my grandfather. I simply believe that war is insanity. War exemplifies the barbarianism of our species. We were attacked. I'm not sure that war is the best means to combat terrorism. I'm not even sure we are reprimanding the correct people. Somewhere some villager in Afghanistan is simply going about their day, and bombs are flying down from the sky. This villager has no knowledge of the villain whom their country is supposedly harboring. We are bombing this country because the villain Bin Laden is supposedly hiding there. I'm just not sure.

I have been attacked, and I don't believe the best way to end violence is to attack back. Yes, we must defend ourselves. Women must defend themselves against abusers. Children can learn skills to help protect them from abusers. Long term, the best way to combat violence is via education. We must enlighten and educate to lift up our species, or our violent barbarianism will destroy us.

It is better to add to the light than fight the darkness. If we are doing any bombing or blasting, we must blast light into the ignorant and dark crevices of our civilization and our world.

October 8, 2001

I didn't sleep much last night. I am strangely upset that we are at war. It is complicated for me. I know all the propaganda that we've been fed: they hate us because of our freedom. I don't know if I buy it entirely. I'm glad I'm not a leader in our country right now. I don't think I could vote in favor of this action. Is war the most viable solution?

In the middle of the night I reread what I wrote yesterday. I decided this is my new mantra:

"Better to add to the light than fight the darkness."

November 20, 2001

My mother called today and asked if I wanted to go to a basketball game at the University of Utah. My sister-in-law has had sugar diabetes most of her life. She had some surgery, and my brother didn't want to go. As my mother and I were walking into the arena, I asked about my sister-in-law's surgery. My mom told me she had a toe amputated.

I felt a chill move through my chest.

November 22, 2001

My dad invited me to go out to my brother's house for Thanksgiving. I think it's because it might snow, and they are nervous about driving in it. My sister-in-law had her toe amputated and I am surprised that they were having Thanksgiving dinner there. Although my brother ordered it from Marie Calendar's Restaurant it is still a big deal.

My sister-in-law was sitting on the couch with her leg propped up and a blanket over her foot. I told her how sorry I was about this and gestured to her foot. She smiled.

My brother was extremely nervous. I recall how Karen Fisher described him as "Hyper-Vigilant." Karen said that with all my sister-in-law's health problems, my brother was waiting for the other shoe to drop. At the time, I thought that's how our entire childhood was; we were all waiting for the other shoe to drop.

November 26, 2001

My sister-in-law had heart surgery today. I couldn't stand the thought of my brother in that waiting room by himself.

He was genuinely shocked when I walked in to support him. I told him I was there to support him. We didn't say much. I sat with him the entire afternoon.

December 14, 2001

It's dark. An early-morning call. My sister-in-law's heart stopped beating. My brother performed CPR until the paramedics arrived. She's on her way to the hospital now.

I stare in silence.

Another call. A broken voice sputters the words that she didn't make it. She's gone.

My parents go to the hospital to be with their son. My nephews are motherless. I ask about them. No one knows. They were home watching when the ambulance drives away. They are alone. No one answers the phone.

My father calls to tell me they'll be helping my brother all day. They are going to the cemetery to pick out a plot and then to the mortuary to pick out a casket. It's cold today. My dad has congestive heart failure. I worry. He'll be walking around in the cold all day.

I tell my niece I'm worried that this will be too much for my dad.

I still don't know about my nephews.

The funeral is Monday.

December 16, 2001

I drive my parents to the viewing. My father looks ashen. He weeps openly as he embraces the visitors. My mother stands steadfast and reserved. She gracefully greets the guests. She never sheds a tear.

All my nieces, nephews, uncles, aunts, and cousins speak with me. Many of the extended family do not know that there is a rift between my siblings. They all asked me to take care of my brother. If only....

I give my brother a hug. He couldn't talk.

After the viewing, I take my parents to dinner. They haven't had a good meal in days. They both eat everything. I order more for them. My father puts his fork down, looks into my eyes, pauses, and says, "Thank you." I smile and say, "You are welcome."

He says, "I don't mean for dinner tonight. Thank you for everything. Thank you for the love, generosity, and forgiveness you have shown us all." I reached across the table and put my hand on his hand. I meet his eyes and say, "Thank you too. What you've done the last few years is remarkable. You are a living testament that people can change. Thank you too."

He looks down. When he looks back at me, tears are streaming down his face.

December 17, 2001

Today my father gives the family prayer before they close my sister-in-law's casket. He is one of the tallest men in the family, and his white hair blazes gloriously as he stands before us.

The chapel is overflowing with people.

At the cemetery, my father doesn't feel up to walking to the grave. I wrap a blanket over him. I kiss him on the cheek. As I close the door, I think, "Now please don't die while we are gone."

The cemetery is snowy. I carefully kicked some snow away to clear a path for my mother. Others followed behind us.

When we came back, my father gives me a weak smile.

December 18, 2001

I am driving; Laurel calls on my cell phone. She says, "April, pull over."

She continues, "Is the car off?"

I say, "Yeah, what's going on?"

In a tender and loving voice, Laurel says, "April, your father died."

My niece, Tom's daughter, called Laurel because no one could get hold of me. She asked Laurel to call me. I can't think of a better way for me to hear this news.

I ask Laurel to call the people I was planning to meet and cancel the appointment. Then I drive to my parents' house. Everyone is here – all my nieces, nephews, siblings, a couple of my dad's brothers. Even Tom's widow is here.

My sister-in-law (I still refer to Tom's widow as my sister-in-law, although she's been remarried for years) meets me and says, "Come with me."

She takes me up to my parents' bedroom: to my father's body. He looks peaceful. Asleep. I tell him that I know he's earned this peaceful parting. "I hope you are forever encircled in the arms of love."

I quickly find out what happened. My father went to the doctor this morning for one of his treatments for his heart. He came home and told my mother that he was tired. He said he was exhausted from the funeral. He wanted to lie down for a few minutes.

My mother made him a sandwich and decided to take it up to him in the bedroom. When she got there, he was gone.

He did earn that peaceful parting. He didn't suffer in death. He had enough suffering in life.

December 21, 2001

My family had two funerals in less than a week. My siblings forced the funeral to be a day and a half after his death. Two days after my sister-in-law's funeral. They claimed it had to do with the holidays. They decreed the schedule and left.

I knelt in front of my mother as they carried my father's body down the stairs. She stressed she didn't want to watch that. I held her hand, gazed into her eyes and told her when she could look.

Then, my sister-in-law, sat with my mother and planned the funeral. My sister-in-law is such a sweet person. However, after a couple of hours, she rolled her eyes and said, "I can't believe Byron and Melinda just left this with you."

I swallowed. I tried to explain my understanding of my siblings' inability to deal with anything painful. Quickly, sweep it away. If there was a rug handy, it would all be swept under it. My sister-in-law chuckled and said, "That's a very nice way to explain it. You are too kind."

My mother asked me to stay with her that night. I was planning to stay in my old bedroom. I heard her muffled cries and gathered her in my arms until she fell asleep. I didn't sleep a wink.

Since my father fell on his knees at Gramps's funeral—and begged my forgiveness—I knew I would speak at his funeral. The thoughts of what I would say had been jumbling around in my head for over five years. Now, because I was at my mother's side every moment, I didn't feel like I had adequately organized those thoughts. My goal was to talk about what a war hero he was, and how he typically pronounced things in black and white terms.

In my talk I emphasized that he was hardly a black and white person. He was complicated with many strengths and tragic flaws. I said that I hoped he had been able to forgive himself.

At the cemetery, as the bugle call finished Taps, one of my older cousins from the Daniels's side approached and said, "Your dad was tough. But, in a few short minutes, you captured him. I understand. I love you. I want my daughters to know you."

I knew of her family. Her mother was bedridden, until my uncle, my dad's oldest brother passed. It seemed my aunt miraculously pulled herself out of bed and began gardening. My aunt became a master gardener for the American Horticultural Society. Her Bearded Irises won awards. I also knew bits of my cousin's story. My cousin had a hard life. Married and divorced an abusive husband. Her eyes were eerily familiar. Like family. Of course, I'd meet with her. Absolutely I would get to know her daughters. I tucked a business card in my cousin's coat pocket. Hugged her then took my mother's arm and guided her to the limo.

Carol

I ALWAYS KNEW THAT HANK in his own perverted way was surviving. I dreamt. I was Hank's mother in the dream, not his real mother but me, who I am now—only he was my son. In the dream I loved him, and I knew if I loved him I must kill him before he ravaged more. I shot him in the dream and woke to a feeling of emptiness and waste.

"I have to forgive him," I thought. "And the children have to own everything that has happened, accept it as part of who they are. Otherwise, they cannot accept themselves."

We had told the grandchildren they were heroes because by talking they were saving other children. Watching them in the years since then I have learned that the greatest heroism of all is the courage to be oneself. April has learned that too. In large measure she accepts her life.

David Hechler says, "It has been suggested that, given the vast array of crime and violence which can be traced to those who were sexually abused as children, child sexual abuse represents a greater threat to this country's future than cancer or nuclear war. Hyperbole? Time will tell."

How many people are going to believe a statement like that?

Who believes April's life? April is in new territory. She is letting the world see child sex abuse, its aftereffects.

Hopefully, because my grandchildren have spewed up rotten fruit early, they will not have to endure the layers and layers of pain and learning April has described.

April

I WALKED TO CUCINA'S TODAY. I got my usual order and then decided to treat myself to one of their delicious homemade brownies. When I ordered, I was told they were all sold out. They usually have a large tray stacked high with the brownies. I looked at the server, stunned and said, "Sold out? That's never happened before." He smiled and nodded his head to the corner of the room, and said, "That guy over there bought them all."

I turned to see a man sitting in a big comfy couch surrounded by an entourage of people. I looked back at the café employee and said, "Do you know who that is?" He shrugged and said, "Someone for the Olympics." I said, "That's Desmond Tutu. He can have as many brownies as he wants. I wish I'd bought them all for him."

Tentatively, I walked over. Immediately, two large men jumped up. His bodyguards. The Archbishop gazed over and waved me to him. I said, "I am deeply humbled to meet you. Your words of hope and forgiveness saved my life a few years ago."

His head bowed as he uttered a simple blessing on my behalf.

The opening ceremonies for the Olympics were tonight. It was inspiring and hopeful. One of the most moving parts was when they brought out the tattered and fire-singed flag from the fallen World Trade Centers. Archbishop Desmond Tutu was an Olympic Flag bearer—the man who saved my life and shares my passion for Cucina's brownies. I was mesmerized as I watched a local Utah boy begin the show by skating with a lantern across the backlit ice battling a special effects storm symbolizing the Child of Light's overcoming adversity.

Months before my father died, my parents bought several tickets to various Olympic events. My mother still wants to see everything, and she's letting my siblings and me take turns going with her. I saw an ice hockey game and watched the Dutch skate for gold. My favorite event was bundling up for the amazing ski jump competition.

The Olympic ski jumping event was particularly fun to watch with my mother because as a young girl she jumped off the largest ski jump in the world in Norway. She landed on old wooden skis. It's a feat that none of her children have been able to match.

My mother was a maverick in her youth. Paying her way through college and getting a university education in far-away Minnesota—at a time when many women didn't even consider an education.

I wish she had been braver with my father. Now that he's gone, she seems to be blossoming.

February 22, 2002

Laurel brought her entire family up for an Olympic weekend. They got here last night. The boys were enraptured with a multi-player computer game upstairs, Laurel asked to see the boots. I had hidden them in the storage area of the basement. When I brought them to her, tears sprang in her eyes. "Oh, they are so little! Can you believe that big buff guy upstairs once wore these?" We both laughed. With a chuckle she continued, "Well, we'll see if he ever gets married…." All the boys are popular, but Parker has a special following of cute girls. She sighed and handed the boots back to me. I carefully concealed them in a brown grocery bag and hid them.

This morning, we got up quite early to head to the mountains for the Men's Gold Medal round of the 50-kilometer cross-county ski event. We all hiked to get a good view of where the athletes raced by. I was cheering for the Norwegians. Then I took the boys over to Park City for an afternoon of downhill skiing. They've transitioned to snowboarding and teased me extensively for being an old lady and still skiing. I swear, I'm going to learn to snowboard. Old, sheesh!

February 24, 2002

The Olympics ended today. I was one of the naysayers, thinking they'd be too expensive; and I kind of wanted to keep our incredible outdoor recreation a secret. But having the Olympics here was fun. It was fun to see the city alive with events and people.

I live within walking distance of the stadium where the opening and closing ceremonies were held. I won't miss the planes, helicopters and drones flying over my house, though.

May 1, 2002

I sold my Mercedes 450SL. I loved that car, but it felt like the right time. Last summer, I pulled into a gas station and a guy was at the pump filling up his boat. I felt a twinge of envy. I said to him, "Looks like you're going to have a good day." He laughed and said, "And you as well." I did have the top down, but I only went home and parked it in the garage. Now I'm looking for a good little water ski boat.

June 5, 2002

Today, there were tons of helicopters and planes circling the house. A couple of women knocked on my door asking if I'd seen a young blonde girl. They showed me a picture. She was abducted from her home last night.

I told them that I just got home, but they were more than welcome to come in and look around. They asked me to check everywhere, just in case. They handed me a flyer and asked me to post it. The young girl is named Elizabeth, and she goes to the junior high school down the street.

I walked through the house, even checking the basement and the garage. Nothing. I know these next few hours are critical to find her. There are lots of people out looking. Oh, I hope they find her. She's in my prayers.

June 7, 2002

All my married nieces and nephews came over tonight for a barbecue. Everyone is talking about Elizabeth Smart's abduction, and there are still people canvassing the neighborhood.

My nephew is a mellow and gentle young man. As we were talking about this abduction my nephew blurted out, "If anyone took my son, I'd kill them." His voice broke as he tried to explain himself, "The love parents have for their children is powerful and profound, I don't think I could control myself. I'd kill them."

July 3, 2002

I found the perfect ski boat. I bought it and went directly to St. George. Now, I'm at Lake Powell with my nephews. I let each of them bring a friend. I'm here with eight boys. The day was glorious. I can't believe how good Burton is getting. It's his first time on a wakeboard, and he loves it. He's jumping the wake, easily switching in mid-air and landing a 180. Burton's friend is also a good boat driver, so I don't have to do all the work. I sit back, relax, and enjoy the show. Of course, occasionally, take a few runs myself!

Later:

It's dark. We camped on the beach, and I turned in early. I'm listening to the gentle waves hit the shore. The younger boys have already gone to sleep. The older boys are all gathered around the fire, laughing and roasting marshmallows.

Right after Elizabeth Smart was abducted, the family released a video of her laughing and cheesing it up at Lake Powell. She's a little younger than Parker. If she's still alive, I pray that wherever she is, joyous moments she had with her family at Lake Powell can sustain her now. I pray she's alive.

July 14, 2002

I bumped into a childhood friend. We went to elementary school together. She's a successful businessperson now, living with her partner in Park City. She gave me her card and insisted on taking me to lunch.

I shy away from contact with people from that old neighborhood. Reluctantly, I went.

She asked how I was doing, and the conversation wove to my family.

I told her that my father had passed away. She asked me how I felt about it. Most people immediately express condolences. I looked up at her.

She said, "I read your book."

I looked away and said, "Oh."

She said, "I've been looking for you for 10 years. I finally decided that you probably wrote the book and split. I envisioned you in Europe somewhere living with all that art and enjoying the Alps."

I smiled.

We talked for hours. The restaurant transitioned from lunch to dinner.

She told me that when she read the book, she already knew most of the stories—especially the ones with the teenagers in the neighborhood. She looked me directly in the eye and said, "Was I there?"

I paused for a very long time. I had to get myself back there. I remembered faces, events, minute details of objects. Smells. I couldn't remember if she was there.

Her urgency was tangible. She had to know. I went through as many of my old neighborhood memories as I could. I couldn't remember.

She exclaimed, "If I knew everything that happened to you, before I even read about them, I had to have been there."

I nodded, "That makes sense, but my memories don't have you there. You could have been there, and I just don't have it now. I'm sorry."

Then she told me she never forgot some of the events. She tried not to think about them. Then she said, "Some things I would like to forget, but haven't been able to bury them. She told me a few of the things that happened to her. Many of the same teenage boys and specifics of certain places. As she was speaking, it all made sense. I believe I was there and that we were abused together in that old neighborhood. Speaking with her did not jar my memory.

As we were wrapping up, I asked her if she was in therapy. She said that she wasn't in psychotherapy. The last few years, she'd battled Stage 3 cancer. She'd had radiation, chemo, the works. She told me her personal theory about cancer. She thought that every cell in the human body has the potential to turn cancerous. She said that no one is sure what the "trigger" is to cause a cell to go rogue with cancer. She said that there is a lot of evidence of exposure to certain chemicals and conditions. She mentioned the well-known studies of asbestos exposure causing mesothelioma, cigarettes to lung cancer, and even the government's testing of the atom bomb—and all the "down-winders" who died of cancer in Southern Utah.

After a short pause she said, "I don't know what triggered my cancer."

I understood. We promised to stay in touch. As I was walking to my car, I thought that maybe one day I'd tell her my private belief about Tom's death. I wasn't sure. It might sound a little hokey.

August 18, 2002

I took my mom to Chuck-A-Rama for dinner today. While we were there, I noticed a religious family all dressed up in long robes, like the Burkas that Muslim women wear. Only this family was white. I know that many people have converted to the Muslim religion, but it seemed out of place at Chuck-A-Rama on a hot Sunday afternoon in Salt Lake City, Utah.

When I visit Laurel in St. George, I see many polygamous women. You easily spot them. When *Paperdolls* first came out, a group of women who escaped a polygamous group came to a book signing that Carol did. They told her that many of the women and children in polygamous groups are sexually abused.

I'm not sure if this family was a polygamous family or a different religious group. I haven't seen a similar garb. It didn't feel right.

As I stared at this family, I met the eye of the young girl. I wanted to walk up to her and say, "Please come with me. Just because you were born in this family doesn't mean you have to stay."

The young girl kept looking at me as if she understood. She looked like she was in her early teens. Did she go to school in that garb? Did she go to school at all? That's all she needed, to be homeschooled by these loons. I tried so hard to not be judgmental, but the whole scene gave me the creeps.

I told my mom that I wanted to say something to them. She patted my hand and recited a portion of the serenity prayer, "Know the difference to know the things you can change in and the things you can't." I got the message. This is a free country and people can practice whatever religion they want. But this didn't feel right. The girl kept looking at me.

I wonder what would have happened if I had approached her? Probably her father would have jumped up and confronted me. I believe everyone has a right to religious freedom, but I highly doubt the wife is free to decide for herself; and I know that young daughter is not.

Carol

LORRAINE'S DAUGHTER, ISABEL, SLEPT OVER last night is back in Salt Lake on a college break. She came over last night for dinner with Norton and me. Isabel usually avoids a situation implying intimacy. Even now she sometimes flinches when she is touched.

However, we were having a good conversation when April arrived with a friend. I didn't know they were coming, but the friend had a crisis of memory. I left the table and took April and her friend to the study. The friend told a little of her childhood abuse memories to April and me and then sat huddled in a big chair sobbing uncontrollably. Isabel must have heard her because she left Norton and came in. Isabel had met April before. She knows that Hank abused April and now this friend too.

April and I were immobile. There are times when someone's pain seems so great you don't know if they want you near. Isabel knew. Today she put her arms around April's friend and held her. She patted her back and said over and over again, "It will be all right." She was kneeling, and her arms had to have become tired. Finally after a very long time, the sobs eased into silence. April and the friend left.

"Isabel," I said, holding her close. "You are so lucky that you remembered and told when you were little."

Isabel looked up at me. "No," she said. "The lucky ones are the ones who never had it happen."

April

I HAVE BROUGHT MY FRIEND to see Carol. She is sitting in a cushy armchair.

From a distance I say, "You're not crazy."

Carol asks her if she has slept. "No," she cries, "it keeps coming." Carol makes arrangements with a therapist at a hospital.

My friend sobs something about me. Something about me being her mirror. I long to hold her, but I know my fears at her stage. A touch was a weapon.

Isabel comes in and without hesitation enfolds her. Isabel wraps her young arms around my friend; the woman leans on Isabel. In broken tears she says, "Isabel—I want you to know—it's because of you—I'm trying. You said life is worth living." Isabel gently rocks her.

I look down. I feel the moisture of my own tears. Slowly my eyes rise to the large, gold-leafed mirror on the wall. I see the reflection of young Isabel holding the woman. I look into the mirror and see a small smile on my lips. I cannot see the scars on my face. I see Isabel's strength in her eyes framed in the gold-leafed mirror mounted on the wall.

My friend is going to the hospital.

"I wish I could give you something before you go—something for you to have—something for all of us, the children."

Dawn will soon come. And peace with gossamer—butterflies on meadow flowers and wind upon your hair—caressing you. I hope the ever changing beach renews you. Golden skies beyond a gray sphere bringing you warmth, hope, and strength. I thank you for the reflection you return. I wish you could see yourself through my eyes—the beauty and the hidden beauty—I know all the love you send out into the lives of others will flow back into your own. I pray for your healing: your restoration...your *palingenesia*... your recurrence of birth.

While waiting for an appointment today I glanced through the local paper. My eyes almost burned through the paper when I saw the name of the "stake president." Now he's the *former* stake president.

Apparently, he took it upon himself to write a letter to the Board of Pardons on behalf of one of the convicted pedophiles in the Scott's neighborhood. Until this afternoon, I didn't know anyone had been convicted from that neighborhood.

The stake president told me that the Church couldn't do anything unless there was a legal conviction because the Church couldn't afford the liability. Here's proof there was a conviction.

He lied to my face about the "market drying up" and fired me. He testified that he had spoken with the Apostle Neal Maxwell about the outbreak of sexual abuse in his area. According to the stake president, Neal Maxwell said, "When there's this much smoke there's fire. I leave it to you to find the truth."

The stake president told me that he couldn't do anything because there were only children who could testify in Court. He said that the Scotts didn't want their children/grandchildren to be subject to vigorous prosecution integration. There wasn't a trial or conviction and subsequently he couldn't do anything.

All along he knew there was a trial and a conviction.

The reason his name came up in this Deseret News article is because the former stake president wrote this prior to the convicted pedophile's parole hearing:

> "...many questions unanswered...regarding what, if anything, really happened."
>
> "I interviewed ███████ after having six sets of parents complain regarding the pressure she was placing on their children during her interviews," [Schmied] also wrote. "These parents felt ███████ was using techniques to confuse and cause their children to question their own knowledge of what really occurred."
>
> ███ did not respond to requests to be interviewed for this story.
> —*September 18, 2002*
> *Deseret News*

This former stake president is the same man who I called after Hank committed suicide. The same man who quoted the bible in response to the news, "It were better for him that a millstone were hanged about his neck, and he cast into the sea, than that he should offend one of these little ones." After citing that barbaric verse, he congratulated me on what an incredible job I was doing for my new company.

I have no idea why he's lied so much. He lied directly to my face about why he fired me (he cost his company millions to replace me by purchasing another bank in Boise). He previously told me that the Church wouldn't do anything regarding "all the smoke" about the sexual abuse in his area without legal precedent. Today I discover he had to have known there was a legal conviction.

Now, this same man writes a letter, as the former stake president, on behalf of a convicted perpetrator stating something that supposedly others had said about the treatment. I'm certainly not an attorney, but I'm pretty sure that quoting something that someone else said is hearsay. Especially when the people being quoted are still alive and their statements can be verified.

And, what makes him suddenly the interviewer? Did he interview the therapist for his/her temple recommend or tithing settlement? The way the Deseret News wrote this it made it seem like the former stake president interviewed the therapist in his/her capacity as a therapist and was questioning his/her abilities and techniques. The former stake president is in business; finance to be precise. I'd hate to see what he would say about my most recent mammogram, dental procedure, or any other type of test or treatment. From a layperson's perspective those tests and treatments would all be described as confusing and painful.

Why would he do this? Why did he lie to me? I used to think he lied to me because he was ashamed of his lack of courage or ability to do anything regarding the epidemic of sexual abuse in his area. Now, after Greg Schmeid, the former stake president, wrote this letter to a convicted pedophile's parole board, I'm not so sure.

September 21, 2002

We're at Lake Mead. Burton is really happy. He has such a dry sense of humor. One must pay attention and then his subtlety is hilarious. For the little kids, he tells such cute jokes:

"What is brown and sticky?" "A stick."

"Two muffins were in the oven. One muffin said to the other: 'It's getting really hot in here.' The other muffin exclaimed, 'Whoa, a talking muffin!'"

Then, he launched into his rendition of when Parker assaulted him with his cowboy boots and his mom had to take them away. Parker was sitting on the bow of the boat. He looked directly at Laurel, exclaimed that he was "damaged for life," shook his head and looked away. Laurel and I quickly met eyes and smiled.

After lunch, Parker went out on the tube. He was lying flat on his stomach and holding onto the rope. Burton was driving to the boat and turning every which way to throw Parker off. Parker is strong. He's the quarterback on the high school football team, and his arms are ripped. As Laurel was watching, she exclaimed, "My Strippling Warriors."

I smiled. Laurel was referencing a story in the Book of Mormon. It's about young men who were great warriors and always obeyed their mothers. Someone gave Burton a T-Shirt that had a cartoon of a big, buff guy on the front that read, "Strippling Warrior." On the back it says, "Mama's boy!" Burton wears it with pride.

We boated until the sunset receded behind the mountains. My whole body ached from the few runs I took, but I don't think the boys were tired. They pulled the boat up on the ramp, the boys wiped down the boat, put everything away, and covered it. I paused. This moment can never be repeated. What a perfect day.

I remembered back to my struggles a few years ago and thought about how I contemplated taking my life. My time in Coronado confirmed to me that I must take mental pictures of the goodness in my life. Then, psychically, I etch them in my heart. I thought of all the mental snap shots I took of the weekend, and re-registered them. I mentally carved these golden moments onto the walls of my soul. As I started the car and began pulling the boat back to St. George, I glanced at Laurel, and then looked at everyone in the car. Tired and happy boys: Burton about to embark on a two-year mission to South America, Parker ready to lead his football team to State, Jason conquering the piano, and Paul ready to start his last year of elementary school. These incredible moments will be etched in me forever.

November 1, 2002

Burton is now in Brazil for two years. It was hard to see him go. It was difficult for Laurel. As we watched his plane ascend into the sky Laurel whispered to me, "The Church really asks a lot of families."

Today, Laurel got her first letter from Burton. He arrived safely. He's at the training center and they can have as much food as they want. He wrote, "I was pleasantly surprised that they had a big bowl of vanilla pudding. And you know how I love vanilla pudding. I piled it high on my plate. When I sat down, I took a big spoonful of the pudding. To my horror, it was mayonnaise."

Laurel is laughing. I know she misses him more than she can even describe. But at least she's smiling now.

November 16, 2002

Parker's football team almost made it to the state finals. It was such an exciting game. After the game, Parker didn't come out of the bus. Finally, Laurel went into the school bus. Parker was in the back of the bus, all by himself, crying.

The popular, handsome, quarterback Parker was blaming himself. While Laurel was in the bus with Parker, I watched the entire team gather their belongings, wipe away tears, shake hands or even hug one another. All these big burly guys were wiping away tears.

Until this moment, I never knew that the big, buff football players cried when they lost.

Like a slap in my face, I realized I'd been holding onto an extremely outdated perception of teenage boys. My brother couldn't even cry when Tom died. Inaccurately, I thought that when boys hit puberty, they quit crying. I thought they felt less or something. I am embarrassed. Somewhere, deep in my unconscious, I still feared them, like the abused little girl once I was. Talk about an ah-ha moment. Not all teenage boys are bad. In fact, probably only a small fraction are abusers. I am relieved I can continue to shed my inaccurate-scar-lined viewpoint. Although I felt bad for Parker, I felt like a ton of bricks was lifted off my shoulders. Most young men are good. Most people are good. Most simply want to be loved, be okay, be productive and experience some happiness.

When Parker finally emerged from the bus, I felt like his experience had given me one of the greatest gifts of my life. With tears welling over, I watched Parker call his team together, and I heard his sincere apology. It's a team sport. They wouldn't let him take the blame. No one blamed anyone. It was a great season. Parker came over and gave me a hug and thanked me for coming. I know he'll never really understand, but I tried to tell him I was incredibly grateful to have been there.

As we were driving home, Laurel and I talked about how hard it is to watch Parker suffer through disappointment and loss. Laurel said, "As hard as it is for him to lose, it is good for him to learn how to lose. Life does involve loss, disappoint-ment, and pain. I hope he doesn't experience more than his share of it throughout his life, but it's good for him to know that he can handle it and not be afraid of it."

Laurel is my hero.

December 7, 2002

Every year, Laurel brings the boys up to go skiing with me. They always board. The last few times, they teased me about being an old lady and just skiing. Last winter, unbeknownst to Burton and Parker, I enrolled in a workshop for snowboarding. I spent six full days basically falling on my face. After my first lesson, I wasn't sure I could do it again. I hurt in places I didn't even know had muscles!

I slowly started to get the hang of it. Last night, Laurel brought the boys up so we could hit the slopes early this morning. They did their usual teasing routine about my age and skiing, I looked at them and said, "I think I'll try snowboarding today."

"No, Aunt April, we don't get to go very often, and we'll spend the whole day just waiting for you. We didn't mean it, you're not old, please ski."

I smiled to myself, walked up to the rental counter and rented a board. I was lucky that the boys were so busy getting their gear situated that they didn't notice I knew exactly what size board to get. The whole way up the lift, they were prepar-ing me.

"Aunt April, when we get off the lift, you just try to stay straight. We'll both go to the right."

I slid right off the lift and then connected my S-turns all the way down the first hill. I turned around to wait for them, shrugged my shoulders and said, "Mmm, it's not that hard."

Both boys were so shocked their jaws were gaping wide open. At lunch, Parker called his mom.

"Mom, you have to try snowboarding! If Aunt April can do it, you can! She kept right up with us! You'd love it. You have to come with us next time!"

Parker handed me the phone and said, "My mom wants to talk to you." Laurel knew I had taken the class and how hard it was. When I picked up the phone, Laurel said, "Thanks. Thanks for that." We'll never tell them. Maybe in my will, I'll jot a note about it for them.

December 18, 2002

My mom just called. She sounded like she did when she called me early in the morning of 9-11. She asked me if I saw David Fuller's obituary in the paper. David Fuller lived across the street from my childhood home. He is the guy who locked me in the rabbit cage and peed on me when I was little. I told her I hadn't seen it, and I doubt I'll look it up. Years ago, in our family meeting, I told her that he'd abused me then locked me naked in a rabbit cage. On the phone just now, my mom didn't notice my response. I didn't have one. I couldn't care less. I'm kind of pleased that I don't have any emotion when his name is brought up.

My mom said that she called the Fuller's house to offer her condolences. June Fuller is currently my mother's visiting teaching companion. When my mom called, June answered and said, "It's all over the papers. It's so horrible." And hung up on my mother. My mom asked me if I'd seen anything in the papers. I hadn't, I don't care.

Maybe those old childhood wounds have healed. Overall, a great day; work is going well. I'm looking forward to more snow for the resorts and I might treat myself to a new snowboard for Christmas. I am blessed.

December 21, 2002

My mom called. She said that when my brother got back in town, he did some research on the Internet and found out what happened to David Fuller. Before I could say anything, my mother read this whole article:

"Police: Local Man Meets Girl Via 'Net, Kills Her
Both Found Dead In Arkansas Storage Unit
POSTED: 10:35 am PST December 6, 2002
UPDATED: 5:43 pm PST December 6, 2002
CONWAY, Ark. — A San Diego man allegedly killed a 13-year-old girl with whom he had struck up a relationship on the Internet, then turned the gun on himself during a SWAT operation in Arkansas, 10News reported.

The girl was reported missing from her home in Holland, Ark., north of Little Rock on Tuesday. The bodies of Kacie Woody (pictured, left) and (David) Fuller (pictured, right) (47) were found at a storage garage in the town of Conway, Ark., according to 10News.

Investigators searching for Fuller Wednesday at his rented storage garage heard a shot coming from inside his van, police said. SWAT officers tried unsuccessfully for two hours to get Fuller out of the van. The officers then stormed the van where they found the bodies of Fuller and Woody. Authorities said that Fuller had struck up an Internet relationship with the girl some weeks ago.

"We don't believe Kacie invited him to come to Arkansas or knew he was coming," said Deputy Jack Pike, spokesman for the Faulkner County Sheriff's Department. "We believe she was abducted from her home. We found her eyeglasses broken and a chair out of place," ... Kacie's brother last saw her at their home Tuesday evening and later determined she was missing. Their father called police when he could not find her.

Pike said that the search for Kacie intensified after Fuller was identified as a suspect in her abduction. Late Wednesday afternoon, investigators found Fuller's name on a storage unit rental agreement in Conway about 15 miles from Holland.

Pike said that officers weren't expecting to find Fuller at the garage.

Pike also noted that it wasn't clear how long Woody had been dead."

—San Diego Union Tribune

My mother kept saying, "Can you imagine? No wonder June was distraught. Can you imagine?" The air drained from my lungs. I'm not sure how long it was before I could breathe. I don't remember if I said this to my mother or not, but I kept thinking, "No, I can't imagine. Yes, I can imagine." Somewhere in my conversation with my mom, I reminded her that David Fuller locked me in the rabbit cage.

She remembered. She gasped. We both cried.

I'm stunned, and I'm not surprised. I'm devastated.

December 22, 2002

I searched the internet. One news broadcaster interviewed an FBI agent who said that Fuller acted with such planning and precision this was probably not his first crime. The FBI agent said there could be hundreds.

The walls in my office felt like they were collapsing in on me. I had to get out. The day was freezing but I walked and walked.

"Hundreds."

I thought of Carol's daughter Susy, in her adult rage, spray painting warnings on Hank's house. Those warnings didn't stop Hank. He continued until his new wife told him he would spend the rest of his life in jail. Then, Hank ended it himself.

David Fuller ended it himself, only when the swat team was closing in on him.

My words of hope, light, therapy, and change are in vain. Only death or jail will stop them.

Later:

I copied the hyperlink of a broadcast of that San Diego television station and e-mailed it to the woman from my childhood neighborhood with whom I had lunch last summer. Within minutes, my phone was ringing. She was shocked but not surprised.

"April, you have to write about this."

I told her I was thinking of flying to Arkansas to meet with Kacie Woody's family. I had no idea why. She cautioned me that they might not welcome someone from Utah. Someone who knew what a monster he was. She told me that they might blame me. She even cautioned me to call my attorney in case there was a liability.

There was that word again: "Liability."

The "stake president" told me he didn't want to pursue a Church court against Hank because he didn't want the Church to be liable. Hank was an attorney, the "stake president" was worried that Hank would sue. Could I be liable for what I knew and not revealed? I feel like if I had done more, maybe someone somewhere would have blown the whistle on David Fuller. Maybe someone could have stopped him. Maybe Kacie Woody would still be alive.

Although I changed David Fuller's name in *Paperdolls*, many knew it was him. No one could do anything about him: Shame on us. Shame on our fear of "liability." Shame on our denial systems. Shame on our legal systems.

And way more than a "shame on" to David Fuller. I hope he rots in hell.

And God rest Kacie Woody's beautiful soul. Beautiful, vivacious Kacie Woody. Please be in a beautiful place in Heaven. I am so sorry. I am so sorry I couldn't have done more to protect you.

Oh dear God, please hear my prayer. Please dear God, please, let her know she is loved and innocent and remembered. Please let her know that I and many others will try to do something so that what happened to her will not happen to beautiful, innocent, wonderful souls like her again. Please God, please comfort her soul and let her know. Please, dear God, hear my prayer.

December 23, 2002

It snowed today. After work, I went to my mother's house and shoveled her front walk. I gazed over to the Fuller's. The house was dark. Their driveway covered in snow. I wondered what was happening behind those darkened windows. I walked across the street. I cleared the snow surrounding their home. I didn't want it to freeze over before they got out.

I want to go to Arkansas to offer my sincere condolences to Kacie Woody's family. I talked to Laurel about visiting them. She said that if she had lost one of her children, in any way, the last thing she would want would be a stranger flying across the country to offer their sympathy. Then she said, "I don't know if there will ever be a good time, April. I'm not sure I would ever want to meet anyone who knew the barbarian who slaughtered my child—even if you were abused by the same barbarian."

December 24, 2002

Christmas Eve, I have my family over for dinner in the April version of the Norwegian tradition. My grandmother used to make a formal seven-course meal on Christmas Eve. I had it catered. It went well, my mother really enjoyed it.

I'm sitting here looking at the twinkling lights of my way-too-big-for-the-room Christmas tree. The fire is crackling, and I'm listening to Christmas music in the background.

I know as I sit in this sanctuary of serenity there are families in turmoil. Somewhere an alcoholic is raging and ripping the family apart. A young child might be in bed, not excited for Santa Claus, but in fear of a monster taking them in the night.

I pray for comfort for Elizabeth Smart's family and if Elizabeth is still alive, please let her be in a place of safety. I have no idea what is worse, the grief and anguish the Woody family is experiencing or the pain of the unknown the Smarts' suffer.

I keep thinking of Kacie Woody's family. I wish I could do something. More importantly, I wish I could have done something to get David Fuller off the streets. Many people have told me that *Paperdolls* did a lot of good and that it helped a lot of people. Kacie Woody is dead. A lot of good that did her. I feel like all my work, all my sacrifices and all that I've lost since writing *Paperdolls* was in vain.

February 22, 2003

I saw a big billboard with Elizabeth Smart's picture on it. I know those billboards on I-15 aren't cheap. I doubt the family will ever give up. Kacie Woody and Elizabeth Smart are about the same age.

I fear Elizabeth is dead also. If she's not, I can't imagine the torment she's enduring. We may never know what happened to her. I pray for her soul and I pray for comfort to her family.

March 12, 2003

It's my birthday and I took the day off to go snowboarding. Since it's a Wednesday and in middle of the week, I couldn't get anyone else to get the day off and join me. It didn't matter, I simply had to treat myself and go. It was such a gloriously wonderful day. I'm still an intermediate snowboarder, and Snowbird has some incredibly steep runs. There's usually a way down for intermediate riders like me, but it was really steep for a relative novice on a snowboard. I was falling all over the place and loving every minute of it. I was getting pretty tired from picking myself up, and my phone kept ringing and ringing. I vowed I wouldn't answer it on my birthday, but I figured it was probably an emergency. Since I needed a break, I sat down on the soft side of Wilbere Ridge. I had over 25 messages. After a few birthday greetings, I started getting messages "Elizabeth Smart is found, and she's alive!"

I wept openly.

I floated down the rest of the mountain.

Elizabeth Smart is alive. What a miracle. This news is the best birthday present I could ever imagine! Elizabeth Smart is alive, and she's doing fairly well.

March 14, 2003

The mayor and Elizabeth Smart's father are having a big celebration in honor of Elizabeth Smart at Liberty Park tonight. It seems that is all anyone can talk about. It truly is a miracle, but now I'm getting concerned for Elizabeth. She's only 14. She needs time to heal. It's wonderful that she has so much support and love in the community and the world, but I'm concerned. She needs time.

I wrote this letter to the mayor of Salt Lake City:

Give Elizabeth Her Privacy

When I heard the news that Elizabeth Smart was alive and physically well, I wept. Tears of joy, relief, and a humble reverence for the resilience of the human soul, or her soul, of her precious spirit. Miracles do happen.

For so many months, this story has become part of us. By us, I mean the public at large: not in the Smart Family, her close neighbors and chosen friends. I mean us. We, who would never have known of her—if she hadn't been yanked from her bed in the middle of the night at knife point.

We've held her in our hearts, we've prayed for her family, and we've rejoiced in the miracle of her return.

We know she is safe. We all know that she has a tough road ahead of her. It will take time for her to adjust, get acclimated to her family again, to begin to sort out her own life and to heal.

To show our love for her, let us respect her privacy. She is a teenager, who has been through a lot. It is not our right to know all of it. She does not belong to us. She needs space and privacy.

The Smarts are not public people, and Elizabeth certainly did not choose to become a celebrity. Again, she is not a self-chosen celebrity, a sports star or an Elected Official. She is a teenager who has suffered a violent crime. Let us respect that.

She does not deserve to be exploited.

Let us hold the memory of the miracle of her return in our hearts forever. And let her have the space, privacy and boundaries that were her right as a private person in our society and are especially granted to minors.

Let us not forget that this is her life. She is a human being, entitled to all that entails. Let us bless her with privacy.

Let her have her life back. Let her begin to feel a sense of control of herself once again. If she chooses, sometime down the road in her adult life, to tell us her story—let her decide.

Cherish the memory of her miracle by holding those whom you love closely to your heart. Tell your loved ones you love them. Appreciate the miracles in your own life. Let her be.

Please write to your local papers and media outlets and encourage them to show restraint. Elizabeth doesn't belong to us. She deserves her life back. Don't let her life become, as Patty Hearst recently stated on CNN, "entertainment for the masses."

March 16, 2003

I keep trying to stop myself, but I am watching the news about Elizabeth Smart. I feel like a hypocrite. I want to give her privacy, and I'm one of the many gawking with morbid curiosity. In my gentler moments with myself, I understand that her homecoming is truly a miracle.

Today they showed some pictures of her captor when he was younger. I stopped breathing. I know that young man. Maybe, maybe it's because there is so much attention to this, I'm just making it up. The weird straggly-haired homeless man, I didn't recognize. But when the news showed a picture of him as a clean-cut, blue-eyed, teenager…I stopped breathing. I know that face. Maybe I'm wrong, but I think he came to our house one night with one of Tom's friends. I think he went to high school with my brother, but then he got put in some other school … because he showed himself to another little girl. Tom's friend said that I would never tell like the other little girl did.

I'm not sure, I could be making connections that aren't there.

I called Laurel. Laurel's husband also went to school during the same time period as my older brothers. My brothers' and Laurel's husband ran in totally different circles. There were over 1,000 kids in each grade, so I can easily understand that they didn't know one another. However, after the teenage photo of Brian David Mitchell flashed across the screen, Laurel's husband checked his old high school yearbook. There he was, Brian Mitchell. Hank, Brain Mitchell and my brothers are all listed in that same yearbook. David Fuller was a year younger and wasn't in this yearbook. But I know he was friends with all these guys.

There is so much publicity I'm not sure it's real. Maybe he wasn't there. My memory is faint on this. I'm not sure. It's eerie that he was in the same school during the same time period with this group of misfit teenage boys, where sexual abuse ran rampant.

April 17, 2003

All the excitement about Elizabeth Smart's return has started to die down. Thank goodness for her.

Occasionally, I am still stunned that David Fuller, one of my most torturous perpetrators grew up to be an adult with even more evil to inflict. My eyes fill with tears every time I think of Kacie Woody. My regret is tangible. I wish I could have done more. In my caustic moods, I wish I truly had been crazy and made the whole thing up. Then David Fuller's treachery would have been a figment of my imagination; he wouldn't have grown up to be a monster. Kacie Woody would still be alive. But, sadly, I'm not insane. I didn't make it up. Davy Fuller did abuse me, he did lock me naked in a rabbit cage for hours. His evil nature did escalate to child abduction and murder.

I wonder if my process of coming to terms with the evil that David Fuller committed is tainting my memories about the presence of Brian David Mitchell in my childhood home. I have one memory that is crystal clear of that face, with Tom's friend, at my front door. They took me to the basement where we played nasty. Maybe my mind is playing tricks on me. Maybe knowing what Hank did as an adult and what David Fuller did as an adult are over-stimulating my brain. I feel like I'm short-circuiting when I see those pictures of Brian Mitchell as a young man though. The scruffy Jesus-wanna-be that kidnapped Elizabeth Smart does not invoke even a semblance of a memory for me.

Now I truly have to break away from all this. My memories won't change a thing. It doesn't matter that Brian Mitchell and David Fuller went to the same high school. It doesn't matter that one of them definitely abused me as a child, and possibly the other. It doesn't matter at all. It's eerie and I have to let it go.

I'm continuing my growth, my quest to be whole, and hopefully to a path towards enlightenment. It doesn't matter if I have a fragment of a memory with someone who looks like the exact same guy as the photos of young Brian Mitchell. Elizabeth is home, and I pray for her continued recovery and growth. Kacie Woody is dead, and I still wish I could have done more to protect her. Somehow, some way, I have to let go of that haunting fact: I wish I could have done something more to save her. I couldn't. David Fuller is eternally responsible for those acts.

July 24, 2003

I spent the day boating with Parker, Jason and Paul. Parker brought along a few of his friends. They are all such good kids. Sometimes I must pinch myself because

I know that Laurel's kids aren't that extraordinary. Compared to the sick teenage boys my brothers were—and all their friends—I formed a skewed view of average teenage boys. Sometimes Laurel must remind me that these guys are just normal boys. Good kids, but normal, simply growing up and finding their place in the world. My childhood was the one that was extraordinary.

I miss Burton, and I know that the youngest, Paul, really misses him also. I took a fun video of Paul trying to jump half the wake. Hopefully we'll be able to send it to Burton at Christmas time.

Although today was such a wonderful day, tonight I'm kind of melancholy. Sometimes I wish I had my own family. My own children. I decided years ago that I was simply too broken to ever have been a good mother. I'd probably smother my children and immobilize them so that they could not learn on their own. I consistently battle my own demons: don't be afraid, people are good, you are worthwhile. I couldn't pass that dysfunction down. Yes, I have regrets. However, I love, have fun, and overall relish my unique life. I love sharing it with the special souls with whom I am connected.

October 6, 2003

This afternoon I had a chance to give back to my friend Jennifer and her dad. It's a glorious autumn afternoon, the sun is shining beautifully, and the leaves are blanketing the mountains in a patchwork of yellows, reds, and oranges. Jennifer and I took the Boss to Jordanelle Reservoir. He loved it. He was feeling good enough to drive the boat, and he ripped around the lake like a teenager, laughing the entire time.

We let the sun warm our shoulders, then an old song by Steve Winwood, *Higher Love*, came on. Jennifer reached over, cranked up the stereo, took her father's hand and said, "Dad, let's dance!"

As long as I live, I will never forget the water glistening like diamonds, the mountains ablaze with color as they danced on my boat on this glorious autumn day.

March 16, 2004

Jennifer called me to let me know that her father has been placed in hospice care, and he's not expected to live long. She said that her dad wants to see me. She gave me the address of the care facility and told me to go there sooner rather than later.

I cleared my schedule this afternoon. He doesn't even look like the same person. He has always been the epitome of life, activity and hope. I wheeled him into the waiting area for the view of the snow-filled mountains. He couldn't talk much; he was simply too weak.

After a while, he said, "Don't you lose hope. Enjoy life. Pass it on." My voice broke slightly as I said, "Dum spiro, spero."

With effort, he nodded and said, "Dum spiro, spero." While I breathe, I hope.

March 21, 2004

Jennifer's father passed away. The moment he passed, the horses in the field by the hospice center starting running. Jennifer's certain her father was over there riding them.

March 31, 2004

The funeral today was beautiful. There were hundreds of people there paying tribute to a man that made this world a better place and helped so many learn to contribute, love and enjoy life. At the cemetery, the Air Force commemorated his life with a full 21-gun salute and a "Missing Man Formation Fly-past."

Four fighter jets fly directly over the cemetery in a V Formation. Then as they pass by, one jet abruptly pulls up towards the heavens. The one jet pulling up represents the departure and symbolizes his ascent into Heaven.

Before the service, everyone wrote a small message to Boss. The message was carefully inserted into a helium balloon. After the fighter jets passed, we all released our balloons. My note said, "Dum Spiro, Spero."

May 13, 2004

Not a day goes by when I don't think of Kacie Woody. I think she would have been in high school now. Damn that David Fuller. Damn all the people who didn't believe me. Dammit.

May 31, 2004

Lilly is now in high school. I took her with some of her friends boating at East Canyon. Lilly was with one friend out on the tube, and they were laughing so hard I could hear them over the roaring boat engine. Oh, the joy!

Suffice it to say, I'm sure that my fears about little Lilly were simply fears. My memories hadn't been triggered back then. I read that frequently women start remembering their own abuse when they had children the same age. Lilly wasn't my child, but we spent extensive time together. Seeing her beautiful, innocent zest for life was certainly one of the catalysts for me to begin to remember.

Now as I gaze at Lilly, with her laughter and her joy, I still have a few tugs on my heart: one of gratitude for her beautiful life and another more solemn remembrance of Kacie Woody. I don't think a day goes by that I don't think of Kacie Woody. When I think of her, I am now imprisoned by anguish and regret that I could have done more. Now I carry with me a solemn reverence in her remembrance. Her memory is with me always.

I laugh as Lilly dives into the water; I recall seeing that video the family of Elizabeth Smart released days after her abduction. Elizabeth was cheesing it up on the shores of Lake Powell. Oh, how I hope that she is free to joyously play on the beaches and dance in the sunshine unencumbered by memories of her months of hell.

October 8, 2004

I'm in St. George hanging out with the boys while their parents are in South America picking up Burton from his mission. Jason is in his first year of high school now and is in the marching band. He has marching band practice at 6 a.m. We're up before it's light, driving to practice. Laurel told me that I could sleep during practice. I packed up my pillow and blanket ready for a nice snooze. And well, I'm pretty sure Laurel is laughing her head off right now. I'm in the parking lot with my pillow against the car window. This is marching band practice. They are outside with very loud bugles, tubas, and drums. Not a chance for sleep.

October 15, 2004

Burton is home! He got off the plane, and Paul ran into his arms! Paul is in 7th grade now and is a bit too big to easily pick up. Burton did it anyway. He swung his youngest brother around, then gave him a big bear hug. I couldn't blink back the tears.

Laurel always tells me that her family is not extraordinary. She knows a lot of families that are just as good, just as wonderfully loving, and healthy as hers. I try to believe her, but then I hear stories about my real sister-in-law threatening to give up her son for adoption or the Division of Family services taking away Melinda's sons. I simply struggle to not frame up Laurel and her family as a miracle. She corrects me every single time I say her family is incredible. I'm in awe of an average family. I feel such joy at their averageness.

May 8, 2005

Burton has been excited to get the boat out of winter storage and launched. This week we went to Lake Mead with a group of his friends, and of course, his younger brothers Jason and Paul. Burton was amazing. He landed every single flip he tried! It was like Burton wasn't missing a day of wakeboarding, nor taking two years off for his church mission. I said something to him about how surprised I am that he's still so good. Burton's eyes gleamed, threw an M&M in the air and caught it in his mouth and said, "Ah, it's just healthy living!"

Burton has this motto that he yells to his little brothers when they go out into the water, "Go big or go home!" Today, after Paul jumped in the water, Burton looked over at me and said, "This one is for Boss." Then, he called to the back of the boat, "Hey, Paul, dum spiro, spero!"

We could hear Paul grumbling, "Whatever in the heck that is."

Burton hollered, "While I breathe, I hope!"

Burton leaned over and said to his younger brother, "Remember Boss? Well, when he was a prisoner of war in Germany, that's what the guys would say to each other, 'While I breathe, I hope.'"

Paul looked up at his older brother and said, "Burton, that's really cool."

As Paul got the rope ready and I popped the engine into gear, Paul yelled to me, "Aunt April: 'dum spiro, spero!'"

I slammed the throttle down, and Paul popped up. He cut outside the wake and quickly cut right back in. When he hit the outside of the wake, he flew over the entire thing! Burton and all his friends were whooping and cheering. Paul then kicked a quick 180 and landed on the other side of the wake. I'm positive that Boss was smiling from Heaven.

September 24, 2005

I volunteer with a group to help repair homes in downtown Salt Lake. I paint. While chatting with another volunteer he asked where I was from and where I went to high school. Usually, I don't answer. He persisted. I finally told him.

Surprised, he said, "I'm probably a lot older than you are, but that's where I went to school also." He was in high school with my brothers. I didn't say a word. Then he shrugged and said, "I'm embarrassed about how some of my classmates turned out."

Clearly, he wanted to tell me about them. I didn't say a word. He told me that his high school buddies got into drugs and all sorts of weird stuff.

Trying to end the conversation, I shrugged, "That's too bad."

He continued, "Yeah, some of them scrambled their brains out. I see one guy around downtown. He doesn't recognize anyone."

We worked in silence for a few minutes then he asked, "I was good friends with Dave Fuller. Didn't he live near you? I wonder what happened to him."

My blood turned to ice. I said, "He's dead. My brother saw it in the paper."

A few hours later as we were washing out our paintbrushes, I asked, "Do you know if David Fuller was friends with Brian Mitchell?"

After a long pause, he said, "Mitchell, that sounds familiar." I didn't want to say, "Yeah, it's familiar because he kidnapped Elizabeth Smart." I waited. He continued, "Brian Mitchell, yeah, he's a couple of years older, yeah I remember him. They did hang out together. One time Fuller boasted that he dropped acid with Mitchell. That's about when I bailed. Way too heavy for me. Like I said those guys were on a bad path."

They did know each other. I have no idea why I was compelled to ask. It doesn't change anything. Kacie Woody is still gone, and Elizabeth was still abducted.

Maybe it isn't accurate, but according to one guy who knew David Fuller during his teenage years, Brian Mitchell and David Fuller did drugs together. I hope that's all they did together.

Carol

ELIZABETH SMART HAD A COMPELLING interview on CNN today. Elizabeth gathered tremendous strength from her own mother including profound advice on punishing her perpetrators. The day after Elizabeth was returned to her family, Lois Smart said, "Elizabeth, what this man has done to you is terrible. There aren't words strong enough to describe how wicked and evil he is. He has taken 9 months of your life that you can never get back again. Don't give him another minute."

Her mother's advice continued: "The best punishment you can ever give him is to be happy, is to follow your dreams and do exactly what you want to do."

I look at Yvonne, Susy, Lorraine's and Jake's children and they all seem to be doing so well. But that's just on the surface. Occasionally lingering effects of the abuse manifest in painful and unexpected ways. It enrages me.

I think of the greatest leaders of the twentieth century—Gandhi, Martin Luther King, Nelson Mandela—and they seem to share an amazing ability to project healing and forgiveness. Maybe we've made some progress in the west—since the not too far distant past when an honor code demanded satisfaction in the form of an apology or a duel. A lot of the greatest literature addressed terrible violations of the human body and soul. Roger Chillingsroth in *The Scarlet Letter* is destroyed because he can't forgive. King Lear never manages to verbalize repentance to Cordelia. Othello and Hamlet must enact the code of their own culture even when it leads to death, and "The Grand Inquisitor" section of *The Brothers Karamazov* is as great as any literature can be. Trying to find peace, I re-read all these works, but Conrad's words in *The Heart of Darkness*, "the horror, oh the horror" best reflect my own feelings and somehow give me the most comfort.

In Bloemfontein, South Africa, there's a monument erected by the Boers who lost the terrible war there with the British and whose families were massacred by them. On the grey granite are engraved the sentences, "We will never forget. We will never forgive." In Jerusalem, the Holocaust monument says only "We will never forget."

We will never forget. Norton and I have known murderous rage towards Hank. But I truly believe the most remarkable words Christ or anyone else ever uttered were, "Forgive them, for they know not what they do." Stopping violence implies forgiveness. I believe forgiveness is the highest moral virtue to which we can aspire.

But if Hank had not died, could I ever have forgiven him? I don't think so. I really don't.

April

IT'S BEEN 10 YEARS SINCE Gramps passed away. It seems like it was yesterday. Every week, I walk the dogs up to my grandparents' grave. On my way up to their headstone I pass many famous people buried in this cemetery: Mormon prophets, apostles, and other well-known individuals from Utah history. None of them are as important to me as my grandparents. In the fall, I usually plant a few tulip bulbs. They are in full bloom today.

I murmured a silent prayer to thank my grandparents for everything they had given me. They instilled a love of the outdoors, an appreciation for the majestic mountains surrounding us, and an appreciation and love of literature, music, and the arts. Once I gave my grandmother a handmade card. I drew flowers on the outside and wrote on the inside: "With art, we are not alone." Gramps quoted it frequently.

I thought of Carol in the Paris at the L'Orangerie weeping in front of the huge panels of Monet's "Water Lillies." For a moment, I was with her. Weeping as I stood at the foot of these majestic mountains. Weeping because I miss my grandparents yet shedding tears of gratitude for all that they had given me. Out loud, I said, "Thank you for giving me a safe place filled with warmth and love—especially in those times when I was a child and needed you so very much. Thank you for holding me and telling me all will be well. Thank you for helping me see that despite the insanity of man, life is beautiful and worth living. I promise to notice more, to appreciate all the beauty and live with intent. To enjoy this beautiful life, you sacrificed so very much to provide for me. Thank you."

As I walked back to my house, I could hear Edvard Grieg's "Morning" playing in my mind. Grieg was a Norwegian and one of my grandparents' favorite composers. The sounds of the oboe and the flute echoed through my soul as I recalled my grandparents' exclamations and excited descriptions of Grieg, his Norwegian background and their love of this song. In college I saw Ibsen's play "Peer Gynt." Interestingly the song served as a background as the hero awoke to realize he was abandoned and stranded in the desert. His friends abandoned him in the night. Treachery and deception is a common theme in art and in the human existence. Yet here I walked, buoyed up by the song, the memories of those whom I cherished deeply sustaining me as I re-committed to embracing the wonder and beauty of this life. Maybe that's why my grandparents played "Morning" so often for me. They knew I had been deceived and abandoned. But they also knew that life is precious, beautiful, and good. And for that, I thank them.

February 17, 2007

PARKER IS IN TOWN for the weekend. He's dating a darling young woman who is attending the University of Utah. He woke me up early this morning, sat on the edge of my bed and told me that he thinks she's "the one." He's completely twitterpated. It's adorable. I am so happy for him. Parker is a handsome, kind, and caring guy. Of course, I'm bias beyond biased, but any girl would be so lucky to have him. In fact, if she is the one, I know there will be some hearts breaking in St. George.

I didn't offer him any advice. I'm not exactly in any place to give marital advice. I just listened to him. I am thrilled with his joy. He's concerned because he has to get through school. But he's pretty sure she's the one for him. They'll work it out.

February 18, 2007

I met Parker's girlfriend. She's wonderful. She made dinner for us. She loves my kitchen and wants to come over and cook again.

I often joke that when I was growing up our kitchen was a war zone; therefore, I don't cook. I always laugh that one of the important aspects of cooking is to stay in the kitchen. It's kind of hard to cook anything if you don't stay in the kitchen— hence, I simply don't cook. I'm thrilled that Parker's girlfriend wants to come over here and cook! She's quite a great cook to boot!

JOY

i thank You God for most this amazing
day....
and for everything which is natural
which is infinite which is yes

—e.e. cummings

April

I CALLED BURTON TODAY AND told him that I had Parker's boots. I heard him gasp on the phone. He said, "All these years! You've had them all these years? What? I thought my mom chucked them in St. George!" I assured him that the legendary boots' story happened at my house, I was going to give them back to Parker tomorrow at the wedding breakfast. Burton couldn't stop laughing, especially when I told him that his mom said, "Maybe, maybe I could give them back after Parker gets married."

I asked Burton if he would help me at the Wedding Breakfast tomorrow when I give the boots back— because he was the victim of the infamous kicks that led to the cowboy boots being banished from Parker's life. He laughed and said, "Sure! And I'll be sure to tell the entirely true version of the story!"

Oh dear, Burton is hilarious; this ought to be good! I'm excited. This is one of the best things I've ever done!

Later:

As I was driving to St. George, Laurel called. She was laughing. She was at a wedding dinner-barbecue tonight at Snow Canyon State Park. It was in honor of the pending nuptials, like a wedding dinner some do the night before a wedding. During the dinner, somehow the story of the boots was brought up. Laurel knows I'm giving them back to him tomorrow. The story of the boots gets funnier with each iteration.

I told her that I was going to get Burton to help me tomorrow. Laurel laughed and said, "Burton didn't say a thing tonight! Parker brought it up. He told the entire wedding party that his mother had damaged him for life by taking away his beloved cowboy boots. He even said that he'd never do that to any of his kids, because it was so traumatic."

August 4, 2007

As I did with my niece, Tom's daughter, and with Burton's wedding, I did one of those genealogy pictures, showing the bride and the groom's parents, grandparents, great-grandparents, and great-great grandparents of each of the couples' wedding days. Since I had already done one for Burton's wedding, I only had to add the bride's side. I now have a tradition set, and I give this genealogy picture to the bride and groom at their wedding breakfast.

Only this time, when I got up to present Parker and his bride's genealogy picture, I had an extra special surprise. There were quite a few people at the luncheon, so they gave me a microphone. I stood up and asked Burton to come up. He was prepared and told his version of the infamous boots story. The whole thing was better than I ever imagined.

Burton is extremely funny. He has a dry wit, and one must really look at him to be able to tell he's joking. Fortunately, all the family and friends at the wedding breakfast knew his humor. He began by stating that Parker wasn't always the valiant Knight before us now. When he was younger, he had a brash side that manifest in the form of boots with extra weaponry attached in the form of spikes.

The exaggerated embellishment went on and on. Burton was a victim to Parker's violent outbursts of kicking. There was bleeding. Ambulances called. Until finally their mother saved Burton's life by taking the boots away.

The entire place was howling with laughter. After things started to settle down, I started to say something. Adorned in his full wedding tuxedo, Parker stood up to defend himself. He calmly said that he's always been a stable and kind guy. There was no blood. No spikes. No ambulances. But, when he was a toddler, Burton bumped into him. His mother saw it and of course he got the blame, and his mother damaged him for life by taking away his favorite Cowboy Boots.

The audience was slapping their knees and wiping tears from their eyes with laughter.

I'm still standing there, waiting to finish the story. When Laurel demanded the microphone. I handed it to her, and she explained the true story.

"Yes, Parker had his favorite boots, and he had a slight problem of kicking his older brother when he had them on." She calmly explained that she sat Parker down and told him how she understood that he loved his cowboy boots, but that if he had them on he couldn't kick anyone—especially Burton. She told him that if he kicked Burton 3 more times, she'd take away his boots and throw them away forever. She concluded, "He kicked him 3 times. I took the boots and chucked rgwn in the garbage."

She handed the microphone back to me and I said, *"In my garbage."*

I heard some gasps in the crowd. Parker's bride was within ear shot and she whispered, "She has your boots!" Parker shook his head and said, "No way."

I continued the story. Explaining that I was a bit of a nuisance to Laurel. I begged her to give the boots back. I was emphatic that Parker had suffered enough. Laurel was adamant stating "April, you are not helping. This is how you teach actions have consequences and boundaries." I shrugged acknowledging that she did have a point. After a few second pause I said, "That probably should have been the end of it. But it was at my house, and that wasn't fun."

I continued, "So, I waited until the next morning. In the morning, in my estimation long after the life altering incident, I begged her again. 'Please Laurel, please, let me give them back.'"

Exasperated, Laurel finally said, "Maybe...maybe when he gets married."

There were several gasps from the audience.

"That was enough for me. I tucked those boots away and kept them." I grinned and raised my eyebrows. The room exploded with laughter.

Laurel stood up holding the boots, walked to Parker and said, "Here's your boots!"

Parker's eyes glowed like an astonished child. He held them up and said, "I've been dupped for 20 years!" He carefully looked at them as said, "They are exactly as I remember them. Ha! There are no spikes!" He tilted them to the side and a tiny rock fell out of the heel. He shouted, "They still have rocks in them!"

Maybe not the best thing I've ever done. But one that brings me complete joy.

Carol

YESTERDAY I TALKED TO A college student at a voting booth. He asked me: "Are you as enraged as I am at the shit that's going down?" Yes, I am. But I need more than his fury. Maybe I need Christ—not Christ carrying a plate of home-baked cookies to a neighbor nor even nursing the dying in Calcutta, but him saying," Forgive them, for they know not ..."

I find myself, when things are bad, demanding of some God, "Be there! Exist!" I don't much care what myth Being takes form in, but for me there must exist Space large enough for me—for Hank—Hank's mother—The Apostle's Children—April's father. Please exist. That will be enough.

April

I'M HOME FROM ST. GEORGE now. I waited over 21 years to give those boots back. Now, in some strange way, I miss them. I'll miss hiding them every time Laurel and the boys visit. I'll miss looking at them on my glass shelf. And I guess, well, I'll miss watching Parker grow up.

October 1, 2007

15 years ago, I redecorated the upstairs apartment. Back then, I painted, wallpapered, made it light, bright and mine. I've been planning some renovations. I want the dropped ceilings removed, restore the hardwood floors, reinsulate, redo the wiring and plumbing, and possibly add a skylight. I hired a contractor to do this restoration.

Once they get started, we might run into some surprises with this old house. But right now, that's the plan. I'm really excited!

October 21, 2007

Whoa! The entire upstairs floor of my house has been gutted to the frames. I kept two main support walls on the inside. Once the dropped ceilings were removed, a bunch of black soot fell. That's from the old days when the house was heated with a coal burning stove. I had no idea all that black soot was still there. This old house represents the healing of my psyche. My psyche still has nooks and crannies harboring old toxic waste handed down for generations. I continuously knock down walls. I clean out the old dysfunction. Occasionally I find treasures. Which I take out and nurture.

November 21, 2007

Thanksgiving in New York! Jennifer and I decided to meet here. Yesterday, we went to Ground Zero where the World Trade Center Towers used to stand. Sobering. It took a while for me to shake the sadness. Walking back to the subway, I noticed that the energy of the city alleviated the feeling of desolation I had at

Ground Zero. New Yorkers are rebuilding. New York's resilience is contagious and inspiring.

I want to bottle up this energy and take it home. I'd give it to all child sex abuse survivors. We don't have to be held hostage by the past or live-in fear of what might happen.

November 22, 2007

A Thanksgiving dinner cruise on the Hudson. The lights of Manhattan are magical from this perspective. Circling the Statue of Liberty, I step out on the chilly deck. I imagine my grandmother gazing at Lady Liberty on her long journey from Norway.

I think of part of the poem engraved on the pedestal: "Give me your tired, your poor, your huddled masses, yearning to breathe free...."

The first time I saw the Statue of Liberty, I was in elementary school. I was tired and longed for Lady Liberty to wave her torch, like a magic wand, and give me reprieve from my wretched life. Now I am free. I bless everything she represents. I thank my grandmother's courage. My grandmother was only 21 when she first saw this statue. My grandmother didn't know a word of English, but had a heart filled with hope and love. My heart is swells with gratitude: *dum spiro, spero.*

Standing in the long line for a taxi. A harbor breeze slices cold. I see a homeless woman teetering along with a shopping cart filled with stuff. The cart tips. The woman kneels and struggles to gather her belongings. I run out to assist her. Two others from the taxi line join me. The woman startles. Calmly I hold my hands out, "We are here to help." One man quickly lifts the cart, another picks up her stuff, I help her up. We escort the woman across the busy street. With a heavy Brooklyn accent one smiles, "Usually tourists are afraid to help. Have a nice Thanksgiving."

November 24, 2007

I had such a wonderful time in New York. With the excitement of a little kid, I loved looking down at the big balloons of the Macy's day parade, I loved fulfilling a lifelong wish: ice skating in Central Park. I blink back tears when I think of those fearless firefighters running up the towers on 9/11. The event that means the most was three strangers joining together to help a homeless woman in the street. No questions: it's what you do. Do the right thing.

Humans are such an odd species. We can be cruel. The cruel ones are generally the most broken. Most of us seem to have some degree of understanding that at any given moment we could be the one who is down in need of a helping hand up—and we extend our hands.

This morning my contractor called and asked if he could meet with me in person. I swallowed hard. It's never good when your contractor says that he must meet. Immediately, I was concerned that he found something else wrong and was worried about the repair costs. He asked if we could meet at a nearby deli because he didn't want his employees to overhear our conversation. I knew it was going to be bad.

He led with, "As you know, I employ a couple of women. What I'm about to tell you needs to remain confidential."

"Of course."

He proceeded to tell me that one of his women employees currently lives at a women's shelter for battered women. For her to live there, she must attend group therapy sessions like, "How to not fall in love with a jerk."

I smiled when he said it. I know that battered women need to learn why they keep falling in love with abusers. My contractor paused. He was struggling with his words. He finally blurted out, "The thing is, in one of her groups, she's reading a book about sexual abuse in Mormon neighborhoods."

My heart stopped beating.

He continued, "You know that beautiful piece of etched glass that took us a day to remove and protect?"

Silently, I nodded.

"The woman who wrote this book also has a piece of etched glass, with the exact same quote from 1040 A.D. Last week, I heard my women employees talking about it. They are curious. Did you write a book about sexual abuse called, *Paperdolls?*"

I was still for a couple of minutes. The poem etched on the glass that is etched through my soul: *"God within me God without. How shall I ever be in doubt? There is no place where I my go, and not see Gods face not know...."*

I envisioned a group of women, trying to heal from the abuse of their husbands, partners and lovers reading my book. Of course, they had *Paperdolls* as a resource at the shelter. Women sexually abused as children frequently land in abusive relationships as adults. Should I tell? I value my privacy so much. I want to be known as me, not just a sexual abuse survivor. But I didn't want to lie. I also didn't want to get thrust into some role as a counselor or quasi therapist—or worse, a hero.

Carefully I said, "I'm familiar with that book. I think there's a very good reason the author wrote under a pseudonym."

I didn't acknowledge it or lie about it. He already knows. Who has an obscure poem from 1040 AD etched in glass in their bedroom? I didn't want to open the door for conversation about it. So, I left it at that. I have no idea what he said to his employee. Secretly, I hope my words have given her the courage to break the psychological chains that have bound her and rebuild her own beautiful life—in her beautifully unique way.

January 28, 2008

I read the news today: "Man Accused of Sex Abuse." I looked at the picture of the man arrested. My paternal cousin, Richard Marcroft. I recently saw him at a funeral. The article quotes the county prosecutor, "The incidents have been going on for years. It happened so frequently it was too numerous to name ... We could have filed far more."

My heart hammers against my chest. The Beatles song, "A Day in the Life" starts playing in my mind: "I read the news today, oh boy...." I call my mother. Byron is aware of the arrest and the charges.

Going on for years? Could have filed more? And they didn't? I smack my desk. My hand stings from the pain. I print the article, scribble a quick note across the top: "This is my paternal cousin. My brother is still close to him. Kacie Woody, Elizabeth Smart, now this! Didn't our book help at all?" I mail it to Carol.

February 4, 2008

The wind woke me up last night. Sounds like sirens whistling between the houses. Outside the trees were swaying with the turbulence. A flash of lightning lit up the dark sky and instantly a boom of thunder. Snow exploded from the sky. A blizzard. I wandered back to bed feeling cozy under the comforter and quickly fell asleep.

Morning brought clear blue skies and over a foot of fresh snow in the yard - a blue bird day. My morning schedule was quickly adjusted. I headed to the mountains.

Fresh tracks and blue skies, I floated through light, fluffy, powdered snow all morning. After the exhilarating day, I clambered onto a bus to get down the canyon with the rest of the powder hounds.

A blonde haired, blued eyed man across the aisle smiled. We exchanged superlatives about the morning, and I noticed he had a foreign accent. It didn't sound Norwegian or German. I found out he escaped from the U.S.S.R. The entire bus started listening. He said there's nothing like freedom. He said to live in a state of fear is indescribable. He had many family and friends who were simply taken away in the middle of the night. They were not heard from again.

A teenager whispered, "Last night's scary storm doesn't compare."

The Russian smiled, grabbed a handful of flakey snow off his sleeve and exclaimed, "Ahh, the Rocky Mountains. Nothing compares to this magical snow!"

The bus erupted with whoops and hollers of agreement.

I gazed down. Some even in the USA live with that type of fear. I know there are souls living in fear of the next strike, the next assault and the next torturous act. Right here in Utah, in the land of the free, right now.

I stopped home for a quick shower before heading to the office. Smiling, I looked up at the construction workers on the top floor. I heard loud whispers, "She's home!"

Shock stopped me still when I walked in the door. The entire kitchen ceiling had collapsed. There was a huge, gaping hole all the way through to the bathroom above. A piece of painter's clear plastic was tacked to the ceiling, the support beams between the floors were intact. Nothing else.

Curious, I went upstairs. In the bathroom, slowly I looked down at the huge gaping hole in the floor. With a tiny smile and a tilt of my head I said, "How was your morning?"

The Site Lead sheepishly explained as they were pulling up the old laminate flooring, they noticed everything underneath was soaking wet with a putrid stench. He added a colorful adjective about the smell. The sewer line from the toilet had a small leak; it had probably been leaking for years. They yanked up a particularly soggy patch, and suddenly everything crashed downward covering the entire kitchen. They'd spent the morning cleaning. I could barely smell the stink. I'm going to need to repair and replace the sewage line and then rebuild the ceiling/floor structure.

Old houses. I've viewed this old house as symbolic of healing, restoration, and decay.

The stench reminds me of my cousin.

February 11, 2008

Carol called first thing this morning. She's been traveling. She called as soon as she received my note and the article about my cousin. She could sense my rage. She strongly suggested that I continue writing. I have always kept a journal.

With Kacie Woody's death, the possible connection with Elizabeth Smart's abductor, and now this, maybe we should publish some type of a sequel. People still ask Carol about me; she says they genuinely care. They also ask if anything ever happened to Hank. They ask about Karen Fisher. Maybe we should write a bit more. My cousin ... Richard Marcroft with crimes "too numerous to name ... they could have filed more ..."

My big question: WHY DIDN'T THEY FILE MORE? Fingers got too tired to type all the incidents? I wrote a flipping book about the abuse in my family, and here it is ... continuing ...

May 10, 2008

My neighbor turned 50 this past week, and he always wanted to go skydiving. For his fiftieth birthday, his wife surprised him with a skydiving package. His wife called admitting that she was too nervous to jump out of a plane. She asked me if I could go with him.

Skydiving had never been one of my "must do" items, but I'm not afraid. This morning, we jumped out of a plane. My neighbor paid to have it videotaped. I am glad that he did because they captured several scenes with me racing out the plane window.

I loved it! The thrill of racing downward at 113 M.P.H., then pulling the chute to a floating descent downward was incredible! I never imagined it could be so fun.

May 11, 2008

My neighbor thanked me for going skydiving with her husband. She paused and said, "I do have to ask you one question. We watched the video last night, and everyone on the plane looked terrified. You looked so calm, like it didn't even faze you. Were you nervous at all?"

I smiled. I said, "As the plane was ascending, I started to get excited. Kind of like how exciting it is to take the first lift on a powder day. But, no, I wasn't really nervous."

As I walked away, I thought, that's a positive aspect from suffering the abuse I experienced as a child. I know I have survived the worst possible pain I can endure. Things can make me nervous, but I know I can survive anything.

After *Paperdolls* was published, a reporter asked me, "You are so strong. Do you think surviving your childhood made you this strong?"

Quickly I said, "Possibly, but I don't believe anyone needs to suffer in this fashion to gain strength. Strength and character can be developed in a myriad of healthier ways than suffering sex abuse. Probably the only positive thing I personally have gained from the abuse I suffered as a child is the knowledge that I can endure just about anything. However, I think people can gain that knowledge in much healthier ways."

July 15, 2008

Melinda's adult daughter, my niece, called me today. She started the conversation with, "April, the only reason I'm calling you is because I know that if I do, you'll do something about it."

I sat down, then carefully replied, "What's going on?"

She said, "It's Jared." She was referring to her half-brother.

My hand tightened on the receiver. Jared was the one who tried to burn his house down in 1992—after he'd spent several weeks staying with my parents. My sister had Jared committed to a psychiatric hospital. He was four years old. This happened a few months after the book was published. When I found out, I called the psychiatric hospital and told his doctor that I was April Daniels, and that Jared was my nephew. My sister pulled my nephew from the hospital the next day because I had "muddied the waters" with his diagnosis.

Now his older sister was calling about my 20-year-old nephew. I wasn't allowed to know many specifics about him since I "took it upon myself to call the loony bin where he'd been committed." My family rarely spoke of him in my presence. I'd heard that he'd been thrown out of school for fighting or drugs, he'd been in and out of drug rehab, and that my sister was afraid of him.

My niece said, "His girlfriend's mother called me and is frantic. Her daughter is missing. She thinks Jared took her somewhere. This girl is 18, and the police won't do anything because the girl is legally an adult. My niece told me that this girlfriend is sweet, but she is a little slow. Jared dominates her. My niece said that she thought Jared had her at my mother's cabin. I hung up the phone and called my sister.

I told her that if she didn't go up to East Canyon, I would. If I found him up there holding this girl, I'd call the police. Melinda left the office and drove to East Canyon. When she got there, she saw Jared's car. She carefully pulled away and called the police.

When the police got there, the place was trashed with beer cans and booze bottles thrown everywhere. There was drug paraphernalia. There was evidence of "a lot of sex." Jared professed that his grandmother let him stay there, but he forgot his key so he broke in. The police called my mom, and she pressed charges.

My mother is heartbroken that she had to press charges against her grandson. However, my mother has sat through thousands of AA meetings. She knows what must be done.

When the police were able to question the girl, she said that she was not being held against her will—although her eyes kept darting to the police car where they were holding Jared.

I know that I tried to do the right thing for Jared when he was four years old. My sister had him committed to a psych hospital because of his anger issues. When I found out, I called my therapist to tell her. My therapist advised me to call that hospital and let the doctors know the family history. My therapist also helped me craft exactly what to say and how to say it.

At the time, I was quite angry with my sister. For heaven's sake, during the family meeting, Karen Fisher advised my siblings to never let my father be alone with their children. Then my sister simply lets her son stay there for a few weeks while she's on a cruise? After her return 4-year-old Jared screams he hates her and tries to burn the house down? I certainly don't know all the facts but informing the doctor that there was a history of sexual abuse in Jared's family seemed like something that might have helped that little four-year-old boy.

The Scotts immediately got all their grandchildren in therapy, and now those kids are Ivy League graduates, some with graduate degrees and MD's. They are incredibly bright and productive members of our society. While my nephew, whom I believe was screaming for help after he was victimized, is now an abuser.

November 7, 2008

A year of construction and my upstairs is finally done. We exceeded the original bid because once they were able to see underneath the layers and get to the framing, the structure, wiring and plumbing they found several more major jobs that had to be completed. The leak in the sewer line causing the bathroom flooring to collapse comes to mind. Then they found old "tube and knob" wiring still utilized in one of the upstairs bedrooms. In the 1970s an electrician supposedly came in and rewired the entire house. I guess he got tired when it came to the attic and simply used the old stuff that was already there.

This house represents my psyche. Again, I must ask, how much old wiring, old ways of thinking and old ways of thought are still utilized in my brain?

My contractor told me that it would have been faster and cheaper to tear it down and build a new house. No way. I must restore this house.

After we knocked out several non-weight bearing walls, the entire upstairs could have been a big loft. I loved the light and the openness. I considered keeping it like that, but I decided that I needed a guest room. I added a wall and at the very top, I put a window between the two rooms. The window has a new piece of etched glass with my mantra:

"Better to add to the light than fight the darkness."

Shortly after 9/11, the U.S. started bombing Afghanistan. The President called it "Shock and Awe." It was disconcerting. I'm still not sure it was the right thing to do. After a night filled with angst, that quote came to me with inspiring clarity. It is my prayer for the living. It is how I want to be remembered. I want it engraved on my tombstone. For now, it's etched on a piece of glass bringing even more light into the sanctuary of my daily life.

November 17, 2008

Carol and I went to lunch today. I asked her if she wanted to see the house. My General Contractor was upstairs picking up tools and doing a final walk through. I've become quite good friends with my contractor, and I was thrilled to have him meet Carol. He showed Carol some of his favorite parts. He showed her the new etched glass. He was so thrilled. He bellowed; "April wrote that! Isn't it beautiful?" A knowing smile crossed Carol's face as she said, "That's such an April quote."

Carol

AFTER OUR LUNCH TODAY, APRIL asked if I wanted to see her restored home. The major construction project was almost completed. This time she did the entire home. She hired a General Contractor and took parts of the house to its original framing. It's still April, but more. It fits where she is in her life now. Open and free. In an upstairs room, she had Gramps's old wooden ladders with two planks in between. She lined the planks with mirrors making a fabulous shelf. There were statues, Lladró figurines, sketches, and paintings on the shelves. In the center, under glass, was the paper doll her grandmother had drawn for her mother. I was stunned. I had forgotten that April found this precious paper doll in her attic. She had preserved it with meticulous care. April quietly said, "To remind me to never forget. Forgiveness doesn't mean 'forgive and forget.' It means I don't have to carry around that toxic pain anymore."

Her contractor was making some final adjustments and walked into the room. He saw that we were standing by the shelves and said that he wanted to throw out those old rickety ladders, but April insisted on keeping them. He boomed, "Now look at them, it's art!"

April quietly said, "With art, we are not alone."

We debated for a moment about who originally said that quote. April thought it might have been C.S. Lewis or Friedrich Nietzsche. I didn't know. I replied, "It's a great quote. I think April Daniels said it."

As I was driving home, I thought of how April has been able to forgive. I know her well. She said it's not like it never happened. She hasn't erased their actions or granted them a pardon. April said she forgave her abusers, and others, for herself. She has released the dark toxicity her abusers inflicted upon her. With sincerity she said she felt like her perpetrators robbed her of the first 30 years of her life. She wants the rest of her life to be hers.

April showed me a quote by Maya Angelo: 'It's one of the greatest gifts you can give yourself, to forgive.'

The paradigm of forgiving for oneself seems sacrilegious: "To err is human, to forgive divine." Forgiveness is the highest moral law. His "Forgive them, for they know not ..." gives Christ moral precedence over all the other religious prophets. Is forgiveness letting go? Do I have to do that? Isn't stopping violence enough?

Because I hate him. I would kill Hank if I could. I don't know how to let go. I wrote stories for the grandchildren. I'll continue to write stories. They are one way to heal.

April

ELIZABETH SMART TESTIFIED IN BRIAN David Mitchell's competency hearing today. After the competency hearing, a reporter asked Ed Smart if Elizabeth was afraid to face her perpetrator. Ed Smart replied, "She actually wanted to face him and, in fact, I think she asked Brett [Tolman, the U.S. attorney for Utah] if he could be muzzled and have to sit there to watch it."

I literally cheered out loud when I heard that Elizabeth Smart requested that her perpetrator be muzzled so he'd have to stay in the courtroom and hear her testimony.

Bravo Elizabeth Smart.

I read Elizabeth Smart's entire testimony at the competency hearing. Some of the phrases that Mitchell said to her are extremely familiar. I'm not positive that he abused me as a young girl also, but some of his phraseology was used by my teenage perpetrators. And they did go to the same high school. I'll never know for sure, but the odds are high that some of the perps knew one another.

One aspect of the timeline haunts me. Mitchell took Elizabeth to San Diego when the weather got cold in Utah. For a couple of weeks, Elizabeth and the wife were left alone camping in the hills. What if Mitchell and David Fuller were friends? What if they were longtime friends from their teenage years? Fuller lived in San Diego at the same time Mitchell took Elizabeth there. Is it just a coincidence that two guys, about the same age, attended the same high school—at almost the same time—and both abducted 13 and 14-year-old girls from their homes? And then both horribly abused their victims?

I will never know for sure, and the only person now who really would know is Mitchell himself. He's playing the wacko card so hard, you could never get a straight answer out of him. But what if, what if Mitchell met up with Fuller in San Diego. Then Fuller decided to go to Arkansas and abduct Kacie Woody? Possibly I'm just connecting dots that should never be connected, but it is an eerie coincidence.

I'm in New York City right now. I love New York. I love the hustle and the energy of the city. I love the art. I love the people. I'm here with Jennifer. Tonight, we saw a play with Daniel Craig and Hugh Jackman called *A Steady Rain.*

The play only had two props: two chairs for the actors. That's it. The rest was the skill of the actors and the power of their ability to deliver the playwright's words. I was riveted. I still am so moved, I am speechless.

Our seats were on the front row. At the end of the show, when the actors came out for their bows, Hugh Jackman bent over, looked up at me, and winked. I don't think it was because I'm attractive, I think it was because he could tell how moved I was. I still am. I can't even think about this play without tearing up.

March 12, 2012

A birthday lunch at the Bistro! I like to ski on my birthday, but we're having an early spring. I'm gazing at purple crocuses peeping above patches of snow. How small and fragile the bulbs were that I planted last fall. Looked like small nuts. After months of frozen darkness, they poke up reminding that life transcends. I might go for a bike ride instead of skiing on the slush.

In Israel, I bought a pendant with the Hebrew symbols for life. It jingles on my wrist as the phone rings. The caller ID: Salt Lake Fire Department. Paramedics are with my mother on a grassy meridian. They found her slumped over the steering wheel.

I arrive to find my mother shaken, embarrassed. She vows she'll check her blood sugar before she drives. A paramedic takes me aside, "We are going to recommend that she stops driving." I swallow.

My birthday lunch is focused on my mother. Laurel whispers, "April you don't even see it, do you?" Perplexed, I shake my head, "Uh, no, what?"

"Your mother always takes center stage. Especially if you are around."

Laurel has mentioned this before; it's more obvious today because it is my birthday. Laurel continues, "Never mind, I've learned you always defend the underdog, and for some reason you view your mother as an underdog. She's not."

Fair enough. She's an empowered, independent, strong woman now. The mother I grew up with stayed in the shadows of my father. She hasn't been in the shadows for years.

March 27, 2012

My mom's driving privileges have been suspended. The State's notice provided the process for it to be reinstated. Her doctor must provide a statement that she's okay to drive. She's optimistic that she has her diabetes under control, and she'll be able to drive soon.

Driving represents independence. She didn't accept my lame effort to minimize it: "Lots of people in New York don't even have a driver's license. When Jennifer lived there, she let her license lapse. She took the subway everywhere."

My mom let me ramble on and when I finished, she said, "We don't live in New York."

I burst out laughing. I love her dry sense of humor.

April 7, 2012

The doctor didn't grant my mother permission to drive. She's down. My sister and I make a driving schedule. We'll take turns driving her to work, church, and her regular appointments. We might rotate in some of my nieces and nephews. Everyone we contact is happy to help. After I explain the arrangement to my mom she seems relieved. With a slight smile she says, "Well, I guess I don't have to move to New York."

September 16, 2012

Laurel is wearing a patch over her eye because she had a biopsy. There's a mass in her brain. It's concerning. The grandkids think she's a pirate! Burton is back east finishing up school, so they've been Skyping with grandma. The patch is a big hit. Laurel is exhausted after she Skypes, but she always wants them to remember her as the fun one.

Later, when Laurel and I were alone in the car, she swallowed and said, "I am only going to say this once, because I can't say it again. I always thought you'd go first. With all your skin cancer and residuals from your childhood. In case it's not, I'm counting on your memory to let them know about me."

I swallowed back the tears. My memory is legendary. Laurel jokes that I have a photographic memory. I don't think so, but for important things, like remembering what Burton wore as his Halloween costume in 1989, I remember. Maybe it's because I journal so much. I don't know, but Laurel professes that I remember way more than she does, and now she's counting on it.

September 17, 2012

I'm going down to St. George this weekend and stay through next week. Laurel scoffs that she doesn't need me there, but sheesh, she has a brain mass. I'm going.

I called Carol to let her know about Laurel. By and by, we have been working on the revised edition of *Paperdolls*. Carol was stunned because Laurel is so young. Carol agreed that I need to be there.

I also called my mom. When I go out of town, my mom looks after my little dogs. After my golden retriever died, it broke my heart that I couldn't just pick him up and hold him. Little dogs live longer and are much easier to scoop up and hold. However, my little girl, Princess, isn't acting well. She's 16 years old and has been extremely lethargic the last couple of weeks. If this were any other situation, I wouldn't leave her. But it's Laurel. And Laurel has a brain mass. Princess is my baby, but Laurel is Laurel. I must go.

September 20, 2012

Laurel's husband has always been so sure of himself, so decisive, so confident. He says he's very hopeful, but I can tell he's concerned. It's hard to describe. He's calmer, more attentive. It's like he's trying to absorb everything, take it all in, notice everything about his beloved wife.

Laurel seems to be doing better. She's resting and seems more relaxed at home. One thing I've always known: Laurel is beloved in this area. It seems like everyone is checking in on her. Wonderful people are always calling and dropping by to see if there is anything they can do to help. Most of the time, she feels good enough to see them.

September 21, 2012

I've been checking in with my mom several times a day. She is doing well, and my cute little dog seems to be doing all right too. Princess is not running around, but she has gone outside and lounged in the sunshine. That's always been one of Princess's favorite things to do: bask in a ray of sunshine. Princess hasn't been eating. So, my niece picked up a syringe and my mother has been using the syringe to feed Princess Pedialyte and chicken broth. My mother thinks it's helping. I hope Princess can hold on until I get back.

Today I asked my mother to put the phone down by Princess's ear. I know it's silly, but I just had to tell Princess how much I loved her, how proud I was that she was being so good for Grandma, and that if it was any other situation, I'd be there with her. But it's Laurel, and Laurel has a brain tumor and is sick and needs my help right now.

Maybe this didn't even happen, but my mom said that Princess seemed to perk up. Princess cuddled into my mom's lap for the rest of the evening.

September 25, 2012

I was upstairs when my mother called. My mother was crying. She said, "It's Princess."

My mother told me that Princess had diarrhea and went all over herself. She couldn't hold herself up. My mother was holding her and waiting for my niece to get there. They are going to take Princess to the vet. My mother said, "I don't have the heart to try to wash her off. I think the water and soap would upset her." I told her to wrap Princess in a warm towel and hold her. I let the tears stream down my face. I said, "Mom, I have my phone with me, but I have to make Laurel dinner. Please call me as soon as you get to the vet."

I went to the kitchen and was pleasantly surprised to see Laurel sitting at the kitchen table. She could tell something was wrong. I told her that Princess had some diarrhea and that my niece was going to help my mom take her to the vet.

During dinner my mom called, sobbing. My mom was sure that Princess had died in her arms. My mother was still holding her, and Princess let out a tiny gasp and went limp. My mother kept crying, "Maybe she's not dead. No, I think she's gone. Oh April, I am so sorry." My mother doesn't cry. She didn't cry when my brother died. She didn't cry when my father died. Then in broken sobs my mother kept repeating, "I'm sorry April, I tried. Please forgive me." I kept assuring her that it wasn't her fault. That I knew she did everything she could. I told my mother that I loved her, and I knew how hard it was for her to do this for Princess and for me. My mother gave out inaudible gasps. She was devastated. I told my mother that she could put Princess down and wait for my niece to help her. My mother said, "I'm going to hold her, I won't put her down."

My niece called a few minutes later. Princess was gone. My niece took Princess's body, cleaned it up, and gently brushed out her beautiful hair. She told me that she was really worried about Grandma (my mom). My niece said that she was going to stay with my mom until I got back.

During this entire phone call, it was as if I had been psychically transported to my mother's house. I was right there with here, holding her and talking her through this. When I ended the call, I was somewhat startled to realize I was sitting at dinner with Laurel and her husband. Laurel put her arm around me and told me that they'd clean up. I simply nodded.

September 26, 2012

Laurel is doing better, so I flew home today. I asked one of my neighbors to help me dig a rather deep hole in my back yard. My mother and I found a beautiful wooden jewelry box. I lined it with Princess's favorite flannel blanket and added rose petals. I laid Princess in the box, and we buried her. I marked the grave with a garden steppingstone embossed with a butterfly.

My mother cried. I know how difficult it was for her to weep last night. Strangely, I'm comforted. It's comforting to experience her humanness.

September 27, 2012

I was too tired to unpack yesterday, so I did it this morning. Tucked inside my suitcase was a card in Laurel's handwriting:

Dear April,

I've always known that Heavenly Father placed you in my life for a reason—probably so that I could have an example and make it back to Heaven. Tonight, I witnessed a heavenly moment. Light from above surrounded you as you talked to your mother assuring her that she did everything she could do, that you loved her, and forgave her. Your sadness and pain was tangible, yet you were filled with such love. Light filled the room. It was Heaven on earth—right here in my kitchen. I am humbled and honored to be your friend.

Love,
Laurel

When I was on the phone with my mother, it was emotional. I don't remember my exact words. My mother was distraught because Princess died under her care. Now I think Princess's death symbolized much more. For everything: for my childhood filled with abuse and loss. My mother is afraid that I'll never forgive her. From my mother's perspective, she let me down again. She didn't. She did everything she could, and I forgave her. I forgave her for everything.

October 11, 2012

I'm driving to Los Angeles. Jennifer has some legal challenges and I'm going to support her. Plus, it's a beautiful fall day. I enjoy long drives like this, occasionally. I'm listening to music. A simple song starts and my eyes well with tears. I'm sure the song was about some sappy love affair gone wrong, but the lyrics bore straight through my heart as I thought of my mother. I played it over and over and wept. It's how I feel about my mother. It's better to give up fighting for anything more from her. She given all that she can give. I'm weary of trying. She has my forgiveness. It's called *Unreconciled.*

November 7, 2012

A dear friend was playing tennis last Saturday. After the game, she had a heart attack and died. After I heard the news, I went to my mother's house to let her know. We both wept at the loss of this young, vibrant friend. Apparently, this wonderful healthy young woman had undiagnosed diabetes. Something with which my family is all too familiar.

Today is the viewing. I arrive at my mom's and her little dog Timmy frantically runs to me. He's agitated, barking and running towards my mom's room and back to me. Something is wrong. I race to my mother's bedroom. My mom is face down on the floor, unconscious. I try to take her blood sugar level with her glucometer; it only flashes "ERR LOW." I call 9-1-1. The paramedics arrive within minutes. The glucose injection does nothing. The ambulance door closes. I'm not far behind.

Arriving at the Emergency Room, I am immediately escorted to my mother's room. It's vacant. I fall into a chair as I realize this might be the exact room where my friend was pronounced dead last weekend. The cold cadence of empty machines echoes through the sterile room.

Parker casually strolls in and gives me a hug. It's his last semester at the U. Laurel must have called him. He's studying while I write. My eyes are tearing up writing this: I don't know what I'd do without Laurel. Her boys are my nephews. Her generosity sharing her family with me is such an extraordinary gift.

The wheels of my mom's bed squeal and stop. Parker is standing holding her hand. She smiles. Parker asks if she'd like a blessing. She nods. Parker finds another man to assist. Two young men blessed a frightened old woman with comfort and love.

November 8, 2012

My mother was released from the hospital this morning. Yesterday morning, she must have given herself a shot of insulin then didn't eat enough carbs to compensate. Before she was released, a case worker pulled me aside and told me it's time to explore options about her living situation. He said she's doing so well, but this event might be a good time to initiate a conversation with her about not living alone anymore.

After my mother was situated at home, I gently broached the subject of her living situation. She exclaimed, "I won't live in a home. I don't want to be around all those old people."

I burst out laughing and noticed her subtle smile. She has such a dry wit. Then she said, "Well, as much as I'd like to, it's obvious I can't live alone. You could rent out your house and move in here. She continued, "This is more valuable, and it has a better yard. Plus, this is yours. Once I'm gone, it will be yours anyway."

I have always thought that I could never live in that house. I've healed and grown so very much. But I think that would be asking way too much of myself. To live again in the where so much abuse happened.

I told her that I'd prefer she move in with me, since I'd recently upgraded most of my house. I asked her if she wanted to move in with Melinda or Byron. We'd already talked about it previously, but I wanted to be sure. She simply wasn't comfortable with either of them. I can understand that.

My mother added that Melinda was really pushing her to move into a "home." She said, "I love Melinda, don't get me wrong, but she doesn't know me. I've told her so many times that I'd rather die than go into a home. Anytime we go out to lunch, she brings it up. Sometimes I don't even want to go to lunch with her, I don't want to hear it."

I surprise myself when I am shocked that my siblings are the same after all these years. I think of the "Allegory of the Cave," I recall my old den of years long gone: Chasing the shadows that aren't real. My siblings are still there.

Congratulating themselves on glories of winning the shadow game. They have been given numerous opportunities to climb out of the darkness of the cave. The pain of adjusting to the light is too much for them.

It's old habits of not feeling or seeing or thinking or something. I used to give Melinda some slack, but now, she's 60 plus years old. She's way past using excuses from our family of origin for her inability to connect. She's responsible for not cultivating those tools for herself. Maybe when she was 16, or even in her twenties, she had an excuse. Now she's responsible for her entrenched shallowness and superficial reality.

I completely understand why my mother doesn't want to live with Melinda. Byron is another story. His is another superficial reality. Byron does have better communication skills. However, he physically avoids anything uncomfortable. He simply leaves the room or leaves town.

Right now, both are out of town. Both travel, quite luxuriously, and quite frequently. They don't even know my mom was in the hospital.

All my therapists, friends, anyone in my support system flinches when my mother says she wants to move in with me. The fact is: years ago, I promised her. Maybe it's simply my old training as a child to take care of the alcoholic parent. Maybe it's a need I have to connect with her. Maybe I want to take care of her in ways she never took care of me. Maybe it's just the right thing to do. She is my mother. Yes, she was incredibly dysfunctional, and still has many blind spots, but she's come a long way. I can't deny her growth. And maybe it's coming full circle. Like in Plato's allegory of the Cave. I've been outside. I see color and dimension. I feel the warmth of the sun on my face. I know what's real. My mother wants out of the den of shadows. I pity those afraid to leave the cave. She craves the light. I'm here to help her. It's the least I can do for someone who gave me life.

I told her that she could move in with me, and then we could take some time and fix up her place. Then we could decide if we'd sell her house or rent it out. My mom preferred renting her house. She said, "April, I want to live with you. However, if we don't sell it and fix it up, you could rent it out and have a steady stream of income for the rest of your life. I don't know if we should sell because it's much more valuable that your house."

I carefully listened to her. She had a point. Residual income for the rest of my life sounded appealing. Holding onto that house, no matter the value, is not.

November 29, 2012

I can't get Kacie Woody out of my mind. It's been 10 years since her tragic death. Laurel says that if any of her children suffered the tragic ending that Kacie did— she would never want to hear from anyone who even remotely knew the monster who took her child. I understand. But I still want to reach out. If I never hear back from Kacie's family, I understand. I wrote this letter. I'm not sure if I'll send it.

Dear Mr. Woody,

For over ten years, I have thought of your beautiful daughter, Kacie, every single day. I have hesitated to contact you because I wasn't sure how you would receive this message. Please know that words cannot adequately convey my deepest sympathy.

My childhood home was directly across the street from the monster who took your angel, Kacie, from this earth. This same monster sexually abused me when I was a little girl. He was several years older than I, but the damage he inflicted upon me during his teenage years was substantial. I have survived, and in many ways thrived.

Over twenty years ago, I wrote a book about surviving my abuse. My message was to warn others that there are predators of children everywhere and to send a message of hope to other survivors, like me.

My grief has been tangible regarding Kacie. In some small way, I wish to honor Kacie and her life.

It has been over 20 years since our book *Paperdolls* was published. An updated edition will be released. My co-author and I have both written more about the major events that have happened during the last two decades. I have written a great deal about Kacie and the tragic circumstances of her death, particularly my feelings of despair and my unabated longing that I could have done more to protect her and to prevent her tragic departure.

In short, not enough people believed me; or, those who mattered the most, and could have possibly done something to stop him, did not believe me. Words simply cannot express the depth of my sorrow.

I have intentionally written under a pseudonym because I wish to maintain a relatively normal life unencumbered by the shroud of sexual abuse. Privacy is something I cherish and have been able to enjoy for the majority of my adult life. If you wish to connect with me further, please feel free to do so. If you do not wish to hear from me or anyone in Utah, with even a remote tie to that monster who took Kacie away, I understand.

I extend to you my deepest sympathy and love. I long for Kacie's beautiful life, cut so very short, to be remembered. Hopefully, my words will etch her memory into the hearts of an untold number of souls forever.

Sincerely,
April Daniels

January 1, 2013

I mailed the letter to Kacie Woody's family. I haven't heard anything, and I doubt I will.

March 27, 2013

It's Easter weekend and I'm in St. George with Laurel and her family. Some mutual friends came by, and it was nice to catch up. Sadly, their daughter passed away and they were now raising their grandson. During our conversation, they said they have been trying to get their grandson admitted to my old elementary school. Apparently, it is one of the highest rated schools in the State. I had no idea. They said they'd even been looking at homes within the boundaries for that school.

I said, "My mom might be interested in selling or renting."

I gave them an abridged version of her age and diabetic issues. They said they were renting now and preferred to buy. I promised 'em I'd talk to my mom about it.

April 1, 2013

The friends interested in my mother's home have already called this morning. I'm going to take my mom to dinner tonight to tell her about this potentially new development.

Later: My mom doesn't want to sell. She is ready to move in with me. To get it ready to rent would be another 3-6 months. We decided that she'd meet with them and see how it plays out.

April 5, 2013

We love them. My mom is concerned about me and the residual income I could lose by selling. She's sharp about money. We both think we should see what they offer and go from there.

April 7, 2013

They offered quite a bit, as is. My mom won't even have to clean all her stuff out. She can take what she wants, then they'll take care of everything else. Including the renovations. The drawback, it's soon.

I highly doubt I could ever live in that house again, but residual income for life is something to consider. I used to dream about watching that house being bulldozed down. Now, I can see the beauty and the value of it. Even as is. I think that's growth. Despite my abusive and damaging upbringing, there still is value. Not much is completely black and white, including my childhood.

There have been times in my life where I felt that my choices were to pick the least toxic option. It feels good to have positive choices. If we rent and fix up, residual income for life. If we sell, there won't be all the cleanup and renovation work—plus we get a fairly nice pay-out. It's a matter of extensive work now vs money now. I must take into consideration that my mom will be moving in with me. She is doing well, working every day, but she's moving in because she can't be alone. I will have new adjustments and different perspectives regarding her to consider. Would I have time to work on that house, plus adjust to my new normal with my mom in my house, plus work full time? Time to dig out my old Ben Franklin "Pros and Cons" sheet. That's the only way I'll be able to make the best decision for me.

April 17, 2013

We are selling. I did the pro and cons sheet, and the residual income is better for me—if I trusted my siblings more. I'd like to think they have done their work and are not the damaged, resentful children in adult bodies that I knew 20 years ago—but I don't know for sure. I don't know them. It seems that if they'd done their work, they would reach out to me. Much like my mother has gravitated to me. She loves them, but she wants to be with me.

I'm trying not to have preconceived notions about them, but I just don't know them. If we keep the house, and rent it out, it could open the doors to some weirdness from the siblings. If we sell—I hope it will close a psychological door for everyone. Okay, maybe it will help diminish the chances of them being weird about sentimental stuff. I just don't know where they are, and I'd like to reduce the chances of weirdness.

My mom and I talked about it in depth. If she moves in with me, I don't have space for all her stuff. I was very firm that we weren't going to simply put it all in storage. I want to deal with the heirlooms, the valuables and all that right now.

My mother and I agreed that we'd let my siblings walk through her house and write down anything they wanted. Anything. Melinda has been up several times and hasn't wanted anything. Byron hasn't had time. After they note anything, they want, we'll open it up to my nieces and nephews. I'm confident we'll be taking quite a bit to charity or leaving a lot for the new owners to discard.

I hope this helps diminish the chance that my siblings get weird after she passes. I have a hunch they haven't done any internal work. Probably, they are still wounded little children in 60+ year old bodies. When my mother passes, I fear those wounded children within will scream. I don't want those screams projected onto me in the name of some sterling silver our grandparents brought over from Norway.

My mother wants to live with me. They both offered to have her live with them. Melinda even has an entire floor of her house with a separate kitchen for my mother. After my mother refused to even think about moving in with either of them, Melinda got fairly pushy about putting my mother in a home. My mom told me how much that hurt her. My mom guessed it was because neither of them are comfortable with me. My mom said, "What can I say? They'll just have to deal with it. I know you'll be as gracious and kind as you always are. This is their problem."

May 26, 2013

My mother is mostly moved in. I'm convinced the only way to deal with all the personal possessions is to do it this way. There isn't any emotion or loss involved. If you want it, it's yours. If you don't, and don't have room for it, we'll donate it or discard it.

I watched Jennifer's family after their parents passed. I think the emotions are higher for the sentimental stuff after the actual loss of the remaining parent. They bickered about old Christmas toys and ornaments. Now, they all realize it was silly.

My siblings — and their children — are so much more dysfunctional. I really don't want to deal with someone asking me for some trinket at my mother's graveside. After seeing what happened with Jennifer's family, it could easily happen with mine. If they want it, they can take it now.

Now, I'm free to help my mother in this next stage of her life, on my terms. And, of course, this is on her terms also. I think this will be hard, but it feels better that we both have a choice. It will be an adjustment for me to be helping her, while still honoring her independence. I'll figure it out.

June 13, 2013

My mother officially moved in last week. Jennifer was planning to go to Portland to visit her family; she invited me. I had some trepidation about leaving.

Walking out the door, Jennifer joked, "Now no wild parties."

With a deadpan straight face, my mother said, "Well, why not?"

Simultaneously Jennifer and I both said, "She'll be fine."

I telephoned the next morning.

"April, did you know there's a nest on your front porch? I'm waiting for Melinda and I'm watching this cute robin feed her babies. I almost don't want to go to work!"

A dragon boat glides across the Willamette River. I picture my mother on the front porch watching a red-breasted robin feed her newly hatched babies.

"Yes, mom, I know. I saw her building the nest a couple of weeks ago. I didn't know the eggs hatched. Mom, it's your front porch now too."

"I don't know about that."

"Mom, I want you to feel at home. That's one of the reasons I left for a few days, so you can settle in and not feel like a guest."

I'm spending most of my time at the hotel, resting, reading, and reflecting as I walk along the river.

June 16, 2013

My mother is reading in the backyard. There is a gentle breeze, the birds are frolicking by the birdfeeder, and I can hear a soft gurgle of water trickling in the fountain. Her little dog, Timmy, is on her lap.

I asked her last night how she was feeling. She said, "I don't know how to describe it. I'm moving on to the next stage of my life and I'm at peace."

I'm sure this will be an adjustment. I'm glad the move is over. It's a relief to have her here.

August 7, 2013

I'm vigilant to the point of almost constant anxiety. I feel like I have electric shocks running up and down my arms. Sleep is elusive. I hope that my angst isn't coming out to other people: my friends, clients, or my mother. I went to the doctor today and got a prescription for Zoloft. I hope it helps with this anxiety.

My mom seems to be settling in quite well. She has her own room, area, even entrance. Her view of the backyard is peaceful and serene. She comes home from work, takes a little nap, then reads most afternoons. She is a voracious reader. For her birthday a couple of years ago, I got her an e-reader, a Nook Book. She finishes a book every other day. I usually download half a dozen books at a time. Discussing books, we've read is one of our favorite things to do together.

She recently read a good book, *The Help*. I enjoyed the book, until I read how many in the black community felt about it. My mother and I had a lively discussion about it. A white person describing the black experience is not realistic. My mother nodded, placed her e-reader on the table and said, "I never thought about that. That is so true!"

I was feeling good about our discussion and casually added, "I scoff whenever I read a man's version of a woman's experience with sexual assault. I realize that sexual assault is not limited to one race or one gender. However, it has been my experience that white men are the predominate perpetrators."

My words brought our conversation to a halt. She nodded. Looked down at her hand and nervously tugged at a hangnail on her thumb.

Although I can talk about the sexual abuse of my childhood, she can't. She tries. But when I say something, it's like I've slapped her in the face. Unreconciled. She's come as far as she can, and I forgive her.

I reach for her e-reader. I find a particularly funny part in the book. We laugh. Then, I tell my mother a story from when I was little. My grandmother was taking care of me and I asked about Martin Luther King, Jr. and the civil rights movement.

My grandmother exclaimed, "Uff da mai"

My mother laughed. That was one of her mother's favorite sayings. It means, "nonsense or phooey."

My mother smiled and said that her mother thought Americans were ignorant and cruel to anyone different, especially anyone with a different skin color. My mother quoted her mother's words, "We are from Norway. We don't get as much sun therefore our skin is lighter. People who come from areas with more sun have more pigmentation in their skin to help combat the intense sun. That's all. The rest is nonsense. No group of people is better than any others because they have different pigmentation in their skin."

My mother grew up listening to her parents' rant about ignorant Americans. Her parents said that the prejudice in America is archaic. Gramps was working at the Hotel Utah when Marian Anderson performed with the Utah Opera. Gramps was indignant as he watched her scurry in the kitchen entrance and take the freight elevator to her room. He almost lost his job over it. America's glorious contralto should have been able to waltz through the main entrance of the Hotel Utah. My grandparents were particularly disheartened with Utah because the Mormon Church had promised them abundance if they left their beautiful homeland in Norway and came to help build up Zion. Unfortunately, when my grandparents arrived in Utah, they were treated badly. Immigrants were not treated as equal children of God. The ladies in the ward mocked my grandmother for her accent. Many ridiculed my grandfather for "taking the good jobs." Mormon converts of color can be treated with even worse disdain.

September 14, 2013

The heat has finally broken and it's such a beautiful day. My mother carried an assortment of flowers from the garden all the way through the cemetery to her brother's grave. She tended to the grave, brushed off some grass clippings and cleaned the headstone. Then, she carefully arranged the flowers in the vase. She stood silently then, she looked up, while blinking back tears, said, "Poor Art."

November 18, 2013

When Melinda picked up my mother for work today, I took a quick picture of them. It's my mother's 88th birthday. Not many 88-year-olds still work every day. Jennifer picked out some cute clothes for her birthday. She looks adorable in the picture.

She's doing well. She walks her little dog, checks her e-mail, chats with friends, and of course reads. Reading is a positive addiction.

Speaking of addictions, her attendance at her home group in AA has diminished. She says that she's uncomfortable asking Melinda or any of my nieces to drive her. She only goes when I take her. She also said that sometimes she doesn't hear the women as well. I asked if she wanted to get hearing aids, but she's too embarrassed. She continued that sometimes she feels like she doesn't need the meetings.

I quickly thought of all the women we've met. The ones who run to her, hug her, the ones who she sponsors and the ones who rely on her for inspiration and courage. I told her that she might not feel like she needs it, but she has no idea how many need her. She nodded.

Then I reminded her about our reparation's agreement. We agreed years ago that for her to make amends with me is to give to others in her 12-Step groups. She only has to show up.

I'm going to adjust my schedule so I can take her at least once a week.

November 22, 2013

Shingles. I have shingles. Apparently if you had chicken pocks when you were little, you can get them—and they are caused weakened immune systems and stress. Trying not to be stressed is stressing me out.

The good news is that I have such a high tolerance to pain. They kind of bugged me and I thought maybe I was allergic to something. When I went to the dermatologist, he barely looked at the rash and blurted out, "Shingles." I've had them for a couple of weeks, so there wasn't anything he could do. He gave me some cream and a prescription. I told him I didn't need anything for the pain. Sometimes it really shocks people in the medical profession when I don't need any pain meds.

I am going to shine that introspective light into the dark recesses of my mind and figure out what is rattling around stressing me. I hate going there. Psychological pain is so much worse than physical pain. And, I loathe not having it all together and being okay. I have come so far, and overall, I'm doing so well. I really don't want to mess around in the past. But I'm sick from something that is well known to be inflamed by stress. The big change has been my mother moving in here, but I swear, it hasn't been that hard. She's self-sufficient. She works every day. She has a great sense of humor. She helps and contributes. She's really a delight. It doesn't make any sense for me to be so stressed.

November 28, 2013

Thanksgiving: I used to loathe this holiday. Now, it's my favorite. A day to unabashedly profess all that I have and all that fills my heart with gratitude: I am grateful that I still have the courage to dust off the cobwebs lurking in my psyche. I'm grateful that I can take out my fears and reframe them as an adult. I am grateful for the golden and red leaves of autumn. I'm grateful for all the love in my life. I'm grateful that my mother has tried, really tried, to be here for me. And I'm grateful that I can start seeing her for who she is in my life now. She's here. She needs me and I'm working hard at reframing any residual resentment from long ago that she wasn't there for me when I needed her most—as a child. I'm an adult now. I am strong. I am loving and I can forgive.

Forgiveness was such a topic in my therapy with Karen. Forgiveness is so important and it's so important for me. To let go of all those latent feelings that are anchoring my soul. I'm grateful that I can be free. I am in the process of identifying, reframing, and letting go of those lingering resentments about my mother not being there for me. I relish the freedom from the psychological shackles of the abuse. Of course, it's not like it didn't happen. But I am grateful how much of it I can let go. How much I've healed. How much I've grown. I am grateful. I am thankful. I love Thanksgiving.

December 24, 2013

The shingles are mostly gone. With the shingles and all that I'm working on psychologically, I almost didn't have the annual Christmas Eve dinner this year. Instead, I catered it. It's more expensive, but the caterers do it all. They did all the decorations, set up the banquet tables and chairs, brought in all the food—and then cleaned up. I felt like a guest, not the host. I was able to observe and interact with everyone more than I have ever before.

My mother was glowing. All the various families took pictures with her. Calmness came over me as I watched her posing picture after picture. She looked cute in her Christmas sweater, holding her little dog. She has a gorgeous smile. The camera can't capture her laughter filling the room or her gentleness with the little ones. I am deliberately re-recording my perspective of her. I am open to seeing her for who she is now. To the needy little girl lurking in the shadows of my psyche, I say, "Be still my soul. All is well. See her for who she is now. Enjoy her essence. Respect her journey. You deserve to experience the joy of your mother. Absorb it. Let this perspective of her growth — flourish in your psyche. Let peace and love be the foundation of your perspective of your mother."

I'm gazing at the fire. I recall Karen Fisher's voice, "Feelings lag behind knowing." I've struggled with this concept for years. It's frustrating to know something and then still have feelings that don't match the knowledge. I have forgiven my Mother. The drive to California when I played "Unreconciled" on repeat, I wept. I forgave her. My innermost feelings have lagged behind my decision. Hence the shingles, the anxiety, the tenseness. I know I have forgiven her. Now, I feel it too.

January 16, 2014

Frequently when I go skiing/riding I ask my mom if she'd like to ride with me. Cradled at the base of the majestic mountain lodge she enjoys drinking a hot cocoa watching the skiers and reading her latest book.

Today she wants to ski.

As we drive up Big Cottonwood Canyon, she talks about the possibility of renting equipment. As she spoke, I mentally review a checklist of what needs to be done. I brought snowboard equipment. I am not an expert on a board. I need to hire a private instructor for her. She's 88 years old and I have no idea how long it's been since she's been on skis. Yes, a private instructor. She doesn't need lessons, but I'd feel much more comfortable having a professional guiding her.

She's already wearing her military grade polypropylene underwear, her snow pants, her mittens and her beanie. We need to rent a helmet. I have extra goggles but I'm going to insist on a helmet. She excitedly is talking about how mittens are warmer than gloves. The heat of your fingers together helps warm up the whole mitten. I reflect on the metaphor: *together is better than separate.*

She senses my hesitation. She admonishes me that she has the "bone density of a 25-year-old." If she slips or falls, she'll be fine.

I have extra knee pads and wrist guards. I'll hire a private instructor.

I'm on board (not merely my snowboard). If she wants to ski today – let her. I want to take precautions for her safety. While she's getting fitted for her equipment, I arrange for the private instructor.

We have two instructors. When I walk in the ski school and explain the situation two instructors jump to the counter. One guy quickly wanted to teach my mom's "lesson." Then, another young woman swallowed and said, "Can I help? No charge. I'd love to help on this one." She's joining for free. I'll give them a large tip.

My mom is ecstatic. She starts on the bunny hill. She's sandwiched between her two instructors on the lift up. She's beaming and waving.

There have been numerous times throughout my life where my mother and I have reversed roles. This is one of them. She glides off the lift and doesn't even stop. Both instructors are beaming now too.

There's a small crowd watching.

She waves her ski pole at some kids. I hear cheers.

She's escorted to the front of the lift line. The lifties are laughing as they gently place the chair under my mom for the next trip up. She turns to me and shoos me away. She calls, "Go have fun April. They'll text you when I'm tired."

I blink back tears and grab my board. I think of when I started snowboarding. My nephews teased me about being an old lady and merely skiing. I doubt I'll ever tell them about all the lessons I took and how many fly swatters I suffered learning. "Fly swatters" are what I named those falls where I was slammed face first into the snow. Oh, it was so worth it: to see their faces and I glided off the lift and made a perfect S turn in front of them.

I am my mother's daughter.

About an hour later, I get the text. They are on the upper mountain and beginning their descent. She fell once and got right back up. She doesn't want to overdue and would like to rest in the lodge until I'm done.

At the bottom, the resort photographer is snapping pictures of my mother's gentle turns. Her skis are parallel and slightly apart.

She gives me a hockey stop and sprays me with snow.

Well done, Mom. Well done.

Her instructors, more like guides, help her out of her equipment. Both want pictures with her.

When she takes off her helmet, she admonishes that there will be no more pictures. Not with her hair looking like this. I try to tip the instructors and they push my hand away, "No, we should tip you. We'll remember this forever."

Smiling, I whisper, "I will too."

Happy Seventeenth of May! It's the Norwegian constitution day. It's also my grandmother's birthday. My mom tells that when she was little, she always thought the whole country was throwing her mother a party with parades, parties around bonfires — all night long. My grandmother certainly deserved it.

Today, I have the flag out and my mom sang: Ja, Vi Elsker Dette Landet (Yes, We Love This Land). It's simply adorable.

Gramps called the 17th of May "Petunia Day." We always bought my grandmother a flat of petunias for her birthday. I've kept the tradition.

I'm planting while my mom is reading on the outdoor chaise.

She stands and her voice breaks. "This book...." And walks into the kitchen to replenish her diet coke. When she returns, she continues....

"It's just this book. It's..." and her voice fades.

I sit. Aloud, she reads:

"There has always been a sliver of panic in him, deeply buried, when it comes to his daughter: a fear that he is no good as a father, that he is doing everything wrong. That he never quite understood the rules. ...There is pride, too, though–pride that he has done it alone. That his daughter is so curious, so resilient. There is the humility of being a father to someone so powerful, as if he were only a narrow conduit for another, greater thing. That's how it feels right now, he thinks, kneeling beside her, rinsing her hair: as though his love for his daughter will outstrip the limits of his body. The walls could fall away, even the whole city, and the brightness of that feeling would not wane."

—*Anthony Doerr,*
All the Light We Cannot See

My mother's voice breaks as she stumbles out the words, "That's how I feel about you."

I reach for her hand and gaze into her eyes and whisper, "Thank you."

WISDOM

"Even in our sleep,
pain which cannot forget falls
drop by drop upon the heart,
until, in our own despair,
against our will,
comes wisdom
through the awful grace of God."

—Aeschylus

April

MY MOTHER HAS *THE SALT Lake Tribune* delivered every morning. I hear her open the front door. Walk down the front stairs and retrieve the paper. I've called several times to make sure the paper is thrown close to the front porch. I tip well to keep it that way.

I hear her move in the kitchen. I can picture her preparing her toast, cereal sprinkled with fresh fruit, orange juice and a banana. She has all her pills laid out, her insulin ready, the paper is in place and her day commences. Listening to her, reminds me of listening to Gramps in the exact same kitchen preparing his breakfast with the same solid routine.

A few moments later, I hear her cry. I race downstairs. She looks up from the paper, "Oh April, Eric Nelson died." Eric's death was inevitable. I'd often wondered if he'd already died. I used to see him wandering the streets of downtown. I wrote about him *in Paperdolls*, I wondered if he'd lost his mind with the drugs those guys took. To my knowledge, Eric was never a perpetrator in the abuse. But he was there. He watched. He never had the strength to stand up to the peer pressure and stop it. He was manipulated and intimidated by guys like Brian David Mitchell, Hank and David Fuller. He was a gentle soul caught in a quagmire of evil. I have no idea of his torment.

When my mother first went through Rehab at Olympus View Hospital in 1987, Eric's parents were there. They had started a non-profit for the mentally ill called the Alliance House. Eric had been diagnosed with schizophrenia. My uncle Art suffered from schizophrenia also, until he shot himself in 1983. My mother and Eric's mother built a strong and deep bond. My mother had lost a son, Tom. Because of her alcoholism, my mother never processed her grief of Tom's death until she got clean and sober. Drugs and alcohol stop emotional growth. As my mother finally dealt with the loss of her beloved son, Eric's mother held my mother in her grief, and said, "There are some things worse than death."

My mother told me later that she knew Eric's mother was referring to the torture Eric was suffering. Now, Eric's tormented mind is put to rest.

I drive my mother to work. She clipped the obituary and was going to give it to Byron. Eric and Byron were best friends in junior high until the group of treacherous boys turned on Byron. They lit our front yard on fire. No one knew why, and Byron retreated to his room and never told a soul. Maybe he told Tom at the time, we don't know. I'd like to think that maybe, maybe Byron tried to stop them. Maybe Byron did try to stop my abuse. I'd like to think so.

Of course, I don't know for sure if Eric's mental illness was a result of the sexual abuse he witnessed in the upper class neighborhood of my youth. I'll never know. Maybe it's merely a tragic coincidence.

March 5, 2015

The full moon is illuminating my bedroom. The trees sway with a light breeze. I watch. And, think of my mother quoting Eric's mother, "Some things are worse than death." I understand that sentiment. But in my heart, I resist. Life is sacred. Human life is particularly sacred to me. I'm not afraid of death. But death is never the answer. No one is in so much torment or pain that death is better. I cannot accept that. If Eric's mind was slaughtered in part, however remote, of the abuse in our childhood neighborhood—there had to have been a way for him to transcend that. Maybe the drugs altered his neurological transmissions terminally. Maybe if he hadn't been part of that quagmire of pain, maybe he would never have taken drugs, maybe his mind wouldn't have been obliterated by schizophrenia. I'll never know.

I know that life is sacred. I doubt there are things worse than death because I know we can heal. Maybe Eric couldn't heal, at least at this time. Maybe one day we'll have the ability to heal minds ravaged by dementia or schizophrenia. Until then, we must stay on this planet. We must stay alive. Life is sacred. I feel so strongly about this because I came so close to killing myself. So many in my childhood neighborhood opted for that. Were their psyches so damaged they couldn't hang on until help arrived? Or hope?

I know I stayed for a variety of reasons: intense therapy, medication, and tulip bulbs. Yep, tulip bulbs. I plant those little, brown, bulbs in the fall and I know, months later they will emerge from the frozen dirt as glorious colorful tulips. One really can't see that in the bulb unless you know. Unless someone tells you or you've seen it for yourself. Many times, I felt like I was that brown, little, insignificant bulb. I worried that the frozen ground would kill me. I simply had to have faith. Spring has always come, and I have had moments of utter bliss in the sunshine.

For me, I know that I survived the worst possible thing imaginable when I survived the abuse of my childhood. Then, I survived dealing with it as an adult. Certainly, that wasn't as hard as the actual abuse as a child but dealing with it all as an adult was extremely painful. The only thing I can say is get through it. It's worth it. Going through that pain as an adult, is excruciating. Worse than anything except the actual abuse itself. But now, I know, I survived and healed from that. I know because I survived that—I can survive anything.

Occasionally, I hesitate to say something like that. I don't want some deviant abuser using that as a justification for abusing another, especially a child. I cringe when I hear of coaches or parents inflicting pain because it will "make the kid stronger." Utter nonsense. There are many ways one can help a child, a pupil or a regular person gain strength. Inflicting pain and abuse isn't one of them. There is absolutely no excuse for abusing another.

I pause a long time. The moon has moved halfway across the sky. I wonder how long I've been reflecting on Eric, abuse, healing, and hope. I know another thing for sure. Carol's granddaughter was right.

Carol once had a conversation with her granddaughter, Isabel, about the abuse. Carol was trying to explain that we are fortunate to get help and heal.

"No," Isabel said. "The lucky ones are the ones who never had it happen."

Carol

LIKE ALL HUMAN EVIL, HANK'S actions will have effects for generations on members of our family, even for the now unborn. Destruction should never be minimized or rationalized. Despite the poverty of anyone's emotional or physical life, I believe that person has some measure of choice and responsibility. I couldn't bear to live in a world that had proved such choice illusionary. At the same time, it's very real that there's no way I can comprehend Hank's mind. Before his suicide, maybe his last thought was "Into Thy hands I commend my spirit." Maybe it was, "Are you satisfied now, Norton and Carol?" Maybe it was blame directed at his own abuser, his mother. Maybe it could have been, "Forgive me. Please forgive me," addressed to God and to all those whom he'd hurt so badly. Maybe it was simply, "Thank God I don't have to suffer anymore." For a long l time wanted him to burn in Hell or any other such available place. I especially wanted him to comprehend for all eternity what he had done.

I long for solace to anyone I've ever encountered. And, to the monsters, like Hank, it's a great weight lifted to be able to pity their pain and hope that one day they can feel it. Dr. Scott Peck calls this "legitimate suffering." Only by feeling their own anguish will they know some degree of relief. If eternal life is real, I hope every monster who ever lived can somehow find a degree of peace, relief, or salvation somewhere.

I hope Hank meets some power, some bright medieval angel "Because the Holy Ghost over the bent World broods with crimson breast and with ah! Bright wings."

I hope Hank meets some power, some bright medieval angel "Because the Holy Ghost over the bent World broods with crimson breast and with ah! Bright wings."

April

March 12, 2015

THE BULBS ARE EXPLODING WITH color. My front yard is filled with purple crocus's, yellow daffodils, and red tulips. I was standing on the front sidewalk looking at all the colors. A car driving down the street stopped. The driver and passenger got out and asked if they could take a picture. They said it was "stunning."

My mom came home from work and beamed. She exclaimed that it was our own "little Holland" right here in the Avenues. We're going to walk down to Cucina for a birthday lunch. (Once again, it's too warm to ski.) I reminded my mother that it's been 12 years since Elizabeth Smart was "found." My mom knows that Brian David Mitchell went to high school with my brothers. She also knows that they knew him and were "friends" with him before he had to go into juvie for abusing a 5-year-old girl. We heard of the incredible awkward moment at one of the high school reunions. One of the awards was for the "most famous" person from their class. Mitchell's competency hearing and trial had happened the year prior. The most famous person from that class was Mitchell. The crowd rumbled. The woman announcing quickly realized the embarrassing fact, she quickly changed and announced, "Here is the most influential person from our high school class who contributed positively to society." A journalist for the local paper was quickly acknowledged.

Later: I've been reflecting on Eric and his family. How they must have suffered all these years, watching their gentle son and brother destroyed by demons in his own mind.

I think of his sister, who is my age. After high school, we went to Israel together. On our way to Jerusalem, we toured Europe for a couple of weeks. We flew to Paris. The night we arrived, six of us from the same high school ventured out. We wanted to see the Arc de Triomphe at night. We took the subway. As the subway train arrived, we heard a commotion a couple of cars away. We didn't know what was happening and continued to enter the car. The train started and suddenly a group of French guys bolted through the doors from the adjoining car. It seemed they were in a gang. They were whooping and screaming. There were about a dozen of them. They surrounded us and started to maul us, sexually. Carol's daughter, Susy, was sitting down and she was kicking and screaming at them. The more she kicked and screamed the more the boys grabbed her. Eric's younger sister was hysterical. She was sobbing and screaming. They were ripping open her clothes. I was standing near the door. Two of the gang got behind me and blocked the door. The subway reached the next stop, and we couldn't get out. No one could. There were probably 20 French people sitting in the car. They kept their eyes down. No one got off the train. I was frozen. Until we were barred from exiting at that stop I hadn't moved. Like a deer in headlights. Since I was in the back, no one had touched me. Then, one of the leaders reached through the group and grabbed my breast. Something happened inside of me. I snapped. I'd been swimming and lifting weights at the time and I was *very* strong. Stronger than many men. When I snapped, I lunged at the leader. With my left hand, I pushed him with all my might. He flew to the other side of the car. He hit the opposite door and looked stunned. I came after him.

I was screaming, "Come on! Come on!" I had my fists up. He started to move towards me, and when I lunged at him, he quickly took steps backward.

Right then, the train got to the next stop, and the doors opened. I was still trying to fight the leader. Susy and another had to pull me out of the car. I didn't calm down until we were outside the subway station.

Since we got off the subway early, we had no desire to go back on a train. We decided to walk back to our hotel. We were all pretty shook and stayed on extremely well-lit areas.

Years later, Susy asked me if I remembered the incident. I looked at her like, "How could I possibly forget?" Susy said, I really remember Eric's sister. And I remember you got us out of there."

Susy and I don't know if Eric's sister was abused. Susy said that based on her reaction that night, maybe she was. It's like she went into an altered state or hysterics. I'm still not sure. I remember saying something to Susy like, "I know I was abused, and I certainly didn't have the *same* reaction. But something really snapped in me. If you guys hadn't pulled me off that train, I think I could have killed him."

May 11, 2015

My mother still goes to AA meetings as often as possible. She has a home group that she attends weekly. It's a woman's group and she loves those ladies. She still sponsors a couple of women. She takes their calls anytime, day or night. She says that staying sober is the hardest thing she's ever done. She says that she is truly powerless to her addiction to alcohol and prescription pills. She still craves it. Her mantra is, "One day at a time." All those days have added up.

Today, she came home with her 27-year chip. 27 years! She was beaming as she showed it to me. She said, "When I first got sober, I couldn't imagine going 27 days without a drink. Now, it's been 27 years!" In AA the date of their last drink is their birthday. She took a birthday cake to her home group. She laughed as she was leaving and exclaimed, "This is truly my birthday. This is reason to celebrate."

May 22, 2015

My mother and I were planning to go up to the cabin for Memorial Day Weekend. Then, on Monday I was going to fly to New York for a few days. Jennifer was able to get front row tickets to see "The Audience" starring Helen Mirren. The play is getting rave reviews and I'm really looking forward to it. A once in a lifetime experience.

This morning, my mother was getting ready to go to the lake. I quickly ran to the store to pick up a few last-minute items. At about 10 minutes to noon, I called her to see if she wanted me to pick up lunch. She said she was finishing packing the cooler and we could get something on the way.

When I came in the door, I called to her. No response. I raced to the kitchen and found her lying on the kitchen floor. I assumed she didn't eat, and she dropped out from low blood sugar. She was conscious, but she couldn't talk. That happens sometimes if she's dropping out. Only she wasn't all sweaty.

I knelt on the floor, and I tested her blood sugar. Her sugars were fine, about 130. I called Melinda. Melinda suggested wiping her fingers clean in case she had some juice or something on them then, testing again. I did and everything was still fine. I lifted my mother up. She could help me with her left arm and left leg, but her right arm and leg wouldn't move. I got behind her and wrapped my arms around her tummy. I moved my right leg and lifted her right leg, so we could walk. We shuffled to the bedroom, and I got her on the bed.

I called 9-1-1.

I told the dispatcher what was happening, and I wasn't sure if she'd had a stroke. The dispatcher instructed me to ask my mom to raise her arms. Only her left arm moved. I asked my mother to say a simple sentence. It was very garbled. The dispatcher asked if that was normal. I said, "She speaks with eloquence. She still goes to work every day." Then, the dispatcher instructed me to ask my mother to smile.

Half a smile—the right side of her face collapsed.

The dispatcher said she'd stay on the line with me until the paramedics arrived. I asked my mom to try not to move and I quickly put my mom's little dog outside. Then, I ran to the front door and opened it.

A swarm of paramedics arrived within minutes. They confirmed the stroke. My house has tiny rooms, so they placed my mom on a chair type stretcher to carry her out. I held her hand as she was loaded into the ambulance. Her eyes were locked on me. I put my other hand over hers and said, "Mom, everything is going to be okay."

I saw Melinda pull up. I looked at my mom and said, "Mom, Melinda is here. I'm going to ride up with her. We'll be right behind you." She nodded.

I said, "Everything is going to be okay. I'll be right there. I love you. Don't be afraid. Everything will be okay."

The ambulance door closed. One of the paramedics gave me a hug. Then, he looked right at me and said, "Where should we take her? LDS Hospital? U of

U Medical Center? I had no idea. He continued, "U of U Hospital is 5 minutes closer."

I nodded and said, "Go there." He hugged me again and ran to the front of the ambulance.

When Melinda and I got to the hospital, they rushed us into the ER room. A doctor raced out and said, "In 10 seconds or less tell me about your mother." I rattled off that she's 89, still works every day, has diabetes, and takes meds for high blood pressure."

The doctor confirmed a stroke. He wanted to know when she had it. I told him that I talked to her at 11:50 AM and found her on the floor at 12:20 PM. It happened during that half an hour. I apologized for wasting all that time messing around with her blood sugar. He held up his hand and said, "It's okay, we can give her TPA 3 hours after the stroke. "It was edging on 2 PM. We granted permission for the TPA and a scan. About 5 minutes later, he came running down the hall again.

He said, "She's got a clot in the upper left portion of her brain. TPA will not get rid of it. We must operate. She has a 50/50 chance of survival. I don't know what will happen if she doesn't have the operation, but her quality of life with be substantially diminished. Fortunately, one of our top neurosurgeons is available, he's teaching a class and he's on his way over. He can remove the clot if you give us permission.

Without hesitation, Melinda and I both nodded in agreement. I signed the consent forms, and another doctor escorted us to the neurology surgery waiting room. Melinda had been texting and calling Byron. Byron was planning on going to Hawaii. I was relieved that he hadn't left yet.

Several hours later, the neurosurgeon came out. He told us that the surgery went well. He had the clot in a jar for us to see. It was about the size of my little fingernail. He said that if it hadn't been removed it would have been 100% fatal. My mother was out of the surgery recovery and moved to the neurological intensive care unit.

When Melinda and I walked in, my mother smiled. It was almost a full smile. The ICU staff started questioning my mother, with things like, "What's your name?" Do you know where you are? What day is it?"

My mother answered flawlessly. After a while, she started reciting the answers before they even asked. It was funny, and most importantly, my mom knew she was being funny. The head of the ICU came in and said that this progress is what they like to see. However, she needs to stay in the Intensive Care Unit.

I am spending the night.

Later:

It's dark. My mom is asleep. I'm listening to the rhythmic cadence of the machinery. Eerily quiet except for the equipment sounds measuring her heart, her breath and a slew of other monitoring devices.

As I gaze at the twinkling lights of the city I think of the silence. Silence has many different meanings in our language. This is not a comfortable silence. It's not a fearful silence like the one imposed on me as a child to keep quiet about the abuse. Maya Angelo couldn't speak for several years after she was raped as a little girl.

Silence.

One of Tom's favorite songs was "The Sounds of Silence" by Simon and Garfunkel. He'd play it repeatedly in his room. Once I heard him crying while he listened to it. Tom's daughter came by to see my mother today. I'll have to remember to tell her about her dad's favorite songs.

I think this is a sad silence.

Earlier, Byron's two oldest sons visited.

My mother asked about Byron. I was uncomfortable. My nephews looked at each other, paused, then explained that their father was in Hawaii. My mom said, "Oh, oh, that's right. I forgot he was going." My nephews smiled and said something like, "Don't ask us about our dad's traveling. He's always flying somewhere." I didn't say a word. I knew that he was still home when he got the messages. No need to tell my mom that her son knew she'd had a stroke, knew she was going into surgery with a 50-50 chance of survival and that he decided to get on a plane to Hawaii anyway.

May 24, 2015

Sigh. I called the airline about my ticket to New York. When I explained that my mother had a stroke, they credited all the funds for my ticket back into my account. I am disappointed. I'll never be able to see Helen Mirren on the front row of this incredible play. I've been planning it for months. The reviews say she'll probably get a Tony for this performance. However, I know I would really regret it if my mother suddenly died while I was having a good old time in the Big Apple.

This is only a play. She is my mother. I've forgiven her for the things she missed with her sophisticated denial system. Overall, I've reframed and rebuilt my relationship with her. Occasionally, when that needy little girl inside me reacts to something, I take a few breaths, remind myself that I'm an adult now and I'm going to conduct myself in the most loving and honorable way possible.

I have chosen to stay here with her. I've chosen to be her advocate and help her. If the machines start buzzing too much in the middle of the night, I go get the night nurses to check whatever is buzzing. If she wakes up, and seems disoriented, I hold her hand and let her know I'm here.

Melinda has been here also. We've been taking turns. I'm here most of the time, but she has helped. Last night, when I returned, I paused for a moment before I came in the room. I gazed through the big glass windows. Our mother was sound asleep. Melinda was in a chair right by the bed, reading, holding our mother's hand.

May 28, 2015

My mom has been walking up and down the hallway with the physical therapist. She passed the "swallow test" and was moved to a regular room. The nurse had her arm and was walking her back to bed. My mom leaned against the door and whispered, "I can't breathe."

The nurse looked at me and said, "Has this happened before?"

I shook my head.

She called another doctor. They gave her an EKG. She had a heart attack. More tests. More doctors. More plans.

May 31, 2015

The medical consensus is that they are going to let my mom recover more from her stroke, then deal with her heart. She's going home in a couple of days. A social worker came in to evaluate the situation and make recommendations. I think he was there to evaluate me. To make sure I could handle it.

I'm not sure all that this will entail, but I know with Gramps, I handled it. Anytime I'm faced with difficulty, I reflect upon the abuse I suffered as a child. My self-talk: "Nothing is as bad as that. I survived that. I can survive anything. This will be difficult, but not even close to the worst I have endured."

June 2, 2015

She's home. I was feeling some anxiety about administering all these medications properly. Before we checked out of the hospital, a pharmacist reviewed all her meds with me. It took the pharmacist half an hour to explain them all. I have pages of instructions. These meds are potent; I can't mess up.

I decided to make a spreadsheet color coding her meds. The colors match five designated time slots: Morning, Breakfast, Lunch, Dinner, Evening. I used a sharpie and colored the top of each pill bottle in a designated color. I printed out the spreadsheet, and it's on the kitchen counter. I cleared out an entire shelf in the kitchen and displayed the meds from left to right. Left is the morning; right is the evening.

If someone helps me, I will show them this system, and insist they follow it.

Necessity truly is the mother of invention. The meds have been one of my big concerns. Now, I am more comfortable that I won't make a mistake, and it might be easier to have others assist me. I hope all her children spend some time with her.

June 7, 2015

Byron is home from Hawaii. Melinda told me that he wants to stop by to visit our mom. I'm still pretty upset with him, but I know how important it is to my mom to see him. She has been asking about him several times a day. I asked Melinda if she could come over when Byron comes by. This is for my mother, and she deserves to see all who she loves.

Melinda and her husband came by, and I casually told my mom I had to run a couple of errands. My mother said, "But, you'll miss Byron." I smiled, and said, "I know Mom, but I haven't had a chance to get to the store since you've been home. Since Melinda is here, I'd really like get a couple of things done."

She nodded and understood.

Outside of my mother's room, I asked Melinda to call me after Byron left.

I wasn't even to the store when Melinda called.

"5 minutes."

"What?"

"Byron was here 5 minutes. Come and gone."

"He's been and gone? Are you kidding me? What? Why?"

"Byron told mom that he rushed from the airport to see her and was so glad she looked so well. Then, he said he had really bad jet lag and had to go."

I was speechless: Bad jet lag?

After a long time, I said, "Well, I must be away for at least 15 or 20 minutes. Mom will know I was simply avoiding Byron. Do you need anything?"

"A brother with a heart."

After I came home, I prepared dinner. I set up a tray by her bed. After she ate a few bites of dinner, she said she couldn't eat any more. I moved the tray, sat down by her and said, "Mom, I know that Byron's short visit must have been disappointing. I know it must have hurt that he didn't spend more time with you."

I reached around her then as she leaned in, I held her in my arms. I felt the wetness of her tears on my shoulder. I held her until she fell asleep.

Later: It's about 3 AM. My shirt is dry, but I still feel my mother's tears on my shoulder. I look up and see the water-colored paper doll my grandmother made for my mother. The one I found in the attic all those years ago. I've kept for it reminds me of how fragile we are and how beautifully resilient. It has given me such hope and strength. I gently retrieve the glass container holding the paper doll. I slowly and carefully descend the stairs to my mother's room. She's sleeping soundly. She has a cross stitched "Serenity Prayer" on a shelf. I've seen her gaze at it numerous times. She can see it from anywhere in her room. I place the paper doll on that shelf next to her prayer.

June 15, 2015

I sent an email to my siblings. I asked them to meet tonight so we could discuss Mom's care. I need help and I also know my mother longs for more connection with her son. At the meeting, my brother was pious, condescending, and he even played the victim card. Byron's monotone voice filled the room for several minutes, "My life is hell. I have no personal time. I'm always out of town for the business and when I'm home, things are torture. I have a disabled son."

Melinda quickly jumped to appease him. She said, "Yes, your situation is different with children at home."

I said, "It's not like you have little children at home. Your youngest is in college." I stopped myself before we burst into an argument that my mother might overhear. I refrained from saying it, but I thought, "As far as this so-called disabled child, I don't see it. All your kids are at the University. I highly doubt you even think anyone is disabled. The 'no personal time' claim is ridiculous. You can't tell me your time in Hawaii was for business."

My body language and facial expressions probably said something. Certainly not enough. I'm pretty sure even he knows it was a sham.

After my siblings left, I checked on my mother. She was awake. I'm not sure if she heard Byron's pitiful soliloquy. Our eyes met and she didn't say a word. I glanced at the needlepoint of the serenity prayer, "God grant me the serenity to accept the things I cannot change...."

"Thank you for bringing down my mother's...paper doll."

June 16, 2015

Melinda called this morning trying to placate me about last night. She was trying to express that she understood me, then she said, "You are in an entirely different position. The roles have reversed. Mom has always been the caregiver and now you've switched roles."

Stunned, I literally bit my tongue. I made myself take a few deep breaths and I said, "Melinda, our mother was an active alcoholic my entire childhood and most of my adult life. I've always been the caregiver. Remember, I spent years learning how not be the caregiver and co-dependent with both of our parents by doing jobs they were supposed to do."

"Oh, that's right."

Sometimes, I wonder if Melinda's insights come from a cereal box.

June 20, 2015

I am wondering if my caregiving is simply my default role. Is this something I do in times of crises? I don't think so. I consciously chose to care for my grandfather, and I have consciously chosen to care for my mother.

June 28, 2015

The discharge prescriptions included sodium. I've been following those meds. Now, my mother is really retaining water. She's up 30 lbs. it looks like it's mostly water retention. When I touch her legs, my imprint stays on her skin. It's soggy, like her legs are filled with fluid. Liquid is seeping out of the pores on her legs. I'm draining her catheter several times a day. I called the doctor and asked about the sodium. No one has responded. This can't be right.

Through it all, she's doing her exercises. Her legs are so bloated I don't know how she can lift them, but she's doing it. She wants to keep her muscle tone, so that when she gets her new heart valve, she can get back to work.

I admire her perseverance.

June 30, 2015

The home health care nurse came by this morning, she heard liquid in my mother's lungs. I rushed her to the hospital. I'm sitting in the ER with her now. Sodium is a standard prescription given after a stroke. It's not standard for a heart condition. They might have messed up when she was released a couple of weeks ago.

Later:

I'm writing from my mom's hospital room. In the cardiac ward. She really doesn't want to be here. I promised her that once we get this water retention under control, she's out.

Her floor nurse came in and we talked for a few minutes. She said that she had a patient who had a stroke and was prescribed sodium that caused water retention. She is only a nurse, but she's quite confident once a cardiologist looks at this, there will be no more sodium.

A resident cardiologist finally came in and he literally scratched his head at the sodium prescription. She's off it now. She'll stay through the night, to see if the retention of all this fluid starts diminishing. I'm spending the night. My mom is much more aware, and she's upset she's here.

July 2, 2015

My mother has lost 9 pounds already. It's that silly sodium pill. I'm not impressed with the cardio unit. I want to just pull her out. Melinda says that if we don't get a doctor's release, her insurance and/or Medicare won't pay for it.

July 3, 2015

It's almost 6 PM and my mother was finally released. While we were waiting, I started researching cardiologists at IHC. That's a different hospital system. It was not necessary for her to be in the hospital for two extra days. They can't claim it was to watch her. At least it's over. She needs a heart valve, and I've started the groundwork of moving her to different cardiac care.

Later:

She's settled in the backyard listening to the fountain and holding her little dog Timmy. I'm sitting with her writing. She smiles, "I want to go to back to work soon."

Carol

If I can stop one heart from breaking,
I shall not live in vain;
If I can ease one life the aching,
Or cool one pain,
Or help one fainting robin
Unto his nest again,
I shall not live in vain.

—Emily Dickenson

OUR FIGHT HAS NOT BEEN in vain. Norton's vision in this battle has been by changing laws and statues supporting victims of sexual assault to achieve justice legally. He serves on boards of national organizations tirelessly working to change inert and archaic political and religious systems. I attack from a higher profile therapeutically mainly to help prevent the sexual abuse of children. I am also active in making perpetrators and those who cover for them accountable. I serve on non-profit boards and foundations to help fund and organize the ongoing battle against child abuse.

April has kept her efforts focused to survivors of sexual assault. Her battle is personal. It fits her. April continues to heal and grow. Her example has helped others in ways April probably will never fully understand. But I know. I've talked to them. April's efforts have not been in vain.

I spoke with April today. Her mother had a massive stroke a couple of months ago. April's relationship with her mother is intimate and healing as well. That's April's way. I am in awe of April's understanding and ability to forgive. We have had many conversations about it on the pretense that I was concerned for April; however, I realized I am yearning for my children to forgive me in a way that April has forgiven her mother.

April gets how sophisticated her mother's denial system is and despite how painful it is for her mother to penetrate her own denial system—her mother tries. That's enough for April. She understands the paradox of her mother. Her mother is a mentor and hero to many in the Alcoholics Anonymous 12 Step Program. She's saved many lives. But, for decades of April's life, her mother was not present. April gets it. April forgives her.

I hope my children and grandchildren forgive me too.

313

April

THINGS ARE ABOUT THE SAME for my mom—possibly better. My brother doesn't see her much, he came by last night before he left for a Mediterranean Cruise. He said she looks better with more color in her face. I hope my face did not show color, because I'm certain it would have been red faced anger. I think she was thrilled that he stopped by. I am committed to providing my mother with a serene atmosphere. I have decided to compartmentalize my feelings about his trips and his bloated sense of superiority and importance.

My mother is still quite tired but has been working hard with her physical therapy. She's hopeful about the valve replacement surgery. She wants her muscles to be strong so she can get back to work.

Since she's been home, she's still needed a catheter. We've gone to a urologist and it's frozen. Of course, that's not the technical term, but that's what I said when it was getting explained to me. In time, her bladder should start working properly again. For now the catheter will be there to prevent embarrassing situations for her.

For some people, adversity accentuates their weaknesses. For my mother, it brings out her strengths. I think for me also. After caring for Gramps, I knew I could do it. But this is much more intense. And it has refined me; I'm more present in the moment. My appreciation and sense of wonder and beauty of life has grown.

We both have a calmness and do what's needed to be done. Occasionally, if I get too tired, I remind myself to be patient and kind. My mom is slightly hard of hearing I know I must annunciate well and speak up. Sometimes I worry that I sound like I'm yelling.

It's Sunday and certain members of the ward come over to give my mother the Sacrament. She insists on getting ready for it. I helped her bathe. She is in a nicer house dress. She's on the rocking chair and I'm doing her hair for her. I turn on some hymns. One of her favorite hymns is "Nearer my God to Thee." I have a beautiful version sung by BYU's Vocal Point a cappella choir. I look at her reflection in the mirror. Her eyes are closed, and her lips are softly moving with the words:

"...on joyful wing. Cleaving the sky, Sun, moon, and stars forgot, Upward I fly, Still all my song shall be Nearer, my God, to thee"

August 18, 2015

I'm sitting in the large waiting area at IHC in Murray; my mother is getting a Cat Scan (CT). She has a couple of other tests to see if she's eligible for a procedure to replace her heart valve. It's not open-heart surgery, and not that invasive. If she passes these tests, there's less than a 1% chance of complications.

If she gets a new valve, she'll probably feel better rather quickly. The doctor even said that she can get the quality of life she had a year ago. A year? I'd be happy with last May.

Later: Well, it looks like she needs a couple of stints in her heart before she can have this heart valve operation. We are leaving the decision up to her. She wants to go back to work. I'm concerned. I will support whatever she decides. I'd like her to live longer, but another surgery? More hospitals? It's a lot. I want to make sure it's her call.

August 19, 2015

My mother decided she wants to have the stints put in so she can have the valve operation. Two more heart surgeries. The first one is scheduled.

I remember my father changing Tom from St. Marks hospital when I was a teenager. His care was dramatically better at LDS Hospital in 1975. No one dared take on the white coats except my dad. In a way, I feel like I'm channeling his strength in moving my mother to the cardio unit at IHC rather than keeping her at the U.

Incidentally, I am extremely proud of myself that I can see the qualities that my father gave me and be grateful for them. He was strong, determined, decisive and smart. It doesn't give him a pass on the abuse or the dominant tyrant he was, at times. I never felt sad when he died. Maybe because I'd dealt with all those feelings so intensely prior to his death. Maybe because he didn't give me a lot that I lost. I don't know. I simply know I'm grateful for where I am in my relationship with him. Not much angst or pain, and grateful that I can accept his attributes.

October 8, 2015

Melinda and I are at the cafeteria at the IHC Medical Center in Murray. The sun is rising above the buildings. Melinda says she didn't know Mom's surgery was for Stents. I carefully place my fork on my plate at gaze at her.

"What did you think this procedure was today?"

She shrugged.

"Melinda, after Mom's CT Scan in August, the surgeon told us she'd have to have the stents put in before they can even consider the heart valve."

"Oh, that's when I was in Norway!"

I nod. Remember when you came back, mom and I carefully explained to you everything. You can also log into her online account to review all the notes.

"Oh, yes, I might do that."

"I don't want to burden you, but it's important that you understand this. This is our Mother. Your Mother. Like we told you before, Mom decided for herself. I don't want you or Byron to ever feel like you were excluded or didn't understand. Your voice is important."

Melinda didn't say a word.

Later:

The surgeon placed my mother in intensive care. Simply because of her age. The surgery went well; however, he couldn't get the last stent in place. He said, "She is one tough cookie. I tried 3 or 4 times, her chest moved, but her heart and breathing remained strong. The last one had too much blockage and I couldn't get it placed."

The doctor told us that we'll have to discuss whether to proceed with the valve. For now, she must rest and recuperate.

She just woke up and looked at me. I stood by her bed and gave her a sip of water. She asked how everything went and I told her fine. She said, "Then why am I still here?"

October 31, 2015

My nieces and nephews bring their kids to visit my mom when she's home. She's their great grandmother and she knows them well. She adorns her orange pumpkin hat and her black witch sweatshirt. She gives them handfuls of candy.

"Oh, so cute!" she exclaims. Frequently she slips in some Norwegian, "Oh så søt" which translates to about the same.

Tom's daughter catches me alone and wants to know if her grandmother is going to have the valve surgery. I tell her that it's riskier now, but she decided that she wants to have it. I'm certain my eyes convey concern because I finish with, "She gets to make these decisions." My niece nods.

November 18, 2015

At breakfast today, my mother announces, "April, in case anyone remembers my birthday, I'd like to have a cake ready. Will you go to Costco and pick up one, and some ice cream?"

I had already ordered two. I simply nod and say, "Sure thing."

I should have had a guest book. There were so many people here all day, I couldn't keep track.

"In case anyone remembers...." We ran out of two large cakes from Costco.

November 20, 2015

One moment from my mother's birthday has haunted me. I've replayed it several times now. One of my neighbors asked where my father grew up. My mother told her. We did the "do you know?" interaction that people do. Then my mother told her that she still has a nephew that lives in the area. My mother said, "Did you know the Marcrofts, on Lakeview?" My neighbor nodded. My mother continued, "That's my husband's sister, who has passed."

The neighbor said, "Isn't it a shame about their son? He's in jail for abusing kids!"

Until that moment, I didn't know if my mother ever heard about Richard. My brother, Byron was standing by the cake. I glanced at him and could not tell if he was listening. After Tom died, Byron spent a great deal of time at the Marcroft's home.

Slowly, I looked at my neighbor and nodded, then said, "I'm aware of this. It's horrific."

I looked at my mother. She heard every word.

Internally, my blood boiled. I wrote about my cousin extensively in January 2008. Obviously, I'm still furious with him. My first cousin. In jail. A pedophile. This pedophile cousin sat right behind me at a family funeral—as President Monson spoke. President Monson was a member of the First Presidency of the Church of Jesus Christ of Latter-Day Saints at the time of this family funeral. How dare this pedophile even walk in the Church, let alone sit and listen to an inspiring talk from one of the First Presidency?

Time will never heal my anger against pedophiles.

November 27, 2015

Melinda came over for a couple of hours yesterday so I could take a few runs. The resort was crowded but it was still delightful to get on my skis. Today, I'm making Turkey Soup. Well, I'm my mother's hands. She's sitting at the kitchen table instructing me. She's a fabulous cook, and it's one of the first times I've enjoyed being in the kitchen.

As we were letting the soup cook, I started to set up her audio book. She held up her hand and said, "April, wait a minute, I have to ask you something."

My mother's breath grew labored. Slowly she panted, "That woman who asked me about... your cousin... I couldn't talk... I didn't know. Thank you... for telling the truth. I'm sorry... I'm so sorry."

My eyes welled.

My mother reached for my hand with labored breath, "You are courage. No one has more. I don't know... I don't deserve you."

317

I think she meant, "I don't know what I did to deserve you." I didn't ask her for clarification. It was enough.

Later:

Tom's daughter spoke with me tonight after watching basketball with my mom. My niece said, "I heard you on Grandma's birthday talking with that woman about Richard Marcroft, your cousin."

I nodded.

She continued, "I was standing near Byron at the dining room table, he was slicing a piece of cake and his hand started shaking so badly that he dropped the cake."

My brother is typically so calm I've joked he functions on an inhibited flat line. I mean the guy is a complete monotone.

My niece nodded vigorously. She then said, "I have to ask, was my father involved?"

She continued, "I thought this might be a good chance to talk. My kids are taking good care of grandma."

We walked to the kitchen. I told her. I told her everything that happened with Tom and what I believed.

I told her that I have absolutely no proof for this, but I believe her dad loved her so much that he didn't ever want to hurt her. I told her that our Bishop told me that Tom had gone to him before Tom went into the National Guard. That Bishop told me that Tom repented for everything he had done. The bishop emphasized that Tom even came in before he was called on his mission to make sure he was really forgiven. After Tom's mission, and during his temple marriage interview, Tom asked again, he had to make sure he was forgiven.

Then, I continued, "But I think Tom knew it was more than a lay Bishop could fix. I think when your mom got pregnant with you, Tom panicked. He bought a huge life insurance policy, much to my father's chagrin (my dad didn't think he could afford it). Then, a couple of months later he got sick. Like he couldn't breathe sick. Your parents were married in June. Your mom got pregnant quickly. Tom bought the life insurance in August. He got sick at the end of September. By January, he was still sick, and they did X-Rays and found a huge tumor across both his lungs.

My niece knew most of the details about the tumors, the cancer, the Kobalt treatments, the radiation pneumonia. But she'd never heard my interpretation of it.

I told her, "Two weeks before Tom died, he was given a 90% chance of complete cure." It wasn't a 90% chance that he'd live. It was a 90% of complete cure.

To celebrate, my siblings all went skiing. To this day, Melinda says she feels guilty about it. She wishes they'd never gone. Because Tom got a cold. His immune system was so shot that the cold moved to pneumonia with lightning speed.

My niece knew all these facts.

She also knew that her dad's lungs collapsed, and because of all the radiation he had, they couldn't inflate them. And Tom died one month before her birth.

Carol

TODAY I AM TENDING ISABEL'S new baby, her second little boy. He is playing with my medallion necklace from Crete, the one with the embossed snake winding around the woman. I wonder what I think it means. The Fall and Sin.

I want to build a wall around this beautiful baby no one will ever break through—would I build it if I could? I hope not. This child has a right to meet and claim whatever happens to him.

What kind of reality will this child know? What kind of world?

I can't understand the equations or vocabulary of quantum physics. But I can grasp some of the concepts. Physicists have found that human observation of electrons makes a difference as to whether the electrons manifest themselves as waves or particles. Electrons behave differently depending on whether or not they are being watched by humans. Human mind affects physical matter. This isn't ESP or levitating spoons. This is a breakthrough, the discovery of a scientific paradox which shouldn't be. This is the possibility that human intelligence is a force affecting the universe as much as gravity.

What does this mean about us? Is it possible that we are marvelously unique? Not just an evolutionary end product but marvelously unique?

I am in awe that we have consciousness. Intelligence, freedom, choice, free-choice—with all its consequences for evil and for goodness.

April

THE LARGE BLUE SPRUCE IN my front yard is lit up with multi-colored lights. A giant Christmas tree. I saw a couple walking by. One reached in their jacket and took out a phone and snapped a picture of the big tree. My mother smiled. I built a fire in the living room, turned on soft Christmas music, pulled back the blinds, and my mother and I sat on the couch for a long time. She reached over and held my hand.

She asked for the walker because she's tired. I swallowed and our eyes met. With each step, she breathed heavily. Between breaths she said, "Ikke vær redd, lille. Alt vil bli bra." It translates to "Do not be afraid little one. All will be well."

A feeling of foreboding chills my soul. I send my siblings each a text and told them that something has shifted. I encouraged both to visit her soon.

November 30, 2015

I hear a loud clank and a thud downstairs. I race into my mother's room. Her walker is across her legs, diagonally. She is trying to kick it upright. Her shins are bleeding. She's trying to stand up. I hold her.

"Mom, wait. Your legs are tangled in the walker. Wait. Let me help you."

She contorts. She's fighting me. I hold her and bring her to a sitting position on the edge of the bed. I move the walker a few inches away, so it doesn't bang her shins. She looks out the window and says, "I can't…."

Does she mean breathe?

She says again, "I can't….G…G…g…."

I hold her. Her muscles are all tense. She's trying to say something. "I can't…"

Yes, she means, "Breathe."

I exclaim, "Mom, just relax here. I'll get the medicine."

She struggles to stand. She falls again. I guide her to the bed.

Why is she fighting me? I hold her. I'll hold her until she catches her breath and calms down.

"I can't…GO…I can't… April! I can't….April."

Then her breathing stops.

Her body relaxes. Her head falls to my shoulder.

320

I have no idea how long I hold her. Finally, I call my neighbor, the Contractor, and ask for his help. It's after 1 AM. He races over. Checks her pulse and confirms she's gone. I call Melinda. I call Home Health Care and they send a nurse over. Melinda asks about the funeral home. I tell her that the one we had for Gramps's will be fine. Someone told Tom's widow, she came over. Byron calls. He asks to talk to me. I don't want to talk to him, but Tom's widow begs me. I get on the phone and Byron tells me he knew she was going to die. I don't say anything, but wonder "If you knew, why did you leave town?" The mortuary arrives. Tom's widow leads me to the living room. I don't take my eyes from the lights on the tree as they remove my mother's body.

Around 5 AM, everyone leaves. I'm alone. I go to my bed and try to sleep. Instead, I sob. My whole-body racks with the sobs.

December 7, 2015

Laurel's hand on my shoulder interrupts my thoughts. I'm transfixed in front of my mother's flower laden casket. Laurel says she's going to visit her father's grave. "Take as much time as you need April."

The last light of day reflects off the rose wood of my mother's coffin.

I think of my grandmother's paper doll. The one I found in the attic. The same one I've kept all these years—safely under glass. She watched over me, reminding me to never forget. Representing our seemingly fragile souls capable of unending resilience, forgiveness, love, truth, and light.

After my mother's stroke, I placed the paper doll on my mother's nightstand. Often, I caught her staring at it. The doll, hand painted by her mother stood sentry over her.

The sky is ablaze with a fiery red and orange as the sun sets. Such a long day. I pick a rose from the top of her casket. I'll keep this rose, to remind me to never forget. I won't forget. I'd like to keep this rose from my mother's grave. Because this morning, I said good-bye to our paper doll. I requested to be the last one to say goodbye and close her casket. The funeral directors seemed surprised, but I could tell from their expressions they were impressed.

An hour before the funeral, there was a public visitation for family and friends. We had an open casket. After everyone except close friends and family left, we had a private prayer. Before the casket was closed, any close friends or family who felt like it, could take a moment with my mother's body to say good-bye.

Some touched her face, some whispered something to her, others wept. After everyone was done, I looked around the room. I gestured if anyone else wanted to say good-bye.

Then, I approach the casket. I hold my grandmother's hand painted paper doll. My eyes well as I think of saying goodbye to my mother and our sentry. The fragile, beautiful doll my grandmother brought from Norway.

I remove my mother's glasses and gently cover her head and face. Then, I carefully place the paper doll in my mother's casket, next to her heart. I slowly reach up and bring the lid of the casket down.

The End

AUTHORS' EPILOGUES

The tiny air currents
that a butterfly creates
travel across thousands of miles,
jostling other breezes as they go
and eventually changing the weather.

—Edward Lorenz, as cited in Gloria Steinem's
Revolution From Within

THE SUCCESS OF *PAPERDOLLS* OVER the years is an indication to April and me of how hungry many people are for true accounts of child abuse. We expected to receive declamations that our story was too bizarre to be true, but there have been none. Instead, we received many responses saying, "This could be my story."

Since *Paperdolls* was first published, the babysitter "Geraldine" has committed suicide, as well as one of her fellow perpetrator "boyfriends" (Tinkleface).

Hank's second wife tried to sue the Mormon Church because they hid their knowledge of his pedophilia from her and kept him as a temple worthy priesthood holder. One of her abused daughter's was permanently physically damaged and can't have children. One son she had with Hank killed himself.

Lorraine's children attempted to bring a civil suit against the Apostle's daughter and son-in-law. The suit was ultimately dismissed by the Utah Supreme Court because the statute of limitations had passed. Utah is the only state in the country to have ruled that child sexual abuse cases cannot be filed retroactively. If other states rules as Utah did the Boy Scout Sex Abuse and the Catholic Priest abuse would never have been uncovered.

Six women have contacted me with their accounts of Hank's abuse of them as children. Like April, these women had repressed all memory of the abuse until adulthood. One of these women endured a physically abusive marriage for many years, two struggled with severe eating disorders throughout their teenage years, and one was hospitalized twice for bulimia and suicide attempts. Another woman has had debilitating panic attacks for years. Some of these survivors of Hank's abuse have difficulty in sexual relationships. Each of them has appeared as successful to the external world. All are attractive; several have graduate degrees and good jobs, while some have children and are married to successful men. These women have put their lives together pretty well, thanks in part to years of therapy.

My own grandchildren have done remarkably well, in large measure through years of therapy and hard work. They were encouraged to talk of their experiences when they were little and as they matured. Today they are all productive people and loving parents. I'm exceedingly proud of them and grateful for all the help they have had.

All who have experienced sexual abuse will always be engaged in the healing process. All of us need to process our individual stories and claim our own truths. Dark secrets need to surface, or they will ultimately destroy.

People ask April and me what can be done to halt child sexual abuse. I tell them that when the shroud of secrecy is broken, children will speak and be believed.

—Carol Scott

CAROL'S EYES HELD MINE. SHE asked me to speak at her funeral. My eyes misted as I whispered, "I'd be honored." Norton took a bite of a dinner roll and said, "That's settled. You did such an amazing job on your mother's that's all Carol has talked about since."

I doubt I could do this incredible woman justice. I looked at Carol, softly said, "You are so much more than the woman who co-authored *Paperdolls*. I'll try to ensure that the bond of our relationship, the message of hope to survivors of sexual abuse, isn't the only thing I talk about." Norton laughed and said, "Well, make sure it's in there, it altered the course of our lives."

Carol patted my hand and said, "Don't worry April, hopefully it won't be soon. Norton and I don't want to be apart. I don't want to live without him, and he doesn't want to live without me."

She brought her teacup down with a small click on the saucer. Her black hair now white framing those piercing green eyes.

"I wanted to make sure you say yes, before time gets away from us."

The conversation then ebbed and flowed to various topics. It took a while to catch up. I'll never get used to the joy in my heart when I hear about the grandkids. They are doing well.

Carol and I often talked about how significant it was that they were able to get therapy and help at such a young age.

Many children who are victimized never get help. My childhood neighbor-hood contained many precious souls who never made it to adulthood. Early deaths, drugs, run-aways, suicides...the list goes on...

I think of my sister, Melinda. Outwardly, she seems to be doing alright. If one gets close though, that veneer of wellness fades. She seems nervous, agitated, like she's waiting for the other shoe to drop. She doesn't understand why her sons teeter on the edges of society, a step away from returning to jail or prison.

Many from my old neighbor have committed atrocities as adults. I know of three of the teenagers who abused me as a child who devolved their abuse to savage levels: David Fuller, Brian David Mitchell, and Hank Carstensen.

Hank was a main perpetrator in Carol's and my life. Hank abused me when he was an older teenager, and I was a child. As an adult, Hank committed monstrous acts against his children and many of the Scott's children and grandchildren. Now, with Hank dead, Carol's side has healed and enjoyed growth and degrees of con-tentment. My family, not so much. Most are still imprisoned in a cave, thinking reality is shadows projected on the wall. Like "Plato's Allegory of the Cave."

As we were walking to our cars, Carol turned and handed me a business card. It had a name and phone number on it. She said, "This man keeps calling. He knew Lorraine and Hank when the sexual abuse was first discovered. I think he wants to talk about it. Could you call him?"

I swallowed. The card read, "David E. Hardy, Attorney-at-law."

Carol handled all the press, inquiries, and attention garnered since *Paperdolls* was published in 1992. Carol supported many with therapy expenses from pro-ceeds of the book.

I took the card and noticed her hand tremor. It was obvious she couldn't han-dle the inquiries anymore. Norton joked, "it sucks getting old."

The next day, I called. I identified myself and said that Carol Scott asked me to call. David Hardy boomed, "Oh my! April Daniels! I feel like I've hit the lottery or something. Can we meet? I'll come to your house!"

This felt rushed. I scheduled a meeting a few days later and set the location in a public spot downtown.

I rounded up a couple of friends. One was my hair stylist. She'd read *"Paperdolls"* and said she couldn't put it down. She's protective of my identity. I also contacted a therapist who worked with Karen Fisher before her death. A few years ago, this therapist contacted me to see if I'd be willing to help a group "make the Church accountable." I told her what I truly believe: the Church is filled with lay clergy who are untrained and frequently make mistakes. I've heard it's better in the years since *Paperdolls* was published, however I knew many of these men are ignorant making egregious mistakes.

I was surprised that both my stylist and Karen Fisher's cohort agreed to come with me.

We met at Little America Cafeteria

David explained why he wanted to meet.

Recently a news story broke about a young female missionary at the Missionary Training Center (MTC) in 1984. The MTC President at the time sexually assaulted her. Time does not heal all wounds. 30 years after the event, the woman met with her former mission president and confronted him. She recorded the conversation. The guy admitted everything in the recording.

I had heard the story on the news but didn't follow it closely. David explained why this story had affected him so deeply: Many in the news were attacking the victim and defending the former Mission President. Attacking the victim is something I knew all too well. It's called DARVO (Deny, Attack, and Reverse Victim and Offender). It seems anyone who tells the truth of their own victimization knows about DARVO. I certainly had my fair share of it. It's counterintuitive that DARVO happens. This woman had the former MTC President on tape admitting it all. And people still attacked her, the victim. David Hardy was outraged.

I swept a few crumbs from the table. I noticed that there were no crumbs to sweep, but I nervously brushed my hand across the table anyway. I wasn't sure why he wanted to meet with me. Then, the rest of his story came out.

When David Hardy heard the vicious attacks on this woman, something ignited in his heart. His shame was like bile rising in his throat as he remembered 1986. He helped the Church cover up the tragic abuse of the children in my co-author's neighborhood. His actions from that time gnawed at his soul.

In Carol's portion of the book, she wrote about the Apostle's daughter and her husband. David Hardy knew them both. I told David that I knew about them from reading Carol's portion, but that's all I knew. He knew Carol's portion well. Much more than I did. *Paperdolls* was first published in 1992.

In 1986, David's law office was downtown, near the Church Office Building. One day David's older brother, Ralph Hardy, telephoned David. Ralph was a high-powered attorney in Washington D.C. David said that his brother helped the LDS Church with major policy, lobbying or problems at a national level. David smiled and said, "In many ways, my brother was the Church's fixer."

The waitress stopped to take our orders. I appreciated the break to try to digest this information. After the waitress left, David continued.

When David received the call from his older brother, Ralph, Ralph told David that he would be receiving a fax. Ralph instructed David to hand deliver this fax to the Apostle identified in Carol's portion of the book. While sitting in the Little America Café, David said the name of the Apostle. Carol had never told me who that Apostle was. I'm sure my face conveyed my shock and skepticism. I swallowed. I needed a moment. I excused myself and went to the rest room. I washed my face. Before I returned to the table, I mentally adorned my "critical thinking hat." I was going to listen as objectively and as openly as I could. There is a difference between critical thinking and analysis and emotional "knee jerk" reactions. As much as I didn't want to hear more, I vowed to listen.

When I returned to the table, David continued relating his experiences from 1986. When the fax came from Ralph, David verified it had come through clearly. He looked at the letter and couldn't stop reading. The letter started out with a sincere acknowledgement of sympathy for the tragedy that befell this Apostle's family. The facsimile continued with an outline of specific instructions on what this Apostle was to do, say and specifically what not to say in regarding the allegations of his daughter and son-in-law's involvement with sexual abuse of children in the Scott's neighborhood. In David Hardy's neighborhood. The entire missive was a loss control plan to diminish the likelihood of a lawsuit. It was a defensive road map to keep the matter out of the public domain and the news.

I asked, "Was there a plan to help the children? Or the victims?"

"No."

I was unsure. Certainly, the Church proclaiming to be the only true Church of Jesus Christ would have a plan to help the children. Suffer the children and all that.

David continued with his actions in 1986. After David read Ralph's letter to the apostle, David carefully folded it and placed it in a secure envelope. David executed his orders flawlessly. He placed the envelope directly in the hand of one the twelve most powerful and righteous men on earth.

Now, over 30 years later, that obedience haunted David E. Hardy. He was aware that the children's lives had been ravaged during the last decades. David told of insurmountable pain of the victims including drugs, mental illness, and several suicides. He knew that the Scott family had been spiritually and emotionally wounded by the betrayal. He knew that Norton almost killed himself because of this spiritual abuse. David informed me that Hank's son, from his second marriage, had committed suicide. Hank had killed himself when his 2nd wife found irrefutable medical evidence that their 3-year-old son had been raped. David informed me that this same son committed suicide when he reached his teenage years.

David was seeking a way to atone for his part in the cover-up. I couldn't help him. My vision blurred. The table tilted. I was glad I was sitting because I might have fallen. Another suicide. Another needless death.

I knew of numerous crimes committed by those inhumane perpetrators who once lived in my childhood neighborhood. Sometimes it felt like my efforts were for naught. The suicides, the deaths, and the murders continued.

I thought of Kacie Woody. Another innocent annihilated by David Fuller, who grew up across the street from me. I thought of the horrors that happened to innocent Elizabeth Smart, who was also abducted from her home by yet another one of the perpetrators from my childhood.

David continued to tell me of the drug addictions, illnesses and early deaths of those children who were abused in the Scott's neighborhood when Hank and his cohorts united in their evil deceit. I knew that the Scott's grandchildren were doing quite well. I felt their healing occurred because they got help when they were young. It never occurred to me that the other children in that neighborhood didn't get help. Many suffered fates like many in my old neighborhood. Early deaths, drugs.... all of it.

Hardy's eyes welled. Until this moment, I thought that the reason nothing happened to the perpetrators in the Scott's neighborhood was because the stake president decided not to pursue any actions against the perpetrators. That stake president told me he didn't want to expose the Church to that liability. He took pride in making such a tragic error, professing that he had protected the Church from undue liability and lawsuits. Now it seemed, he was merely a pawn in a sophisticated defensive plan.

I turned to the therapist who worked with Karen Fisher and said, "I'm sorry. I didn't know. I thought they were naïve and stupid."

She said, "It seems that the members of the Church at the grassroots level are far more loving and Christian than those on the high echelon of the institution."

I shook my head in dismay. Doesn't anyone protect the children? I recalled that Norton and Carol had worked hard to get the Church to put in a hotline for Mormon Bishops to call when a sexual abuse case was reported. The hotline went to LDS Social Services to help the victims.

Hardy laughed. He had been a Bishop. He said the hotline goes to the Church's law firm, Kirton McConkie. He said that when he was a Bishop he called the hotline several times. Each time he was informed not to report the abuse. There was no help offered for the victims.

This hotline seemed like such a good idea. A hotline to help the children. But a call to a law office? Please, don't let this be true.

I swallowed. It felt like I was swallowing my rage, again. I refused to do that now.

I told the story of David Fuller abducting, raping and murdering Kacie Woody. I told them that David Fuller had brutely abused me when I was a little girl. I explained that he was friends with my brothers and their friends. I reminded them that Hank was friends with David Fuller and Brian David Mitchell. They were a weird group of teenage boys who abused little children. I knew some of those guys grew up to be even more evil perpetrators. Their crimes expanded to be more insidious, toxic, and evil.

Instead of shouting, I whispered: Crimes against humanity.

After my monologue, the table was eerily quiet.

No one spoke as the server refilled our water glasses.

I continued, with my own speculation: David Fuller lived in San Diego at the same time Brian David Mitchell took Elizabeth Smart to San Diego. There was a period when Mitchell left Elizabeth and Wanda alone for a couple of weeks. Could Mitchell have met up with his old high school buddy Davy Fuller?

The therapist who knew Karen Fisher years ago, clinched and unclenched her hands. My friend, the hair stylist, gasped and slapped her hand to her forehead.

I held my hands up and said, "I'm not saying it happened. I just saying it's a weird coincidence. Here's what I know. They were sick friends in high school bonded by inflicting pain on animals and children. They even dropped acid together. Decades later, these once high school buddies land in the same place and the same time. Mitchell with beautiful, young Elizabeth Smart. At this exact same time, Fuller decides to abduct the charismatic and lively teenager, Kacie Woody. Do I even need to point out that Kacie and Elizabeth were about the same age? It's an eerie and ugly coincidence, for sure."

David stated, "Well, my cousin is Ed Smart. Is it alright with you if I call him, tell him about this, and see if he would be willing to ask Elizabeth about it? If she remembered anything from her time in San Diego with her captors?"

A couple of months later, I felt a lump in my left breast. After some tests, I got the call that it was stage 2, malignant breast cancer. It had to be removed, then radiation and possibly chemo. That's a tough call to get. I wrote a lot and fell on my long-standing mantra, "If I survived the abuse of my childhood, I can survive this. Even if this prognosis is terminal, nothing is as bad as what I suffered as a child."

Before my surgery, I decided to visit Jennifer in Los Angeles. I was writing while listening to Jennifer play the piano. Unexpectedly, David Hardy phoned. I hadn't heard from him since the dinner at Little America. He explained that Elizabeth had been working with Warner Brothers on a television series. Elizabeth had an opportunity to host her own show. It was going to be titled "Crimes That Never Should Have Happened." She wanted to start with her story, and how it never should have never happened. She wanted to interview me.

"David, I know this is bizarre, but I am in Burbank right now. I can see the Warner Brothers lot from my friend's apartment."

Instantly, "You are kidding me!"

I said, "I'm going to the beach today, but I could walk over there tomorrow and talk to them."

Jennifer came with me, and we met a few people at Warner Brothers. The main producer kept saying, "I can't believe April Daniels is here. Right now. Two days ago, we were trying to find out how to find you. Then, Elizabeth said her dad might know and here you are. Everyone was saying, "It must have been meant to be."

Meeting with the Warner Brother's producers was easier than when I first talked to David Hardy at Little America. I told them about David Fuller. I brought the letter that I wrote to Kacie Woody's father. I told them that I knew Brian David Mitchell and David Fuller went to the same high school and that they were both involved in the abuse in my childhood neighborhood. I told them of the three teenage perpetrators who grew up to be monsters.

I didn't tell them that I had just been diagnosed with Breast Cancer. I didn't mention that I was having surgery as soon as I got home. I was resolved that I would do anything I could to help Elizabeth. I know that the main reason I have such a rich full life is because others have helped me. I believe that one of the reasons I've survived, is because I was meant to let other survivors know that if I can do it—anyone can.

I had my surgery. My surgeon met with a tumor board, and unfortunately the tumor had grown. The board recommended chemotherapy. Laurel was with me, and she gave me a hug and said, "Well, let's just plan on making the most of the next few months, no matter how crappy they might be."

I finished the chemo when the producer from Warner Brother's called again. They wanted to do the interview with Elizabeth and me, complete with the film crew. I told the producer that I had recently completed chemotherapy. I'd love to go to LA again, but I couldn't because I had to start radiation.

Within an hour, the producer called back. The film crew was coming to Salt Lake City.

The film crew was greeted by a snow dump. A couple of feet in the mountains and a foot of powder at the airport. The producer called from the hotel and said her LA film crew was outside trying to have a snowball fight, but the snow was too flakey and wouldn't stick in a ball. I laughed. Fresh Utah powder isn't ideal to make a snowball, but skiing or riding it is heavenly. The producer continued to explain that a well-known director was flying in from New York. He would be directing this interview between Elizabeth Smart and me.

Aside from no hair, pale complexion, I looked fine. I was more concerned about the first time I would ever show my face on camera. I wished Carol could still do these interviews.

Shortly after the breast cancer diagnosis, I went to see Carol. Her daughter, Susy warned me that she might not remember me. Susy brought me into her mom's room and said, "Mom, you have a visitor!" Carol sat up and said, "April! Come sit down! How are you?" I didn't tell her immediately. But, after a few minutes, I told her about my breast cancer diagnosis. She uttered, "Damn."

Carol said, "Isn't this your fourth different type of cancer?"

I nodded.

She put her hand over mine and said, "There's extensive research confirming that trauma alters chromosomes and physical cells. The propensity for children who suffered trauma in those developmental years to experience significant health issues as adults is significantly higher. We still have a lot of work to do."

Carol might have a hard time remembering what she wore the previous day, but as far as her professional aptitude and knowledge was concerned, she was as sharp as ever.

Remembering that Carol had done television and radio interviews numerous times, helped as I walked into the recording studio.

The contraption they had us sit in for the interview looked like something from outer space. It was more convoluted than the radiation treatment machines. I looked at Elizabeth, shrugged my shoulders and said, "I don't know how you do this"

There were sound guys adjusting microphones and checking lights. The director bellowed, "Just act natural." We burst out laughing. Elizabeth whispered, "You'll get used to it."

Elizabeth had several index cards with questions to ask me. Thankfully she started easy. Possibly because I was visibly uncomfortable. She said, "After all these years, you've never shown your face of camera, why now?"

Since I was thinking about Carol, I told Elizabeth about her. "Typically Carol handled the publicity and inquiries. I'd much rather be skiing than sitting right here."

Elizabeth quickly responded, "Even with your cancer treatments, you've been skiing?"

I chuckled, "Yes. I only last a couple of hours, but I've gone. I've even convinced one of the radiation techs to take lessons."

"What about the other seasons? What do you like to do?"

My face lit up, "I love to putter in the garden. I also love waterskiing and wakeboarding."

Elizabeth smiled and said, "I love to garden also, do you grow vegetables?"

I said, "I love fresh vegetables. But I need my flowers. I simply don't have enough garden space for it all. I chose flowers. All sorts of flowers. In the spring I call my little front yard a patch of Holland. I've seen cars stop, and people get out to take pictures of all the flowers. It's lovely."

She paused and said, "Do you know why you love flowers so much?"

I nodded.

The director said, "Words please."

I said, "Yes, I do."

I continued, "When I was Beehive, that's the name the LDS Church calls girls in the 7th grade classes, around 12 years old. I had a horrible lesson in my Beehive class. I told the story I wrote about in *Paperdolls*, the chastity lesson that used a daisy to demonstrate what happens to you if you let a boy kiss you or touch your sacred body. The teacher said our bodies are a sacred temple. The lesson progressed until a bare ugly bulb was left, without any petals. That's what happens if you let a boy go 'all the way.'"

Ever since I saw that ugly image at such a young age, when I was suffering incomprehensible sexual abuse and incest, I've loved flowers—everywhere. Inside the house, the garden, everywhere. In *Paperdolls*, I even wrote about how upset I was when I went to church in St. George with Laurel, and some woman was giving the exact same lesson. I practically made a scene right there in Laurel's ward. I was shaking. I know Laurel took action to try to get that lesson removed from Church manuals and lesson plans.

Elizabeth said, "I had the exact same lesson."

I almost came out of my chair. I totally forgot the cameras, makeup, and the microphone clipped to my jacket.

"What?"

I made such a big deal about it; I was certain that nonsense wasn't taught anymore.

Elizabeth said, "I've made a big deal about it also. I don't think it's in the manuals, but there still might be some rogue teacher who thinks it's a clever visual."

My whole body jolted.

The director said, "We need to adjust April's microphone. April, could you please try to stop moving your arms so much?"

I took a few deep breaths as they fixed the microphone.

We got back to the more scripted questions. She asked what the response was when *Paperdolls* was first published. I told her I was stunned. I told her that when it was first published, I thought it would simply be a book that therapists used to help survivors deal with their trauma. I explained how jarring it was when it was the lead on the evening news.

Later, many others, especially women, started reaching out, telling their stories, I felt like it would be like Jericho—the walls would fall because of our voices.

Elizabeth's face lit up and said, "That sounds good to me!"

"In time, I realized how angry some were that I wrote the book. I explained that I tried to understand why they are angry, but I never really understood. Why not give a voice of hope to others so they can heal? Why is that so threatening?"

Elizabeth shrugged and said, "I don't know either."

She glanced at the index cards and said, "One of the consistent questions is 'How is April?' We touched upon it earlier, but I want to ensure we cover that. How are you? Do you still wrestle with any demons from the abuse you suffered as a child?'

I said, "Not very much. It's not like it didn't happen, but overall, I'm doing quite well. I have things, everyday life things, that many people have, but that's all part of it. These things are what make life so wonderful.

"Do you ever get triggered now?"

"Not really. I have a couple of lingering things that I've simply accepted as an idiosyncrasy."

'Can you give me an example?"

"I can't close my eyes in the shower. Usually, I have red eyes after I shower because I get shampoo in my eyes. It goes away after a few minutes, so it's no big deal."

'What's a bad day for you now?'

"The day I got the call about my breast cancer. That was a bad day. I continued, "I don't want to minimize anyone's experience. Cancer and cancer treatments are tough. But, for me, it's not even in the top five of the hardest things I've been through."

Elizabeth nodded, "I bet."

"Whenever I face a tough time, I think of the abuse and dealing with its ramifications, and I remember that if I survived that I can survive anything. I thought of that when the doctor called with my diagnosis."

I told her that on the first session of chemotherapy, the patient is usually placed in a private room in case there is a strong reaction to the infusion. I explained that my first session was the day of Dr. Christine Blasely Ford's testimony in front of the Senate Judiciary Committee. I watched Dr. Ford's entire, eloquent, and compelling testimony. Since I had a private room, several nurses and hospital workers kept coming in to watch it also. Fortunately, I didn't have a negative reaction to the chemo, but there was a strong reaction to Dr. Ford's testimony.

"How so?"

"Dr. Ford's testimony was credible. Her testimony was calm, well-founded, and logical. For me, the excuse that Brett Kavanaugh was a college kid when this happened doesn't fly. I experienced torturous abuse from *teenage* sexual predators who devolved into adulthood as kidnappers, rapists, and murderers. In my layperson's understanding, those hearings were basically a job interview and given my experience with *teenage* assailants, I think an older *college aged* sexual predator doesn't qualify for the job. In our entire nation, there must be numerous stronger options for a seat on the highest court of the land."

Since Elizabeth and I were talking about United States Senators, I told her one of the first quotes I ever memorized. I was a little kid, and Martin Luther King, Jr. had just been assassinated. I sucked my thumb until I was 8 years old. I remember, sitting there, sucking my thumb when the news showed Robert Kennedy making the sad announcement about Martin Luther King's death. Bobby Kennedy quoted one of his favorite poets, Aeschylus:

"Even in our sleep, pain which cannot forget falls drop by drop upon the heart until, in our own despair, against our will, comes wisdom through the awful grace of God."

The Director asked for a short break. When we came back, I realized that he'd checked to verify that's what Bobby Kennedy said when he announced Martin Luther King's death. He inquired, "How did you remember that?"

I told him that as a child, I knew despair and that quote always gave me hope.

After the break, Elizabeth continued:

"Were you surprised with the threats, including death threats Dr. Christine Ford received after her testimony?"

With resignation I said, "Not surprised at all. The reality is that retaliation is a *Dark Energy* option for attacking the victim. There's a therapeutic name for it: DRAVO. Basically, the perpetrator is convinced they are the victim."

Elizabeth asked if I thought there would be a backlash against the #MeToo Movement. Another sober response. "Yes, there will be. I'm not sure what it will be, but it will happen. But we must continue speaking the truth. Dr. Ford believed it was her civic duty. Now, I think it's our duty to humanity."

"I think you're right."

Elizabeth asked about my childhood neighborhood. She specifically asked about Brian David Mitchell.

I explained that I recalled Brian David Mitchell with one of my brother Tom's friends. I also recalled him with David Fuller in the old neighborhood.

Elizabeth asked if I was aware that Brian David Mitchell was caught molesting a 5-year-old girl in that neighborhood and had been sent to Juvenile Delinquent prison. I told her I was aware of that because I read the transcript of Brian David Mitchell's competency hearing. I cringed with Mitchell's father testified that his son hadn't done anything to the little girl, just exposed himself.

Elizabeth looked up and asked, "Were you that little girl?"

"No."

She asked if I knew who it was, I told her I had an idea but wasn't certain, so I didn't want to speculate on camera.

I told Elizabeth that after she was found, there were pictures all over the news of her kidnapper. I didn't recognize that weird Jesus wannabe. Then, I told her that a news story showed pictures of him when he was first married to Wanda.

The hair on the back of my neck rose when I saw the young version of Elizabeth's assailant.

I knew him.

I recalled the news story in 2003 showing a video with him and Wanda at some church party. They were dressed up as a shower, dancing around the cultural hall. When I heard Mitchell's voice it was as if I time traveled back decades to myself as a little girl. *I knew him.* He'd been to my childhood home. In our basement. Before the news clip finished, I called Laurel and asked her to check her husband's yearbooks from high school. He wasn't in the later years, but he was in the sophomore yearbook.

I remembered, when he came over to my house, Brian David Mitchell held me and made me promise not to tell. I was naked. He told me that another girl told and got in big trouble. As a little girl, I thought the other little girl got in big trouble for telling.

Brian David Mitchell went to juvenile detention, then when he was released, he went to a different high school. Elizabeth was aware of that. It was part of Mitchell's legal proceedings. We talked about the other well-known perpetrators that came out of my childhood neighborhood.

David Fuller and Hank Carstensen.

I still struggle when I talk about Kacie Woody. Tears eked out. We took a short break as the makeup person fixed my smears. The producer came over and said, "Will you read part of the letter you wrote to Kacie Woody's father?"

Portions of the letter were highlighted.

We resumed, and Elizabeth set it up by saying, "Would you please read portions of the letter you wrote to Mr. Woody?"

I knew it so well, I barely needed to look down at the sheet.

Dear Mr. Woody,

"... I have thought of your beautiful daughter, Kacie, every single day. Please know that words cannot adequately convey my deepest sympathy.

My childhood home was directly across the street from the monster who took your angel, Kacie, from this earth. This same monster sexually abused me when I was a little girl. He was several years older than I, but the damage he inflicted upon me during his teenage years was substantial.

Over twenty years ago, I wrote a book about surviving my abuse. My message was to warn others that there are predators of children at large and to send a message of hope to other survivors, like me.

An updated edition will be released. My co-author and I have both written more about the major events that have happened since its original release.

I have written a great deal about Kacie and the tragic circumstances of her death, particularly my feelings of despair and my unabated longing that I could have done more to protect her and to prevent her tragic departure.

... not enough people believed me; or those who mattered the most, and could have possibly done something to stop him, did not believe me. Words simply cannot express the depth of my sorrow."

I heard sniffles. I looked up to see the makeup artist weeping. The Director wiped his eyes. There were no more words.

The Director broke the silence by announcing that we needed to take the crew up to my childhood neighborhood. They wanted shots of Elizabeth and I walking around the neighborhood. There were many people in that neighborhood I still knew. I smiled as I thought of their reaction to seeing Elizabeth and I walking the neighborhood with a film crew behind us.

Elizabeth rearranged car seats in the back to accommodate two film guys, both in the back seat. One filming Elizabeth and one with a camera focused on me. After we were seated, the director said that he didn't want long periods of silence and instructed us to have a causal conversation.

Elizabeth was relaxed driving up to the snowy benches of Salt Lake and I almost forgot that there was a couple of camera guys in the backseat. As we were driving up to the east side at the base of the mountains, Elizabeth asked me what my favorite flower was. I laughed, "Oh, I don't know if I have a favorite! I love them all. I guess I'm partial to daisies because that's the flower my Beehive teacher ripped up when I was in 7ᵗʰ grade."

I heard the click of a metronome then realized Elizabeth was signaling for a left turn. As the steering wheel rotated, she said, "You know, I really think they've stopped teaching that."

"I certainly hope so. I'm not Pollyanna or anything, but I certainly hope we can do a bit more than stopping Beehive teachers from ripping up flowers."

We both laughed.

Elizabeth said, "I've met a lot of survivors, and you are the most positive and optimistic one I've ever met."

I shrugged my shoulders and replied with something like, "I'm sure there are plenty like me."

She said, "No, you are quite remarkable."

"I don't think so, I really could be anyone. If I can do it, anyone can."

As we headed up 39ᵗʰ South, I told Elizabeth about my feelings when I saw the "The tomb of the unknown soldier." Now, I truly feel my experience could be anyone's. Gratefully, I'm not dead. But there's nothing special about my healing. I reiterated: If I can do it, anyone can.

I remembered the director's instructions to keep a conversation going. I asked, "Would you like to hear about the best thing I've ever done? And it's not the book, my higher education, or my career. However, it's the very best thing I've ever done."

As she turned the steering wheel turning onto Wasatch Boulevard she nodded and said, "Of course."

I told her the boots story. I explained that Burton and Parker are about her age now, but the notorious events happened when they were 3 and 5 years old. I delighted in the details about how much Parker loved his little boots and wore them all the time. The problem was that he kept kicking his older brother Burton with them. I love retelling the story, and probably embellish it a bit. I explained what a great Mother Laurel was (and still is) and how she laid down the law. Laurel gave Parker three chances to stop kicking Burton with those boots. Unfortunately, the 3ʳᵈ time happened at my house. I shrugged my shoulders and said, "I swear she had eyes in the back of her head. How she saw that last kick, I'll never know."

Elizabeth chuckled.

I continued the lavish story, "With mother-like speed, she swooped in and took those boots before Parker could even get his leg back down. Her continuation landed the boots in my trash!"

I retold how Parker's little eyes welled with tears. How smug Burton was. I explained that when the boys were not within hearing range, I begged Laurel to give them back.

Elizabeth laughed and said, "This sounds like my mother! I would have done exactly what Laurel did!"

I heard snickering from the back.

I noticed we were getting close to my childhood home. I quickly ended the story with Laurel's proclamation that maybe I could give the boots back when Parker got married. "So, I tucked them away for over 20 years, and gave them back to him on his wedding day!"

I sighed and said, "Ahh, best thing I've ever done."

Elizabeth exclaimed, "Did Parker have any idea you had them?"

"No! Totally shocked him when we gave those boots back to him at his Wedding Breakfast."

I told her I was thinking of naming the new release of **Paperdolls,** to be **Paperdolls and Cowboy Boots.** I said that the whole topic depicts one of the ugliest sides of humanity. I want to show survivors that we can survive and thrive, but also experience joy.

We stopped in front of my childhood home. Elizabeth turned and said, "That's wonderful, I like that. I really like that."

I showed her where David Fuller lived and where the irrigation creek runs under the road. That's where so much abuse happened with Davy Fuller.

We weren't laughing anymore.

The camera guys were filming everywhere I pointed. We drove a few houses up to the elementary school. I showed Elizabeth the scrub oak where my older neighbor saved me from the boys. Andrea McCall took me home and to subdue my tears cut out paper dolls. That's one of the reasons we decided on the title of the book. I looked at Elizabeth and added, "I insisted the title be misspelled, all one word, Paperdolls, because we are all connected."

I chuckled and said, "That misspelling really bothered one of the editors from the national publishers in 1993. I wouldn't relent."

We drove higher and I pointed out a few of the more well-known family homes in the neighborhood. She recognized the names. Then we stopped in front of Scott's old home. I said, "This is where they lived when Lorraine and Hank met."

It's one of the biggest houses on the hill. Elizabeth commented that she thinks it's important that people know abuse isn't confined to certain socio-economic classes.

The director sent a message and asked if we could stop and walk around. I walked for a bit, but quickly grew fatigued. The chemo, radiation, and now the emotion of this interview might have been more taxing than I realized. I waited in the car and noticed some of my old neighbors slowing down as they drove by.

As we headed back to the studio, Elizabeth asked about my pseudonym.

"April showers bring May flowers."

We were at a stop light. Elizabeth met my eye and I swear her eyes were twinkling when she said, "I get it." Then continued, "What about Daniels?"

"Why Daniel surviving the lion's den, of course."

Before the light turned green, Elizabeth and I shared a smile. I nodded and said, "Words please."

I heard the director's chuckle in my ear prompter.

The main producer was waiting for us at the studio. While we were gone, she had written up a few more questions for Elizabeth to ask. Back into the contraption, this time I wasn't nervous at all. I trust Elizabeth Smart.

Elizabeth looked through the cards, then said, "Your abuse was at a much younger age than I experienced, and I always had the support of my family." She paused and continued, "Yours was for such a long time. You suffered in your own home. I don't know if I could have survived if my family hadn't supported me. I don't know if I'd be here if my family was part of the abuse."

I responded with, "Don't underestimate the trauma of your experience. We can't compare pain."

Another speechless moment.

Elizabeth flipped through more cards, then looked up and said, "Do you have any advice for other survivors? I nodded.

From behind the cameras we heard, "Words please."

I repeated myself saying, "If I can do it anyone can. There's nothing special about me. Get therapy. Push through the pain. And, it is painful, but it's worth it. Life is worth living. Live. Stay on this earth."

Elizabeth asked if I had any words for perpetrators.

"Not really. It's not like I don't care about the perpetrators. I mean, I know most of them have been abused as well. But, if someone is an abuser, my advice to those perpetrators is: 'stop whatever you are doing, right now. Call 9-1-1. You must stop murdering souls.'"

I watched as Elizabeth brought up the last card. She said, "I know we all can't blow our trumpets and have the walls of Jericho fall, but what do you think we can do, to change society's denial of this atrocity?"

Elizabeth waited for my response. Finally, I ask, "Are you familiar with Plato's 'Allegory of the Cave'?"

"No."

I explained that it's an allegory written by Plato of what Socrates said, a long time ago. Like 400 BC. I mentioned that there are thousands of poignant and meaningful interpretations. I have an interpretation of it, for those being sexual abused, or for those growing up in insanity—using this historical allegory.

Elizabeth says, "I'd like to hear it."

"As a reminder, picture a time about 400 BC. Imagine a few prisoners held in a dark, dingy cave.

I continue, "The prisoners are bound so that they can't see anything except the cave wall in front of them. There's a large fire behind the prisoners. Occasionally, an object is held in front of the fire, the light of the fire projects a shadow on the wall. The only thing the prisoners ever see are shadows.

"Think about these poor souls back in 400 BC, living in a cave their entire lives, only seeing those shadows. Eventually, the prisoners started playing a game of guessing the names of the shadows. "

"Socrates offers some hope. One day, for some reason, one prisoner is released from bondage.

"Imagine her moving her limbs from their confined position. The blood flowing through her legs and arms. Maybe it hurts. Picture her turning her head and seeing the fire for the first time and cowering in fear from the brightness. Socrates tells of her crawling on her hands and knees up the stairs and falling outside the cave. The light is too much. Too bright. Too painful. She crawls out of the cave and collapses.

"A long time later, she can squint her eyes to see. Eventually she can fully open her eyes in the daylight.

"She sees a flower, with dimension and color and smell. She explores and sees so many wonderful things. She is no longer afraid. She is euphoric. Everywhere she looks or walks, or runs is stunningly beautiful.

"One day, she hears a songbird singing in a tree. She looks at the tree. She looks down at her path. She sees the shadow of the tree on the rock in her pathway. She realizes that when she was imprisoned in the cave, she saw shadows of these multidimensional, colorful trees. She saw the shadow of a bird and never heard the songs, or saw the colors, or witnessed the miracle of a bird in flight.

"It dawns on her that her entire life, up to the time she was released, she thought the shadows were real.

"She remembers there are still prisoners in the cave.

She feels such love for them. She must go back to tell them. To free them. She must tell them that there are colors, singing and flying birds, scent filled flowers, and a blue sky that frequently has gorgeous white clouds floating above us. She must tell them that there are things she can touch and feel, see, smell, even taste.

She must tell them about dancing in the light.

She skips back to the cave and exuberantly exclaims to those still imprisoned.

"These are shadows! Wait until you see and touch and feel the real flowers!" Flowers have an amazing scent that I can't describe. She tries to explain all the marvels outside the cave.

She tries to stand in front of them so they can see her. They flinch and close their eyes. She tries to touch a woman's arm. The prisoner shrieks.

She doesn't want to hurt them. They don't understand.

She can't explain something they've never experienced. She finally pleads for them to simply believe her. To follow her up the stairs and out of the cave.

No one moves. One of the prisoners exclaims that she is crazy. The prisoners' shudder in fear. If anyone leaves the cave, they will go crazy. They tell her to sit down, come to her senses, and join in their guessing game.

She can't. After seeing color and dimension and light, she can't pretend that gray shadows are real.

She begins to leave, and one brave prisoner asks to join her. She gently helps this one out. Explaining that it takes time to adjust to the light and to not be afraid. They wait. Slowly the other prisoner realizes what has been said about light and color and dimension is true.

This new friend is free and dances with glee.

Sometime later, she tries to bring another prisoner to freedom. This time, this prisoner can't adjust to the light. It's too painful and runs back into the cave telling everyone that indeed, anyone who leaves the cave is crazy.

Occasionally, simply because she loves this colorful world so much, she courageously goes back into the cave. the prisoners cruelly spit hateful words to her. She simply states that she's telling the truth. There's a magnificent world outside the cave. She offers to help. She tells them they don't even need to go with her. They just need courage to leave and realize it takes time to adjust. They'll find their own glorious reality and life in the light.

Sometimes, some follow. Sometimes some leave on their own. They wait to adjust. Outside the cave is glorious. Words cannot even describe how different it is than staring at shadows on a wall.

"Of course, sometimes being outside has challenges. Even pain. One can get stung by a bee or stub their toes, but overall, it's a heavenly existence outside of the cave.

I pause and look at Elizabeth, "Thank you for going back into the cave. Thank you for trying to save them."

A sacred silence. Finally, the director says, "That's a wrap."

As I'm removing all the wires and microphones, Elizabeth gives me a hug. I say, "Please take care of yourself. Please spend most of your time in the light. You can't save everyone."

With a smile she says, "It doesn't mean I can't try."

"When a butterfly flaps its wings...."

"It can change the weather across the world."

—*April Daniels*